D0876176

McCarthy's Americans

McCarthy's Americans

Red Scare Politics in State and Nation, 1935–1965

M. J. Heale

The University of Georgia Press
Athens

Published in the United States of America in 1998 by
The University of Georgia Press, Athens, Georgia 30602

First published in Great Britain in 1998 by Macmillan Press Ltd.

Library of Congress Cataloging in Publication Data
Heale, M. J.
McCarthy's Americans : red scare politics in state and nation,
1935–1965 / M.J. Heale.
p.   cm.
Includes bibliographical references and index.
ISBN 0–8203–2026–9
1. Anti-communist movements—United States—History—20th century.
2. Anti-communist movements—United States—States—History—20th
century.   3. McCarthy, Joseph, 1908–1957.   4. Internal security—United
States—History—20th century.   5. United States—Politics
and government—1933–1945.   6. United States—Politics and
government—1945–1989.   7. Michigan—Politics and government.
8. Massachusetts—Politics and government.   9. Georgia—Politics and
government.   I. Title.
E743.5.H39 1998
973.9—dc21   97–41118
                                                            CIP

Printed in Great Britain

For my wife, Lesley

CONTENTS

ACKNOWLEDGEMENTS

This book experienced rather a long gestation period, the consequence both of distractions from other projects and duties and of the intermittent nature of opportunities to visit the United States for research purposes. It is now difficult to recall all the debts incurred along the way, but the book owes much to the generosity of others. A fellowship from the American Council of Learned Societies helped to launch the study, and grants from the British Academy, the American Philosophical Society and Lancaster University kept it going. The value of such grants was immeasurably enhanced by the hospitality of various American hosts, several of whom were able to bring their own perceptions to bear on my subject. I wish to record my gratitude to Ziva and Michael Anshel, Jean Thomas, Alger Hiss, Bob and Joan Fisher, Dick and Katheryne McCormick, Ellen and Alvin Cohan, Robert and Arsha Rubyan, and the successive Keepers of the Matthiessen Room, Eliot House, Harvard, George Abbott White and Alan Heimert.

A considerable debt is owed to those patient scholars who kindly read all or part of the manuscript. Ellen Schrecker's incomparable knowledge of McCarthyite matters saved me from many a slip, and Gareth Davies, a pupil when this project was conceived and now a colleague, completed a diplomatic role reversal in sharpening both my prose and my ideas. Dan T. Carter, Patrick Renshaw and Tony Badger also gave generously of their time and knowledge. Another debt is owed to the many people who over the years gave me encouragement or provided a forum for my thoughts, among them Herbert Nicholas, Marcus Cunliffe, Charlotte Erickson, Owen Dudley Edwards, John Thompson, John Ashworth, Richard Crockatt, Eric Homberger, Peter Boyle, Peter Ling, Bob Reinders, Maldwyn Jones, Peter Parish, Robert Harrison, Jack Pole, Stanley Kutler, James Gilbert, George Calcott, Alasdair Kean, and Inderjeet Parmar.

My greatest debt as always is to my wife Lesley, who shared this book throughout even as its pursuit required my overlong absences. It is dedicated to her with love.

MJH
New Year's Eve, 1996

viii

ABBREVIATIONS

The following abbreviations and acronyms are used in the text.

ACLU	American Civil Liberties Union
ACTU	Association of Catholic Trade Unionists
ADA	Americans for Democratic Action
AFL	American Federation of Labor
AFL–CIO	American Federation of Labor–Congress of Industrial Organizations
AMVETS	American Veterans of World War II
AVC	American Veterans Committee
AYD	American Youth for Democracy
CIO	Congress of Industrial Organizations
CIO–PAC	Congress of Industrial Organizations–Political Action Committee
CLUM	Civil Liberties Union of Massachusetts
CP	Communist Party (of USA)
CRC	Civil Rights Congress
CUAC	California Un-American Activities Committee
DAR	Daughters of the American Revolution
FBI	Federal Bureau of Investigation
FEPC	Fair Employment Practices Committee
GCE	Georgia Commission on Education
GE	General Electric Company
GM	General Motors
GOP	Grand Old Party
HUAC	House Committee on Un-American Activities
IFLWU	International Fur and Leather Workers Union
ILWU	International Longshoremen's and Warehousemen's Union
IUE	International Union of Electrical Workers
LWV	League of Women Voters
MIT	Massachusetts Institute of Technology
NAACP	National Association for the Advancement of Colored People
NLRB	National Labor Relations Board
NSL	National Student League

OUAC	Ohio Un-American Activities Commission
PTA	Parent and Teacher's Association
SCEF	Southern Conference Educational Board
SCHW	Southern Conference for Human Welfare
SISS	Senate Internal Security Subcommittee
SNCC	Student Nonviolent Coordinating Committee
SRC	Southern Regional Conference
UAW	Union of Automobile Workers
UE	United Electrical, Radio and Machine Workers of America
UPW	United Public Workers
VFW	Veterans of Foreign Wars
YWCA	Young Women's Christian Association

PREFACE

Some years ago a conference held at Harvard University on the topic 'Anticommunism and the US' was advertised by a poster presenting the brooding, baleful face of Senator Joe McCarthy. The image was a powerful one but it was also misleading, because, as most of the conference participants knew perfectly well, the late Senator had done little or nothing to create the phenomenon he had come to personify. McCarthy is not synonymous with McCarthyism, even less with American anticommunism, and his troubled presence has sometimes obscured those historical processes that helped to make his career possible. Over the last generation several scholars have sought to reach beyond the image, and a number of superb studies now illuminate parts of what might be called McCarthy's hinterland, but the process remains incomplete. Probably no area has been as patchily addressed as that represented by the basic building blocks of the American system of government, the American states themselves. No major episode in American political history can be fully understood without a knowledge of what was happening outside Washington, and the purpose of this book is to look beyond the McCarthyites of Capitol Hill to their counterparts in the states. Among other things, the study provides yet further evidence of the irrelevance of Senator McCarthy to the movement which bears his name.

One limitation of the term McCarthyism is that it slights the long history of red scare politics in the United States before Joe McCarthy's high-pitched whine was first heard in the United States Senate. Domestic anticommunism, that tendency to espy a red enemy within, has been a primary feature of American politics since the late nineteenth century. At times the fear of subversion, or at least the exploitation of that fear, has been so intense and pervasive as to constitute a red scare, as in the Haymarket Affair of 1886–87, the Palmer Raids of 1919–20, and the McCarthyism of the early 1950s. This is not the place to explore the political and cultural roots of American anticommunism, but any study of a particular episode needs to be aware of that resilient tradition. More than most societies, Americans have been defined by shared values rather than by ancient institutions, and have thus always been sensitive to the prospect of ideological subversion. The peculiar burden placed on political ideology in the United States has been the greater because of the variegated nature of its people. A diverse society has not easily cohered, and conceptions of Americanism have been pressed into service in attempts to strengthen the social fabric. But patriotism can take different forms, and may divide as well as unite. Both the American Civil Liberties Union and the John Birch Society have grounded their legitimacy in American conceptions of freedom. The actors encountered in this book may seem capable of the most egregiously partisan and cynical behaviour, but they were also conditioned by values which stretched back to the beginnings of the American republic. Red scares have been part of the American political process, inseparable from its instrumentality and its ideology, not aberrations or the products of mindless hysteria or the spawn of gifted demagogues.

But even the red scare associated with Senator McCarthy was not triggered by his celebrated speech at Wheeling, West Virginia, in February 1950. Several scholars have pointed to the significance of episodes and policies associated with President Harry Truman's first beleaguered term, and some have emphasized the rightward thrusts of American politics during the later part of the New Deal, as illustrated by the foundation of the House Committee on Un-American Activities (HUAC) in 1938. (A fuller discussion of McCarthy historiography is offered in the Conclusion.) A focus on state politics emphasizes the value of this longer perspective. One way of perceiving the Senator's excesses is as part of a political cycle which first emerged in the mid-1930s and took two decades or more to run its course. In several states, the political configurations which were to make possible the red scare politics of the Cold War years had first taken shape in the 1930s, if not earlier. McCarthyism was not so much an aberration as a product of long-term processes that favoured conservative politics. In some states, indeed, McCarthyite political formations survived after a fashion and were provoked to new spasms by the radicalism of the 1960s. The revitalized conservatism of Richard Nixon and Ronald Reagan was not created in a vacuum and owed something to tensions which Senator McCarthy and the little

McCarthys in the states had exploited. They had helped to expose the fragility of what is sometimes known as the New Deal political order.

If McCarthyism was in part made possible by an older rightward trend in American politics, key events of the 1940s and 1950s undoubtedly furthered the cause. Scholars have rightly pointed to the demoralizing impact of the course of foreign affairs on both public opinion and policy-makers, most evidenced by the extension of Soviet control over eastern Europe after the Second World War and by the unnerving 'loss' of China and the revelation of Soviet possession of the A-bomb in 1949. The responses of the Truman administration and of the public at large to the escalating threat of world communism helped Senator McCarthy and his brethren to move from the political wings to centre stage. Yet a state-level examination raises questions both about the critical junctures in international relations and about the Senator's influence. For one thing, anticommunist politics did not emerge simultaneously throughout the land. In some states red scares arrived early and in others late, suggesting that external stimuli of themselves have limited explanatory power, that as much attention needs to be paid to internal political pressures. But if there was a foreign crisis which had a clear impact on state politics it was the outbreak of the Korean War. Because McCarthy's heyday was almost coincident with the Korean War, it is difficult to disentangle the influence of the two on the extensive political terrain outside Washington, but the evidence suggests that Korea was more important than McCarthy (or even other foreign policy reverses) in precipitating anticommunist programmes.

It may be that both national and state governments exaggerated the prospect of a Third World War in these years. But anxiety over Korea cannot simply be dismissed as irrational. Recently some scholars, while contemptuous of the irresponsible antics of Senator McCarthy, have presented moderate anticommunism on the foreign and domestic fronts as a reasonable response to a real and present danger. They have identified a threat not only in the murderous Soviet regime but also inside the United States, where there was both an active Communist party which sympathized with the Soviet Union and authentic Soviet espionage. This view implies a correlation between Communist

and anticommunist activity, and whether one existed is a question
that can be asked of state politics. The following pages do reveal
something of such a connection. But the evidence also suggests
that the rationality of anticommunist behaviour often reflected
more a self–regarding partisanship than a selfless patriotism. The
threat of domestic communism was invariably magnified by the
operations and culture of American politics.

A study of state politics also makes possible a consideration
of other important questions scholars have raised about
McCarthyism. It has been held that McCarthyism was primarily
the product of populist or grassroots pressures revolting against
a political establishment, that is a form of mass insurgency fuelled
by status anxieties or resentments. More recently responsibility
has instead been substantially assigned to various elites, whether
presidential administrations or powerful institutions like the FBI.
The political establishment in Washington or the major parties
engaged in conventional partisan politics, in this view, far from
being the targets of grassroots anger, were the prime creators of
this Frankenstein's Monster. Yet, with some valuable exceptions,
neither perspective has been much informed by research at state
or local level. If it is necessary to establish whether McCarthyism
was a populist phenomenon, welling upwards through the
American political system, or an elitist phenomenon, introduced
at the top and trickling downwards, it seems logical to examine
the states, for they were the arenas in which local and national
pressures met. This question helped to inspire this study,
although it may now be doubted whether it is a very useful one,
for it assumes a tidier political system than that possessed by the
United States, in which the whirls and eddies of political currents
are not easily charted. McCarthyism, like other American political
movements, was not static. It varied according to place and
changed in character over time. It will be suggested in the
following pages that the populist–elitist dichotomy is largely a
false one. A populist impulse was of critical importance at times,
just as at other times elitist pressures were the dominant ones.
Further, the two frequently interacted in a dynamic that neither
wholly controlled.

But a study of the states should reveal more than the direction
of McCarthyite pressures. The state arena provides a context in
which at least some of the ingredients of red scare politics might

be identified and their interaction examined. Quite apart from the inseparability of national and state politics, it was also the case that the state McCarthyites often blazed the trails for their federal counterparts. Controlling sedition and subversion, after all, had traditionally been a state responsibility, and by the time the federal government formally moved into this sphere with the Smith Act of 1940, the state statute books bristled with laws directed at anarchists and Communists. (This also provides a reason for focusing on states rather than local communities. More studies of community red scares are necessary, and this book will draw attention in particular to the role of large cities in the generation of McCarthyism, but cities are legally the creations of states, and governmental programmes to combat communism were framed primarily at state level.) Congressmen fought the red menace with HUAC, but several states had their own little HUACs, some of which anticipated the techniques used by the various congressional inquisitors of the 1950s. Loyalty oaths were widely deployed by the states before President Truman introduced his loyalty programme for federal employees in 1947; the Communist party was even outlawed by one state some years before Congress contrived to do something similar with the Communist Control Act of 1954. This is not to suggest that the federal measures and probes of the 1940s and 1950s owed their force to state example. Sometimes the states took the initiative and sometimes the federal government did, and the latter could generally exert more influence. The dynamics of party politics, the Cold War and the national security state did exert powerful pressures from the centre, but they also need to be seen as operating in a constitutional structure which allowed the states significant autonomy. Indeed, this author has argued elsewhere that it was the very flimsiness of the federal government which in part explains the historic strength of anticommunism in the United States.

For the most part in this book the term red scare politics is preferred to the term McCarthyism. Some limitations of the term McCarthyism have already been indicated; it sits poorly with a story which began before the Second World War and continued after the Wisconsin senator's death. Further, in some accounts the term has been used to direct attention to the political purge of the Cold War era and its victims. That is a vital issue which other scholars have addressed, and it is not the intention here to document every judicial proceeding or job loss. The term red scare politics is meant to suggest a somewhat different concern, one which allows a focus on the operations of state politics, which may witness the redbaiting of party opponents as well as the hounding of suspect employees. Attention here is paid more to the ways in which governments sought to protect their states from red subversion, an essentially political process, than to the often sad fates of those who fell victim to these programmes.

One problem confronting any scholar who addresses the history or politics of the American states is that there are today 50 of them. There is room for 50 studies of red scare politics (for the territories, especially Hawaii, did not escape the experience), had authors, publishers and readers the patience for them. One solution is to offer an overview, generalizing broadly about the state experience, and one or two brave scholars have attempted this in essay-length surveys. The difficulty with this approach is achieving the complexity and intensity needed to enhance understanding of McCarthyite politics. The other solution is to undertake one or more case studies, which may add depth but at the expense of comprehensiveness. This book seeks to achieve a balance between these two approaches. Part I offers an overview of the states generally, one which attempts to delineate the broad contours and suggest the patterns that might be discerned in a myriad of anticommunist activity. Parts II, III and IV offer case studies of three states in different parts of the Union. While there were some similarities in the way in which the Communist issue worked its way through the political culture of each of these states, there were major differences too and a distinctive story to tell in each case. To a large extent this book has become a comparative study of state (or regional) political cultures, using McCarthyism as the instrument of dissection. Part V returns to an overview and offers a conclusion.

McCarthyism – or red scare politics – was a complex phenomenon, and can be explained only by addressing the American political structure as a whole and by reference to a variety of pressures. While the political passions which peaked in the 1950s had their roots in the 1930s, it makes no sense to try to understand them without considerable attention to the Cold War and the imperatives of the national security state. Without these later pressures the anticommunist persuasion, strong though it already was, would not have achieved the potency it did. But there were other essential ingredients too, among them what in another context has been called reactionary populism. Historians have lately been recognizing that the conservative rejection of the celebrated consensualism of the 1950s was not confined to the unreconstructed rich, and that distaste for New Deal liberalism or the liberal consensus extended to many workers (and to some of the middle and professional classes too). A form of reactionary politics also flourished in the South, and again Senator McCarthy and his ilk would not have enjoyed the prominence they did without the critical role played by this section in the American political system. Yet complex phenomenon though McCarthyism was, ultimately the red scare politics of the 1940s and 1950s were an expression of a kind of political fundamentalism, or rather of a variety of fundamentalisms. The focus of some early scholars on the fears of those of modest status may have been somewhat misleading, for anxieties were liberally distributed throughout society. The term status anxiety may be inappropriate, but at many levels there were people and interests clinging fiercely to traditional forms. In different and subtle ways, the precepts of class, race and religion were militating against the emergence of a genuinely multicultural society. For many Americans, McCarthyism was a cry of pain for the sundry worlds they had lost.

PART I

RED SCARE POLITICS IN THE STATES

McCarthyism has sometimes been linked to a conservative revival originating in a reaction against the New Deal; another view has located responsibility in governmental and elite actions of questionable necessity; a third has found some justification for communist-control measures in the suspicious behaviour of a Soviet-aligned Communist party. The evidence from the states suggests that each of these approaches can tell a part of the story.

When the Truman administration launched the prosecution of Communist party leaders in 1948, when Senator McCarthy began waving his lists of allegedly subversive government employees in 1950, and when the Senate Internal Security Subcommittee (SISS) began to interrogate university professors about their political opinions in 1951, they were giving aid and comfort to anticommunist activists across the land. Those public officials and private citizens in every community who suspected that America's great experiment in democratic freedom was being undone by an insidious Communist conspiracy, and those who calculated that they could make political capital out of such suspicions, could only take heart from this legitimization of their cause from on high. Yet the federal government was a relatively late recruit to the war on domestic communism. During the Depression a few states had contemplated curbs on the 'reds' they perceived behind protest activity. Senator McCarthy's demagogic activities had been anticipated by state Senator Jack B. Tenney of California, whose indiscriminate redbaiting caused his political colleagues to repudiate him five years before McCarthy's colleagues followed suit; and while the SISS's scrutiny sent a *frisson* through the American academy, the first serious professorial bloodletting in the Cold War period occurred at the University of Washington in 1948, prompted by a state investigating committee. Even that had been preceded by a purge of New York City colleges in the early 1940s, again at the behest of state inquisitors.

Some states, like the United States Congress itself, had begun to introduce protections against domestic communism even before American entry into the Second World War. Many citizens had been disturbed by the relative vigour of the Communist party during the 1930s, when hundreds of thousands of members had probably passed through its 'revolving door', albeit often speedily, and when its popular front strategy had allowed it some contact with American liberals, even a few in government. When the Soviet Union after all became an ally of the United States during the war, there were significant constituencies – including much of organized labour – that remained adamantly unreconciled to either domestic or Soviet communism. In the troubled postwar period the Truman administration moved closer to these groups. The White House began to perceive the Soviet Union as replacing Nazi Germany as the epitome of totalitarian expansionism, and when governments in Greece and Turkey were threatened by Communist influence, Truman determined on an epochal change to American foreign policy. Enunciating the Truman Doctrine in a combative speech before Congress in March 1947, he insisted that 'it must be the policy of the United States to support free peoples who are resisting attempted subjugation by armed minorities or by outside pressures'. When soon after Truman announced the federal loyalty programme, it seemed that he was branding both domestic and international communism the enemy of American democracy. The advent of Communist regimes in Czechoslovakia and China in 1948 and 1949 respectively seemed to vindicate the image of a voracious Soviet menace while calling into question the administration's capacity to contain it. Foreign policy reverses also suggested to some that there were indeed Soviet agents in the United States working to subvert American institutions and policies, and with the outbreak of the Korean War both national and state governments turned once more to strengthening their internal security defences.

There was nothing very surprising in the fact that the states were taking measures to combat communism. The function of protecting the American polity from subversion and insurrection had traditionally been primarily a state one. At the time of the Red Scare following the First World War, Attorney General A. Mitchell Palmer had been unable to secure a federal sedition act and it had been the states that had busied themselves with such legislation. If not exactly a state preserve, red scare politics could claim a long pedigree at state level, and in the Cold War years the states reasserted their prerogative.

They employed no single method of combating communism. One or two states contemplated introducing the death penalty for Communists, though none nerved itself to carry through this ferocious solution. Several set up their own investigating committees, and some of these rivalled Washington's own House Committee on Un-American Activities (HUAC) for the recklessness with which they interrogated witnesses, named names and ruined careers. Some states attempted to ban Communist meetings or put obstacles in the way of Communist or other allegedly subversive candidates being placed on the ballot. Education was a major responsibility of state governments, and red scares thus often focused on colleges or schools. Protecting children from the wiles of wicked subversives was an abiding concern, and some states found ways of removing radical teachers from the classroom while others strengthened their techniques for impregnating children with patriotic principles. But a state could be penetrated by those trying surreptitiously to effect its destruction at almost any point, and frequently all public employees were subjected to surveillance. And there was more to red scare politics than identifying those citizens, if any, who gave their first allegiance to the Soviet Union, for the red scare was a well-tried tactic for discrediting political rivals. While these varieties of anticommunist activity were widespread in these years, they were not arbitrary or capricious. They were forms of purposeful behaviour, best understood in a political context.

The extraordinary diversity of measures deployed by the states to combat communism almost defies analysis. But broadly there were three approaches. The one that precipitated greatest publicity and worried civil libertarians most was the investigating or redhunting committee, which in fact appeared at state level before the notoriety of the technique was escalated by HUAC. The 'little HUAC', like its congressional counterpart, operated largely on the assumption that exposure was the best means of frustrating the red menace. The politics of exposure held a strong appeal for a superpatriotic minority and for those who saw a partisan advantage. A second approach, much the most pervasive, was the loyalty oath; this was designed to harness patriotic sentiments to the public service, and to isolate those whose loyalty was in question. At the height of the Cold War, when the politics of patriotism became all but irresistible, American citizens were swearing allegiance to their state and nation on a scale unparalleled in hot wars. The third broad approach favoured by the states was the communist-control law, that is legislation designed to regulate the lives of American residents of supposedly subversive intent, such as by prohibiting certain kinds of organization or behaviour. Not all states resorted to the politics of regulation, but for a season they seemed to offer a mode of combating communism and harassing dissidents. There was some overlap between these three approaches, and several states employed a mixture of them, but they were not pursued with equal vigour by all states at all times. Some states were readier to resort to red scare politics than others, and there were periods when certain approaches were preferred to others. An analysis of the variegated measures introduced by the states to combat communism, therefore, serves not only to identify the constituent elements but also the larger rhythms of red scare politics in the United States.

These three approaches to containing communism paralleled and were intertwined with those that were being developed at federal level, and any federal initiative was likely to set a powerful legitimizing example. The investigating committee was most notoriously exemplified by the House Committee on Un-American Activities, established on a temporary basis in 1938 and made permanent in 1945. Its celebrated probe of Hollywood in 1947 was abruptly terminated after it had attracted criticism, but its power was demonstrated when the unfriendly Hollywood Ten were given prison sentences for contempt of Congress. With the Korean War the Senate decided that it too needed to investigate subversion, and to this end in 1951 it established the Senate Internal Security Subcommittee, which was soon busying itself in particular with exposing red academics. It was not until 1953 that Joe McCarthy secured the chairmanship of a redhunting committee, which is the purpose to which he turned the hitherto obscure Permanent Subcommittee on Investigations of the Government Operations Committee. In the event, he was to expose more of himself than of a Communist plot.

The politics of exposure had initially been directed by HUAC at Franklin Roosevelt's New Deal, and during Harry Truman's tenure the Democratic administration remained the subject of hostile attention by congressional conservatives, who complained of its failure to take seriously the Communist threat. President Truman sought to pre-empt his critics by embracing the politics of patriotism. In 1947 he adopted a loyalty programme to screen federal employees for 'disloyalty' to the United States. This programme did not rely on an oath as such, but employees had to fill in loyalty forms, including a questionnaire, and could be subject to interrogation by loyalty boards. Thus thoughts and associations were being proscribed, and one bar to government service could be membership of any group on the list of subversive organizations that the Attorney General was now required to maintain. The publication of the celebrated list, compiled largely on hearsay evidence, put a weapon into the hands of official and unofficial redhunters across the country. Truman had hoped that the loyalty programme would both deflect the redhunting committees and avert a resort to communist-control laws, though on occasion he invoked coercive techniques himself. An early form of regulation had been the Smith Act of 1940, which had its imitators in the states, and which sought to make it illegal knowingly to advocate the overthrow of the government by force. Used against Trotskyites and 'native fascists' during the war, this sedition law was given added weight in 1948 by the decision of the Truman administration to use it against top American Communists. Truman did resist another communist-control measure, the 1950 Internal Security Act requiring Communist organizations and their members to register with the authorities, but it was passed over his veto. This meant that not only government employees (and top CP officers) but also private citizens were being subjected to political surveillance. A few states were already experimenting with the politics of regulation, and others were prompted to action by the new federal model. The activities of Communists across the country were thus already seriously circumscribed by the time that Congress passed the Communist Control Act of 1954, which finally declared the CP to be 'the agency of a hostile foreign power'.

In both state and nation the phenomenon of anticommunism underwent important changes over time. Among the roots of red scare politics was a conservative rejection of the New Deal and progressive reform, sometimes accompanied by a populistic suspicion of those in authority. Such conservative and maverick elements tended at first to operate on the political fringes, but around 1950 governments were being recruited to a more vigorous embrace of the anticommunist cause, particularly in states in which there were clusters of Communists. Such pre-emption of the issue, however, sometimes by authorities of moderate disposition who hoped to control it, could result in the unlocking of a Pandora's Box. And while many of the resultant programmes were more symbolic than substantive, what is sometimes overlooked is their institutional legacy, one which served to enhance the authority of the national security state.

1

THE POLITICS OF EXPOSURE: INVESTIGATING COMMITTEES

Among the most sinister figures in western culture is that of the witch-finder, whose capacity to evoke fear rests in large part on the combination of authority with arbitrary power. Arthur Miller's play, *The Crucible*, directly linked the witchcraze of the seventeenth century to the American political inquisitions of the 1950s. There were probably more effective ways of protecting the polity from subversion, but none was more cherished by its champions and more reviled by its opponents than the investigating committee. The deep emotions it aroused owed something to folk memories of the witch-finder, but also to the recognition that such a device could easily be turned to political and partisan purposes.

In the Cold War period over a dozen states imitated Congress in establishing their own legislative committees, the 'little Dies committees' or 'little Thomas committees' as they were sometimes known, or, as we might call them, the 'little HUACs'. Their proclaimed purpose was usually to investigate 'un-American activities' (never un-Californian or un-Ohioan activities), signalling their willingness to enrol in the common cause against the red menace. These committees were less robust than HUAC itself, typically surviving only two or three years, although California's inquisitors stalked the state for an extraordinary three decades. A few were stillborn, but the most active of them framed anticommunist legislation, staged highly publicized hearings featuring both friendly and unfriendly witnesses, published reports naming names, and sometimes provided a focus for a state's anticommunist crusade. But their agenda extended well beyond uncovering reds.

The great majority of states put into place some kind of anticommunist machinery in these years, most often loyalty oaths for public employees. Such anticommunist rituals however, may not be evidence for much more than the pervasiveness of the anticommunist persuasion. More revealing are the more active crusades against the red menace launched by several states. An examination of the activities of the little HUACs, and of their timing and location, helps us to establish the contours of anticommunist politics. A major root of such politics, as Earl Latham argued many years ago, was a conservative thrust for office originating in the 1930s if not earlier. At their formation little HUACs were often free-booting right-wing vehicles for assaulting liberal groups and reformist administrations, but in due course they were to become instruments of the reigning authorities.[1]

The emergence of little HUACs

Like HUAC, such committees first appeared on the eve of the Second World War, as part of that 'little red scare' which was punctured by the wartime alliance between the Soviet Union and the United States. With the advent of the Cold War a rash of 'little HUACs' busied themselves with the red menace, the most notorious of them being California's Tenney Committee, although almost as reviled by civil libertarians were Washington state's Canwell Committee and Illinois' Broyles Commission. By the 1950s the zeal for investigating committees had abated a little, and the committees themselves may have been marginally better behaved, but the Ohio Un-American Activities Committee and the Bowker Commission in Massachusetts engaged in some energetic redbaiting, while the late 1950s and early 1960s witnessed a flurry of such committees in the Deep South. By 1965 the day of the little HUAC was essentially over, although ageing committees lingered until the end of the decade in California and Hawaii. Some local idiosyncrasies apart, the phenomenon of little HUACs waxed and waned with the larger red scare.

The vitality of little HUACs owed something to American democratic ideals. The legislative power to investigate was itself part of the Anglo-American libertarian heritage. British parliamentarians had long been jealous of their right to inquire into the public management, and Congress had conducted its first investigation in 1792. Such inquiries soon moved beyond the executive branch as it became clear that lawmaking needed to be properly informed, and it came to be accepted that legislative investigations might also be used to inform public opinion. It was in the 1930s that Congress greatly expanded its investigative operations, as the Nye Committee pursued the 'merchants of death' who had allegedly been responsible for the American involvement in the First World War, as the La Follette Committee sought to expose violations of labour rights – and as the Dies Committee struck back at such Progressive inquisitors and the New Deal. While the parameters of these probes remained the subject of intense dispute, by the 1940s Congress had provided the states with ample precedents for legislative investigations. With the evil of totalitarianism (whether fascist or communist) increasingly being perceived as the enemy of democracy, the legislative right of free inquiry acquired an enhanced legitimacy.[2]

Not that the state legislatures needed very much encouragement from Congress, particularly in the sphere of hunting subversives. At the time of the Red Scare following the First World War, policing sedition had been more a state than a federal responsibility, one which the New York legislature had sought to discharge by dispatching a committee to investigate the Bolshevik menace. The Lusk Committee not only raided socialist sanctuaries but also produced a gigantic report of over 4000 pages, mostly reproductions of documents published by left-wing groups, a treasure-trove which was to be plundered by antiradicals for decades to come. In the mid-1930s, when the Hearst newspapers and the American Legion were inveighing against red professors, state legislatures were sometimes prompted to scrutinize the colleges, as when the Wisconsin legislature branded the University of Wisconsin 'an ultra liberal institution in which communistic teachings were encouraged', and the Arkansas legislature probed alleged radical activities at Commonwealth College, a small labour school. In New Deal America such probes in any case were fairly easily shaken off. The publicity of 1935 served only to attract further irreverent students to Commonwealth College, among them the young Orval Faubus; a sedition bill aimed at the college was defeated in the legislature.[3]

By the late 1930s a more pronounced anticommunist politics was emerging, part of that conservative reaction which put an end to the New Deal. In Congress this was illustrated by the emergence of HUAC, proposed by Martin Dies in 1937 and established in May 1938 by the lower house's conservative bloc of Republicans and dissident Democrats. At its birth the committee contained five Democrats and two Republicans and was chaired by Dies, a Texas Democrat who had joined the southern revolt against the New Deal. Outraged at Communist activity in the burgeoning Congress of Industrial Organizations (CIO), these conservative Democrats and Republicans were soon chafing at Roosevelt's dalliance with labour and the popular front, and added such New Deal agencies as the National Labor Relations Board to their targets. Similar conservative convulsions were disturbing a number of states, one of which even anticipated the House of Representatives in establishing a little HUAC. Early in 1937 a Special Commission to Investigate the Activities ... of Communistic, Fascist, Nazi and Other Subversive Organizations was founded in Massachusetts, and despite the ecumenical cast of its title quickly developed as an anticommunist and anti-popular front vehicle. Chaired by a Republican, its most belligerent member was a conservative Democrat. It summoned popular front radicals before it, some of whom were to endure decades of redbaiting when they were named in its 1938 report. After the Nazi–Soviet Pact and the outbreak of war in Europe cast the Soviet Union yet more starkly as the enemy of civilization, American Communists were rendered even more vulnerable. Congress enacted its own sedition law – the Smith Act – in the fearful summer of 1940. The New York legislature set up the Rapp–Coudert Committee to investigate subversive activities in colleges and schools. In California several former New Deal Democrats broke with the reform administration of Governor Culbert Olson, among them the ambitious Sam Yorty. One of their creations was the Yorty Committee to investigate the State Relief Administration, a primary symbol of Olson's 'little New Deal' and said to be infested with Communists. A conservative backlash was also experienced in Oklahoma, whose senate in 1941 appointed a committee to investigate subversive activities, primarily among university teachers, after the governor had claimed 'positive proof' that 'many' faculty members were 'Communists'.[4]

Two of the bodies spawned by the 'little red scare' deserve particular note. The Rapp–Coudert Committee, as Ellen Schrecker has shown, not only precipitated an unprecedentedly large purge of college teachers, but was also something of a training school for later federal and state committees, pioneering techniques of investigation, interrogation and exposure, and providing invaluable experience for such personnel as Robert Morris, who was to be chief counsel of the McCarran and Jenner Committees in the 1950s. Less well-disciplined was the Yorty Committee, which in 1941 was reconstituted as the Joint Fact-Finding Committee on Un-American Activities under the chairmanship of the former songwriter and bandleader Jack B. Tenney, the composer of 'Mexicali Rose'. The Tenney Committee anticipated J. Parnell Thomas and Joseph R. McCarthy in the recklessness with which it conducted investigations, summoning and abusing dozens of witnesses and publicly branding hundreds of organizations as communistic. Its thick reports were widely circulated, and anticommunist groups through the Cold War era were to use them in the same way as they used other 'official' lists of so-called subversives – to harass those unfortunate enough to be 'named as Communists'.[5]

The Tenney Committee apart, none of these early committees survived the Second World War, but the advent of the Cold War precipitated the greatest ever rash of little HUACs. 'There is certainly an increase of interest in the various legislatures in establishing "un-American activities committees"', observed an officer of the American Civil Liberties Union (ACLU) in April 1947. Although the growing friction between the United States and the Soviet Union intensified red scare pressures, the conservative currents of the late 1940s represented a resumption of those of the late 1930s, as the New Deal tradition and popular front groups again came under siege. In Congress a newly Republican HUAC gained a higher profile for itself than ever with its attacks on the Truman administration and the camp followers of the New Deal. Inspired partly by this example, California's Tenney Committee stepped up its assaults on the state's educators, labour activists and entertainers. In 1947 Washington state created a committee, which soon won some celebrity for its part in procuring the dismissal of three professors at the University of Washington. In the same year, little HUACs

were also created in Michigan, Illinois and New Jersey, while civil
libertarians in Ohio managed to thwart a proposed investigation
of education. 'I know there are communists'; protested its
sponsor, 'I just can't lay my finger on them.' Perhaps encouraged
by the high profile of the Tenney Committee, the Arizona lower
house also established a Committee on Un-American Activities,
which in 1948 was busy fashioning loyalty oaths; in Montana the
Republican senate set up a study group to determine whether
such a committee was necessary. In 1949 the legislatures of New
Hampshire and Oklahoma created their own little HUACs,
although in both cases they appear to have been compromise
substitutes for fiercer probes directed at universities. 'The house
has showed me it is not in favor of stamping out communism',
shouted the chairman of the Oklahoma HUAC after he failed to
secure the full redhunting licence he had sought. Not to be
outdone was the territory of Hawaii, which in 1949 established its
own committee to ferret out Communists. A little later, in 1950
and 1951 respectively, Massachusetts and Ohio followed suit.[6]

This eruption of little HUACs in the late 1940s thus preceded
the conviction of Alger Hiss and the outbreak of the Korean War.
These state inquisitors were prowling the land before the heyday
of McCarthyism, and while they may have contributed to it they
were hardly the product of it. Yet they were the creations of their
time. The popularity of investigating committees in these years
was related in particular to perceptions of the Communist threat
and to the conservative counterattack on the New Deal order.

The doctrine of exposure
Both the little HUACs and HUAC itself were drawing sustenance
from the contemporary doctrine that exposure was the most
effective answer to the red menace. As the Cold War darkened
conservatives were to reach for more coercive instruments, but
for the moment an informed public was to be the first line of
defence. The pre-war Massachusetts committee had concluded
that 'the greatest protection' for the US lay in 'educational
enlightenment and a penetrating understanding of the actual
methods and objectives of the Communist lies'. During the 1930s
CP membership in the United States had risen towards 100 000,
Communists had won strategic positions in several industrial
unions and in some welfare, civil rights, and cultural organiza-

tions, and were to be found on the nation's campuses and in the professions. The secrecy of many about their affiliation had long been the cause of some distrust, and when in 1945 the organization rejected cooperation with any liberals who did not support the Soviet Union, the extent of Communist influence in American public life occasioned wide concern. But victory in the Second World War had helped to strengthen confidence in American democracy, and in the immediate postwar period it seemed enough to rely on America's free processes to dispel the threat of a fifth column. This was the message of the grander authorities on communism. J. Edgar Hoover himself was sceptical of proposals to outlaw the Communist party (CP), which could simply change its name. 'I feel that once public opinion is thoroughly aroused as it is today', Hoover told HUAC when he first dignified it with his presence in March 1947, 'victory will be assured once Communists are identified and exposed.' The US Chamber of Commerce, which was flooding the country with anticommunist pamphlets, pressed a similar strategy to meet the menace of communism: 'If its machinations were exposed to the public, if its front groups had the mask torn from them, its influence domestically would rapidly shrink.' The opinion of many lawyers was expressed in 1948 by the New York State Bar Association, which resolved that 'it is better to oppose the Communist movement by debate, publicity and other traditional American methods ... rather than by legislating against the Communist Party as such'.[7]

Local anticommunist activists seized on the doctrine of exposure. 'Exposure and publicity are the two things that subversives cannot endure', reported the Tenney Committee in 1945: 'They "wither away", like Marx's imaginary last state, in an informed community.' In Michigan Governor Kim Sigler debated with fellow state officials the best means of combating communism, arguing that the most effective technique was keeping the people constantly informed 'on the facts of Communist activities in this country'. He cited a recent exposé in the *Detroit News* as 'the best kind of information to spread before the American people'. Washington state's Canwell Committee echoed this view: 'We feel and have felt at all times that Communism cannot function in the light of day. We feel that with the publicity given their activities, during the course of this hearing, that the people of the State of Washington will properly and adequately take care of the Communists ...'[8]

The doctrine of exposure was the more attractive to many of its proponents because of the political agenda it served. The flurry of little HUACs in the period 1947–51 owed much to a reaction against the political experiments of the 1930s, and this resurgent conservatism helps to explain both their timing and their location. For politicians, whether Democratic or Republican, who wanted to break down the New Deal political order, the techniques of investigation and exposure had an obvious utility. Reform configurations might be discredited if Communists could be identified in popular front groups or labour unions. Little HUACs (like HUAC itself) had first appeared before the Second World War as a conservative tide turned against New Deal administrations. Checked by the wartime Allied cause, the conservative revival soon resumed and was intensified by the deteriorating Cold War. Whether pressed by politicians of any party label anxious to repudiate New Deal or progressive politics, or by Republicans bent on harassing a Democratic administration, this revitalized conservatism was drawn naturally to the politics of exposure.

Reliance on techniques of exposure assumed that there was something to expose. Usually there was – investigating committees which uncovered nothing were a political liability. Thus little HUACs did not appear at random; they were most often found in states which did contain clusters of Communists, or other radicals. According to FBI estimates for the year 1950, ten states sheltered at least a thousand CP members, led by New York with an estimated 25000. Of the ten, six sported little HUACs sometime in the 1940s (California, New York, Illinois, New Jersey, Michigan, and Washington), and another two (Ohio and Massachusetts) followed suit in the early 1950s. The two remaining states with concentrations of Communists were Pennsylvania and Connecticut, and the former adopted a communist-control programme of a different kind, while Connecticut barely made the 'top ten' of CP states with only a thousand members within its borders. The CP emerged from the Second World War in reasonably good heart, at least until the imperatives of Cold War demanded its Stalinization, and progressive political formations briefly glimmered in a number of these states.[9]

'Such states tended to be urban-industrial states, for the CP recruited from trade unionists, educators, welfare workers, students, and racial and ethnic minorities. The pluralistic socio-economic characteristics of these states also tended to promote polarized or competitive political systems, affording party politicians a temptation to capitalize on the CP presence. The urban-industrial states, too, were the ones most likely to exhibit the characteristics provoking the conservative counterattack – a New Deal or popular front heritage or some support for Henry Wallace's Progressive insurgency of 1947–48. The Communists in these states had frequently worked with liberal Democrats, trade unionists, or other reformers. When the CP itself rejected popular front politics and paraded its sympathies for the Soviet Union during the early Cold War, both it and its erstwhile allies were rendered even more vulnerable. Not infrequently the little HUACs which emerged in these circumstances were rather maverick bodies, the creation of low-status politicos who were dissatisfied with the existing political order.[10]

The Tenney Committee was one such loose cannon, enjoying little respect even in the senate which sponsored it and at odds with the moderate administration of Governor Earl Warren. It early became the most notorious of the little HUACs, inspiring the couplet: 'A Communist is any / Who disagrees with Tenney.' In a series of disorderly hearings in Oakland in November 1947, for example, Tenney seemed eager to establish a Communist network embracing the Bay area's waterfront unions, the California Labor School, and the University of California. This 'exposé' of the liberal–labour–radical nexus of northern California was accompanied by bizarre scenes, as witnesses and attorneys threatened to resort to fisticuffs, a CIO lawyer was dragged to the back of the room by state patrolmen, and spectators were ejected for applauding. In 1948, aping the US Attorney General, the Tenney Committee published its own hit list of 'Communist Front Organizations', which was so sloppily composed that it embraced some undeniably patriotic groups as well as the old popular front, labour and communistic bodies that Tenney was targeting. Liberal or progressive fellow legislators were also occasionally named.[11]

Other little HUACs of the late 1940s also took aim at the progressive impulse. Like the Tenney Committee, Washington's Canwell Committee focused less on the CP itself than on the role of Communists in somewhat more respectable institutions, notably the Washington Pension Fund, the University of

Washington, the Seattle Repertory Playhouse – even the state legislature was said to have contained a Communist cell. Having discharged its duty of exposing 'Communist' professors, the committee left it to the university to find ways of sacking them, a fate which overtook three. Elsewhere, too, schools, labour unions and 'Communist fronts' were subjected to unfriendly scrutiny. The Broyles Commission in Illinois held its most celebrated confrontation with Roosevelt College and the University of Chicago, after the legislature had been disrupted by a group of student demonstrators. 'That crowd was the dirtiest, greasiest bunch of young people I have ever seen', fumed one Cook County solon. 'If they're dirty outside, how can they be clean inside?' The committee's obsession with front groups was catered to by its hired inquisitor, Dr J. B. Matthews, who proved to his own satisfaction that some 60 members of the university had been affiliated with 135 'Communist fronts'. Performing a similar function for the Callahan Committee in Michigan was the professional ex-Communist witness Joseph Kornfeder, who fingered various Detroit unions and Michigan campuses.[12]

These rather cavalier proceedings were usually directed at what remained of the spirit of political reform. Popular front politics had been prominent in California in the 1930s, when Communists had cooperated with prominent liberal Democrats, and in 1948 Henry Wallace's partisans there were able to build an exceptionally broad organization in the state. In Washington state too Democrats had embraced left-wing causes in the late 1930s, such as the Washington Commonwealth Federation and the Washington Pension Union. James A. Farley had even spoken of 'the forty-seven states and the Soviet of Washington', and its Democratic party has been described as 'a kind of united front organization'. In both states popular front activities were associated with advances in the labour movement, not least by Harry Bridges's International Longshoremen's and Warehousemen's Union, in which there was a strong Communist presence. The ILWU was also becoming a major force in Hawaii, whose Democratic governor (like Olson in California) had initially cooperated with its radical leaders. In the immediate postwar period, the Hawaiian ILWU was identified with the expanding progressive wing of the Democratic party, to the distress of old-guard Democrats. These connections again became the natural hunting ground for the territory's little HUAC on its creation in 1949.[13]

The little HUACs, of course, were not the only means of combating communism (or of reform causes), and some states with strong New Deal and Progressive traditions, such as Minnesota and New York, resorted to other techniques. Sometimes local political configurations reflected those in Washington DC, where conservative Republicans in Congress were redbaiting the Truman administration and seeking to discredit the New and Fair Deals. This was particularly evident in the industrial Midwest, where the relative strength of the Wallace movement in such states as Illinois and Michigan antagonized conservatives. In the years 1949–53, when the midwestern red scare was at its height, Michigan, Illinois and Ohio all had Democratic governors, for the most part confronting Republican legislatures. As James Truett Selcraig has shown, in rollcalls in midwestern legislatures Republicans supported anticommunist measures – including little HUACs – much more solidly than did Democrats. In Ohio the little HUAC was chaired by the Republican house speaker who, criticized by both the Cincinnati ACLU and the CP, responded that 'birds of a feather flock together'. Its subsequent programme was carried over the veto of the governor. In Illinois Governor Adlai Stevenson was initially reported to be quietly resisting the Broyles Commission, and when Senator Broyles subsequently pushed a stringent anticommunist bill through the legislature, Stevenson won the admiration of intellectuals throughout the country with an eloquent veto.[14]

The little HUACs of the late 1940s owed some of their confidence to their capacity to aid and abet one another. An anticommunist network was being created, particularly on a regional basis. The Canwell Committee took its official name and much of its stated mission from the Californian committee. Members of the Tenney Committee attended the Canwell Committee's hearings on the University of Washington, listening 'with intense interest'. Tenney and his vice-chairman Hugh Burns also travelled to Springfield, Illinois, in May 1948 to confer with members of the Broyles Commission, and the two bodies arranged to exchange copies of their reports. Jack Tenney visited Hawaii in 1949, offering his services in the creation of the territory's little HUAC, and the Hawaiian Committee in due course quoted regularly from the reports of the Tenney and Canwell Committees. When Governor Kim Sigler launched an anticommunist offensive in Michigan in 1947–48, members of the

California and Washington committees soon made contact with him. Also giving discreet assistance to members of this network was the FBI.[15]

By 1948 there was sufficient accord within this anticommunist fraternity for it to attempt a joint venture. A national conference of little HUACs, it was thought, would strengthen the bonds between the various state bodies, which might hold annual conventions and develop 'an integrated program that will once and for all put a stop to those treasonable individuals and organizations that are working 24 hours a day, 365 days a year to destroy this government of ours'. The proposal originated with state Senator Thomas H. Bienz of the Canwell Committee, and met with a favourable response: the Tenney and Canwell committees jointly sponsored an Interstate Legislative Conference on Un-American Activities, which duly met in Los Angeles in September 1948. The legislatures or governors of ten states sent representatives, as did several patriotic and veterans groups. These two days represented the high point of little HUAC history, as the representatives listened to one another's ideas for combating communism, their proceedings dignified by congratulatory speeches from such celebrities as Karl Baarslag of the American Legion and Richard Nixon of HUAC. They broke up pledging to meet again in 1949, but that was not to be. By then the Tenney and Canwell committees were in trouble.[16]

Briefly in the late 1940s the little HUACs seemed to be winning a grudging legitimacy. Like HUAC itself, they were not exactly elite creations, and a part of their vigour may be attributed to a populistic distaste for those in authority. But primarily the outbreak of little HUACs in the industrial states at this time can be credited to that larger conservative revival which sought to turn back the New Deal and the advances in the labour movement. For this purpose the techniques of exposure served well; when a conservative consensus settled on the country in the 1950s there was less need for little HUACs.

By about 1949 the enthusiasm for the politics of exposure had peaked. While the McCarthyite atmosphere of the early 1950s ensured that some little HUACs continued to function, state legislatures resorted to them more sparingly. One reason for this was that new methods for containing communism were coming into favour; another was that the consensual politics of the 1950s had less room for maverick bodies. But with the disappearance of

popular front or progressive politics, as illustrated by the humili-
ation of the Wallace movement, the techniques of exposure were
losing their attraction. In any case the behaviour of the
freewheeling committees was giving anticommunism a bad name.

In California the Tenney Committee made enemies more
readily than it made friends. Its notorious 1948 report, the
compendious list of alleged Communist front organizations,
encountered critics on the right as well as the left. The anticommunist Los Angeles *Daily News* upbraided the committee for 'over
zealously' bracketing 'scores of good citizens' with known
Communists. Even the country's leading anticommunist
newsletter, *Counterattack*, felt obliged to correct errors in the
report, lecturing the committee that it had found 'a perfect recipe
for DISCREDITING your work and making enemies for it
instead of friends'. By 1949 Tenney's fellow legislators – some of
them not best pleased at being described as Communist 'dupes
and dopes' – were turning against him. One recalled: 'By himself,
Tenney couldn't sway the legislature very much. I know that to a
lot of us the last two years that he had the committee, the question
was, "How do you dilute it down?" Or, "How do you minimize his
appropriation?"' The committee itself was allowed to survive, but
the price was Tenney surrendering the chairmanship. Other
investigators were meeting similar fates. The furore stirred up by
the Canwell Committee embarrassed the state's political
leadership, and the legislature ended its funding in 1949 while
Canwell himself lost a race for the state senate. The Illinois legislature also retreated after the chancellor of the University of
Chicago had discomfited the Broyles Commission, which was
terminated and its legislative proposals rebuffed. Broyles had
alienated the legislative leadership, and his request for an appropriation of $75000 to continue his mission caused particular
outrage, not least because he had failed to account for the money
he had already spent on 'joyrides' and 'renegade communists'.
The Oklahoma probe also occasioned the legislature some embarrassment, as when the committee chairman began the interrogation of each witness with the question 'Where was you borned
at?' The legislative elders, anxious to give the nation 'a better
picture of Oklahoma', put an end to the proceedings. Michigan's
Callahan Committee also contrived to stumble into the theatre of
the absurd. Its probe was consummated by a trial for contempt of
a recalcitrant student before the entire state senate, which made

itself 'the laughing stock of the whole country' in the view of one
of its members. Senator Matthew Callahan failed to secure re-
election in 1948 and his committee expired. The Arizona
committee too ceased to function.[17]

By the end of the decade the politics of exposure were losing
credibility (thanks partly to the antics of HUAC under J. Parnell
Thomas as well as the erratic state committees). Where little
HUACs were irresistible, the state authorities were trying to
contain them. New Jersey had hit on a restraining device as early
as 1947, when the legislature allowed the governor to appoint the
committee, and he nominated a respected educational administrator as chair and avoided political hacks; the committee agreed
in 1948 to conduct its proceedings 'without publicity' and then
contrived to take another five years to produce its anodyne
report. The political leaders of both New Hampshire and
Massachusetts reluctantly bowed to the authorization of little
HUACs in 1949 and 1950 respectively, the former achieving the
desired result when the committee concluded that no further
action was necessary; the exposure of Communists, it suggested,
was a federal responsibility. The Massachusetts committees of
1950 and 1951 also kept a low profile, holding no public hearings
and engaging in no redbaiting histrionics, although the outbreak
of the Korean War rendered it politically impossible to dismiss the
red menace. Something of an exception was the territory of
Hawaii, where the powerful ILWU seemed to signal a Communist
presence, attracting the attention not only of HUAC itself but also
of the Senate's Committee on Interior and Insular Affairs, which
recommended in 1948 that statehood be 'deferred indefinitely,
until communism in the Territory may be brought under effective
control'. Anxious to remove any obstacle to statehood, in 1949
Hawaii established its own Commission on Subversive Activities,
although in due course its activities too were limited by a
reduction in its appropriation.[18]

Co-option by the state

A few little HUACs did survive into the 1950s, and a few were
founded then, but they were tending to undergo a subtle change
in character. Less reckless than the freewheeling committees of
the 1940s, the 1950s agencies tended to be closer to the state
political establishments. Not only were the little HUACs anxious

to distance themselves from the cavalier ways of Jack B. Tenney, but for the most part the state governments of the early Eisenhower years were themselves more conservative than their predecessors. The Cold War and the Korean War had created a consensus in which there was little room for liberalism and in which communism was the acknowledged common enemy. The few little HUACs that operated in these years tended to function as part of the reigning order rather than as irritants of it. Massachusetts saw the reconstitution of its little HUAC in 1953, and by 1954 it was empowered by the support of Governor Christian Herter. The Bowker Commission, as it was known, was able to operate in the mid-1950s with both legislative and executive support. In New Hampshire, although the 1949 committee had found no Communist menace, a 1951 law empowered Attorney General Louis C. Wyman to develop a communist-control programme, and in 1953 he secured major revisions to it, giving him clearer legislative authority to subpoena witnesses and to require testimony under oath, and, crucially, to make public such information as he received. Wyman defined his function as 'a delegated legislative fact-finding investigation', in short, a kind of one-man little HUAC. He was encouraged in his activities by the businessman-governor Hugh Gregg, a McCarthy admirer, and was himself a protégé of Senator Styles Bridges. These investigators were not semi-detached demagogues like Tenney or Broyles; they were close to the ruling circles of the state, intent on preying on the powerless.[19]

California's committee again best exemplifies the evolution of little HUACs in these years. After Tenney had been forced off the committee, the chairmanship fell to Hugh Burns, another sometime New Dealer who had swung to the right. A far more astute politician than his predecessor, the clubbable Democrat Burns rose steadily in seniority, became president pro tem of the senate in 1956, and later was momentarily to serve as acting governor of the state when its two highest officials were simulta-neously absent, enabling Governor Ronald Reagan to grace him with the title Governor-Emeritus of California on his retirement. Burns chaired the committee with the circumspection expected of him, and it was never the loose cannon it had been under Tenney. He doubtless enjoyed the prominence the committee gave him, and he seems to have cherished the political support it won from the state's businessmen and veterans, whom Burns credited with the committee's longevity. But increasingly the committee was passing into other hands: control of it was largely being exercised by its chief counsel, Richard E. Combs.[20]

Combs – like Yorty, Tenney and Burns – had also been active in Democratic politics in the 1930s, and as a lawyer had represented victims of the Depression. He had been recruited by Sam Yorty as chief counsel for his 1940 committee, and he had continued to serve the committee through its various metamorphoses. By the time the complacent Burns became chairman, Combs had acquired considerable expertise, and in due course was to be consulted by officials in the federal and other state governments on ways of combating subversion. When he retired in 1970 he was thought to be the longest-serving state legislative aide in the whole United States, which suggests one reason for the long survival of the committee – it provided Combs with an income. (The committee furnished 'comfortable retirement slots for deserving political workers', according to one irritated senate leader.) But, like J. Edgar Hoover and Dr J. B. Matthews, Combs liked to think of himself as a professional, and like them he culti-vated informants, methodically maintained compendious dossiers on suspect individuals or groups, and crafted data-filled reports.[21]

Guided by Combs and Burns, the committee in the 1950s held fewer public hearings and gained a measure of respectability, in effect becoming an arm of the state's internal security system. In 1952 the so-called 'California Plan' was unveiled – a form of collab-oration between the state's campuses and the committee to vet faculty members and other employees – following a meeting of college presidents with the committee. Each campus was meant to have its own security liaison officer to work with the committee. Combs was soon boasting of removing over a hundred suspect Communists from educational institutions, a figure that the trigger-happy Tenney must have envied. He hoped to sprinkle the state's campuses, and presumably other public institutions, with ex-FBI men who would report to him, although the furore following the announcement of the California Plan seems to have frustrated any systematic surveillance programme. While the University of California, for example, did appoint a statewide security officer who liaised with Combs, it was soon claiming that his concern was only with security clearances in relation to defence contracts. Nonetheless, bodies such as the Los Angeles city housing authority, the city's board of education, the Pacific Gas and Electricity Company, and even the Los Angeles County Medical Association, for a period cooperated with the committee, abetting investigations, opening their files, and dismissing fingered employees. State agencies sometimes checked the committee's files before making appointments. Directly or indirectly the Burns Committee may have been responsible for denying jobs to several hundred people. The Los Angeles board of education not only asked the committee to conduct an investigation of its 26 000 employees but also provided it with funds to do so. In 1956 the committee lent its services to the San Francisco Public Library, which had asked it to vet a gift of books from the National Library of Peking. For some of the 1950s at least, the governor's office also checked state appointments against Combs's files. These files were updated with reports sent in daily to Combs by his unpaid informants across the state. Protected by the growing seniority of Senator Burns, a committee which had once served as a platform for the demagogic posturings of Jack Tenney was being turned into a bureaucratic surveillance system. Its energies went into compiling dossiers rather than framing legislation, and altogether it gathered 'subversive' files on some 20 000 people, including an unlikely Richard M. Nixon. It went out of existence in 1971 on Burns's retirement when the new president pro tem of the senate was outraged to find that it had been maintaining dossiers on two dozen fellow legislators, himself included.[22]

No other state committee managed to entrench itself in quite the same way as the Burns Committee. Nonetheless such committees as survived into the 1950s were less capricious than their predecessors and more likely to serve the internal security interests of the state authorities. The Hawaii committee screened the records of public employees, some 56 600 of them between 1951 and 1961. The Ohio committee chose to go out of existence once it had secured legislation to have the Attorney-General's office take over its surveillance responsibilities. In Massachusetts the commission established in 1953 soon secured police cooperation in checking the loyalties of the hundreds of suspect citizens reported to it. Discreet political surveillance was gradually replacing exposure as the function of the redhunters.[23]

The evolution of the remaining little HUACs into organs of the establishment was also evident in their shifting choice of targets. In the early postwar period university campuses had been the favourite stalking-ground of the little HUACs, as when the Canwell Committee probed the University of Washington or the Broyles Commission had its tense confrontations with Roosevelt College and the University of Chicago. The campuses and other educational institutions, with their minorities of student protesters and radical academics, never lost their lure for the little HUACs, but with the deepening of the Cold War, attention tended to shift to labour. In 1950 the CIO completed its purge of Communist-led unions, which then became susceptible to raids by other unions on their members, a process easily abetted by redbaiting politicians. Furthermore, the outbreak of the Korean War underlined the potential for industrial sabotage, or at least provided an excuse for probing the left-wing unions. Thus the Ohio Committee (OUAC), while not neglectful of education, paid considerable attention to the 'Communist-domination of industrial groups', especially in plants 'engaged in war work', most notably in the activities of the United Electrical Workers (UE). James B. Carey, the powerful anticommunist CIO leader who had organized an alternative to UE, energetically urged OUAC on. Carey also surfaced in Massachusetts, where he testified before the Bowker Commission, assisting it too in the harassment of UE workers. In New Hampshire, Attorney General Wyman similarly found targets additional to the state campuses, such as the relics of the Progressive party and the left-wing unions. In Hawaii too the focus came to be even more exclusively on labour, the little HUAC concluding in 1955 that 'Communist activity in Hawaii now appears to be centered almost entirely around the ILWU, its satellite union, the UPW, and the "Honolulu Record", weekly newspaper largely subsidized by the ILWU'.[24]

Those unions expelled by the CIO, of course, were easy pickings. The little HUACs of the 1950s were displaying scant initiative. Close to the ruling authorities of a state, they were abetting a process whereby employers and anticommunist unions were clubbing a dying labour radicalism. They were not so much 'exposing' subversives as justifying their own existence by engaging in the undemanding game of tormenting those already tagged as 'red'. The little HUACs, initially conceived by disaffected conservatives striking back at New Deal and popular front politics, had been absorbed into the establishment, a part of the consensual politics of the 1950s which put dissidence beyond the pale.

A disturbing postscript to the history of the little HUACs was played out in the South. As noted earlier, such committees were most commonly associated with the urban-industrial states, and in their heyday none appeared in the South, which had less of a popular front or labour tradition to rebuff. The South was relatively unmoved by Senator Joseph McCarthy's campaign, and Nathan Glazer and Seymour Lipset even concluded from a poll analysis that it was 'the most anti-McCarthy section in the country'. Even in Texas, an industrial commission appointed by Governor Allan Shivers was unable to find any current Communist activity in the state's unions, and Shivers himself in January 1954 said that the absence of Communists rendered a little HUAC unnecessary.[25]

But a few months later came the Supreme Court's celebrated decision in the *Brown* case, calling for the desegregation of southern schools. Many southern leaders responded with sightings of Communist subversion, and a number of legislatures established investigating committees to expose the aliens who were plotting revolution. Sometimes calling themselves legislative investigating committees, a few such bodies were explicitly designated as un-American activities committees. They directed their energies towards proving that civil rights groups were part of a larger Communist plot. Thus in 1958 Florida's little HUAC eagerly listened to the peripatetic Dr J. B. Matthews testifying to the large number of NAACP (National Association for the Advancement of Colored People) officers who had been associated with Communist fronts or activities, and in the following year he performed a similar service for the Mississippi committee. In the early 1960s South Carolina also boasted a little HUAC, which became engaged in a programme to inform citizens 'of the threat of communism to the National security'. By this date little HUACs had disappeared elsewhere in the country, except for California and Hawaii where they lingered on for the rest of the decade. Even in the South the little HUACs were disappearing by the mid-1960s. Fear of the red menace in Florida was being replaced by a concern over another kind of subversion in 1965, when the state's Legislative Investigation Committee turned its attention to 'the extent of infiltration into agencies supported by state funds by practicing homosexuals'.[26]

Conclusion

The history of the little HUACs is illustrative of the larger complex history of red scare politics in the United States. They drew their legitimacy from democratic and libertarian traditions, specifically from the principles of free inquiry and an informed public. Created and named for the most part by state legislatures, they could claim to be agents of the popular branch of government. Such a rationale eased the emergence of red scare politics, and although a few little HUACs were barely active, their presence usually signalled red scare sentiments of some intensity. A state might adopt a loyalty oath as a shield; a little HUAC was a weapon. They tended to appear in the more urban-industrial states, which housed clusters of Communists and other radicals as well as reactionary interests, and which were more likely to possess competitive two-party systems in which recourse to the Communist issue could be hard to resist.

But the eruption of little HUACs in the late 1930s, and again and more strongly in the late 1940s, owed much to that conservative reaction against the New Deal and progressive politics. The targets of these committees at this point were less the CP itself than its popular front allies, real or imaginary, to be found on the campuses, in the unions, or on the liberal wing of the Democratic party. And although highly conservative, there was something populistic about these bodies. They were not normally part of the political establishments of the states in which they appeared, but were rather maverick creations, sometimes the vehicles of demagogues willing to use them to harass or embarrass relatively liberal administrations, like those of Governors Olson and Warren in California or Governor Stevenson in Illinois. Seemingly at their happiest in redbaiting progressive political bodies or constituencies, the little HUACs did little to frame communist-control legislation. Such behaviour, however, did serve to discredit them, and it may be doubted whether much more would have been heard of them had the Korean War not broken out.

As an anticommunist consensus settled on the country in the 1950s, the little HUACs underwent some change in character. If one of their objectives had been to subvert that nascent progressive political formation which seemed to be emerging in some areas at the end of the Second World War, that objective had been achieved before the end of the 1940s. During the Korean War and after the little HUACs – those that survived – assumed a new place in the polity. Increasingly they were tending to merge with the states' ruling orders, functioning more as agents of the establishment than as critics of it. In some cases too they were taking on the role of political surveillance. As the demands of the national security state served to expand the authority and reach of the federal government, so the little HUACs seemed to enjoy a little reflected legitimacy as part of a state security apparatus. In some measure state governments had succeeded in harnessing red scare politics to their own purposes.

2

THE POLITICS OF PATRIOTISM: LOYALTY OATHS

In the 1940s there was a strong partisan dimension to red scare politics. Nationally, the Republican party used the Communist issue to harass the Truman administration, and in the states right-wing groups used it to undermine progressive formations (as Truman supporters also used it to undermine Henry Wallace's Progressive party). The politics of exposure suited these partisan purposes. But by the early 1950s anticommunist politics were taking on a new aspect. With the deepening of the Cold War, and with the outbreak of the Korean War in the summer of 1950, the Communist issue was projected to centre stage. Governmental and right-wing groups moved closer together, contributing to the formation of a pervasive anticommunist consensus which obliged almost everyone to engage at the least in a ritual disavowal of communism. Such emblematic forms of patriotism, however, often adopted as a minimal concession to red scare pressures, once instituted were to prove difficult to dislodge.

In founding a little HUAC a state was usually making an unequivocal declaration of war against domestic radicalism, but only a minority of states resorted to such high profile weaponry. Much the most common means of combating communism was the loyalty oath; some 80 per cent of states were imposing loyalty tests of some kind by 1953, most often by requiring public employees to sign a declaration of loyalty as a condition of their jobs. Millions of affidavits were sworn annually across the country, as teachers, social workers, legislators, doctors, clerks, caretakers, and state and municipal bureaucrats of all kinds insisted on their continued allegiance to nation and state. By the early 1950s the loyalty oath was the states' first line of defence against communism.

The passion for loyalty oaths thus peaked a little later than that for little HUACs, which were at their most visible in 1947–9. It was not until 1949 that there were widespread demands for oaths, demands which at that time were imperfectly met. Their advocates were more successful a little later, 1951 seeing their greatest impact. A number of influences contributed to this resort to loyalty testing, among them an extraordinary partiality for loyalty oaths reaching far back in American history. Most important was the outbreak of the Korean War, which required the mobilization of the citizenry at large in a patriotic repudiation of communism. If little HUACs were often the products of partisan politics, loyalty oaths were more the product of consensus. They became part of what sociologists have called a 'symbolic crusade'.[1]

Loyalty testing assumed many forms. Simple oaths of allegiance to uphold state and national constitutions had long existed for some public employees, but in the Cold War years they were being supplemented by explicit disclaimers of subversive intent. The aim sometimes was to bar subversives from elective office, and candidates found themselves taking loyalty oaths as they filed their election papers. A state could also extend loyalty tests to the various professions or occupations that it regulated, although the licensing power of the state was to give rise to some bizarre requirements, as in the case of the wrestlers and boxers of Indiana who had to take an oath before setting foot in the ring. Oaths also varied in stringency. The most common was that modelled on the federal civil defence oath, swearing support for the American Constitution and disavowing advocacy of the forcible overthrow of government or membership of a group with that objective. But the renunciation of subversion could go further. Oaths sometimes required an explicit denial of membership of the CP or of the bodies on the US Attorney General's notorious list of subversive organizations. In Georgia employees had to name any family member who had ever belonged to a subversive body, and one reportedly cited his father – as a member of the Confederate Army![2]

The growth of loyalty testing

One reason for the pervasiveness of loyalty oaths is that they were a well-established feature of American political culture. They could be said to constitute the glue of nation-making, a part of the process of building colonial societies in the New World and later of creating the United States. The very first document to be printed in the colonies was a loyalty oath, used by Massachusetts Bay Puritans to swear fealty to their Commonwealth, and royal authority soon made oaths to the Crown commonplace throughout the colonies. The convulsions of the War for Independence put pressures on individuals to declare their loyalties, and by 1778 every state had followed George Washington's advice to 'fix upon some oath or affirmation of allegiance'. America's second great civil war let loose an even greater orgy of oath-taking, and the loyalty of some citizens was again disputed during the First World War. After it the Red Scare focused suspicions on the true allegiance of radicals and aliens. The most formidable of the investigations then undertaken, that of the New York legislature's Lusk Committee, identified as critical the ways in which citizens were socialized; 'in the last analysis', it concluded, successful education depended upon 'the character and viewpoint of the teachers'. The committee recommended a law requiring public schoolteachers to secure 'a special certificate certifying that they are persons of good character and that they are loyal to the institutions of the State and Nation', and New York duly introduced a loyalty oath for teachers in 1921.[3]

This preoccupation with the formative role of teachers was an enduring one. In a nation defined less by ancient prescriptions or geographical boundaries than by common values, the role of education in sustaining the political and social order was critical. This sense that Americanness rested on a set of shared beliefs was especially acute in the 1920s, when the ethnic variety of the people seemed to threaten that commonality, as did the country's apparent exposure to alien influences. The public school system came under intense scrutiny, as patriotic groups fretted about impressionable minds and demanded loyalty oaths for teachers and 'Americanized' textbooks. Over half-a-dozen states followed the lead of New York in requiring such oaths. The 1930s saw similar pressures, particularly in the middle of the decade, when the Hearst press, the American Legion, and the Daughters of the

American Revolution (DAR) mounted a campaign against Communist influence in colleges and schools. Several state departments of the Legion submitted loyalty oath bills to their legislatures, and nine states enacted such laws in 1934–5. Often these bills (which usually required no more than a promise to uphold the law and constitution) excited little comment, but sometimes battle broke out between patriots and civil libertarians. In Connecticut two Socialist representatives led a successful fight against a bill. The governor of Maryland effected a Solomonic decision by vetoing an oath bill while explaining 'that it did not have enough teeth in it'. By 1941 about half the states used teachers' loyalty oaths, a few of them relics of the Civil War but the great majority creations of the ideological perturbations which had disturbed American public life since the Red Scare.[4]

Thus it is hardly surprising that the loyalty test once more became a primary means of promoting internal security in the dangerous years from 1949. The existing oaths of allegiance could be amended by the simple addition of a paragraph disavowing any interest in a Communist or violent revolution. Such a recourse would avoid the opprobrium attracted by little HUACs and the expense associated with registration schemes and other elaborate communist-control measures. Further, they would allow everyone to be enlisted in the Cold War. The politics of patriotism would replace the politics of exposure.

In the late 1940s loyalty tests began to supplant little HUACs as a favourite state anticommunist device. Teachers were among the first to suffer, being subjected to oaths in five states in 1949. In Texas a vigorous attempt was made to impose an oath on university students, some of whom, when they lobbied against it, were told by the sponsor: 'You are lower than any skunk who ever crawled on the face of this earth.' But loyalty oaths were now being pressed on other citizens too. Oaths aimed at all public employees were enacted in seven states, and New Jersey was perhaps the first to adopt a loyalty oath for candidates for public office. But the loyalty oath drive was not universally successful in 1949, the American Civil Liberties Union (ACLU) reckoning that more bills had failed than succeeded. Certainly the proposals which aroused greatest controversy were rebuffed. This was in part because they were being pushed by little HUACs whose behaviour was already being widely condemned. In Illinois Paul

Broyles had been promoting anticommunist bills since 1947, and
five of his measures, among them loyalty oath legislation, went
down to defeat again in 1949. Even more spectacularly, the
several loyalty oath bills being pushed by Jack Tenney in
California passed the senate but were rejected by the assembly.[5]

Much more cheering to the advocates of loyalty oaths was the
experience of 1950, for the outbreak of the Korean War in the
summer created a sense of crisis and a number of governors
called their legislatures into emergency session. The United
States, it seemed, was now at war with the red enemy, and in
many states the divisions earlier occasioned by the Communist
issue were replaced by a measure of consensus. Loyalty oaths in
particular were often seen as innocuous. Even an ACLU representative in New Hampshire had advised against making a test
case out of a teacher loyalty oath since he believed that 'any
teacher ... should be willing' to take it. President Truman's call for
a revitalized civil defence programme in effect invited the state
governments to mobilize. He commended to the states the loyalty
oath administered to federal civil defence workers, and this (with
variations) became the most widely used of the state oaths.
California adopted a sweeping loyalty oath in September, a widely
reported measure because of the attention already drawn to the
state by the Tenney Committee and the great oath controversy at
the University of California in 1949. When other state legislatures
met early in 1951 some of them adopted the California version, a
distinctive feature of which was a denial of disloyal activity for the
previous five years. Loyalty oath laws were passed in at least nine
states in 1951. The deluge thinned thereafter but did not stop,
while states with loyalty legislation already in place contrived to
add to it (a favourite pastime of California patriots, ever on the
prowl for new groups to whom oaths could be extended). By the
mid-1950s, with public employees widely subjected to loyalty
testing, there was some tendency for attention to shift to those
occupations or professions licensed by the state – which might
demand proof of loyalty before issuing permission to practise.[6]

By 1953 the great majority of states were using loyalty oaths of
some kind. An ACLU survey of that year identified 42 states
employing loyalty oaths. Only 11 states now used loyalty oaths for
teachers alone, and all public employees were expected to take
oaths in 24 states, as they were also in the territories of Alaska and

Hawaii. The politics of patriotism had penetrated every region of the country, encompassing states of contrasting economic, social and political characters. The few states which resisted this temptation are perhaps more deserving of notice (although they may have been developing other communist-control measures). There were just seven of them, that is Rhode Island, Delaware, Minnesota, Wisconsin, Iowa, Missouri and Wyoming. It was suggested earlier that little HUACs were most likely to appear in the more urban-industrial states, with their clusters of labour and radical groups; conversely, the rural Midwest seems to have been a little more resistant to the politics of patriotism than some other parts of the Union.[7]

While the long tradition of loyalty testing and the patriotic emotions released by the Cold War help to explain the explosion of loyalty oath laws, they do not tell the whole story. There was something patently irrational about the loyalty oath, as some of its sponsors admitted. What was its purpose? Since Communists were held to be totally unscrupulous life forms, worming their way into public employment in order to subvert the great experiment in democratic government, they would presumably lie when obliged to take an oath. Patriotic legislators responded that a Communist who had falsely executed a loyalty affidavit could be charged with perjury, a conviction for which could mean not only loss of employment but also a jail sentence. (This was illustrated in 1950 by the celebrated conviction of Alger Hiss for perjury, after he had denied on oath being a spy.) The loyalty test at the very least should give subversives pause. But even this argument rested on the premise that Communist employees would somehow be found out, despite their reputation for being fiendishly clever. The historical evidence was against the loyalty testers. There had been oath tests for teachers in many states for two or three decades, but perjury convictions or even dismissals for false swearing had been very rare. Massachusetts had employed loyalty oaths for teachers for 15 years by 1950, but none had ever been removed for proven disloyalty. Nonetheless loyalty oaths were eagerly adopted, sometimes as milder alternatives to a little HUAC, but also because they enabled both legislators and citizens to make their own contributions to the great war against Soviet communism.[8]

Politicians accustomed to taking oaths of allegiance often failed to anticipate the resistance that the stronger oaths could provoke, and usually had little sympathy with protests about freedom of speech. Oklahoma legislators told campus protesters at a loyalty oath that they 'should hunt a job elsewhere' and scorned the 'unscrupulous objections of professors'. An Iowan state senator, in proposing an oath bill, said that he was asking nothing more than to 'require teachers, janitors, and other public employees to stand up and be counted as not associated with traitorous activities'. The loyalty oath to many Americans was not so much an instrument as a symbol, a ritual of patriotism which afforded some pride when the nation was in peril. 'I don't know why anyone should object to an oath of office,' said one sponsor of a loyalty bill, 'I get a thrill when I take my oath.'[9]

The politics of patriotism could descend into murkier waters. The demonization of radicals that accompanied the effective outlawry of the CP rendered them highly vulnerable. The Oklahoma Commander of the American Legion, which was deeply implicated in the formulation of the state's loyalty oath bill, sent a telegram to a hesitant governor pointing out that '50 000 Legionnaires ... believe strongly that a bill should be adopted for the protection of our taxpayers who pay for the upkeep of our present form of government. The American Legion is opposed to one nickel of tax money going to the salary of any individual who would speak against democracy and our form of government.' There were a number of messages here, among them that government and public service belonged to the taxpayer, who might reasonably determine conditions of employment, and that Oklahoma's Legionnaires were also 50 000 voters. And there could be even murkier reasons for the adoption of loyalty oaths. When a state like Kansas enacted such measures, it was their symbolic import that mattered. Yet there were communities in which the loyalty oath could be used as a weapon. One was California, with its popular front heritage and its clusters of liberals and radicals, many of whom had once belonged to organizations listed as subversive in the infamous Tenney Report of 1948. Jack Tenney may have lost control of his committee, but that did not lessen his support for loyalty oaths, which could be used to harass those whom he had identified as enemies of his country. A Californian employed by the state – perhaps in its

educational or welfare agencies – who had once been a member
of a popular front group, would have a choice of refusing to take
the oath and losing the job, or taking it and risking being prosecuted for perjury. Richard Combs's intimidatory files were packed
with photostats of the activities and memberships of a wide array
of progressive groups. After his 1949 loyalty bills had gone down
to defeat, an exasperated Tenney revealed that his committee
believed there to be 'about 15000 or more bona fide Communists
in Los Angeles' and 'several times that number of fellow
travelers'.[10]

Political calculations also played their part in the adoption of
loyalty oaths. Public opinion was consistently in favour of loyalty
and other anticommunist measures, and no politician liked to be
seen to be giving comfort to the Communist conspiracy. In one
opinion poll (taken in the summer of 1954 when the anxieties
aroused by the Korean War had eased), 91 per cent of respondents believed that a schoolteacher who was an admitted
Communist should be sacked. A politician about to meet the
electorate needed a strong nerve to resist measures designed to
flush out Communist subversives. A few politicians like Jack
Tenney and Paul Broyles tried to make the anticommunist
crusade their *raison d'être*, although this degree of zeal usually
narrowed their constituency and limited their political careers.
But more centrist politicians often found it prudent to bow to
anticommunist pressures. When Adlai Stevenson as governor of
Illinois won liberal plaudits for eloquently vetoing the Broyles
bills in 1951, he was not running for re-election that year; when
California's Earl Warren in the summer of 1950 decided to join
forces with Jack Tenney in a call for a loyalty oath, he knew that
he would be facing the electorate again in three months. One
reason why the city of Los Angeles was among the first to adopt a
loyalty oath was the perception of the city fathers that the
citizenry would not tolerate otherwise. 'I am coming up for
election next April', one councilman told a reporter. 'I want to
stay in office and if this "cold war" becomes a "hot war", I don't
want to have to try to explain to my constituency why I voted
against this measure.' Similar agonizing characterized the debate
over loyalty oaths in the California legislature in 1949. 'This old
state is celebrating its 100th anniversary this year and we've
gotten along all right without this stuff', said a Democratic assem-

blyman. 'My wife doesn't make me swear allegiance to her every day. She believes in me. ... The people who want to overthrow our Government aren't going to be stopped by any loyalty oath.' He then voted for it. In 1951 the minority leader in the Pennsylvania senate made equally clear his distaste for a loyalty oath bill but announced that he would vote for it so that the Democratic party would not be 'further stigmatized' as 'un-American'. The politics of patriotism in Pennsylvania survived rather a long time. An assemblyman who voted against repealing the loyalty oath as late as 1967 told a reporter in 1994 that 'I had no more courage then than I have today. And no less common sense.'[11]

The California experience
California remains the paramount example of a state wedded to the loyalty oath. No other state enacted as much loyalty legis-lation, and in no other state were there as many victims. In California too the various stimulants to such legislation were highly visible.

California's susceptibility to patriotic and right-wing impulses has been extensively discussed. Both reactionaries and radicals had long flourished in its fertile soil, which was a magnet for millions of Americans in the 1930s and 1940s. The prosperity of this land of opportunity in the Cold War years gave some credence to the ideology of individualism and free enterprise. Patriotic pressures were strongest in southern Californa, where the individualist ethos may have been promoted by rapid economic growth, by a suburban sociology typified by the predominance of single-family homes, and by the weakness of institutional identities or ties, such as those associated with ethnic neighbourhoods or political parties. The striving individuals of this culture, often newcomers to the state and relative strangers to one another, perhaps sought security in ideology, which for some was a patriotic Americanism. Loyalty oaths were a badge of membership, an affirmation of allegiance to an otherwise impal-pable body politic.[12]

California, of course, had earned a reputation for superpatri-otism well before its flirtation with loyalty oaths, which, as elsewhere, did not really develop until 1949. During the 'little red scare' of 1938–41 California had banned the CP from the ballot and established what became known as the Tenney Committee. Loyalty oaths were not a major demand at this time, and did not feature among the dozen anticommunist bills that Tenney introduced into the legislature in 1947. It was the patriotic city fathers of Los Angeles who first demonstrated the potential of this device to the state, and indeed to the nation.[13]

The Truman Doctrine and the federal loyalty programme, both announced in March 1947, excited some attention from Los Angeles politicos. The former dramatically offered American assistance to regimes threatened by communism, while the loyalty programme required the screening of federal employees for 'disloyalty'. The cavortings of HUAC, on which sat southern California's own Richard Nixon, also made an impression in Los Angeles. The Los Angeles city government, warned councilman Ed J. Davenport, 'is already a target for invasion by the Communist party'. In fact it was the more conservative (and rural) county of Los Angeles which acted first, in August 1947, introducing a loyalty oath for employees which required them to disavow both subversive intentions and 150 organizations listed by the Tenney Committee. Davenport urged the city council to follow suit, and collaborated with Tenney and Richard Combs to draft a resilient loyalty ordinance, duly adopted by the council in 1948. 'We at the grass roots of government in the City Council feel safer and more sure of our ground as we meet the agitation that is constantly brought before us ...', explained Ed Davenport. 'We know now we can turn with assurance and safeness to a legislative committee ..., manned by a competent staff and headed by a man like Senator Jack Tenney, our own representative here in the South.' The axis established between the Tenney Committee and local politicians in Los Angeles produced results. Soon recalcitrant county employees were losing their jobs, proof of the efficacy of the loyalty oath.[14]

The success of the Los Angeles ordinances both in sustaining court challenges and in impaling employees was not lost on Jack Tenney, who in 1949 introduced another 13 anticommunist bills, 7 of them proposing loyalty oaths; Tenney cited the Los Angeles experience as 'the basis of most of our bills'. One fateful bill was aimed at the University of California, which had been regularly attacked by the Tenney Committee for its allegedly lax attitude towards Communists. Also unnerving for the university were the recent Canwell Committee hearings in Washington state, which had resulted in three professors losing their jobs. Confronted by the immediate prospect of speaking engagements on campus by Herbert Phillips (one of the dismissed professors) and Harold Laski (the British socialist), the university's board of regents in June 1949 adopted its own loyalty oath. Though milder than Tenney's, the senator acknowledged that it was 'a step in the right direction' and dropped his own bill. For the next three years the convulsions at the University of California disturbed academics across the country, as the refusal of many professors to sign a Communist disclaimer resulted in some thirty losing their jobs. Meanwhile, Tenney's extravagances, and his implication of fellow legislators in the Communist conspiracy, so exasperated the assembly that all his 1949 bills were rejected, while he lost the chairmanship of the little HUAC.[15]

Unlike the university, the state had refused to succumb to the politics of patriotism. The legislature was not due to meet again until 1951, by which time Tenneyism should be no more than a bad memory. But in the event California was indulging in a veritable orgy of oath-taking by the end of 1950, with one Californian in ten (and all state employees) expected to swear loyalty. The Tenney reply to the red menace had triumphed after all.[16]

What precipitated this conversion was the outbreak of the Korean War and Governor Earl Warren's response to it. In Congress, the Korean War speeded the passage of the McCarran Internal Security Act, with its requirement that Communist organizations register, and in a kind of reflex action Ed Davenport introduced a resolution in the Los Angeles city council calling for all Communists in the city to register with the police. 'American boys are now engaged in a shooting war', he explained, and warned that Communists would be 'undermining, impeding, and sabotaging our war production and defense efforts'. Others in the state shared this ominous vision. Even southern California's ACLU activist, the Rev. A. A. Heist, virtually despaired of protecting civil liberties 'when no one knows how soon each of us will be inside of a Communist belly'. When Earl Warren called a special session of the legislature to strengthen civil defence preparations in the summer of 1950, Jack Tenney and his lieutenant in the assembly, Harold Levering, hastily proffered a batch of sweeping communist-control bills.[17]

In some respects Warren shared the apprehensions of the patriotic right. Like many other Californians, he believed the state to be perilously exposed, and he was equally convinced of the hazardous nature of the Cold War. 'Our country is at war, ostensibly with North Korea, but actually with the Soviet Union', he insisted in a broadcast in August. He warned of the possibility of atomic war and urged the need for protection from 'almost certain sabotage on the part of fanatical Communists among us who, while enjoying the liberties of this country, glorify in their disturbed minds the slavery of Soviet Russia'. He had conceded the Tenneyite claim about the presence of dangerous subversives, although he saw little merit in the draconian remedies being urged by the superpatriots, from whom he had previously kept his distance. President Truman, however, had issued 'solemn directives on civil defense ... [which] cannot be treated lightly, particularly by California which has at least three major atom bomb target areas', and had commended the federal loyalty oath. Warren seized on this as an answer to the emergency. A loyalty oath could head off more drastic legislation and would have presidential approbation. Further, by embracing it Warren could dispel the suspicions he had aroused when he resisted the regents' oath at the University of California. Assemblyman John E. Moss congratulated Warren for 'a sane program for handling subversives, notable for its lack of hysteria.'[18]

Warren now made common cause with the patriots, collaborating with Senator Hugh Burns (the new chair of CUAC) and Assemblyman Levering in the preparation of a loyalty oath bill. In the event, the resulting Levering Act went somewhat further than the federal civil defence oath, requiring dissociation from subversive organizations not only currently but for the past five years. It also – sweepingly – made every public employee a 'civil defense worker'. Teeth were provided by a clause withholding paychecks from those who did not sign the oath within 30 days. The bill was not passed without some resistance, a small number of progressive Democrats in both the assembly and the senate opposing the measure. Signalling his conversion to the politics of patriotism, Warren promptly took the oath himself on signing the bill on October 3rd, wanting to be the first to do so, but was beaten to this honour by assemblymen and senators who had rushed to take it even before it had become law. In the fall of

1950, with American boys dying in Korea and Richard Nixon campaigning in California for the US Senate against the 'Pink Lady', Helen Gahagan Douglas, the politics of patriotism were all but irresistible.[19]

Earl Warren had used the loyalty oath to secure a near-consensus on the issue of internal security. He could believe that he had averted more extreme legislation and united the political community behind him. His stance carried some conviction since in the critical year 1940–1 he had also expressed his views on the peculiar vulnerability of California, then favouring the exclusion of the CP from the ballot. But in 1950 conviction coincided with expediency. Warren was running for re-election at a time when Americans were calculating the chances of the Korean War escalating into world war, and the gubernatorial campaign was largely fought on defence issues. The Democratic candidate, James Roosevelt, proposed the creation of 'shadow cities' to house 4 million people in the event of an atomic attack on the West Coast, an idea compared to which Warren's loyalty oath seems eminently sensible. Roosevelt had been on the progressive wing of the Democratic party, and his nomination had upset conservative Democrats such as Hugh Burns. In creating a consensus around the loyalty oath, Warren could hope to win over disaffected Democrats in the fall election. His sense of the imminence of nuclear holocaust remained with him after he had been re-elected: he used his third inaugural to speak of 'the shadow not just of a possible but a probable third world war.'[20]

In forging an accord on a loyalty programme Warren hoped to pre-empt the sweeping proposals of the Tenneyites, but he soon found that he had unlocked a Pandora's Box. This was to be a persisting dilemma for moderate or liberal politicians through the Cold War era, as they struggled to find 'safe' ways of containing the Communist issue but succeeded only in legitimizing and enhancing it. California's legislative session of 1951, which Warren opened with a call for further civil defence preparations, saw the introduction of over thirty bills to 'combat Communism', among them proposals to amend the state constitution by writing the Levering Act into it, to require a non-Communist oath by all candidates for public office, and to extend the Levering oath to any business or profession requiring a licence from the state. The politics of patriotism were becoming the dominant discourse in California in the early 1950s.[21]

A bill to require a loyalty oath by lawyers aroused particular controversy. Lawyers who had been defending victims of the Cold War red scare, whether before investigating committees or the courts, had become the subjects of patriotic wrath, not least in California where some of the more distinguished members of the bar had lent themselves to this suspect cause, as in the case of the Hollywood Ten. When in 1951 Hollywood personalities such as Edward Dmytryk began to admit CP connections, it seemed that California lawyers had indeed been aiding and abetting traitors. Hugh Burns, the bill's sponsor, argued that it would 'smoke out Communist lawyers', who would lose their licences if they refused to take it and could be subject to perjury prosecutions if they did. The bill, he thought, would be a major blow to Communist activity because 'the legal arm of the Communist Party is vital to its existence'. Burns evidently believed that the loyalty oath could be an effective communist-control device, presumably because in the state's popular front past a goodly number of lawyers had revealed their progressive sympathies and were vulnerable to loyalty tests. The *Call-Bulletin* gave the lawyers' oath bill 'a better than even' chance of passing because of 'the recent "confessions" of former Hollywood Communists'. But in taking on the legal profession the patriotic right had ventured too far. Lawyers mobilized against the bill, creating the statewide Lawyers Against Test Oaths for the Bar, other civil liberties groups took up the cause, and the bill was defeated. The bill to extend loyalty oaths to licensed professions met a similar fate. But if on this occasion they were seen off by the professionals, the loyalty testers enjoyed some victories. A Tenney bill to require loyalty oaths from candidates for public office did make it to the statute books, as did the bill to write the Levering Act into the state constitution. This was an important measure, politically and symbolically. Among other things it meant that a loyalty amendment would have to be put to the voters in the 1952 elections.[22]

The lawyers were not the only group to organize. Soon after the Levering Act's passage, a number of threatened professors and public employees had formed the Joint Action Council for Repeal of the Levering Act, which in November 1950 held a major rally in San Francisco. But the old popular front associations of a few of its leaders proved an embarrassment to other civil liberties groups, notably the ACLU. The burden of opposition came to rest on the broader Federation for the Repeal of the Levering Act, an 'organization of organizations' chaired by Dr Eason Monroe, a nonsigning professor dismissed from San Francisco State College. Affiliated to it were various educators, medical and social workers, civil liberties and labour groups. The aim of repeal was quickly overtaken by the events of early 1951, when further loyalty measures were passed and when protesters were faced with the prospect of the referendum on inserting the Levering Act into the state constitution. The referendum became a major focus of the politics of patriotism.[23]

The loyalty issue was also moving into the courts. Since the passage of the Levering Act in September 1950, hundreds of Californians had been losing their jobs, largely because of their refusal to swear the required oath, among them college professors, schoolteachers, social workers, and nurses. By December at least 890 people were known to have defied the Levering oath, the biggest concentration being at the University of California. Some of those dismissed took their cases to the courts, where in due course they reached the California Supreme Court. Judgement was eventually reached in October 1952, when the court upheld the Levering Act but invalidated the regents' oath on the grounds that the state had already 'occupied the field'. The court's reasoning on the validity of the Levering Act was somewhat tortuous, for the state constitution mandated only an oath of allegiance and expressly declared that 'no other oath ... or test, shall be required' of officeholders, but the court concluded that being neither 'religious' nor 'political' the Levering test was not of the prohibited kind. The overthrow of the regents' oath brought little relief to the University of California – because its employees were subject to the Levering oath. At about the same time the US Supreme Court upheld the Los Angeles loyalty oath for city employees. California's loyalty oaths were proving uncomfortably buoyant.[24]

But the Levering oath had still to be written into the state constitution, and on this issue battle was joined. Proposition 5, if approved, would replace the old oath of allegiance in the constitution. Also before the voters in 1952 was Proposition 6, a Tenney-inspired measure to bar 'subversive' persons from the public service. Campaigning strongly for these measures was the conservative press, particularly the Hearst newspapers, the *Los Angeles Times* and the *Oakland Tribune*. Their cause was helped by the publicity attending the California Smith Act trials of 1952 and by a HUAC investigation of Los Angeles in October. Resisting the amendments were the Federation for the Repeal of the Levering Act and the ACLU, which lobbied the legislature, organized mailings and press releases, staged rallies, distributed billboards and made much use of radio spots. As polling day neared they were joined by such bodies as the Democratic State Central Committee, the League of Women Voters, the AFL, the CIO, the California Federation of Teachers, Americans for Democratic Action, and even by Governor Earl Warren. But this display of respectability could not overwhelm the politics of patriotism in California. The voters ratified the amendments, although by the relatively narrow margin of two to one. (The proportion supporting the Levering bill in the legislature had been higher.) One county defiantly rejected both propositions, namely San Joaquin, location of the labour town of Stockton, where the State Federation of Labor, the Grange, and the *Stockton Record* mobilized effectively against the loyalty tests. Although they took some comfort from the size of the 'No' vote, the forces opposing the Levering oath were ravaged by the outcome of the referenda. The oath, already upheld by the California Supreme Court, was now written firmly into the state constitution and seemed all but immovable. In January 1953 the Federation for the Repeal of the Levering Act decided to disband.[25]

With the voters having explicitly endorsed loyalty measures, the 1953 session of the legislature opened with yet another array of anticommunist bills. Despite the hundreds of people who were leaving the public service, the patriotic right still believed that too many subversives were escaping detection. The Burns Committee, as California's little HUAC was now known, was one group to fret over its inability to punish Communists suitably. In its 1953 report it spoke of its 14 years of experience, during which it had learned that 'when it possesses a stack of original documents, such as catalogs of Communist schools, brochures of Communist fronts, ... and reports of Communist activities – all of which repeatedly mention a certain person; and when such a person is subpoenaed and appears at a hearing accompanied by a lawyer with a similar record; and when the witness repeatedly invokes the Fifth Amendment as a refuge when questioned about his Communist affiliations, ... the committee can draw no other conclusion except that the Communist record of the individual as reflected by the committee's files and the pattern of interrogation is entirely accurate.' Angered by the resilience of members of California's old popular front community, and encouraged by the McCarthyite atmosphere of the time, such patriots moved to close the loopholes in the anticommunist armoury, as when they won legislation requiring teachers and other public employees to answer questions about their affiliations before official bodies. And loyalty oaths were still part of the prescription. One law of 1953 required churches, veterans and non-profit organizations to execute loyalty affidavits to retain tax-exempt status, despite Quaker and Unitarian protests. In their zeal to close off every refuge to suspect citizens, the patriotic right had pointed up one of the weaknesses of their programme – that it was more likely to ensnare conscientious objectors of unquestioned loyalty than authentic subversives.[26]

But after the ending of the Korean War the politics of patriotism began to lose some of their vitality in California. Changing Cold War pressures interacted with changing political patterns in the state to create an environment less favourable to the patriotic right. Party organization had long been weak in California, one of the conditions which had helped Earl Warren to forge a consensus on loyalty issues in 1950. Warren, although nominally a Republican, liked to regard himself as nonpartisan, generally assumed a moderate stance, and in the 1950 campaign had made political appearances only before Democrats-for-Warren clubs. Warren's loyalty oath proposals in 1950 had been supported by most legislative Democrats, including party leaders such as Sam Yorty and Hugh Burns. But in the course of the 1950s this consensual style of politics began to break down. Warren himself disappeared to the US Supreme Court, and the Democratic party began to revive. Party divisions sharpened, not least over internal security matters, as some Democratic leaders questioned the utility of communist-control laws, and the patriotic right came to be largely marginalized as a Republican faction.[27]

One sign of the times was the political demise of Jack Tenney, careering into a right-wing wilderness. He had predicted that the election of Dwight Eisenhower in 1952 would be 'the end of the Republic', from which awful fate he had tried to save his country by running as the vice-presidential nominee of Gerald L. K. Smith's Christian National party. In 1954 he lost the Republican primary for his state senate seat, which in November was won by a liberal Democrat. In the gubernatorial campaign that year redbaiting was strongly rebuked by the Democratic candidate, Richard Graves, who in a television address assailed 'character assassins' who were trying 'to create an atmosphere in which it is dangerous to have more than one viewpoint', and accused Governor Goodwin Knight of McCarthyism. Graves was not elected, but his party increased its share of the vote. A part of the Democrats' difficulties in the 1954 campaign was that one Democratic official had admitted to once having been in the CP. One consequence was the yet further extension of loyalty oaths – a 1955 act required them of members of county central committees of political parties. But this brazenly partisan measure tied the politics of patriotism to the Republicans. In October 1955 the California Federation of Young Democrats adopted a recommendation that their party leaders oppose all loyalty oaths. As the Democratic revival continued through the 1950s more politicians cool to loyalty tests assumed office. In 1956 the Democrats were able to organize the state senate for the first time in the twentieth century, electing as president the adroit Hugh Burns, who had cleaved to Warren in 1950 but who was now distancing himself from the politics of patriotism.[28]

Loyalty legislation was beginning to lose its appeal. While an occasional progressive Democrat or schoolteacher might be revealed as being possessed of a radical past, the great majority of the hundreds of public servants who fell foul of the California oath laws of the 1950s were evidently not disloyal. These victims were predominantly those who had declined to take an oath, the Levering Act itself never producing any perjury prosecutions in the 1950s (though two schoolteachers were eventually arraigned under it in 1967). Attorney General Edmund G. Brown as early as 1953 considered loyalty oaths 'practically impossible to enforce', prosecution being both cumbersome and highly expensive, and district attorneys were reported to be 'sidestepping' prosecutions. The law imposing a loyalty oath on churches in particular helped to bring the loyalty crusade into disrepute. While most churches complied, whether because of their own patriotic sentiments or because in this era of church-building they could not afford to forgo any tax privileges, a few resisted. By 1954 a number of Quaker, Jewish, Unitarian, and Lutheran groups had refused to sign. The same law applied to veterans, and a wounded veteran also filed a suit challenging its constitutionality. A Citizens' Committee to Preserve American Freedoms emerged to mobilize labour and religious groups against the loyalty oath laws. A repeal attempt failed in the legislature in 1955, but the highly charged debate again put the patriots on the defensive. The *San Francisco Chronicle* observed that the 1955 session had 'a higher record for respecting, maintaining and defending the liberties of Californians than any Legislature since the end of World War II'. A few months later it was reported that a US Senate committee headed by Tom Hennings, investigating infringements of constitutional rights, was interesting itself in the California church oath law.[29]

By the mid-1950s it was usually possible to stop new loyalty oath laws from reaching the statute books, but those on the books could not be easily removed. Another attempt to repeal the church loyalty oath failed again in 1957. As elsewhere in the country, it was the courts rather than legislators which eventually dismantled the creations of the politics of patriotism. In 1958 the US Supreme Court ruled the church oath law unconstitutional. On other California laws the US Supreme Court seemed slow to act, perhaps because Earl Warren as Chief Justice was not enthusiastic about reviewing laws he had signed as governor. But in the heady atmosphere of the 1960s a number of Californians defiantly refused to sign the Levering oath and found greater public sympathy for their stand. After the US Supreme Court had moved against the loyalty oath laws of other states, the California Supreme Court was finally emboldened in December 1967 to strike down the Levering Act. Some of those Californians who had refused to sign now began to return to their old jobs. One landmark case was that of Dr Eason Monroe, who was dismissed from San Francisco State College in 1950 and who was reinstated by court order in 1972, when he was cordially welcomed back by the right's new hero, President S. I. Hayakawa.[30]

Hawaii, Oklahoma, Pennsylvania

No other state proved quite as zealous as California in the pursuit of loyalty oaths, but only a handful escaped loyalty legislation of some kind. A number of the circumstances which had promoted the politics of patriotism in California were present in other states, if in milder degree. All were subject to the critical influence of federal example, and particularly the presidential request to make adequate civil defence preparations, which could include a loyalty oath. Most possessed groups of superpatriots, their demands amplified by a conservative press, who needed to be either discredited or placated. Also common were clusters of real or imagined radicals, capable of becoming the focus of patriotic fury, against whom old scores might be settled. Principle and expediency often reinforced one another as insecure legislators competed for the honour of a ritual enlistment in the Cold War and as political leaders calculated the advantages of siding with veterans and patriotic societies in an election year. Harassed governing authorities looking for some convenient way to signal the state's patriotism were drawn to loyalty oaths as moderate devices around which a consensus might be fashioned.

One area ardently to embrace the politics of patriotism was the territory of Hawaii. As in California, the presence of old popular front and radical groups (notably the longshoremen's ILWU, designated in 1949 by the CIO as a Communist-led), enraged patriotic conservatives, while the islands' business leaders were never averse to weakening the power of labour. But what also made loyalty a sensitive political issue was the territory's ambition to become a state. In 1949, after a visit by its chairman, the US Senate's Committee on Interior and Insular Affairs recommended that statehood be 'deferred indefinitely, until communism in the Territory may be brought under effective control'. This report coincided with a major dock strike led by the ILWU, and an emergency session of the territorial legislature rushed through a package of anti-subversion measures, including a non-Communist oath for all public employees. When a constitutional convention drafted a constitution for the prospective state, it included a loyalty oath disavowing forcible overthrow. In the spring of 1951, as the Korean War focused attention on the strategic importance of the Pacific, a yet more stringent anticommunist programme was enacted, including further provision for loyalty oaths. Civil libertarians were troubled by the vagueness of the legislation, which not only denied public employment to anyone about whose loyalty there was 'reasonable doubt', but also required employees to file a 'personal history statement' covering 'such information as the [Loyalty] Board shall prescribe'. The governor, his mind on statehood, bought peace by appointing persons of some respectability to the board, including a number of moderates and liberals.[31]

In Oklahoma it was the campuses that irritated patriots. Legislative suspicions of academics and students were of long standing, as witnessed by the 1941 senate probe of the University of Oklahoma. A non-Communist oath for public officials (not teachers) had actually been adopted with little notice in 1945, and trouble only flared in 1949 when a special oath for teachers and students was proposed. It was campus protests at this which precipitated the state's ill-fated little HUAC of 1949. Although the committee was laid down, the global events of 1950 caused patriotic pressures to mount again, and in the fall the state's American Legion demanded an oath for all public employees. At the beginning of the 1951 session and with the example of California before it, such a bill was introduced into the legislature, which it eventually negotiated without a single negative vote, the foreign crisis having induced a momentary consensus. Similar to the California model, the bill also contained dubious provisions of its own, notably in its use of the US Attorney General's celebrated list of subversive organizations, and in requiring signers to take up arms for the state if the need arose. Campus and other opposition to the bill grew after it went to the governor, its unusual features provoking unfavourable or bemused comment, such as how could foreign nationals employed by the state be expected to fight for it? The governor had initially favoured a loyalty oath as a patriotic emblem, in order 'to keep us in line with the thinking of the rest of the country'. But his doubts about the bill grew and he asked for reconsideration by the legislature, precipitating a debate in which the politics of patriotism were shrilly reaffirmed. Legislators wondered what the 'rabble-rousing college teachers were making such a fuss about' and called the protesters 'drones and intellectual bums'. Finally the governor, strongly encouraged by the American Legion, signed the bill, and heads were soon rolling. By July 1951 about a hundred people were thought to have left the state's service, some by resigning or by allowing their contracts to expire.[32]

As in California resistance centred on the campuses, initially the University of Oklahoma and later the Agricultural & Mechanical College, where eight teachers took the matter to the

courts. As in California too, what heightened the political sensitivity of the loyalty oath was the alleged abuse of religious
freedom: conscientious objectors were required to pledge that
they would bear arms in an emergency, as were aliens working for
the state government. The Oklahoma Supreme Court supported
the legislature, arguing that there was no constitutional right to a
public job and that employees had to serve on whatever terms
were set. The case moved on to the US Supreme Court, which in
1952 unanimously struck down the Oklahoma law, following a
principle recently established which held that people should not
be penalized for membership of an organization if unaware of its
subversive intent. But Oklahoma's patriots were not prepared to
let the matter rest there. The conservative press and veterans'
groups pressed for a new oath, and in March 1953 the legislature
adopted another law, with but one lonely senator voting against
it. The revised version required an affirmation that the signer was
not a member of the CP or of any group 'known to me' to favour
violent overthrow, contained a promise not to advocate violence
'by the medium of teaching', and a promise to take up arms or
offer noncombative service in an emergency (thus placating
conscientious objectors). In contrast to the 1951 Act, this measure
encountered little public opposition. Teachers and others were
apparently prepared to pledge that they did not advocate
violence or revolution. A moderation of the law had produced
something close to consensus. The new loyalty oath law went into
effect without disturbance and by 1955 it remained unchallenged
in the courts.[33]

In Pennsylvania a critical role was again played by the governor
who, like Earl Warren, somewhat unexpectedly decided to
attempt to lead the patriot cause. It was also a state in which the
loyalty oath itself was relatively mild, as some of its victims
attested. Only a few lost their jobs because of the measure, but it
briefly occasioned considerable controversy.

The oath bill was fashioned by the state American Legion,
whose representative, Senator Albert R. Pechan, introduced it
into the legislature in January 1951 as public nerves were being
stretched by the Korean War. At first it excited little comment, but
during a long gestation period it acquired new sections,
eventually emerging as a general communist-control bill. But the
loyalty oath provisions remained central and attracted the

greatest controversy. The eventual Pechan Act required all state employees (including teachers) and candidates for elective office to swear loyalty oaths, and also provided for the dismissal of those found to be subversive and the denial of employment to those about whose loyalty there was 'reasonable doubt'. Teachers in universities and colleges were not required to take loyalty oaths as such, but these institutions had to file annual reports on their procedures – which could include oaths – for excluding subversives from their staffs. It was Pennsylvania's radicals who first took exception to the bill, and opposition centred around the Teachers Union of Philadelphia, which did contain CP members. Albert Pechan snarled that 'Communists, pinks, and fellow-travelers' were ganging up against him. But the attention served to broaden the opposition and protests erupted on several campuses. The Pennsylvania State Education Association, with its 60 000 teachers, entered the lists against the bill, as did Quaker groups and respectable newspapers such as the *Philadelphia Inquirer*. At a large meeting in Philadelphia prominent lawyers and businessmen disputed the need for it. The bill looked destined to succumb to these formidable adversaries, but in mid-summer the governor, John S. Fine, threw his weight behind it and called for a 'loyalty program' in strong speeches before the Veterans of Foreign Wars (VFW), the American Veterans of World War II (AMVETS) and the American Legion. This imparted a new impetus to the bill, which became the focus of intense lobbying and which finally became law after it had been watered down, much to Senator Pechan's disgust. Politicians who doubted the need for a loyalty measure thought it prudent to vote for it.[34]

By March 1952 almost all of Pennsylvania's public employees had taken the oath. But there were a few casualties, including eight people who were discharged for refusing the oath, comprising three teachers, three doctors, a nurse and a social worker. Three of them were members of the Society of Friends; none made plausible subversives. One described the wording of the oath as 'relatively innocuous' and another as 'harmless'; they were simply refusing as a matter of principle to sign a measure which promoted conformity and inhibited freedom of discussion. Later in the year the candidates of four minority parties, including the Prohibition party, were refused access to the ballot because they failed to take the loyalty oath. Further, while most colleges and universities had found no difficulty in certifying that they were free of subversives, one, Pennsylvania State College, briefly made a loyalty oath a central part of its procedures, leading to the temporary discharge of one employee. As was often the way, whatever else the Pennsylvania loyalty oath was doing, the people whose jobs it was taking were evidently not Communists.[35]

The Philadelphia branch of the ACLU took up the case of the eight people who had lost their jobs, particularly that of Marie Fitzgerald, a Quaker and a nurse. Her action was unsuccessful, for although the state court recognized that she was 'utterly opposed to communism' it nonetheless upheld the Pechan Act. State courts usually did side with state legislatures on security issues; unfortunately for the nurse her case did not reach the federal courts. But the Pennsylvania casualties remained few in number. By 1955 no one had been discharged as subversive from the state's public employ; indeed, the only victims known to the Philadelphia ACLU were the eight discharged in 1952. The Pechan law remained on the books, despite periodic attacks upon it. More courageous than some Pennsylvania politicians was George M. Leader, who had voted against the Pechan bill in the senate and who in the course of a successful race for governor in 1954 described it as a 'malevolent instrument of discrimination against educational and religious minorities', but the legislature was not emboldened by his example. The law was modified in 1967 but an attempt to repeal the oath provision failed. A ruling by the state attorney general in 1975 freed applicants for state government jobs from taking the oath, but in theory local government workers and schoolteachers were still subject to it, as were candidates for elective office. In practice, most local governments and school districts ceased to apply the oath, although there were occasional reports of it being used, and in 1994 the Democratic and Republican candidates for governor swore the oath. Unless the courts were willing to intervene, state loyalty legislation tended to remain in place.[36]

The slow death of loyalty oaths
If loyalty oaths were the most pervasive kind of anticommunist device, they were also the longest lived. Fashioned as instruments

of consensus, they tended to become part of the political fabric. They could not be dispensed with as readily as little HUACs; changes in political fortunes rarely produced repeal, and legal challenges had less hope of success than was the case with more complicated or draconian legislation. While the glut of loyalty oath bills diminished appreciably in the mid-1950s, those that made it to the statute books tended to stay there for some years. As civil defence measures their utility remained highly questionable. Even in California they were not used to press perjury prosecutions, and the only visible victims were Quakers and other conscientious objectors who refused to take loyalty oaths on principle. And the oaths lent themselves to ridicule. The Texas legislature enacted a loyalty oath after having been exasperated by an opinionated student radical, who thereupon happily took it because it did not require him to renounce the CP by name. The one avowed Communist of Monterey County, California, a 67-year-old caretaker, enthusiastically signed the Levering oath to the fury of local officials, pointing out that he had no need to advocate the violent overthrow of the government because it would 'collapse from its own rottenness'. Yet largely ineffective and derided as the loyalty oath laws were, the state legislatures and even the state courts proved loath to undo them. Political capital was not risked on them.[37]

Only when federal judges were willing to intervene was there much hope of striking down loyalty legislation, as civil rights activists had also been finding with the South's segregation laws. But even the federal courts moved cautiously. The Supreme Court was dismantling other kinds of federal and state communist-control programmes in the late 1950s, but hardly touched loyalty oaths. It did annul Oklahoma's sweeping loyalty oath in 1952, but upheld those of Los Angeles, New Jersey and New York. It was not until the 1960s that the Court more consistently began to chip away at the legislation enacted at the height of the politics of patriotism. In 1960 an Arkansas law (requiring teachers annually to submit a list of the organizations to which they belonged) was annulled because of its 'unlimited and indiscriminate sweep'. In the following year the Court held a Florida loyalty oath law to be too vague. A major decision came in 1964 in the case of *Baggett* v. *Bullitt*, after several dozen staff and student members of the University of Washington had brought a class action suit against two Washington loyalty oath statutes of 1931 and 1955. The US Supreme Court invalidated them because of their 'unduly vague' language, and the ruling strongly encouraged civil liberties groups to press further cases. In 1965 loyalty oaths in Idaho, Oregon and Georgia were struck down or restricted. Another major decision came in 1966, when the Supreme Court by a narrow margin shifted the grounds on which such legislation was tested, deciding in an Arizona case that witting membership of a subversive organization was not enough to attract a penalty – that would require actual engagement in illegal acts. And in 1967 a large part of New York's Feinberg Law was found to be unconstitutional by the Warren Court, which in the same year struck down Maryland's oath. By the late 1960s, following the lead of the Court, the lower federal and state courts were regularly dismantling loyalty oath legislation. Loyalty oaths were not quite a thing of the past, but they were joining the dustbin of history.[38]

3

THE POLITICS OF REGULATION:
COMMUNIST-CONTROL LAWS

By the 1950s the doctrine of exposure was losing credibility. In part this was a consequence of the unsavoury publicity attracted by the Tenney, Canwell and Broyles committees, not to mention HUAC itself. Many states, as we have seen, reached for the easy solution of the loyalty oath, which allowed the emotions of patriotism to be engaged at low cost. But the loyalty oath was often a product of prudence rather than conviction, the preferred option of pragmatic politicians more sensitive to public opinion than to constitutional niceties. True believers in the red menace yearned for a more robust defence of American virtue. There were other reasons too for a hardening in the offensive against domestic communism. The 'losses' of Czechoslovakia and China in the late 1940s and the outbreak of the Korean War in 1950 had heightened the image of an insatiable communist bloc stretching out across the world. Within the United States a series of sensational 'spy trials' competed for the headlines for much of 1949. The eventual convictions of Alger Hiss in January 1950 (technically for perjury but in effect for spying), of Judith Coplon for espionage in March, together with the arrest of Klaus Fuchs in Britain, seemed confirmation enough that the United States had been successfully penetrated by Soviet spies, an impression deepened by the arrests of Julius and Ethel Rosenberg in the summer of 1950. Propagandists on the right seized on these events as evidence of the dangers of tolerating American communism, however far it may have been exposed. Their campaign was eased by the popular alternative image of communism as a sort of loathsome vice, for which the old American remedy of prohibition seemed appropriate. As with other prohibitionist legislation, however, this technique for controlling the red menace was to enjoy limited success.

The redbaiting magazine *Counterattack* summed up the repressive viewpoint:

> *The CP* is a Fifth Column, a Conspiracy.
> *It must* be dealt with as a conspiracy.
> *New laws* are needed for that purpose.
> *But a mental lag* prevents people from catching up with that fact.[1]

By the turn of the decade new laws were being fashioned on this premise. In September 1950 a Congress energized by the Korean War passed the Internal Security or McCarran Act, requiring Communist and Communist-front organizations to register with the government. The states were barely any slower to act. There were laws to exclude the CP from the ballot, to deny public employment to Communists, to oblige Communist organizations and their members to register with the authorities, and even to outlaw the CP entirely. The state of Texas contemplated the death penalty for Communists. In some respects the attempts to deny the CP access to the ballot and to public employment did not differ much from loyalty legislation, since the loyalty oath was frequently the technique used to bar Communists from public life. But several of these laws went further. It was one thing to protect the public service; it was another to criminalize the Communist party or to make its members divulge information about themselves to the state. The state, in short, was seeking to regulate the lives of private citizens.

The politics of regulation were not entirely new. Many states retained regulatory laws from earlier eras. A profusion of laws directed at sedition, anarchy or criminal syndicalism was enacted during the Red Scare of 1917–23, and a further wave of state laws followed in 1939–41, several of them imitations of the Smith Act. But most states adopted some kind of communist-control legislation, if we may so designate those regulatory devices which did not rely on little HUACs or loyalty oaths. A 1953 ACLU survey concluded that there were only seven states free of communist-control legislation of this kind; a few such laws had been enacted before the Second World War, but the majority came after it. The seven unregulated states were Idaho, Nevada, and Utah in the West, North and South Dakota and Nebraska in the Great Plains, and Maine, New England's most rural state. The mountain and Plains states, perhaps, felt little need to regulate communism. For the rest, there were three broad strategies that could be adopted. The first was eliminating Communists from public service; the more ambitious alternatives were to outlaw them or to regulate their activities. Prohibition of the CP best exemplifies the politics of regulation, but first brief attention must be given to more realistic attempts to control it.[2]

Protecting the public service: New York

As a kind of variation on the loyalty oath, several states banned the CP from the ballot and Communists or other subversives from public employment. Frequently, of course, eligibility for these positions was dependent on a loyalty affidavit, although a few states attempted to impose such debarments without using an oath. Several states had enacted bans on the CP's participation in elections during the 'little red scare' of 1939–41, but between 1945 and 1954 as many as 25 states passed laws prohibiting the placing of CP or subversive candidates on the ballot or requiring a disclaimer oath from them; 16 of these were passed in the years 1951–4, when the perception of the CP as an agent of a hostile power was at its strongest. Embracing such disparate states as Wyoming, Indiana, Texas and Alabama, there was no easily identifiable common characteristic prompting this particular response. Similar devices designed to exclude Communists from public employment were enacted in 29 states between 1945 and 1954; 18 of these were passed in the anxious years 1951–4. Many of them, of course, were directed against teachers and deployed loyalty oaths. Like the loyalty oaths too, many of these communist-control measures stemmed from the anticommunist consensus induced by the Korean War.[3]

Excluding subversives from public employment was the defence mechanism adopted by the state with much the largest number of Communists within its borders, in a strategy which resulted in an extraordinary bloodletting. In the Cold War period at least, New York resisted the temptation to let loose a little HUAC or to outlaw the CP, but it fashioned two pieces of legislation designed to protect it from the red menace. One was the 1949 Feinberg Law, intended to cleanse the school system of subversives. A second measure, the security risk law of 1951, facilitated the dismissal of suspect employees from other public agencies by removing the standard civil service protection. With both of these measures, New York went somewhat its own way.[4]

There may have been less of a need for a little HUAC in New York in this period because the Rapp–Coudert Committee of the early 1940s had already trained an unwelcome spotlight on radical teachers. Then over thirty dismissals or resignations had been secured, mainly from City College, but the hunt had been called short by the Second World War. The advent of the Cold War afforded an opportunity to complete the purge. In fact, New York already possessed an old law denying public employment to subversives, but the legislature was persuaded in 1949 that in the school system at least it was not being enforced. Citing 'common report' that the CP had infiltrated the public schools, and finding that it was pledged to teach a 'prescribed party line' too 'subtle' to detect in the classroom, the legislature directed the board of regents 'to take affirmative action to meet this grave menace'. Such action included the submission of annual reports on the loyalty of teachers, and the promulgation of a list of subversive organizations, membership of which would provide prima facie evidence for disqualifying a teacher from employment. In New York City, spurred by a zealous superintendent, school officials soon embarked on the cumbersome process of reporting on employees, while the state board of regents appointed a committee to draw up the required list of subversive organizations. The committee was interrupted in its labours by a legal challenge to the Feinberg Act, but when the law was eventually upheld in 1952 it resumed its public hearings. Finally in September 1953 the list of prohibited organizations was published and was found to contain but two entries – the Communist Party of the USA and the Communist Party of New York. Ironically, however, like many pieces of anticommunist legislation, the Feinberg Law exerted psychological rather than legal force. New York City school officials came to circumvent it, finding that

existing regulations allowed them to dismiss teachers who refused
to answer questions before authorized bodies. Goaded by the
interest that Congressional committees took in the recalcitrant
teachers of New York, the purge resumed and by 1955, on one
estimate, over 250 had resigned or been dismissed. Another
estimate put the number of 'expulsions' through the 1950s of
schoolteachers at 321 and of college teachers at 58. Not until
1967–8 did the US Supreme Court invalidate the laws that had
been used to remove them.[5]

New York was also the only state to adopt a security risk law.
This was passed as an emergency measure during the Korean
War and permitted the transfer or dismissal of employees in
'security positions' or 'security agencies' as designated by the
state's Civil Service Commission. Opposed by a small group of
Democrats in the legislature, critics of the measure were
disturbed by the lack of procedural safeguards and outraged by
the comment of a sponsor that dismissals should not be appealed
because a reversal would put a 'stigma' on the authorities for
'having fired an innocent man'. But to Governor Thomas Dewey
the law represented 'a sincere attempt to combat within the state
government the danger of persons dedicated to foreign
ideologies'. It evidently served some bureaucratic purpose,
because it was renewed annually even after the Korean War had
ended, and by 1956 some 30 per cent of state employees and as
many as 81 per cent of New York City employees were so
classified. Even palaeontologists and sanitary workers were
among those held to be in sensitive positions. The ACLU, the
AFL–CIO and Americans for Democratic Action campaigned
against the law, and Governor Averill Harriman urged its
revision, but the legislature extended it repeatedly. In 1956, of
the 16 legislators who voted against the law 14 were Democrats
from Manhattan or Brooklyn and two were upstate Republicans.
In the late 1950s the coverage of the act was restricted and in
1960 it was finally allowed to expire. Compared to the number of
New York teachers who lost their jobs the effects of the security
risk law were arguably not very drastic, but by 1958 some 85
persons of over 340000 scrutinized had resigned or been
removed or disqualified, most of them in New York City. New
York had devised its own communist-control programme, and
like that of California it had considerable human impact.[6]

Towards prohibition

But excluding Communists from public employment and denying them access to the ballot were not enough to defeat the red menace, at least not according to many patriots. If the CP was indeed an alien conspiracy, bent on the overthrow of American government in the interests of a foreign power, there could be no legitimate place for it within the polity. Variations on this message were pressed endlessly in the late 1940s and early 1950s. HUAC's chief investigator patiently explained in *The Red Plot Against America* that there is a 'Communist conspiracy against the Government and the people of the United States', one which operated 'astutely within the texture of our Constitution and the resilient borders of our native tolerance'. Former Communists such as Louis Budenz were lining up to tell Congressional committees and the public that the CPUSA was indeed part of a conspiracy masterminded in Moscow. 'I want to show beyond question that the Communist party is not a political party in the American or democratic sense', he wrote in a 300-page book, 'but solely a fifth column of the Kremlin.' Karl Mundt, who as a member of HUAC spent some years trying to devise a federal communist-control bill, explained in 1950 that communism was not a party but 'an international conspiracy not employing the ballot at all, but employing such techniques as infiltration, sabotage, intrigue, and force, and what I call conspiratorial cohesion'. He called for both federal and state laws to combat it. There was nothing particularly new in these analyses, but the course of international and domestic politics was giving them greater credence at this time, and the grandest authorities in the land had come to accept them. The federal prosecution of the CP leaders, whose 1949 conviction was upheld by the Supreme Court in 1951, was based on the Smith Act and the assumption that the CP was a Soviet-directed conspiracy dedicated to the overthrow of American democracy. The Internal Security or McCarran Act of 1950, designed according to its author to 'fortify the home front even as we are today fortifying our boys on the battlefield of Korea', similarly treated domestic Communists as subversives and required Communist and Communist-front organizations to register with the government. The loyalty and trustworthiness of American radicals at any point in American society, not simply in government, were being called into question.[7]

There were broadly two remedies proposed by those who wanted to place strict curbs on communism. One was to follow the lead of the Smith Act and try to find ways of outlawing the CP. Because the party could change its name this was not easy, and reliance came to be placed on formulations which made it a crime to advocate the forcible overthrow of government. The rich corpus of Marxist writing could then be plundered to show that members of Communist groups did subscribe to such doctrines. The other route was that pointed by the Mundt–Nixon Bill and then the McCarran Act, putting Communist groups under surveillance by requiring them to register with the authorities and supply information about their members. Between 1945 and 1954 ten states enacted laws seeking to outlaw Communist or 'subversive' organizations, all but one between 1949 and 1954, and eight states adopted laws requiring them to register, all between 1951 and 1954.[8]

The first state in the postwar period to make a serious attempt to put Communists beyond the law was Alabama, where a highly visible effort to re-establish the CP in Birmingham in 1946–7 provoked a hostile response from a white power establishment already disturbed by Operation Dixie (the CIO attempt to unionize southern workers) and the civil rights policies of the Truman administration. The legislature adopted a number of anticommunist measures in 1947, central to which was an unusually comprehensive law which authorized the dissolution of the CP if it was found guilty of advocating the forcible overthrow of government. In 1949 Kansas too adopted its own version of the Smith Act, making the witting advocacy of overthrowing the government punishable by a prison term of up to ten years and a fine of up to $10 000, half the penalties specified by the federal measure. But attempts to outlaw communism did not really gain momentum until Maryland showed the way with its celebrated Ober Act of 1949.[9]

The Maryland experience

Long commemorated as the 'Free State', Maryland could lay some claim to a traditional sensitivity to civil liberties. It had survived the first Red Scare without resort to hysterical measures, had not taken Prohibition very seriously, and had not adopted repressive anti-labour laws. In 1935 an attempt by a Methodist Episcopalian clergyman and an American Legion officer to form an American Loyalty League to combat 'subversive efforts' in the state had failed when a meeting to launch it attracted a small turnout. But the state's tolerant heritage was misleading. By the late 1940s the reigning Democratic party was still perpetuating the power of a white supremacist establishment, and the growth of industry in Baltimore and elsewhere had created a conservative business class only recently challenged by labour organization. The influential Roman Catholic church reflected the antisocialist values of the American Catholic hierarchy, and had been lending its authority to the anticommunist cause in Maryland's labour movement. And by this date the operation of the Communist issue in American politics was serving to strengthen these local conservative forces. The proximity of Washington to Maryland and the employment of many of its residents in the federal government meant that charges focused on the red menace were well publicized. When HUAC staged its celebrated confrontation between Alger Hiss and Whittaker Chambers in 1948, Marylanders became aware that both an alleged and a self-confessed Communist conspirator had resided among them. In 1950 another famous confrontation, that between Senator Joe McCarthy and Maryland's Senator Millard Tydings, intensified the Communist issue in a state which was already moving to defend itself. Determined to rid the Senate of his tiresome critic, McCarthy became deeply implicated in the Maryland senatorial campaign, when unscrupulous anticommunist propaganda was launched at the conservative grandee Tydings, who succumbed to a devastating defeat. Maryland, it seemed, was being convulsed by its own red scare.[10]

The 'Free State', then, was probably more than usually receptive to the anticommunist persuasion in the late 1940s and early 1950s, when it commanded widespread attention for its 'model' communist-control programme. As in several other states, Cold War tensions had first surfaced in 1947, when veterans and Catholic spokesmen were inveighing against the red menace and a little noticed bill to amend the constitution to ban subversives from office passed the legislature without opposition. But its subsequent submission to the electorate in 1948 compelled a public campaign, which became bound up with a broader onslaught on communism. One of the more actively patriotic groups in Baltimore was the Kiwanis, at a meeting of which state Senator Wilmer C. Carter became alarmed by what he heard about the red menace from a former FBI officer. Carter promptly introduced a resolution into the legislature calling on the governor to appoint a commission to prepare legislation 'to expose and expurgate subversive and other illegal activities', and it was speedily adopted in May 1948, primarily because the lawmakers' attention was focused on other matters. The issue was further stirred by the Baltimore school board in June, which decided that Communists could not be accommodated in a school system whose aim was 'to help develop good citizens, loyal to the American way of life'. Its determination to oust subversive teachers was strengthened by the complaints of local politicians about its employment of the wife of the prominent CP leader Philip Frankfeld.[11]

Maryland's lawyers too were becoming worried about official indifference at the Communist threat, and at the end of June the Maryland Bar Association called on lawmakers to prohibit subversive organizations, offering it as their expert view that 'it is within the constitutional powers of Congress and the state legislatures to pass laws outlawing the Communist party'. A powerful advocate of this thesis was Frank B. Ober, whose address to the meeting was widely republished, and whose views commanded attention well beyond the state's borders. Ober's influence rested in part on his stature. He was not an uncouth demagogue engaging in indiscriminate redbaiting; he was a graduate of Princeton and Harvard, a senior partner in a firm founded by a former state governor, and an author of scholarly law articles.

What disturbed Ober was the negligence of government and judiciary, federal and state, in the face of impending danger. The CP, he insisted repeatedly, was not an indigenous growth but 'a conspiratorial organization and the spearhead of a threatened foreign attack upon us'. Given the Soviet success in undermining regimes elsewhere, it was absurd for Americans not to protect their democratic institutions. The Supreme Court in particular was guilty of 'the exaggerated application of civil rights to a field which threatens our national survival'. Even the Mundt–Nixon Bill, with its registration provisions, did not go far enough for Ober: the only security lay in outlawing the CP, and a carefully crafted law could do just that. In developing this robust view (that the preservation of democratic freedoms justified prohibiting disloyal bodies), Ober cited a variety of authorities, including congressional reports, J. Edgar Hoover, and several law review articles. Five days after delivering this address, Ober was appointed by the governor to the chairmanship of the Maryland Commission on Subversive Activities, whose responsibility it was to fashion a communist-control programme for the state. He was joined on it by Wilmer C. Carter, together with nine other legislators and prominent citizens. The governor had appointed Ober in the knowledge that his ambitious personal mission was the proscription of the CP. The federal and several state governments had already experimented with various sedition laws, but none had really claimed to have turned Communists into outlaws. (The federal indictment of the CP leaders under the Smith Act occurred just after Ober's appointment.) Banning the CP would require not only fastidious legislation but also political will – sufficient support for any such measure would need to be mobilized to overcome the explosion of protest from radicals and civil libertarians.[12]

Mobilizing popular support for a vigorous anticommunist programme became the task of state Senator Carter, whose Kiwanis sponsored a number of meetings with representatives of patriotic, veterans, commercial, civic and religious societies in the fall of 1948. The objective was to form an 'organization of organizations' to combat communism, and HUAC's Karl Mundt attended at least one of these meetings, urging state action. The outcome was the Maryland Committee Against Un-American Activities, chaired for a time by Carter, which by December claimed the allegiance of some 55 local groups. This was an unusual body. It was not a little HUAC because it was not a creation of the state; it was a private group of a kind which rarely appeared in red scare politics, a field effectively occupied by existing lobbies such as the American Legion. It was clearly well connected, for a former State Commander of the American Legion succeeded Carter as chairman, and the Baltimore city treasurer joined it. Sponsors included the American Legion, the Baltimore Bar Association, the DAR, the Independent Federation of Catholic Alumnae, and the Public School Association. But equally important was the range of business groups supporting the committee, among them the Association of Commerce, the Maryland Petroleum Industries Association, and the Real Estate Board. CP spokesman Philip Frankfeld claimed the 'real power' behind it to be the 'labor-hating, Big Business employers ... who have never accepted the trade unions'. The new group's objectives were twofold: securing the passage of the constitutional amendment prohibiting subversives from holding public office, and helping the Ober Commission to develop an anti-subversion programme. The committee was well financed, so much so that it was able to employ a paid director and secretary, and local businesses offered it facilities of various sorts. It was this support which made it effective. On its own estimation, the committee distributed over half-a-million handbills and postcards in its campaign for the constitutional amendment. It also placed advertisements in over thirty newspapers, and used its contacts, such as former Baltimore mayor Theodore R. McKeldin, to secure favourable commentary on radio stations. Resistance by civil liberties and liberal groups and the *Baltimore Sun* proved futile and the electorate decisively approved the anticommunist amendment by 202910 votes to 84132. The committee held a celebratory dinner and resolved to stay in existence to support the work of the Ober Commission.[13]

The Ober Commission was buoyed by the referendum vote, which it believed 'definitely and finally indicates the views of the people of our State with respect to any character of subversive activities whatever'. The Commission proceeded not by holding formal hearings or summoning witnesses (it had no subpoena power), but by a careful study of existing laws and legal opinions. It was evidently determined to avoid the histrionics of other little HUACs, emphasizing that its remit was 'to formulate and prepare a legislative program', not to act 'as a fact-finding Commission', a reference to the 'Fact-Finding' Tenney and Canwell Committees which were then receiving so much adverse publicity. The doctrine of exposure, in its view, was insufficient to protect the republic, as evidenced by the advance of communism in other countries in the preceding ten years. The Ober Commission took it as axiomatic that communism in the United States was 'a treasonable conspiracy', and from this premise could only devise a programme to eliminate the CP and other subversive groups. It set its face against any 'investigating commission which might be accused, whether justly or unjustly, of "red baiting" or "witch hunting"'. Execution of the programme was to be entrusted to 'the traditional law enforcement authorities'.[14]

There were three principal strands to the Ober proposals, presented in January 1949. One owed a great deal to the Smith Act, but tried to improve on it by making *advocacy* of the forcible overthrow of government illegal only when committed under 'such circumstances as to constitute a clear and present danger to the security' of the nation or state. To make the thrust of this legislation clearer, it was also made a felony knowingly to participate in a 'foreign subversive organization'. Ober's emphasis on knowing participation in subversion and on the well-tried legal doctrine of a 'clear and present danger' was meant to fortify the proposed law against charges of vagueness. A second and novel feature was the provision of enforcement machinery: the state attorney general's office, via a specially appointed assistant attorney general, was to be responsible for investigating and prosecuting subversion, and offenders could be indicted only when a grand jury was satisfied that there was a case to answer. States had often enough enacted sedition laws without providing enforcement machinery. The Maryland solution was a permanent institutional unit with a clear remit, headed by an experienced lawyer answerable both to the attorney general and to a grand jury. This was to be no police 'red squad': the attorney general's proposal for a police investigator had been firmly rejected in favour of 'a civilian, a trained lawyer who would have the respect of the public'. The third main element in the programme was a loyalty oath required of all candidates for appointive or elective office. Again, care was to be used in the formulation of this oath, and past associations were not to be inquired into. Further, public educational institutions were to be permitted to make their own arrangements for guaranteeing the loyalty of their employees, although they would have to report on their procedures to the state authorities before they could expect funding.[15]

The Ober Commission applauded itself on its finely crafted proposals. It had not attempted to outlaw any organization by name, for its definition of subversion was meant to focus on acts rather than beliefs, thus not (in its view) interfering with free speech or academic freedom. Current members of subversive groups would be given time to recant, any files compiled would be strictly confidential, and responsibility for executing the programme would rest with trained professionals. The Commission's respect for civil liberties, however, had not blinded it to the Communist menace, which would be dealt with severely. Any person found guilty of sedition was subject to a prison term of up to 20 years and a fine of up to $20 000, the same hefty penalties as in the Smith Act. Any organization found to have violated the law was to be dissolved and its records seized.[16]

The Ober proposals were presented to the legislature in January 1949, and warmly welcomed by a public meeting in Annapolis, reportedly attended by a large number of Catholic women. Catholics were also well represented at a public legislative hearing in February, as were the American Legion and the Chamber of Commerce. The Maryland Civil Liberties Committee, Americans for Democratic Action (ADA) and the CP registered their opposition. A Citizens' Committee to resist the measure – citing support from a few union leaders, academics and lawyers – appeared belatedly the same month, but the bill cleared both houses by the middle of March, encountering little opposition and only minor amendments. A lone vote was cast against the bill in the lower house. When a *Washington Post* reporter queried Senator Carter about the legislation, Carter asked to see his credentials, adding darkly 'Maybe you're a Commie'. Frank B. Ober commended his law as 'a model law for the other states'.[17]

Perhaps because of the cautious approach of the Ober Commission, opposition was slow to form and the new legislation was greeted ambivalently even by some of those accounting themselves liberals. *The Baltimore Sun* gave the act a cautious welcome, focusing on the unique provision for enforcement through a trained lawyer in the attorney general's department: 'That lawyer should be a good one. He should have a special knowledge in the field of dissenting opinion. He should strive as mightily to deflect the law from the Marxian idea [i.e. the academic study of Marxism] as he strives to apply it against those who present a clear and present danger of Marxoid subversion of the Government.' E. T. Baker in the *New Republic* uneasily conceded that 'Given a scrupulous prosecutor, Maryland's non-Communist Left can live under the new law, broad as it is'. Conservative groups enthusiastically hailed the law, the redbaiting *Counterattack* describing it as 'the strongest, most carefully drawn anti-Communist law in the country'.[18]

Yet the Ober Law was not to prove the panacea for which patriots yearned. The CP in Baltimore finally succeeded in directing public attention to the measure, and opposition to it grew after enactment. The Citizens' Committee originally formed in February vowed to continue the fight, as did the CP, which was soon claiming the formation of a 'united front' against the law. Opponents intended both to challenge the law in the courts and to force a referendum, so that it might be repealed in the elections of November 1950. The conspicuous involvement of the CP in this campaign probably served to hinder as much as help, since groups like the Maryland Civil Liberties Committee, while opposed to Ober, were distinctly uncomfortable at the idea of working with the Communists, and even with the Citizens' Committee, some of whose members were thought to have 'Communist tendencies'. Nonetheless some early successes were achieved. In August 1949, Circuit Court Judge Joseph Sherbow declared the law unconstitutional as a bill of attainder, agreeing with the complainants that it did proscribe thought as well as overt acts. For the moment the law was immobilized, though in February 1950 the Maryland Court of Appeals reversed the decision and it went into effect. Loyalty oaths began to be exacted of public employees. But in the meantime the Citizens' Committee Against the Ober Law had been collecting petitions for a referendum, which was duly scheduled for November.[19]

The right-wing crusade to drive Communists from the 'Free State' reached its climax in 1950. At the beginning of the year the attorney general, the Ober Commission, and the Maryland Committee Against Un-American Activities were appealing against Judge Sherbow's decision. Arrayed against them were local chapters of the NAACP, the ADA, the AFL, the ACLU, and – rather more conspicuously – of the CP, the Progressive party and several left-wing unions. The Appeals Court's vindication of the law seemed to impart new energy to both sides, as they turned their attentions to campaigns to win the referendum.

Other events simultaneously conspired to raise anticommunist emotions in the state. Its long-serving US Senator, Millard Tydings, came under attack when his subcommittee harshly condemned Senator Joseph McCarthy for his irresponsible behaviour; the anticommunist cause in Maryland was probably also aided when McCarthy used the Tydings hearings to name Johns Hopkins professor Owen Lattimore as 'the top Russian espionage agent' in the United States. Although an impeccable conservative, Tydings found himself ruthlessly redbaited by McCarthy's minions as he ran for re-election, and also found some of his old supporters turning against him. His postbag was filled with letters from constituents deploring his aid to the Communist conspiracy, several of them from voters who claimed to have supported him when Franklin Roosevelt tried to purge him in 1938 but who were prepared to do so no more. That fall too saw the Crusade for Freedom, a national campaign launched by General Lucius D. Clay to protest at Soviet Communism and given added urgency by the outbreak of the Korean War. It involved Americans putting their signatures to the 'Freedom Scroll', and the cause proved particularly popular in Maryland, where the local organization was headed by Brigadier General William C. Purnell, a member of the Maryland Committee Against Un-American Activities (both groups had their headquarters in Baltimore's Southern Hotel). By the end of the year Maryland ranked first per capita in the number of signers to the Freedom Scroll. And yet more patriotic groups were being formed, the most significant being the Minute Women of the United States of America, founded by the Belgian-born sculptress Suzanne Silvercruys Stevenson in Connecticut in 1949. Now spreading to other states, its aim was to mobilize women to support the 'traditional American way of life' and to renounce socialism and communism, particularly by getting its members to harass suspect speakers and bombard officeholders with phone calls and letters. A Maryland branch was formed in October 1950, and by early November was claiming five new members a day.[20]

This was the unpromising background against which Maryland's civil libertarians had to operate in the fall of 1950 as they sought to persuade voters to strike down the Ober Law. By now the campaign was led by the Maryland Civil Liberties Committee, supported by local chapters of teachers and professors, by librarian, Quaker, and social work groups, as well as by the ADA and the YWCA. 'We anti-Communist groups', they explained, '... feel that the large number of conscientious opponents of the Law should be provided with some leadership and support other than from the pro-Communist forces.' Their principal press advertisement emphasized that the Ober Law threatened not Communists but loyal citizens who could become entrapped by the enforcement machinery. But despite a perception that the furore had 'increased interest in civil liberties', these anticommunist civil libertarians were no match for those determined to banish communism. The Maryland Committee Against Un-American Activities was stronger than ever, its 55 sponsoring groups of 1948 having swollen to 102. Local chambers of commerce and other business groups were even more in evidence, as well as several Catholic and ethnic associations and some new patriotic societies, such as the Minute Women. The committee began its campaign early, appointing chairmen in every county in the state, holding public meetings, distributing leaflets, and publishing advertisements in the press. 'Vote For The Ober Law', it insisted. 'Its defeat ... would be a grave and stunning shock to the American men who fought the Reds in the mud and muck of Korea.' It particularly upheld the use of the loyalty oath (the most contentious of the Ober provisions), pointing out that it would enable subversives to be prosecuted for perjury, as had been the fate of Alger Hiss. In the event the citizens of Maryland overwhelmingly upheld the law to abolish communism, by 259 250 votes to 79 120, an even greater majority than had obtained for the milder anticommunist constitutional amendment of 1948. 'The people have backed the law; but they have backed only a decent and orderly enforcement of the law', concluded the *Sun*. 'They have backed an enforcement procedure which clears through the ancient safeguard of the grand jury.'[21]

Apart from the virulent anticommunist sentiments loose in the state in 1950, Maryland's Ober Law was probably endorsed by the electorate because its impact had hardly been draconian. By April 1950 almost all public employees had signed the anti-subversive oath. Only four had refused to do so, not because they were Communists but because they had conscientious objections as Quakers, and were losing their jobs. The law, they said, rejected 'the authority of the Inner Light'. While this proved the civil libertarians' point that it was non-Communists who would be ensnared by the law, the number was too small to trouble many Marylanders, particularly since other Quakers had signed. By the November elections the number of dissenters had grown slightly, but since two new additions had been candidates for the Progressive party, then very much identified as a Communist front, it is doubtful that most citizens felt much outrage. Over the next few years others fell foul of the procedures, but by April 1953 only ten altogether had been dismissed, mainly from colleges, schools and libraries, and none had chosen to make use of the appeal mechanism. An unrecorded number may have 'voluntarily' resigned or declined public employment, but it was difficult for the opponents of the law to point to large-scale casualties.[22]

In fact the state authorities showed little enthusiasm for enforcing the law vigorously, particularly its pioneering provisions for stamping out the CP, although they were obliged to set up the special unit under a new assistant attorney general. Attorney General Hall Hammond made it clear that it was up to local agencies to implement the oath clause, and rather defensively explained to a ward Democratic Club that the law was only 'a psychological attack on communism', a way of directing public attention to the danger, and that its enforcement was 'up to the people'. He assured the meeting that there would be few 'actual cases' of prosecutions. As attorney general, he advised other officials to take no action against those who had refused to file oaths until the courts had resolved the constitutionality of the measure. The lawyer that he appointed to oversee the law, A. Bowie Duckett, took a similarly insouciant view, explaining the lack of prosecutions in the first year of the law in terms of the possibility of its being overturned in November. A year later there had still been no prosecutions, although it was the case that the federal authorities were pursuing six Maryland CP leaders under the Smith Act and were to secure their conviction in April 1952. Duckett's office did compile dossiers on suspect individuals or groups, and probably exchanged information with other government agencies, but otherwise the unit kept a low profile. Parts of the law continued to be challenged in the courts, and there was always some chance that it might be found unconstitutional.[23]

The Republicans showed rather more interest in enforcing the law when they took office following the 1952 elections. The new Assistant Attorney General for Subversion was Marvin H. Smith, who was soon issuing admonitory statements. 'The Communists feast on anything that engenders controversy ...', he explained. 'We do know they have attempted to worm their way into very many organizations.' He insisted that investigations were being conducted constantly, but that developing prosecutions required 'time, patience and perseverance'. The high point of his crusade came in May 1953, when his agents rather conspicuously attended a meeting of the United World Federalists, noting down car licence numbers and taking photographs of speakers. The public response, a mixture of indignation and amusement, prompted Republican Governor Theodore R. McKeldin to condemn the episode. But even Smith was unable to bring prosecutions under the law. To his frustration, he found that potential witnesses were reluctant to give evidence, and he repeatedly and vainly begged for a law to compel witnesses to testify under a grant of immunity; he also wanted attorneys who pleaded the Fifth to be disbarred. Ironically, on this testimony, the so-carefully-devised Ober Law was inoperable because of its own deficiencies. Another turn of political fortune in the November 1954 elections removed Smith and the new regime promised a return to normality. If there was not enough evidence there would be no prosecutions under the Ober Law, promised the incoming attorney general: 'We don't anticipate doing anything spectacular.'[24]

He was true to his word. The anti-subversive unit slowly atrophied, in part because of the lack of enthusiasm of its directors, but also because of the increasing tendency for the federal government to displace the states in the area of internal security. The Smith Act prosecutions of the Maryland CP leaders had deprived the unit of some potential targets. The US Supreme Court's *Nelson* decision in April 1956 effectively wrecked state sedition laws, making prosecutions for subversion primarily a federal responsibility. Maryland's attorney general concluded with some relief that the *Nelson* decision 'apparently left no room for any State action against sedition'. Less philosophical was Frank B. Ober, who complained that the decision appeared to 'deprive the states of all power to protect their own existence against the criminal aspects of the Communist conspiracy'. But the anti-subversion unit did not disappear at once. At its peak under Smith it had employed four officers, and the number gradually declined over a ten-year period. What the office did was to keep files on potential subversives: some 600 names in 1953 grew to 3000 by 1964, by which time right-wing groups were

coming under scrutiny. Federal, state and local governmental
agencies, especially the Baltimore Police Department, sometimes
used this data bank to screen potential employees. By the mid-
1960s the functions of the unit appear to have been minimal. The
Special Assistant Attorney General spent 'all but a small part of his
working time' on other duties, assisted only by a part-time undercover agent whose value might be measured by his pay of $100 a
month. After 1967, when the Supreme Court further circumscribed the Ober Act, the files were not added to, although they
were still there gathering dust as the law required in 1971. There
had never been any prosecutions under the act. Nonetheless the
weakness of the Ober Act became a problem for some in the
1960s: in 1966, responding to a new set of pressures, the
Baltimore police department established its own Intelligence
Section or 'red squad'.[25]

The state's loyalty oath also remained in existence for a period
to irritate some of those who took it, including those in teaching
institutions which used the state's model. Supreme Court
decisions in the early 1960s cast doubt on the validity of the oath,
and academics in particular periodically called for the repeal of
the Ober Law, complaining that it impeded recruitment of top-
flight scholars. Three leading Democratic legislators did
introduce a repeal bill into the 1966 General Assembly. William C.
Purnell, sometime member of the Maryland Committee Against
Un-American Activities and state organizer of the 1950 Crusade
for Freedom, re-emerged flanked by veterans' groups to warn
that repeal of the Ober Act would be 'an obvious invitation to
Communist elements to come to Maryland'. The repeal bill was
shouted down, patriotic emotions being on the rise again because
of demonstrations around the country over the Vietnam War,
while conservative whites were also antagonized by an energetic
civil rights campaign in Baltimore for housing desegregation. As
usual it was the courts rather than the legislature which were left
to undo the loyalty law. In 1967 the US Supreme Court,
reviewing the case of a Quaker who had apparently been denied
a job at the University of Maryland for refusing to take the oath,
declared the oath lacking in precision and thus unconstitutional.
Municipal and other educational bodies in Maryland soon
abandoned their versions of the oath. Based on the 1967 decision,
another federal court in 1970 struck down most of the remaining

provisions of the Ober Act, in particular specifying that its central attempt to outlaw subversive organizations was itself unconstitutional. The Ober Law had never fulfilled the ambitious purpose that its framers had intended, and now it was no more.[26]

Imitations of Ober

Ineffective though the Ober Law was in the long run, its framers must have been gratified at the immediate attention it received. Recommended to other states as a model, it became the most widely imitated communist-control law. Mississippi was quick to follow suit, in 1950 reproducing a large part of the Ober Law in its own statute books, although according to the FBI there was only one Communist in the state. Ohio's little HUAC was much taken with the Ober Law and framed a communist-control programme in 1953 largely based upon it, although the Ober solution could only make the committee redundant. Its records accordingly were turned over to the attorney general's office, although only after the Ober programme had been passed over the veto of the governor, Frank J. Lausche, who feared for 'the reputations of innocent persons actually ruined by rumors, doubts, innuendoes and guilt inferred through association'.[27]

Also modelled on Ober was a 1951 law adopted by New Hampshire, a measure which was arguably more oppressive because it forbade any 'alteration' to state and national constitutions, although responsibility for enforcement was lodged directly with the attorney general rather than a specially appointed assistant. The legislative sponsor of the bill wished he could send Communists 'back to Russia', and failing that 'quarantine them like anyone else having an infectious disease'. Unusually, as previously noted, the New Hampshire experiment moved from an emphasis on controlling or outlawing communism to an emphasis on exposure, and the law was changed in 1953 to further this shift. Much of the responsibility lay with the incumbent attorney general, conservative Republican Louis C. Wyman, a zealous anticommunist, aided by William Loeb's *Manchester Union-Leader*, which made its reference library available to him 'on numerous occasions'. 'I am unable to tolerate in my own mind and heart the presence of Communists within America', he wrote privately, 'whether or not by overt act they have manifested their disloyalty.'

Wyman considered that the 1951 act had limited but not elimi-
nated the CP in New Hampshire. 'An ideology cannot be legis-
lated out of existence', he reasoned. 'Education of the citizens of
the state is essential as to ... the conspiratorial, stealthy, cunning,
techniques used by the Communist Party.' By 1955 there had still
not been any prosecutions for subversion as such. Like Assistant
Attorney General Smith of Maryland, Wyman felt the law to be
inadequate and sought the power to grant immunity to witnesses
in order to compel them to answer questions, but as in Maryland,
the legislature failed to oblige. It did permit continuation of the
investigation, though this was soon overtaken by the *Nelson*
decision, following which Wyman devoted much of his energy to
trying to change the federal law. The most visible casualties of the
New Hampshire inquisition were two witnesses who were prosecuted not for subversion but for contempt for refusing to answer
questions. Dr Paul Sweezy was rescued by the US Supreme Court,
but it declined to offer the same protection to religious leader
Willard Uphaus, director of the World Fellowship. In December
1959 he finally went to prison.[28]

Such casualties apart, the campaign to outlaw communism at
state level probably had little practical effect. Versions of the Ober
Law appeared also in Florida, Georgia, Pennsylvania and
Washington, and it influenced communist-control laws in several
other states. Their function appears to have been largely
symbolic, and the *Nelson* decision in any case rendered them for
the most part redundant.[29]

A few states tried to develop their own means for outlawing the
CP or prohibiting subversion. Indiana in 1951 initially considered
reproducing the Ober Law, but in the event enacted a cruder
measure 'to exterminate Communism and Communists' by
outlawing membership of the party or of any group engaged in
'un-American activities'. But the law was never used to prosecute
anyone and the state's CP continued to function openly from its
headquarters in Indianapolis. Also in 1951, Massachusetts
adopted a modified version of the Ober Law, declaring the CP to
be illegal and making it a punishable offence to remain within it,
but the law did not deter Bay State patriots from bombarding the
legislature with anticommunist measures year after year. When the
state authorities did move against local Communists in 1954, it
used a 1919 anti-sedition statute against seven of them, although

one was charged under the 1951 law. Neither law survived the *Nelson* decision, which prompted the state to abandon its attempts to prosecute Communists. Sometimes more draconian legislation was contemplated. Legislators in Tennessee and Michigan raised the spectre of the death penalty for unlawfully advocating the overthrow of government. The governor of Texas, Allen Shivers, also urged capital punishment for convicted CP members, after a commotion triggered by a CIO strike in which a few old-style Communists had been implicated. The legislature in 1954 more moderately decided on 20 years' imprisonment for violating a law which outlawed the CP and other groups favouring action 'intended' to overthrow government violently. The term 'subversives' was undefined but it was made a felony to be one. Oklahoma copied the Texas law in 1955, and Nebraska outlawed the CP and its successors, 'regardless of the assumed name', as late as 1961. These sweeping measures might catch the headlines, which was perhaps the intention of their authors, and serve to harass radicals, but as with so much communist-control legislation, they were put to little further use.[30]

The device of registration

The other principal variety of communist-control law was that which required the registration of suspect groups or individuals. These laws did not attract the same support or attention as the Ober Law, and were more a reflex action by a number of state authorities than an authentic initiative to extirpate the Communist menace. There were also more doubts about their constitutionality, a California court having found a Los Angeles registration ordinance to be in violation of the constitutional guarantee against self-discrimination. Almost all the registration laws were enacted in the 1950s after the Congress had favoured this remedy in the McCarran Internal Security Act. As with the federal measure, 'subversive' groups were never so obedient as to comply with registration laws, which for the most part were either symbolic measures designed to advertise a state's disapproval of communism or devices used to harass distrusted citizens.[31]

Michigan passed a law as early as 1947 requiring the registration of 'foreign agencies' which had presumably been inspired by the Voorhis Act, but even the state authorities did not take it seriously and it was never enforced. A similar fate befell the state's wide-ranging Trucks Act of 1952, which also contained a registration provision. The registration laws precipitated by the McCarran Act appear to have been particularly popular in western and southern states. California, Montana, New Mexico, and Wyoming all deployed registration laws at some stage. The Nebraska legislature retreated from such a law when the attorney general had doubts about its constitutionality. More self-confident was the state of Delaware, where a registration law, which also required registrants to be fingerprinted, passed both legislative houses unanimously in 1953 and with little public protest. In the South, Alabama, Arkansas, Louisiana, Texas, and North and South Carolina experimented with registration laws. The Texas law, passed without dissent in the 1951 legislature, declared the state 'in imminent danger of Communist espionage and sabotage', required registrants to name all others known to them as Communists, and instructed public employers to fire anyone believed on undefined 'reasonable grounds' to be a Communist.[32]

An attraction of registration laws in the Deep South was that they offered the possibility of controlling black and civil rights activists as much as Communists, and in so far as they were enforced it was these groups that tended to fall foul of them. Two African Americans attempting to register to vote in Louisiana in 1952 were arrested for having failed to register as Communists. 'Man, I'm not a Communist ...', protested one of them, 'I'd pick up a gun and fight 'em in a moment.' (It seems that they had misread the word 'now' for 'not' on the voter registration forms, and had written in the word Communist instead of Democrat.) A decade later the law was used to attack the Southern Conference Educational Fund (a civil rights offspring of the defunct Southern Conference for Human Welfare), which had its headquarters in New Orleans. Prompted by Louisiana's little HUAC, and abetted by Mississippi Senator James O. Eastland (chair of the Senate Internal Security Subcommittee), this assault involved the raiding of SCEF's offices and the arrest of James Dombrowski and two of his associates; the furore aroused by this case led to the registration law being struck down by the US Supreme Court in 1965.

Elsewhere, the city of Birmingham attracted attention in 1950 with an ordinance fashioned by commissioner Eugene 'Bull' Connor requiring Communists to register; Macon and Miami adopted similar measures. In 1951 Alabama enacted the Communist Control Law, extending registration to the whole state, on penalty of fine or imprisonment. This, coupled with other Cold War pressures and Bull Connor's personal attention to Birmingham dissidents, intensified local harassment to such a point that in 1951 the few remaining Communists in the state decided to disband the CP. In 1954 a 64-year-old black janitor, Matthew Knox, was arrested under the law and sentenced to two years in jail. There was no evidence that he was a Communist and he had only been arrested when police pursuing a different investigation had happened to come upon some Marxist literature in his room. The conviction was eventually quashed, but not before Knox had lost his job and become something of a minor celebrity. Knox told a reporter that the police had actually been 'right nice' as they arrested him, one officer asking bemusedly 'Don't you like the American way of life?' 'I told him Yes', Knox explained to the reporter, who queried 'Yes, you do; or yes, you don't?' 'I just told him Yes', Knox replied. 'It weren't no place for starting an argument.'[33]

The limits of control

The dispiriting recounting of communist-control laws and other anticommunist measures can give an impression of an entire United States engulfed in a McCarthyite red scare. But it was possible to resist the anticommunist onslaught. Even where states did enact communist-control legislation, the anticommunist victories were sometimes pyrrhic ones. No one can doubt the power and pervasiveness of anticommunism during the Cold War years, but it did not always carry all before it.

The year 1949 witnessed 'almost an epidemic' of communist-control bills in the state legislatures, but only a few were adopted. The infamous Broyles bills in Illinois were turned back year after year, only a loyalty oath eventually slipping through. The well-organized Chicago division of the ACLU coordinated the resistance by mobilizing some 400 'key organizational representatives throughout the state' and prided itself on its 'systematic and politically-hep campaign'. Iowa also rejected a version of the Ober Law. The Wisconsin legislature too periodically rebuffed stringent anticommunist bills; despite Joe McCarthy's presence, there was also a strong civil libertarian tradition in a state which could field a socialist mayor for its largest city through the 1950s, and the state's socialists and La Follette-style Progressives had long demonstrated their immunity to communism. In Connecticut in the early 1950s the opposition to communist-control bills was sufficient to defeat them, even the American Legion on one occasion lobbying with the civil libertarians. Vermont and Maine repelled similar demands. Bills modelled on the Ober Law and endorsed by the governor were rejected by the Tennessee legislature in 1951 after churchmen, academics, lawyers and the press had waged an effective opposition campaign which dwelt on the libertarian principles of the state's 1796 constitution. In Kentucky the attorney general fought for a bill to outlaw the CP, but the Louisville *Courier-Journal* attacked it as unnecessary and it was defeated in the senate. Almost all states at some time adopted some legislation to protect themselves against Communist subversion (or at least against superpatriotic imprecations), even if only a loyalty oath, but the civil libertarians had their victories too. And when laws were adopted, they frequently proved ineffective. In California and New York in particular, with their relatively large radical communities, hundreds of people lost their jobs, but elsewhere the number of documented casualties was often low. This is not to deny the repressive atmosphere created by such legislation, or the tawdry misuses to which it might be put, but it is important to note that the specific designs of the zealous anticommunists were frequently frustrated. The mouldering files in the office of the Maryland attorney general symbolized the fate of state communist-control laws that had fallen into disuse almost as soon as they were created.[34]

PART II

RED SCARE POLITICS
IN MICHIGAN

During the bleakest days of the Cold War few states were to rival Michigan in the bitterness and intensity of its anticommunist passions. Red scare tactics envenomed election campaigns, elaborate communist-control legislation was enacted and police red squads instituted, and labour unions, the campuses and the public service were disrupted by hunts for subversives. In many states, even in the Midwest, the Communist issue barely invaded the political arena. The citizens of Iowa saw little need for anticommunist crusades, which were located more often in the industrial states. In Michigan, not only were anticommunist pressures strong but they were unusually evident in electoral politics. By the late 1930s Michigan had become a two-party state, and in a period of close competition between Republicans and Democrats red scare tactics were frequently employed. More than was the case in most states, Michigan's party system reflected class differences, as the Republicans became the spokesmen for property-owners and the business community and Democrats forged a close identity with organized labour. The origins of Michigan anticommunism owed much to the emergence of a highly partisan style of politics and to the class conflict which fuelled party competition. The state provides much evidence to support the argument of Michael Paul Rogin and Robert Griffith that McCarthyism was essentially rooted in the dynamics of party politics. Michigan also offers a telling example of the way in which fierce red scare pressures can sometimes be contained, albeit at a cost, in this case by a determined governor, G. Mennen Williams.[1]

The case of Michigan provides an illustration too of the interdependence of national and state anticommunism. A full-blown red scare could not have developed in the state without the impact of outside influences, such as scrutiny by bodies like HUAC or less tangible pressures like the example of federal legislation. Yet equally a red scare could not have ignited had Michigan itself not been combustible. More than in most states there existed in Michigan conditions which encouraged an anticommunist political culture. Local and national anticommunists did not march in lockstep, but each drew strength from the other.

The wellsprings of Michigan anticommunism did not begin flowing with the advent of the Cold War or even of the Great Depression. The socioeconomic structure of the state had long laid a basis for reactionary politics. In the nineteenth century the mushrooming industries of Michigan – lumber, mining, furniture, machinery – had been pioneered by entrepreneurs intolerant of organized labour and had attracted a miscellany of semi-skilled and unskilled immigrants and surplus American farmhands. It was also a fiercely Protestant area, and the anti-Catholic American Protective Association flourished in Detroit in the 1890s. By the early twentieth century a new and remarkably swift industrial revolution, centred on the automobile industry, was transforming the economy. Small and diversified local businesses were replaced by giant firms like Ford and General Motors. In the 1910s and 1920s the population of the state was increasing at a rate of over 30 per cent each decade, about double the national average. The workers who thronged into the expanding factories brought with them little experience of unions, and employers successfully maintained the open shop in the new motor cities. By the mid-1930s Michigan was one of the most industrialized states in the Union, ranking fifth in the value of its manufactured products. The nature of this breathtaking industrial revolution placed the business classes close to the centres of political power and fostered a pervasive business ideology which could recognize paternalistic obligations towards the workforce but which was deeply antipathetic towards political radicalism and independent labour organization. A business-oriented Republican party dominated the state's political councils. The suspicious antiradicalism of corporate executives was to constitute one source of red scare politics through the first half of the twentieth century.[2]

But the working class which was being created itself contained the potential for a popular anticommunism. Displaced farmworkers from the lower Midwest and upper South crowded into the booming industrial cities, the whites among them bringing the racially tinged values of Anglo-Saxon and fundamentalist Protestantism. Their self-consciousness was raised by the tide of immigrants which threatened to engulf them, some of them Canadian or German, but many of them Poles, Russians, Finns, Hungarians, and Italians. Of the state's white population in 1930, about 47 per cent were either foreign-born or were of foreign or mixed parentage. Migrants from the Bible Belt were rubbing shoulders with Roman Catholics, Jews, and members of the Orthodox churches. The church-centred and ethnic-centred cultures of many industrial workers, as well as their relative affluence, rendered them indifferent and even hostile to 'atheistic communism'. Catholic priests and some Protestant ministers regularly condemned socialism, and the Catholicism of many of the state's industrial workers was profoundly to influence the course of anticommunist politics. A few Russians, Lithuanians and Finns did organize small Communist groups, only to encounter much suspicion from within their own communities. This popular anticommunism did not go unnoticed by conservative business and political leaders, and at times elite and populist sentiments were critically to interact in the making of a red scare.[3]

The state's few radicals met antipathy not only from employers, church groups and many workers, but also from the rural hinterland. Michigan's lumbermen, large and small farmers and small-town citizens viewed the mushroom growth of the industrial cities with some distrust. Many were the descendants of the evangelical Yankees and other Americans and northern Europeans who had settled the frontier state in the nineteenth century, and whose God-fearing individualism had made them the backbone of the Republican party. The strange tongues, religions and – in a few cases – political doctrines of the new industrial workers did not always endear them to the predominantly old-stock residents of the farm and forest counties. Overrepresented in the legislature and strongly Republican, rural and small-town conservatives could sometimes make common cause with the motor magnates or clerical superpatriots in assaults on the modest radical enclaves of the cities. But the thrust from the right did not carry all before it. In the event, it was to be a form of liberal anticommunism which eventually triumphed in Michigan.[4]

4

CLASS CONFLICT AND PARTY
POLITICS, 1935–1945

Business suspicion of labour and radicalism was an old tradition in Michigan. The Employers Association of Detroit had been formed in the late nineteenth century, and had become known through the country for its use of thugs and blacklists in destroying every vestige of unionism. Red scare tactics continued to be deployed against radicals and aliens, a pattern which culminated in 1919–20, with the energetic participation of state and city police in the infamous raids ordered by the US Attorney General A. Mitchell Palmer. This was anticommunism of a familiar sort, a product of class conflict and of nativist fears of uncouth foreigners, and directed largely by business interests and conservative politicians at the 'dangerous classes' well beneath them in the polity. Such sentiments remained relatively strong in Michigan's political culture, but before the end of the 1930s anticommunism had begun to assume a new shape. Red scare tactics were no longer directed exclusively at workers and aliens, but also at more privileged targets, some in the universities but more especially within the leadership of a major political party. In 1938, when it seemed to some that Governor Frank Murphy was hounded out of office by a vicious use of red scare tactics, it was demonstrated that even the highest in the land were not immune to the new anticommunist passions. Party competition was coming to rival class conflict in the generation of red scare politics.

Political partisanship cannot easily be distinguished from class fears in this reorientation of anticommunism, because the revival of an effective two-party system in Michigan was itself partly the product of class rivalries. Much of the animus that came to be directed at those reaching high office stemmed from the outrage of a displaced class. It was during the 1930s that business hegemony in Michigan lost its legitimacy, as the devastating effects of the Great Depression shredded the pretensions of the old political order. A crucial consequence of the economic distress was the creation of a powerful, class-conscious labour movement which, while not closely linked to the Communist party, was sufficiently novel to alarm many business, political and church leaders. Further, the precipitate arrival of organized labour, together with the momentum imparted by the New Deal, induced a political realignment in the state in which the Democrats came to challenge the traditional Republican ascendancy. This was to be fundamental to the generation of red scare politics. The revitalization of the two-party system represented a political expression of the new forms of class conflict, as the Democrats became linked to organized labour and the Republicans more clearly to the major corporations. In Michigan, more than in most states, party politics were evolving as a form of class-related interest group politics, and in due course it would be possible for political scientists to speak of unions and management intervening in politics 'within their respective parties'. In such a system, class fears could be readily translated into red scare politics. Yet it would be too crude to equate political anticommunism with Republican conservatism, because the demands of the political system and its sociological base obliged the Democrats to associate themselves with a labour and church-oriented anticommunism. Their own reformist aspirations intensified their desire not to be fatally linked with a Communist party of doubtful loyalty. The imperatives of party politics, in short, enjoined on both major parties an anticommunist stance, thus rendering the CP itself highly vulnerable. The political configurations established in Michigan in the 1930s were to remain in place for at least a generation.[1]

Conservative unease
Red scare tactics would not have become a feature of party politics in Michigan had anticommunism not had popular dimensions. The traditional antiradicalism of the political and business elites

had by the 1920s been supplemented by that of many workers. The Ku Klux Klan briefly flourished in the middle of the decade, preying on aliens, labour organizers and African- Americans, and winning some support in the manufacturing towns to which poor white and Protestant farmers from the lower Midwest and upper South had migrated. There was also an active hostility towards the CP from its rivals in the Socialist party and the American Federation of Labor, sharpened by resentment over Communist attempts to unionize the auto industry. Further, the automobile boom muted the appeal of radicalism and organized labour. The relatively high wages and welfare capitalism of the motor industry provided alternative sources of security, and the better paid skilled workers in particular often shared the ideological perspective of the business leadership. When the Great Crash stripped away the benevolent veneer of the power structure in Michigan, the state's traditional leaders could hope for some allies among the lower orders.[2]

In the early years of the Depression the red menace continued to be identified with insurrection from below, particularly since the CP was active in organizing unemployment demonstrations, and for the most part the state's authorities betrayed the fearful mentality of a beleaguered business class. Successive incidents revealed the collusion between politicians, police forces and corporate interests, sometimes abetted by flickers of nativist reaction within the working class. The infamous Ford Massacre of March 1932 served in particular to expose the nature of the power structure usually found in urban Michigan. A hunger march on Ford's River Rouge plant exploded into gunfire, and four demonstrators (three of them Communists) were shot dead by police or Ford servicemen. The Dearborn police chief had worked for Ford and continued to liaise with its security boss, Harry Bennett. The Wayne County Prosecuting Attorney, Harry Toy – a Republican destined for a long anticommunist career – insisted that responsibility for the massacre rested with the Communists. Ordering a raid on CP headquarters, he also demanded the arrests of William Z. Foster and other CP leaders. The Employers Association of Detroit and the American Legion endorsed the Toy line of blaming Communists and 'outside agitators,' as did a subsequent grand jury. The cry of red subversion had been used to deflect attention from police and business brutality and to discipline an industrial workforce.[3]

During the darkest days of the Depression, which hit the automobile industry with exceptional severity, some employers and public officials could be tempted into even more sinister thuggery. Their instruments were insecure native workers who, competing for jobs with immigrants and blacks, were finding refuge in the Ku Klux Klan. Out of such a milieu there emerged a shadowy organization, the Black Legion, a hooded order which reached a membership of perhaps 100000 in Michigan and Ohio and other parts of the industrial Midwest by the mid-1930s. Formally committed to finding jobs for southern whites, the Legion came to have close ties with corporate interests, police authorities, and some local Republican organizations. It claimed that it wanted only 'to stamp out communism', to which end it flogged labour or Communist activists, bombed or torched their homes, and was implicated in murder. When the Black Legion was eventually exposed in 1936 successive newspaper headlines uncovered the murkiest of its associations: its strength in Detroit and Pontiac, its members in police departments, sheriffs' offices and on city councils, its links with the Packard and Hudson motor companies, its attempts to penetrate union locals. It had functioned as an anti-labour terrorist and espionage group, and its unmasking added credibility to old labour complaints about collusion between the corporations, local authorities and police departments.[4]

Conservative unease also came to focus on labour's suspect allies in the universities. The Crash had called into question the viability of the American free enterprise system, and many intellectuals were captivated anew by the Soviet Union. The red menace no longer consisted simply of a few malcontent workers but had also become an ideology capable of seducing anyone. Michigan campuses contained their share of professors and students drawn to varieties of socialist thought. Since the major universities were public institutions, and often contained representatives of the large corporations on their boards of trustees, they were vulnerable to the anticommunist animus found in some business and political circles. Most Michigan professors managed to conduct themselves with discretion, but student activists could draw unwelcome attention from the state's rulers. The Oxford Union's celebrated peace pledge of 1933 encountered a friendly reception on many American campuses, where anti-war sentiment was being deepened by the revisionist thesis that businessmen and bankers had been responsible for American intervention in the First World War. In 1934 the Communistic National Student League (NSL) called for 'peace strikes' on the country's campuses, and conversely William Randolph Hearst launched his newspaper campaign against radical professors. These national campaigns touched Michigan, where some legislators were becoming agitated by student socialist and pacifist protests. University of Michigan students joined May Day demonstrations in Detroit in 1934, and 'radical' protest meetings were held at Michigan State College. During the pacifist agitation of 1934–5 a record number of Ann Arbor students signed the Oxford Pledge, a campaign which was consummated with the burning of an effigy of William Randolph Hearst on the library steps. The NSL was active in these episodes, though probably more eloquent were the speeches of the young heir to a soap fortune, G. Mennen Williams, and the articles of the student editor, Arthur Miller.[5]

Disturbed by the signs of class revolt in the early 1930s, the state's conservatives moved to protect their world. The Republicans won the gubernatorial and legislative elections of November 1934, and early in 1935 right-wing legislators were looking for ways of striking at both labour and campus radicals, revealing some enduring features of red scare politics.

Republican state legislator Joseph A. Baldwin introduced a bill to outlaw the advocacy of the forcible overthrow of government and to require teaching institutions to support it: both unions and campuses were said to be nurturing red revolution. 'This bill is an open declaration', he shouted during a legislative battle, 'that the people of Michigan will no longer tolerate Communism.' He invited his fellows to choose between the American Legion, the Daughters of the American Revolution and the Veterans of Foreign Wars on his side and on the other 'mostly Communists'. Despite the slap at universities, the Baldwin–Dunckel bill was primarily an attack on labour, capable of crippling strike action. One of its most significant effects was to provoke the formation of the Conference for the Protection of Civil Rights, which, in evolving into the Civil Rights Federation and then the Civil Rights Congress, was long to antagonize the patriotic right.

This body won a public hearing, encouraged extensive lobbying at Lansing, and eventually secured the removal of the bill's most offensive features, although a limited sedition law passed. Potshots were also taken at the campuses. The 1931 teacher loyalty oath law had not applied to college professors, and a bill was introduced to extend it to them. One of its supporters spoke of 'the disloyal teaching going on in the schools' and others cited a CP-led demonstration at Michigan State College. A few brave legislators deplored 'the anticommunist hysteria' displayed in the debate, but large majorities swept the bill into law. While not draconian in their final form, the two 1935 measures sent a warning to labour groups and campus authorities. The latter at least took heed, University of Michigan President Alexander Ruthven issuing a condemnation of 'a few professional agitators', tightening the expulsion rules, and refusing to readmit three NSL members in the fall. The unemployment, labour and student protests of the early Depression years had produced a modest red scare, which left a legislative residue and a few young and pinkish scalps. But these modest victories proved to be the last gasps of a collapsing political order.[6]

A new political universe
The new working-class consciousness in Michigan, a product of the hard times and brutal management tactics, turned many workmen against their employers and towards Franklin Roosevelt's New Deal, which from 1935 became strongly identified with the labour movement. The sensational disclosures about the Black Legion in 1936 did nothing to improve the corporate image in Michigan. That year the Democratic party found an attractive gubernatorial candidate in Frank Murphy, a Catholic and a New Dealer, and Franklin Roosevelt's coat-tails helped him to victory. The Democrats also won control of both houses of the legislature, part of a remarkable Democratic sweep nationally. With the resurgence of the Democratic party went labour militancy, exemplified in particular by the growth of the United Automobile Workers (UAW). A powerful alliance was being forged between a class-conscious organized labour and the Democratic party, one which doomed the business-dominated order in Michigan.[7]

The class base of the state's politics was reflected too in the presence of an active Communist movement. Communists had appeared in Michigan after the First World War, especially among foreign-born workers, and by the end of the 1920s had established a significant presence, in particular in the expanding automobile plants. By the mid-1930s their numbers remained relatively small – there were 630 CP members among auto workers in 1935 – but their prominence in industrial disputes had attracted the wrath of business and political leaders. By this date Michigan Communists were benefiting from the accession of a number of college graduates, some from radical Jewish homes, able to offer highly competent leadership. Confronted by hostile managements, Communist unionists won enviable reputations as organizers and the confidence of many non-CP workers. As the UAW took shape, Communists assumed important positions within it, organizer Wyndham Mortimer becoming its first vice-president. Many CP unionists sought to conceal their party affiliation, but their presence in the UAW in particular could not be disguised. This was the 'popular front' period, when Communists were eager to work with a range of liberals and leftists in a common struggle against fascism, and uneasy coalitions were developed in a number of labour and other organizations, in Michigan as elsewhere. Communists were thus loosely associated with the New Deal alliance between the Democratic party and industrial unionism in Michigan, thereby reinforcing right-wing perceptions of the New Deal as an alien creation.[8]

   In both nation and state it was the celebrated sit-down strikes of 1937 which dramatized the spectacular rise of industrial unionism and the partnership between organized labour and the New Deal. Conservative opinion was predictably appalled both by the challenge to managerial prerogatives and property rights and by the protection afforded the strikers by leading Democratic officials, a reaction which reached well outside business circles. Orthodox Americans of all classes were unsettled by the changes to the status quo. The motor cities of Michigan had long been renowned citadels of the open shop, a potent symbol destroyed by the sit-down strike at the General Motors (GM) plant in Flint, when pressure from Governor Frank Murphy and President Franklin Roosevelt for a negotiated settlement eventually secured recognition for the UAW. The world's largest open-shop business had capitulated, and Chrysler soon followed. Although Ford held out, the motor cities were falling to unionizing drives, as were other industrial centres across the country. The Congress of Industrial Organizations (CIO) became a major force in the land, and UAW membership soared from 88 000 in February 1937 to a phenomenal 400 000 in October.[9]

The insolent challenge of the sit-down, the invasion of property rights, and the refusal of Governor Murphy to enforce a court order against the strikers, represented something close to anarchy or red revolution to the old rulers of the motor cities, whose fears were given some credibility by the central role of some Communist organizers. The Flint city manager reacted by hiring guards to protect the waterworks from Communist sabotage, and a GM newspaper described the strike as 'a vast conspiracy to destroy all for which life is worth living'. Elsewhere too the reaction was sustained and forceful. Anti-union workers and vigilantes created the Flint Alliance, which condemned the sit-down as communistic and alien, and a Protestant Action Association with links to the beleaguered Black Legion was formed in the city in order to drive out the UAW. (A few Flint locals even had to contend with Black Legionnaires within their memberships.) Yet it was not only the business community and local nativists who were alarmed by the Flint strike and the subsequent sit-downs in Detroit and elsewhere. A Gallup Poll of March 1937 showed that 67 per cent believed that the states should outlaw the weapon. The AFL disavowed the sit-down and its vice-president condemned 'communistic and socialistic methods' in industrial disputes. Even Murphy eventually began to voice warnings against Communist influence in the CIO and labour disputes, reacting to correspondents who told him that he had allowed the 'seeds of communism' to be 'nurtured, fertilized and cultivated'. Leading liberal Democrats, looking both to their own survival and that of the reform cause, were developing an anticommunist stance.[10]

What helped to give anticommunism some purchase at the grassroots in industrial Michigan were the conservative religious values to which many workers cleaved. Some church leaders in Detroit joined in the condemnation of the sit-downs. A locally popular Baptist preacher from Texas, Dr Frank Norris, denounced the strike as 'the Moscow plan imported to America', a perspective shared by other Protestant fundamentalists.

More important to the motor cities' large ethnic populations was the attitude of Roman Catholic clerics. The Catholic church had long reviled communism as an enemy, and in 1936 the Pope, intensely disturbed by the course of the Spanish Civil War, had sought to rally Catholics everywhere in an anticommunist crusade. Further, most American Catholics were deeply patriotic, balancing their allegiance to a distant spiritual leader with an Americanism which could hardly be surpassed. The Catholic hierarchy in the United States generally recoiled from the New Deal after the sympathy the administration had evinced for the sit-down strikes, and in Detroit Bishop Michael J. Gallagher, after punctiliously criticizing both sides in the General Motors confrontation, voiced the suspicion 'that it's Soviet planning behind it'. Michigan's most celebrated priest was Father Charles E. Coughlin, broadcasting to his vast radio audience from the Detroit suburb of Royal Oak and popular with many Catholic workers in the auto plants. He spoke of an attempt 'of union labor to Sovietize industry'. In October Coughlin precipitated a great controversy when he warned that 'a good Catholic could no more belong to the CIO than he could embrace the Mohammedan faith', eventually obliging the new Archbishop of Detroit, Edward Mooney, to repudiate him. Mooney skilfully developed a pro-labour yet antiradical stance for his church: 'It is undoubtedly true that there are Communists in the CIO who are making every effort to gain control of the organization for communistic purposes but it is the duty of Catholics in the CIO to relentlessly oppose these efforts.' With the endorsement of Mooney, the Association of Catholic Trade Unionists (ACTU) formed a chapter in Detroit in 1938, and this was to play a significant role in guiding the local labour movement along an anticommunist course. In the following year the first Catholic labour schools appeared in Detroit, designed to promote the church's social teaching and encourage trade union activities among Catholic workers.[11]

   The new political universe taking shape in Michigan left organized labour as an effective counterweight to an outraged big business, with working-class voters revitalizing a previously feeble Democratic party. This political restructuring also had a profound impact on the nature of anticommunism. Red scare tactics, hitherto directed mainly at low-status labour radicals, were now to be used against those high in the polity. This became clear in the gubernatorial campaign of 1938. Frank Murphy, seeking re-election, was irremediably identified with the New Deal, the UAW, and the sit-down strikes. One candidate for the

Republican nomination was Harry S. Toy, the former Ford
Company attorney and Wayne County prosecutor who had
blamed the Ford Massacre on Communists and who had since
served as state attorney general and as a Michigan Supreme
Court justice. Toy urged the prosecution of the strikers' 'communistic leaders' and accused Murphy of failing to 'protect honest
labor from communists'. The Republican nomination in fact went
to ex-governor Frank D. Fitzgerald, but Toy's charges set the tone
for the campaign. Congress's new anticommunist agency, HUAC
or the Dies Committee, helped out, visiting Detroit in October to
conduct hearings on communism in the labour movement and
then listening to Michigan witnesses in Washington. Knights of
Columbus, American Legionnaires, labour spies, and local police
officers paraded before the committee to confirm its suspicions
that the 1937 sit-down strikes had originated in Michigan and
were instigated by 'well-known Communist agitators'. They implicated John L. Lewis, Walter Reuther, University of Michigan
professors and even Albert Einstein in the Communist conspiracy.
Michigan, according to the state's American Legion authority on
subversive activities, was 'one of the most communistically conta-
minated states in the Union.'[12]

The most overcharged testimony attempted to link Governor
Murphy to the Communists. Fred W. Frahm, Detroit police superintendent, reported that Communists were responsible for 75 per
cent of recent Detroit area strikes and that Murphy had
encouraged the strikers. 'I am satisfied the manufacturers want to
deal with the working people', he obediently testified, 'but the
union leaders cannot control the men because of the
Communists.' Judge Paul V. Gadola testified that Murphy had
prevented the execution of a court order against the Flint sit-
down strikers; Flint's city manager, John M. Barringer, averred
that Murphy was guilty of 'treasonable action in not giving us
help when we asked for it'. The effect of Gadola's and Barringer's
testimony was somewhat blunted when they revealed themselves
to be Republicans, the former imprudently blurting out, 'We
didn't have any Democratic judges in Michigan until these
shirttail riders came along.' These witnesses seemed to be
expressing the outrage of a deposed ruling class. The object of
these proceedings could hardly be mistaken, and a furious
Franklin Roosevelt was moved to make his first public assault on

the Dies Committee, which he accused of attempting to influence an election by permitting 'a disgruntled Republican judge, a discharged Republican city manager and a couple of officious police officers' to make unsupported charges against 'a profoundly religious, able and law-abiding governor'. The anti-New Deal Democrats on the committee had not forgotten Roosevelt's recent attempt to purge others of their kind.[13]

Republicans (and other conservatives) in Michigan had been spying reds close to the Murphy administration at least since the sit-down strikes, but the Dies Committee hearings provided them with 'proof' or vindication of a sort. They also provided them with a chance of prising away votes from the Democrats in the cities. The closing weeks of the campaign were dominated by the Communist issue. Frank Fitzgerald repeated charges of reds in the UAW and of their protection by the governor, promised to ban sit-down strikes, and pointed out that the CP had endorsed Murphy. Invoking images of the Communists penetrating the Murphy administration, he charged that it had not done its part 'in driving these people' from 'their present spheres of influence'. He also sought to appeal to Catholic voters. The CP had in fact endorsed Murphy's re-election, inspiring a Republican pamphlet tellingly entitled *Communists Back Murphy in Fight to Turn Michigan Over to Reds*.

The election was being closely watched nationally because Murphy seemed to personify the New Deal and his fate was regarded by some as 'a barometer of what people are thinking about the President'. Whatever Michigan voters were thinking, they gave a decisive victory to Fitzgerald and elected large Republican majorities to both houses of the state legislature. The Democrats probably suffered because their turnout was lower in this presidential 'off year' and because of a broader popular reaction against the New Deal, accentuated by the economic recession of 1937–8. Murphy did lose support in Flint and in other cities where there had been serious labour trouble, and professional politicians thought that his role in the sit-down strikes had done him most harm. The significance of the related Communist issue remains more speculative, and one study of the role of the Dies Committee could not establish clear electoral consequences. Yet several Democrats and Murphy himself believed that the redbaiting tactics had hurt him, notably among

Catholics, and there were disheartening reports about the unfavourable attitudes of priests in Detroit and elsewhere. What was incontrovertible, however, was that Murphy had lost the election after an anti-New Deal and redbaiting campaign. Republican leaders were enormously relieved that there was some prospect of restoring the old business-dominated order and doubtless took note of the electoral advantages of red scare politics.[14]

The little red scare

For the moment the unnerving political world of the New Deal, with its pernicious Democratic–labour alliance, its potent industrial unions, and its red tinge, had been beaten back. The country as a whole was beginning to experience a 'little red scare', in part fuelled by the backlash against the New Deal and labour radicalism and symbolized at the national level by the cavortings of HUAC. The political sociology of Michigan proved receptive to the patriotic cause. Through the 1930s there had been occasional signs of an unholy alliance between business conservatism and nativism, and the superpatriotic emotions which ran high between about 1939 and 1941 at least created the potential for the emergence of a kind of informal broad front of the right, one which might embrace corporate executives, reactionary Republicans, patriotic Catholics and fundamentalist Protestants, right-wing unionists and surviving elements of the Klan. But the political sociology of the state, as it had been reshaped in the 1930s, also gave some force to the left, creating the potential for a popular front embracing the CIO unions, liberal Democrats, African American and civil rights activists, progressive farm and church groups, and the CP. In fact the diversity, fractiousness and mutual suspicion which also characterized both ends of the political spectrum meant that there was no real consolidation on either right or left, but on occasion there was cooperation beween some of the constituent elements. Mainstream politicians found themselves operating in a rather polarized political universe, subject to pressure from activists on both sides. The international events of 1939 aided the forces of the right, largely by disrupting the radical left. The stunning Hitler–Stalin Pact of the summer, followed by the outbreak of war in Europe, seemed to cast

American Communists as accessories to Nazi aggression, popular front accommodations fell apart, and the CP stood perilously alone. Yet the 'little red scare' remained limited in its effects, because a large part of the labour movement was able to demonstrate its loyalty to American institutions.

In Michigan the conservative turn of the 1938 elections was paralleled by the resurgence of nativism. There were reports of the revival of the Black Legion and of other vigilante groups. Father Coughlin continued to blast away at the New Deal, 'communistic Jews' and reds in the CIO and the local UAW. He also organized the Christian Front, which won modest followings among the Catholic inhabitants of large cities, including Detroit and its environs. Among Protestant fundamentalists, Dr Frank Norris of the Detroit Baptist church still had an audience for his racist and anticommunist preachings, and he was augmented by hundreds of fundamentalist worker-preachers. More celebrated was the silver-tongued Gerald L. K. Smith, once associate of both Huey Long and Father Coughlin, who led the Committee of One Million and in 1939 made Detroit his headquarters. There he enjoyed some support from local motor magnates Horace Dodge and Henry Ford and found some receptive if limited audiences for his anticommunist and racist bombast among southern white migrants. Like Coughlin, whose radio network he took over, Smith interested himself in local as well as national affairs, backing Homer Martin in his battles in the UAW and developing a fierce hatred for Walter Reuther. The Committee of One Million, he said, was 'merely trying to educate the people to combat such menaces as communism, nazism, fascism, new dealism, Murphyism and the CIO'.[15]

While one form of anticommunism nestled in that shady nexus between big business and nativism, a quite different form was continuing to take shape in the labour movement. Communists had contributed to the growth of industrial unionism in Michigan, but for the most part that organized labour which so affronted big business did not represent a revolutionary spirit among the working class. The class militancy which had been awakened had turned industrial workers against their employers but not against the political system and not against a reformed capitalist order, one exemplified by the New Deal. Once big labour had become a power in the land, allied to the Democratic party, its Communist helpmates could be seen as a liability, calling into question labour's commitment to the American way. For Michigan's industrial workers, so many of them of immigrant stock, a Catholic heritage pointed up the suspect loyalties of the Communists. Encouraged by the Catholic church, a labour-oriented anticommunism was gathering force which would achieve fuller political expression in the state's postwar Democratic party. In January 1939 Archbishop Mooney urged priests and Catholic workers to show a lively interest in ACTU, the prime purpose of which was 'to make the Catholic membership in the unions an intelligent force for sound unionism in the Christian spirit'. The 'Catholic view' of industrial relations implied an obligation on management and worker alike to strive for a 'constructive' purpose, which is, 'in one word, to achieve cooperation instead of conflict'. Industrial problems were in principle resolvable with good faith on both sides.[16]

ACTU was developing its stance against the background of the well-publicized convulsions in the UAW. The latter's president, the former Baptist preacher Homer Martin, supported by the Hearst press and the clerical superpatriots, had been fighting Communist officials with a ferocity that had cost him much support, and in April 1939 he broke away from the UAW–CIO and led his rump into the AFL, which finally threw itself into organizing auto workers with the help of redbaiting tactics. The Communists in the UAW, concerned about the destructive fire they were attracting, generally deferred to the leadership of the non-Communists, a strategy which eased the rise of the moderate group around Walter Reuther. The anti-Soviet Reuther was developing ties with New Deal Democrats and with ACTU, which in turn strengthened him in his stance against the Communists in the union. Organized labour in Michigan was edging towards what the Detroit ACTU president Paul E. Weber called 'sound unionism'. Those industrial workers who nursed a distrust of communism but were keen to advance their collective bargaining rights could see merit in the Reuther strategy and the alliance with the New Deal.[17]

But at least before the Nazi–Soviet Pact the groups on the left could sometimes make common cause. After the 1938 elections, right-wing Republicans moved to take advantage of their restored control of the legislature, determined to strike at those they thought responsible for undermining the natural order of things.

Senator Joseph A. Baldwin, whose main anti-labour proposals had been hobbled in 1935, had been impressed by HUAC's performance and in January 1939 he introduced what became known as the 'little Dies bill' because it sponsored the appointment of a state commission to investigate 'seditious or subversive activity'. Another sponsor, speaking as a 'member of the American Legion and a citizen', explained that 'We Republicans campaigned in 1938 with the promise that we would investigate and expose un-American activities in Michigan'. Representatives of the American Legion, the VFW and the Lansing Junior Chamber of Commerce lobbied for the bill. But the popular front left was already too strong to be swatted aside. The Civil Rights Federation, which had emerged as a left-wing counterpoise to the far right, worked hard to mobilize progressive labour, church, and farm opposition, and representatives of the National Lawyers Guild, the CIO, the Socialist party, the Farmers Union, the Workers Alliance and the CP went on record against the bill. The leftist colouring of these groups must have aggravated the bill's sponsors, but it died in the senate after the chamber had been jammed with hundreds of protesters.[18]

While the new Republican government undid a number of Murphy's reform measures and introduced anti-labour laws, it made little immediate effort to follow up on the red scare rhetoric of the campaign. Fitzgerald himself died three months after inauguration. The Communist issue remained largely the prerogative of unreconstructed business conservatives of the Baldwin variety. But the crumbling of left-wing groups following the Hitler–Stalin Pact momentarily strengthened the hand of the patriotic right both inside government and out. Fears that the CP was attempting to disrupt defence preparations intensified with the 'defense strikes' of 1940–1. A UAW unionising drive at the Ford River Rouge plant was fought by the Ford management with images of 'a gigantic Communist plot threatening national defense', and although the UAW won, the episode again did something to uncover the extent of the Ford use of spies and thugs and the close connections between company and police. Some observers also glimpsed corporate interests behind renewed thrusts at Communists at the University of Michigan. In the summer of 1940, as France fell to the Nazis and bombs rained down on British cities, President Ruthven warned that the university 'welcomes only students who are convinced that

democracy is the ideal form of government' and would 'deal
firmly ... with subversion or so-called "fifth column" activities'.
Thirteen student activists, ten of them members of the CP-led
American Student Union, were curtly informed that they would
not be readmitted in the fall. *The Nation* dourly pointed out that
the university received its funds largely from the state legislature,
composed of upstate farmers and downstate representatives of
the motor industry, and from wealthy alumnae, and that its board
of regents contained corporation lawyers with close ties to the big
motor companies. These dark days for the left also invited
attempts to drive Communists out of politics. Communist
canvassers were arrested in Kalamazoo, and the Republican
administration threatened to sack state employees who signed
Communist petitions.[19]

The patriotic right, however, failed to capitalize effectively on
the disruption of the left. The mayoral election in Detroit in the
fall of 1939 pitted the incumbent Republican, Richard W.
Reading, against a pro-labour judge, and the campaign
predictably became an exercise in class conflict. 'Failure to vote
tomorrow, and failure to cast your votes against the CIO and the
Communists, may spell the doom of your city', intoned Reading
on the eve of the election. 'With this solemn and sincere warning
I say goodnight.' Reading won re-election but was soon indicted
for graft and bribery, as were others such as police superintendent Fred W. Frahm who had testified so eloquently before
HUAC. The anticommunists were also unable to sustain their
cause at state level. A number of states were seeking to bar the CP
from the ballot in 1940–1, and the Michigan legislators
considered such a measure as the Ford 'defense strike' reached its
peak. The ferocious anticommunist Blanche Winters campaigned
for the measure: 'to hell with democracy', she shouted, explaining
that the word democracy was not in the Constitution. The
proposal passed the lower house by 67 votes to 10, but the Civil
Rights Federation then rallied its forces and managed to defeat
the bill. *The Detroit Times*, a Hearst newspaper, angrily printed the
names of five Detroit senators who had opposed the bill and
screeched that 'Reds Win in Michigan'. The Republicans also lost
the gubernatorial election, although to Murray D. Van Wagoner,
a machine rather than a reform Democrat. Despite the 'little red
scare', labour and the left were holding their own in Michigan.[20]

World war

American intervention in the Second World War had a mixed impact on Michigan politics. As the United States became an ally of the Soviet Union the 'little red scare' faded, but the state's nativist constituencies were also receptive to isolationism and the turbulence on the right continued. At the same time, the transformation of Detroit and other motor cities into the 'arsenal of democracy' demanded new workers, and the massive influx of southern whites and blacks intensified racist tensions. The wartime overcrowding of the cities, the competition for both housing and jobs, added another poison to a discordant sociopolitical environment which could be exploited by agitators of any political complexion.

The Nazi attack on the Soviet Union in 1941 gave American Communists some respite, and the bombing of Pearl Harbor offered them an opportunity to display their patriotism. As the CP swung vigorously behind the American war effort it even enjoyed something of a resurgence, particularly in Michigan, where in 1942 it was recruiting twice as many members each month as in the previous year. But 'sound unionism' was also making some headway. The CP's revival was flagging by the end of the war, the party's subordination of workers' demands to the war effort limiting its appeal, while the Reuther faction in the UAW was consolidating its position through its sensitivity to the rights of labour.[21]

The CP's commitment to the war meant that it was less subject to harassment from the authorities, but it continued to be a target of tireless nativist and right-wing attention. Within Congress, at a time when most politicians were seeking to respect the wartime alliance, some of Michigan's representatives, most notably Democrat John Lesinski and Republicans Clare Hoffman and Arthur H. Vandenberg, remained unrestrained in their condemnation of Communist and Soviet wiles. In the state itself the superpatriots sought to harness the swirl of isolationist and racist emotions. Father Coughlin, under pressure from his superiors, had largely ceased his propagandist activities, but Gerald L. K. Smith reached what was perhaps the peak of his influence. Fiercely isolationist and predicting that there would be a 'communist revolution' after the war, Smith established ties with two of Michigan's leading Republican politicos, Senator

Vandenberg and Congressman Hoffman, and Henry Ford provided him with investigators to compile a list of alleged Communists. In April 1942 Smith launched his monthly *The Cross and the Flag* and later that year disturbed Republican leaders by running in the party's primary for US Senator, polling an impressive if insufficient 109000 votes. Smith's increasing absorption in national politics, however, afforded some relief to Walter Reuther and other local targets, for isolationism was supplanting the issue of CIO reds as his primary cause.[22]

Even murkier than Smith's connections were those of the Ku Klux Klan, which had probably never entirely disappeared from Michigan. In the early 1940s there were persistent reports that the Klan was invading union locals, an extraordinary development given its anti-labour history. The Klan, it was said, was taking its cue from the CP and instructing its members to 'bore from within' the industrial unions to wrest their control from the Communists. Detroit became the centre of a revitalized Klan, its path ironically having been smoothed by Father Coughlin's antisemitic and anticommunist crusade. The Klan also fed on the racist resentment of southern white and Polish American workers in wartime Detroit, where the shortages of housing and jobs, together with the growing numbers of African Americans, were dangerously exacerbating ethnic rivalries. The Klan and redbaiting politicians were implicated in a riot early in 1942, a prelude to the great racial explosion of June 1943, which resulted in 34 deaths. The Detroit public prosecutor, however, preferred to blame the 'radical talk' of the NAACP.[23]

The 1943 race riot was the most spectacular manifestation of the profound stresses which divided Detroit during the war and immediately after. Hundreds of thousands of poor whites and blacks from Appalachia and the South (more whites than blacks) had arrived to compete with the city's immigrant groups for jobs, overwhelming the housing supply and accelerating the physical deterioration of transport and other public facilities. Inflation increased pressure for labour action in what was now the most unionized city in the country, municipal employees agitated for the right to organize, and war's end brought widespread lay-offs, particularly among black workers. Such conditions only served to encourage the urban nativism that reactionaries had long exploited.

The 1943 mayoral campaign, following hard on the race riot, had witnessed the use of anti-red tactics against the labour-endorsed candidate, although the race issue became dominant as the Klan and other backers of Mayor Edward Jeffries presented him as the sounder guardian of white supremacy. Jeffries had trailed in the primary, but such methods contributed to his re-election. Even uglier was the 1945 mayoral election, when the formally nonpartisan Jeffries was pitted against the formidable Richard Frankensteen, the UAW vice-president. Jeffries had the support of local Republicans, the Teamsters, the AFL, the major newspapers, and, if unsolicited, of Gerald L. K. Smith. Meanwhile the CIO's Political Action Committee, local Democrats and the African American press supported Frankensteen, as did the CP. A new popular front seemed to be in the making. After Frankensteen won with a plurality in the primary Jeffries's disturbed backers unleashed a campaign of exceptional virulence, exploiting the anti-black and antisemitic prejudices of many white and ethnic voters. Critical in the politics of Detroit through the postwar period were homeowner groups anxious to prevent African American invasions of their territory and disposed to regard public housing schemes as communistic. Jeffries's partisans harped on Frankensteen's support for federal public housing policy and Jeffries himself on Frankensteen's alleged red tendencies. 'The Trotskyites', he said, were linked to 'the national PAC', who in turn were 'out to use Detroit as a spring-board, as a jumping-off place – for their revolutionary campaign'. Such figures as Gerald L. K. Smith and Homer Martin joined in this refrain, and the *Detroit News* agreed that 'A vote for Jeffries is a vote against Communism'. Jeffries was again elected, and a post-election analysis concluded that the racist and anticommunist propaganda had a significant effect in securing him critical (if often minority) votes in Polish, Irish, Italian and poor native white wards. Many of these voters must have been UAW members. The right had again capitalized on urban discontents; a threatening popular front coalition had been wrecked.[24]

Class and party politics

Even before the advent of the Cold War, then, red scare politics were well advanced in Michigan. The disintegration of the

business-oriented Republican hegemony in the 1930s in itself was
to some evidence of a kind of subversion. The rather abrupt
emergence of a powerful labour movement and the revitalization
of the Democratic party placed class conflict at the centre of
Michigan politics and served to redirect anticommunist sentiments. The fact that there was a vigorous CP presence in the
state, particularly in the labour movement, gave Republican
politicians a strong incentive to suggest that their opponents had
been infiltrated by reds. Anticommunist rhetoric was no longer
being directed exclusively at restive urban workers but also at
those in high places. But anticommunism was not a monopoly of
the corporate interests or the Republican right. An antiradical
patriotism was also being promoted by a variety of religious
leaders, both Catholic and fundamentalist Protestant, who were
cultivating followings in the industrial cities, where there were
large numbers of Roman Catholic immigrants and southern
whites. Such conditions encouraged a measure of collusion
between the different interests. At one level, corporate executives
might conspire with Klan-like figures to terrorize labour activists.
But the most significant form of accommodation was that between
Republican politicos and Catholic or nativist voters. Republican
candidates in statewide and in big city elections needed to reclaim
some working-class votes if they were to win. Hence they
regularly warned 'honest labor' against the wicked machinations
of Soviet-directed Communists.

The labour movement itself, of course, was deeply divided by
the Communist issue. On the right, Homer Martin mercilessly
redbaited his rivals, on occasion colluding with the bosses. More
moderately, the ACTU encouraged workers to espouse 'sound
unionism', a cause exemplified by Walter Reuther in the UAW. A
labour-oriented anticommunism was emerging, one which was
still class conscious in its commitment to the interests of labour
and its suspicion of management but which wanted to modify the
capitalist system rather than overthrow it. The exponents of this
kind of labour philosophy were increasingly determined not to
allow the industrial unions to be directed by Communist officials.

Despite the potential for red scare politics in Michigan, by the
end of the Second World War the victories of the anticommunists
had been limited. The legislature and executive had not
themselves succumbed to a serious anticommunist crusade, in

large part because labour and the left were strong enough to see off the patriotic right. Yet red scare politics had left their mark. The relative closeness of the fit between the two-party system and the class system in Michigan meant that election campaigns were a natural forum for the Communist issue. Republican-supported candidates had apparently won the gubernatorial election of 1938 and the Detroit mayoral election of 1945 with the use of red scares. If the forces represented by organized labour and the Democratic party had so far proved resilient in the face of these pressures, it remained to be seen whether they could withstand the added tensions of Cold War.

5

THE REPUBLICAN OFFENSIVE, 1945–1950

During the second half of the 1940s Republican partisanship was a major source of red scare politics in the country at large. The Truman administration critically helped to legitimize domestic anticommunism with its loyalty programme, its decision to prosecute CP leaders under the Smith Act, and its redbaiting of Henry Wallace during the 1948 campaign. But whatever the responsibility of mainstream Democrats, much of the energy behind anticommunist politics, as a number of scholars have argued, was imparted by Republicans anxious to discredit the New Deal, reduce the power of labour, and restore their own political fortunes. It was pressure from the highly conservative Eightieth Congress which impelled Truman to adopt his questionable loyalty programme, and it was the Republicans' outrage at their loss of the 1948 election which incited them to intensify their use of the Communist issue. They turned increasingly to the Communists-in-government charge in order to harass a Democratic administration compromised by foreign policy reverses in the Cold War.[1]

The Republican offensive in national politics was not invariably paralleled in state politics, but in Michigan the Republicans had already made the cause their own. They had been among the pioneers of red scare tactics in the gubernatorial campaign of 1938, which had seemed no less effective when deployed against a popular front resurgence in Detroit in 1945. The strength of labour and Democratic liberalism in Michigan had served to limit the gains of the anticommunist forces in the decade after 1935, but the harrowing strains of Cold War could only add to Republican temptations to use the Communist issue to restore the state to its natural rulers. Many of the state's Polish Americans, for example, felt that Franklin Roosevelt had cynically betrayed Poland at Yalta, and could prove susceptible to Republican overtures. As the Republicans forced the Communist issue, Michigan's Democrats responded by embracing their own form of anticommunism and denied Communists a place in their party or the associated labour movement. Party competition was coming to overshadow class conflict as the mainspring of red scare politics.

Even before world war was replaced by Cold War the political culture of Michigan was highly vulnerable to a renewed red scare. The CP presence in the state was a real one, and the factional battles inside the UAW in particular drew attention to it. There were perhaps a thousand CP members among the auto workers of Michigan in 1946, scattered around several shop branches in the various motor cities, about 450 of them at Ford. In some local unions such Communists held influential positions in the dominant factions. But it was not simply the labour wars that revealed the existence of Michigan reds. Also arousing suspicion was the prominence in the state of the American Youth for Democracy (AYD), a Communist group which noncommunists had joined during the wartime popular front. The AYD held a veterans' conference in Detroit towards the end of the war, and followed this with a series of pamphlets designed to appeal to students, veterans and blacks. The first peacetime AYD convention met in April 1946 in Detroit, where civil rights issues remained alive in the wake of the great race riot, and it agreed both on a major membership drive and on an assault on race discrimination in Detroit's restaurants.[2]

This radical offensive risked a serious backlash. Soviet expansionism during and after the Second World War caused anguish in Michigan's eastern European communities and also confirmed native-born conservatives in their long-held suspicions. Intertwined with ethnic and nativist anticommunism was that within the labour movement, in which ACTU in particular was conducting a reinvigorated anticommunist campaign among Catholic industrial workers. When Walter Reuther won the UAW–CIO presidency in March 1946, ACTU claimed much of the credit. The ethnic and religious tensions overlay a more fundamental class tension, one reflected in the party system. Organized labour continued to advertise its preference for New Deal Democrats, while the Republicans remained close to the corporate interests even as they reflected the conservatism of rural Michigan. As the world polarized between East and West, the Republicans injected the red scare into the dynamics of party politics.[3]

Kim Sigler and red scare politics

Red scare tactics were not uncommon among Republican party candidates generally in the mid-term elections of 1946. Indeed the GOP national chairman conjured up a battle between 'Communism and Republicanism'. But the Republican gubernatorial campaign in Michigan surpassed most in its resort to redbaiting, as the Republicans seemed to take up where they had left off in 1938. Their candidate was Kim Sigler, who had emerged to prominence in the mid-1940s as a special prosecutor investigating corruption in state government. The party initially turned to him in order to exploit widespread suspicions of misconduct at Lansing, and while Sigler did run on a clean government platform, in the fall he introduced a secondary theme to his campaign, that of the dangerous Communist influence in the state. Indeed, Sigler attempted to link the two. He warned that there had been an 'infiltration of racketeers and communists' in the labour movement, and promised that his administration would make it a 'must' to expose 'racketeers and communist leaders' in Michigan unions. Like other Republicans before him he sought to drive a wedge between 'honest and sincere labor leaders' with whom he would work (and whose followers he hoped would vote for him) and 'the racketeers and communist labor leaders who are destroying labor and America'. He moved on from labour to the Michigan Democratic party itself, which 'Communists and left-wingers' had largely taken over. It was 'a known fact that the Communist Party has charted this area as the spot in which will break that volcano of social revolution, which will be the focal point for their TOD – Take Over Day.' (TOD was to become a favourite piece of Michigan anti-red mythology.) He equated communism with belief in

Washington bureaucracy and urged the defeat of the Democrats so that 'the American Way of Life can be perpetuated'. Michigan Republicans were still running against the New Deal, evoking that natural order in which the privileges of management were not limited by the countervailing force of organized labour.[4]

The irony was that the Democratic gubernatorial candidate in 1946 was Murray D. Van Wagoner, who owed his position to his own personal organization rather than to the CIO, whose state president was withholding support. The Democrats, demoralized and divided during the currently unpopular Truman administration, many of them more interested in federal patronage than state offices, failed adequately to rally behind their candidate. Some AFL leaders supported Sigler, and some old-line Democrats remained unreconciled to the presence of reformers in the party. Henry Wallace's outspoken comments added to their frustrations, for his break with Truman involved an attack on Michigan's Senator Arthur Vandenberg – a Wallace appearance in Detroit in November gave the Republicans yet another opportunity to paint the Democrats red. The anticipated Republican victory was even more resounding in Michigan than in most states. Not only was the Democratic presence in Congress reduced to a rump, but the Republicans won the governorship by the largest margin since 1928, some 95 out of 100 seats in the state lower house and 28 out of 32 seats in the senate. 'And so died the New Deal!', rejoiced the *Detroit News*' ... For more than thirteen years it has regimented and restricted the country, but now it passes.' Yet again, it seemed, the Republicans had successfully used the Communist issue.[5]

Unlike Frank Fitzgerald in 1938, Sigler continued his anticommunist campaign from the governor's mansion, making it a central cause of his administration. Like the Republicans in the 80th Congress, he hoped to turn back the political clock. Even before he took up his duties, the state police were responding to the new mood, warning that Foss Baker, an official of both the United Public Workers (UPW) and the Michigan State Employee Board (representing union locals before the state), was 'definitely a communist and a paid CIO organizer'. This raised the possibility that the state civil service had indeed been penetrated by Communists. Reports were also reaching the governor on local AYD chapters, which had been campaigning against race discrim-

ination in restaurants and for a Fair Employment Practices
Committee (FEPC) bill. Gerald L.K. Smith had warned HUAC in
1946 that AYD was a Communist front, and the civil rights activities of the lively group in Michigan brought it to the attention of
the authorities. Meanwhile, the red presence in the labour
movement was regularly headlined in the press as the CIO drive
against Communist-led unions began to get underway and as the
Reuther group in the UAW employed a liberal anticommunism in
its struggles with the left-centre faction. With his own social
reform agenda to further, Reuther was using anticommunism to
build the political strength of the UAW.[6]

Even before President Truman's declaration of war on
domestic communism in March 1947, Governor Sigler was
leading an assault on the Communists whom he believed infested
Michigan's state payroll, campuses and labour movement. He
began by asking university presidents to take appropriate action
with respect to campus AYD chapters. Soon after, he declared
Foss Baker to be a Communist, and charged him with organizing
state employees 'on the pretense of bringing them into a labor
union when in fact he is interested in the Communist Party'.
Determined to expose Communists in the state's employ, Sigler
directed Attorney General Eugene F. Black to conduct a probe.
While the two recognized that law-abiding CP employees could
not be fired for membership alone, Sigler insisted that he would
sack 'anyone who has engaged in un-American activities', and
Black threatened prosecution under the sedition laws.

As Sigler warmed to his work he decided that he needed to
consult J. Edgar Hoover, and in mid-February he and
Commissioner of State Police Donald S. Leonard travelled to
Washington. There Sigler identified three areas in which
'agitators, radicals and communists' were making inroads in
Michigan, notably among state employees, college students and
labour unions. 'Michigan is the heart of the nation's industry and
of its war potential,' he explained in a typical politician's image of
his state. 'It is the most fruitful field in the country for agents of a
foreign power to move into a strategic position.' He seemed
particularly troubled by the Communist infiltration of labour and
pledged to support the anticommunist factions in their drive:
'They know who the Communists are. I plan to turn the spotlight
on them so there will be no doubt about who they are. That will

help the union membership clean house.' Content to exploit labour turbulence, his technique was to be one of exposure rather than repression. Police Commissioner Leonard also put his time in Washington to good use. FBI Assistant Director Louis B. Nichols coached him on how best to attack Communists: 'a blast should also be taken at the same time against Fascists'. Leonard reported to Sigler that 'I was impressed with the thought that this problem which you are calling to the attention of our Michigan citizens is not a question of political debate but an organized plot to overthrow our Government or align it under Red Russia.' The Washington line was beginning to engage state officials.[7]

This Cold War perspective on domestic communism suited Sigler well enough and he used it to further his campaign. The Hearst-owned *Detroit Times* rallied to his side with a series of articles on subversive activities in Michigan, using material apparently supplied from police files, and the *Detroit News* too followed the governor's lead. In his regular radio broadcast at the beginning of March, Sigler said that the Communists were using a 'Trojan horse' strategy on the United States, seeking to undermine the country by boring from within, using 'the ingenious "front" technique' to recruit unsuspecting citizens. In mid-March the Truman administration announced its own loyalty programme, giving credence to the idea that there were Soviet agents inside the United States, and HUAC embarked on a series of momentous hearings to consider legislation to outlaw the CP, inviting a number of prestigious witnesses such as former ambassador to the Soviet Union, William C. Bullitt, and the AFL head, William Green. Most impressive of all, J. Edgar Hoover agreed to appear, marking the first occasion on which he dignified HUAC with his testimony and also his breach with the Truman administration.

Into this arena strode Kim Sigler, summoned as an 'expert' on communism. He told HUAC that there were 'upward of 15 000 Communists in Michigan', a spectacular improvement on a recent FBI report of 2135, read out his file on Foss Baker, named Democratic state Senator Stanley Nowak as a Communist sympathizer, and capped his testimony by citing 22 Michigan organizations as Communist fronts, including AYD, the Civil Rights Federation, various eastern European workers groups, and the Detroit Council for Youth Service. (This last turned out to be a 'mixup' in police files for which Sigler had to apologize.) But, as before, Sigler's central thrust was that Communists were seeking to dominate the labour movement. He spoke of compiling evidence on the hundred or so 'most notorious Communists', who were manoeuvring to win control of the UAW in order to give Moscow the power to immobilize the industries of Michigan in time of war. HUAC was well pleased with Sigler's testimony. It offered him access to its own files and Congressman Karl Mundt praised him for doing a 'precedent-shattering job' in fighting communism in Michigan, the best in any state. 'I recall that in past years when we had sit-down strikes, and other developments in Michigan we got no support from the then Governor of Michigan', Mundt reminisced pointedly. 'I think Michigan can be proud of the progress made since those days.'[8]

More than any other state governor, Sigler had made anticommunism his cause, and he and HUAC needed one another's endorsement. Such state–federal collaboration – or mutual legitimation – could powerfully intensify a red scare, and Sigler returned to Michigan to survey the damage he had wrought. The UAW was furious, Walter Reuther scathingly condemning him for 'resorting to the traditional Red Scare'. Whether the Sigler attack significantly harmed the Michigan CIO, and in particular the UAW, cannot be gauged, but soon afterwards the Reuther forces pressed ahead with their own anticommunist drive, most notably in urging the enforcement of a clause in the UAW constitution which could be interpreted as barring Communists from office. The impact of the Sigler scare on Foss Baker and the UPW was undeniable. Seven UPW locals withdrew from the Michigan State Employee Board, and eventually Baker quit his UPW post. Experiencing even greater disruption were the AYD chapters on the state's campuses.[9]

Sigler's fingering of the AYD triggered an attack from suspicious legislators, who were no better disposed towards campus radicals than they had been in 1935 or 1940. Leading it was Republican state Senator Matthew F. Callahan of Detroit, who introduced a resolution calling for 'an investigation into alleged communistic activities at Wayne University'. The senate in fact extended the scope of the problem to 'the state of Michigan', linked it to the governor's probe, and entrusted it to Callahan and fellow GOP senators Colin L. Smith and Don Vander Werp. Senator Stanley Nowak alone resisted the measure. Nonetheless Wayne University, which was in the process of being brought into the state university system, remained the primary target, Callahan and Smith hinting that the process might be obstructed and funds blocked unless the university rid itself of its AYD chapter. President David Henry bravely attempted to face the committee down, insisting that he had no evidence that the chapter was 'operating as a communistic group'. Callahan and Smith had their own version of admissible evidence, as when Detroit policemen testified that AYD, which had been picketing restaurants, 'was using Negro students as dupes, and tried to stir up racial strife under the guise of aid to universities'. To Callahan such evidence was proof that AYD was 'part of a plan laid down in Moscow to stir up bloodshed and revolution', and he found Dr Henry's refusal to ban it 'staggering'. David Henry stood his ground, dismissing charges against the national AYD as irrelevant, and was vindicated when the US Justice Department conceded that it had 'no evidence' that AYD was subversive. But Henry's triumph was short-lived, for it was during this imbroglio that J. Edgar Hoover gave his celebrated testimony to HUAC, citing AYD among other groups as a Communist front. Soon after the Justice Department repudiated its earlier letter and informed President Henry that local AYD chapters were Communist recruiting centres. The Justice Department and the FBI were evidently accommodating themselves to Hoover's public line, and the invocation of such authority doomed the Michigan AYDers.[10]

Wayne University finally banned its AYD chapter after it refused to dissociate itself from the national AYD. HUAC broadened the onslaught with the publication of its *Report on American Youth for Democracy*, warning that there was 'a determined effort to disaffect our youth and to turn them against religion, the American home, against the college authorities, and against the American government itself', and calling on state governors and college presidents to expose the organization. The AYD now fell victim to patriotic assaults and state probes across the country; among the campuses banning it were the University of Michigan and Michigan State College. Kim Sigler's red scare, in blazing a path for powerful federal influences, had served to ravage student radicalism.[11]

The success of the legislative assault on the campuses, together with the anticommunist stance of the governor, encouraged Senator Callahan to press on with the red hunt. He sponsored a bill to oblige 'foreign agencies' in the state to register with the authorities. At its first appearance, like the Baldwin–Dunckel bill of 1935, it appeared to be primarily an anti-labour device, for it provided that any union dominated by subversive elements be placed in receivership until 'loyal officials are elected'. Accordingly, even ACTU, Walter Reuther and other anticommunist labour leaders denounced it. The highly partisan nature of legislative anticommunism was demonstrated by the fact that Callahan won the support of all but one of his fellow Republican senators and the opposition of all Democrats but one. But the explosion of labour outrage forced the bill's amendment in the house, and it emerged retaining only the feature requiring the registration of foreign agencies. Michigan's nativist impulses had not disappeared. The governor signed the bill into law, but the matter did not end there. Objecting to the excessive power given to the attorney general, and fearing for such bodies as international unions, church groups and even the English-Speaking Union, the Civil Rights Congress launched a campaign to repeal the act by securing enough signatures to force a referendum. The move was premature, because Attorney General Black, stung by Callahan's criticism that he was staging a 'sit-down strike against the Callahan Act', issued a press statement describing the law as 'monstrous and complete nonsense', incompatible with federal law, and flatly declining to enforce it. Black had earlier been placed in charge of Sigler's red probe, and Callahan was incensed at this betrayal, a step toward 'the dissolution of organized society'. The senate consoled him by continuing his investigating committee and renaming it the Committee on Un-American Activities. Michigan now had its own little HUAC, and it was to return to the cause after Sigler had called for a new round of redhunting in 1948.[12]

While Governor Sigler had helped to unleash the legislative bloodhounds, his own anti-red offensive of 1947 was faltering. He had been embarrassed at having to retract some of his well-publicized testimony before HUAC and to apologize to groups mistakenly named; he had fallen out with his attorney general, who had been charged with the probe but was being drawn into an investigation of alleged corrupt business contributions to Sigler's 1946 campaign; and finally the undiplomatic Sigler was increasingly embroiled in quarrels with the legislature. Yet he had become a prominent symbol of the anticommunist cause. In May

1947 the Midwest Republican State Chairmen's Association followed Sigler in drawing attention to the 'inroads' communism had made in American governmental structures, firmly assigning responsibility to New Deal Democrats. In July American state governors held a conference on improving the quality of citizenship, a goal which Sigler told them could be achieved only by exposing communism on the campuses, relating the proud tale of his campaign against AYD. In September the American Commission of the Navy and Army Union commended Sigler for 'taking a leadership in opposition to Red and Communist activities'. He also acted as a magnet for other anticommunists. Michigan Republican Congressman George A. Dondero offered him aid. Further afield, California's Jack B. Tenney congratulated Sigler on his 'forthright fight against communistic forces' and supplied him with Tenney Committee reports. Thomas H. Bienz of the Washington state HUAC invited him to the 1948 conference of little HUACs. And state Senator Wilmer C. Carter of Maryland, anxious to develop that state's communist-control programme, wrote to Sigler on the suggestion of HUAC officials for information on the Michigan measures. Such networking added to the effectiveness of the anticommunist forces, and the attention paid to Sigler encouraged his self-image as a leader.[13]

Republican anticommunism

By the spring of 1948, as international tensions increased abroad and the larger red scare deepened at home, Kim Sigler was ready to resume his leadership of the cause. His way was paved by the *Detroit News* and its columnist James Sweinhart, who launched a major series of articles under the title 'Communist Plot Exposed'. Sigler was on friendly terms with Sweinhart, feeding him with information on local communism, receiving advance copies of the articles, and later using him to draft correspondence on the Communist issue. Beginning on 7 March 1948, and dominating the front page, the series ran through 29 articles and was subsequently published as a book. It adopted the FBI–HUAC–Sigler premise of a foreign conspiracy, and purported to show 'how the Communists have developed an organization of foreign-born agents and American traitors for the day when they can take over Detroit and other strategic points and establish a police-and-slave state'. The series insisted that Soviet Communists were bent on world domination, presented the American CP as the tool of Moscow, discussed the Canadian spy case of 1945–6 (Canada's proximity heightened interest for Michiganers), and ran photographs of Michigan CP leaders. At least a few local nerves were touched. A number of civic and patriotic groups were inspired to hold meetings on the Communist peril and to call for more exposés. The Detroit superintendent of schools cited the articles in instructing that copies of the US Attorney General's list of subversive organizations be sent to over 30000 employees in the city's public and church schools. More fateful still were the revived anticommunist campaigns of the state governor and Detroit police commissioner.[14]

The launching of the Sweinhart series was marked by a radio-television discussion between three leading Republicans, Governor Sigler, Attorney General Eugene Black, and that veteran of the anticommunist cause Harry Toy, now Detroit police commissioner. Sigler argued that exposure was the most effective method of combating communism, as illustrated by the Sweinhart series. Black held that Communists were concentrating 'on the young people of America' and called for the scrutiny of college textbooks. Harry Toy was the most belligerent, demanding laws 'which would enable us to put in prison those people who conspire to overthrow the United States Government'. At one point he was understood as having said that 'Soviet agents entered this country recently through Canada disguised as Jewish rabbis'. He also disclosed that the Detroit police, in cooperation with the state police and the Michigan National Guard, had worked out a 'plan of mobilization' to combat Michigan Communists should they ever try to take over the state's key industries: 'The Communists have an elaborate plan they call "Take-Over Day," but we're ready for them.' Letters poured into the governor's office commending the offensive.[15]

The Sweinhart series and the broadcast by the three Republican officeholders provided the momentum needed to advance the communist-control programme. Attorney General Black proposed the creation of an anti-subversive division in the state police, and in April Sigler backed a bill to effect this, implicitly reaching beyond his earlier reliance on simple exposure. Not to be outdone was Harry Toy, who announced the revival of the Subversive Activities (or 'Red') Squad in the city police, 'because I am convinced the Communists in this area are planning riots and disorder in the future'. Formed around Lieutenant Harry Michaels and Detective Leo Maciosek (the 'Mic and Mack' of anti-labour repute who had been Dies Committee witnesses), citizens were soon said to be writing to the squad with names of suspected Communists. On one occasion Toy ordered the wholesale seizure of comic books, on the grounds that they were 'Communistic and immoral'. Both Sigler and Toy were thought to be eyeing the Republican gubernatorial nomination, Sigler's quarrels with the legislature having put his renomination in doubt.[16]

Toy soon had an opportunity to mobilize his red squad. On 20 April a murderous shotgun attack was made on Walter Reuther, who survived with severe injuries. Commissioner Toy told his officers to round up the usual suspects, particularly 'Communists or anyone in industry or a union'. To the *Detroit News*, 'with events abroad in mind, the possibility of Communist authorship is all too apparent'. The Detroit police obligingly questioned a number of UAW left-wing leaders and detained one of them, prompting the Civil Rights Congress to ask why members of management and the Ku Klux Klan were not similarly interrogated. (Lacking confidence in the city police, UAW officials attempted to secure an FBI investigation: 'Fellows, Edgar says no', the US Attorney General reported back. 'He says he's not going to send the FBI in every time some nigger woman gets raped.') Neither the perpetrators of this attack nor of that on Victor Reuther a year later were ever brought to justice; the Reuther brothers suspected underworld figures connected with union-busting activities and auto executives. In the event, the affair served only to reinforce class divisions, confirming to labour that the police remained an arm of the business community and to upstanding citizens that Communists were capable of murder.[17]

Increasingly Michigan's conservatives were turning to the police for an answer to the red menace, and this was destined to become a central issue in the state's anticommunist politics. In the United States, unusually, as Michael Rogin has noted of the FBI, responsibility for both criminal detection and political surveillance was combined in the same agency, and this confusion between crime and political dissent was also perpetuated by police forces across the country, so that the boundaries of police action sometimes became a matter of political dispute. In Michigan's motor cities, some of them essentially company towns, the business classes had often enjoyed a close relationship with local police forces, which had perhaps exchanged personnel with company security divisions and employed red squads. Further, Republican legislative proposals, such as the 1935 Baldwin–Dunckel bill and the 1947 Callahan bill, had on presentation tended to treat radicalism as an extension of the labour problem. The Republican attempts to establish subversive activities divisions in the state and city police in the Cold War era suggest that conservative perspectives had not changed much, particularly since the proposals tended to emphasize the extensions of police powers rather than the protection of civil liberties. The hankering for the business-dominated universe which had obtained before the New Deal was also illustrated in the Republican impulse to link the Communist conspiracy to labour-oriented Democrats. The police's subversive activities divisions usually became known as 'red squads', and because labour had long regarded red squads as anti-union devices, proposals to extend them could only encounter extensive labour and liberal opposition. The proper role of the police in combating communism was an issue which was to divide Republicans from Democrats through the early 1950s.[18]

Kim Sigler invited the special session of the legislature convened in April 1948 to consider the establishment of a state 'red squad', as the press characterized it. The proposal, drawn up by the attorney general and Commissioner Leonard, authorized the State Police Commissioner to create a subversive activities investigation division, keep 'confidential files', hire 'informers' outside the department, and keep his staff secret. Critics objected to the very wide powers given to the police commissioner, but the measure passed the lower house (in which Democrats had but token representation) with only one dissenting vote. As it happened, however, the bill was slowed in a senate committee whose chairman doubted its necessity and had not cleared when the legislative session ended, by which time the senate and the governor were wrangling over other matters. For the moment the state police were denied their own red squad, but the proposal was to serve as a model for later Republican responses to the menace of domestic communism.[19]

Meanwhile a few Republican legislators had been able to use the brief spring session of 1948 for their own stabs at local Communists. Some had signalled their distrust of education with a proposal to require teachers to sign a statement disavowing CP membership, although its passage was averted by doubts about its constitutionality. More extraordinary were the antics of Senator Callahan, determined that his anticommunist crusade should not flag. He was frustrated in his desire to revise the stalemated Callahan Act since Governor Sigler had not listed it as a matter for the special session. But Callahan's 'little HUAC' was still in existence and on the prowl for campus Communists. The professional ex-Communist witness Joseph Kornfeder added a little to the committee's stature with testimony that there were Communist groups in various Detroit unions and on Michigan campuses. The president of Michigan State College, in downplaying the significance of campus radicalism, had earlier told the committee that there was only one Communist on campus, and by April the committee had identified this lonely subversive as James Zarichny, a 24-year-old veteran whom it promptly summoned. Callahan's anticommunist zeal drove an increasingly bizarre farce.

Zarichny declined to answer questions about his relationship to the CP, citing his constitutional rights. Callahan denied their relevance since CP membership was not illegal and took the opportunity to define communism as 'an international conspiracy and an atheistic and anti-religious ideology' aimed at the violent overthrow of government. The Callahan Committee cited Zarichny for contempt, only to discover that a contempt hearing had to be held before the full senate, an event unprecedented in Michigan history. Senator Nowak warned that the chamber would be a national 'laughing stock' if it tried a 'young boy' for refusing to reveal which party he belonged to, but the senate stoically proceeded with its duty. Zarichny was found guilty and sentenced to a suspended prison term for the rest of the legislative session, a matter of hours. Like a number of zealous anticommunists in the late 1940s, Callahan did himself more harm than good. He was defeated for renomination in the Republican primary and his Detroit district was subsequently captured by Democrats. But he had left his mark. Zarichny, who had been on probation since his earlier AYD activities, was expelled from Michigan State College some months later for associating with Communists; the student newspaper and Student Council sided with the authorities. Legislative snarls had again damaged campus radicalism.[20]

The executive and legislative thrusts of 1948 had met with only modest success, but enough to keep alive the association between Sigler and the Republicans and the anticommunist cause. The course of international and national affairs guaranteed that the Communist issue would again feature prominently in the fall elections. Despite his squabbles with senate Republicans, Kim Sigler was again the party's gubernatorial candidate. Pitted against him was the young liberal Democrat G. Mennen Williams, one of those peace-minded students who had so troubled the legislators in 1935, a protégé of Frank Murphy, and a favourite of the CIO. Not since Frank Murphy's 1938 campaign was business so clearly arrayed against labour. Sigler's anti-labour and redhunting policies had served to encourage the Michigan CIO to cleave even more tightly to the state Democratic party, and Sigler made much of the sinister nature of the CIO and of Williams's connections with it. Campaigning in labour strongholds, Sigler urged workers to rid themselves of reds in their ranks. He hammered at 'CIO maneuvers to gain control of the state Government', espying a 'pattern of political seizure that has brought ruin to many European countries', and promised 'Continuous efforts to ferret out and curb subversive activities'. The Democratic campaign too reflected the class basis of Michigan politics. Mennen Williams focused on Sigler's anti-labour record and represented him as a tool of the auto dealers, whose illegal contributions to Republican coffers in 1946 were now being embarrassingly revealed. Williams's strong liberal and big labour image gave Sigler some hope of eating into the Democratic vote. Many organization Democrats, who had not cared much for Frank Murphy and his indifference to machine politics, were similarly unenthusiastic about Williams. So too were some AFL unions, and a number of AFL locals, disliking Williams's ties with the CIO's UAW, came out for Sigler. Nonetheless Sigler's attempts to woo labour conservatives did him little good. In an extraordinary and unexpected outcome, paralleling that of the presidential election, Williams defeated Sigler by the substantial margin of 163 000 votes. The Democrats also made significant gains in the state legislative elections, although the

Republicans remained firmly in control of both houses. The Republican exploitation of red scare politics had failed to have its desired effect. The alliance between the CIO and the Democratic party had been consummated in the 1948 campaign and its potency had been demonstrated.[21]

A bizarre subplot to this campaign involved the notorious Callahan Act, which the state's attorney general had derided as unconstitutional and which Sigler and other leading Republicans had admitted was faulty. Yet in 1947 the Communist-led Civil Rights Congress (CRC) had launched a drive to have it put to the voters at large, and had been collecting signatures to this end. The mechanism for a referendum, once triggered, pressed on remorselessly, and belated CRC efforts to halt the process failed, despite the incongruous assistance of the Republican attorney general. The Callahan Act, which neither Democratic nor Republican candidates for executive office had any intention of using, was on the ballot. That electorate which decisively rejected the redbaiting Sigler and part of which put a Democrat in Callahan's seat, upheld the act by a three-fifths vote. The anticommunist genie had been let out of the bottle and Michigan citizens, workers among them, were signalling their hostility to foreign intervention in American politics.[22]

Urban discontents

Mennen Williams's election as governor meant that there would be little pressure for a red scare from the state executive, but anticommunist sentiments continued to course through other parts of the polity, particularly in urban-industrial areas. Popular anticommunism though was undergoing some modification. The religious messiahs had receded from the foreground. Father Coughlin had long since gone silent and at the end of 1947 Gerald L.K. Smith, who had been finding Detroit increasingly incapable of providing receptive audiences, had moved to St Louis. The more moderate anticommunism associated with the Roman Catholic establishment, however, was becoming a widespread orthodoxy, assisted by perceptions of an aggressive Soviet foreign policy and widespread outrage in the state's white ethnic communities over the subjugation of eastern Europe. In 1948 ACTU marked Labor Day for the first time with a religious service, during which a priest invoked Pius XI's 1937 encyclical condemning 'atheistic communism' while upholding 'social justice'; the Roman Catholic church was lauded for offering 'so clear a middle way between unregulated capitalism on the one hand and devastating communism on the other'. As the national CIO moved to expel the Communist-led unions, the Detroit ACTU urged its constituents to remove Communists from office in union locals.[23]

A series of incidents in urban Michigan reflected the growing anticommunist suspicions. The University of Michigan's Workers Educational Service came under attack in 1948, General Motors president Charles E. Wilson describing one of its 'Marxist tinged' courses as consisting of 'personal insults to me and my own position'; its director was subsequently dismissed. At Michigan State, James Zarichny was finally expelled. In December the notorious 'Red Dean' of England's Canterbury Cathedral, Dr Hewlett Johnson, was denied access to the Ford River Rouge plant lest he was 'subjected to unpleasant demonstrations'. The Detroit Police Commissioner, Harry Toy, also attracted national attention when he tried to impose a loyalty oath on newspaper reporters wanting press cards; police records, he explained, indicated that 'several members of the press in Detroit are communists or communistic sympathizers'. Finally, a minor *cause célèbre* emerged in Detroit's water board when George Shenkar, who had once chaired a Marxist study group, was refused promotion when he failed to answer questions about his politics. These local anti-red impulses were given some legitimacy in the spring of 1949 by the Smith Act trials in New York, where Detroit's Carl Winter was one of those charged and an FBI agent testified to attending CP meetings in Detroit.[24]

By the summer the Detroit city fathers were once again fretting about the red menace that threatened their city, their minds concentrated by the approach of the fall elections. Shenkar's continued presence on the payroll irritated them, and the city's civil service commission estimated that there were at least 60 Communists or sympathizers in their employ, many of them members of the United Public Workers, one of the unions being expelled from the CIO. The success of the UPW in organizing city employees was particularly disturbing. The problem for Mayor Van Antwerp was that the city charter prohibited questioning employees about their political beliefs, and membership of the (legal) CP did not itself constitute grounds for dismissal. Detroit's leaders were thus vulnerable to the criticism voiced in the *Detroit Free Press* when it deplored the location of Communists in the transport, lighting and water departments, where 'their potential for damage to essential public services is great'. The mayor responded by appointing the nation's first city Un-American Activities Committee, chaired by Police Commissioner Toy; it quickly reported an estimated 34 subversives on the payroll and recommended a permanent loyalty committee. There was still no way of formally proceeding against CP members, but Van Antwerp wrote to the governor demanding that they at least be excluded from the ballot, and seeking his endorsement of the proposed city loyalty programme. Mennen Williams demurred, urging both caution and further study.[25]

Denied state assistance, city officials pressed ahead with their own solution, an amendment to the city charter to allow a municipal loyalty commission, the screening of employees, and dismissal for disloyalty. Resisted in vain by the governor, and denounced by teacher and especially labour groups as a campaign ploy, the measure nonetheless proved strikingly popular with the city's patriotic electorate. Told by the *Detroit News* that it was 'a Vote on Communism', the citizens approved it by over 75 per cent. From the fall of 1949 Detroit thus had its own unique communist-control programme, constituting first a Loyalty Investigating Committee to conduct probes of city employees, and second a Loyalty Commission to hear any cases that were brought. The city had armed itself against the red menace before Michigan saw fit to do so. Its Americanism was also demonstrated by the outcome of the 1949 mayoral election, when Republican Albert Cobo, known for his anti-Reuther views, heavily defeated the liberal Democrat George Edwards. This surprise result probably owed something to the extensive use of antiradical and racist propaganda. Cultivating the plethora of white neighbourhood groups, Cobo won the votes of many union members after playing on fears of 'Negro invasions' and public housing. Thereafter the UAW largely abandoned its attempts to win this unionized city from its conservative rulers. One victim of the pressures stoked in 1949 was the United Public Workers, which the national CIO had ousted by early 1950 and which by

March was reported to be fast losing members in Detroit and other Michigan cities. In 1951 the Detroit city council was to ban the UPW from the negotiating table.[26]

The troubles in Detroit and the continued spasms in the UAW over its Communist members were not lost on Michiganers outside the metropolitan area. Such publicity seemed to offer either evidence of Communist subversion or opportunities for political gain. Among the electorate, no group had a better claim to patriotic values than the veterans, of whom there were some 800 000 in the state by 1948. Expanded by the Second World War and reinvigorated by the Cold War, veterans who inveighed against the red menace were ignored by politicians at their peril. In April 1950 the American Legion sponsored the Wolverine All-American Conference on Subversive Activities at Lansing. Local and state patriotic and civic groups were well represented in this affair, which provided a platform for such anticommunist notables as Dr J.B. Matthews, Rabbi Benjamin Schultz and Illinois state Senator Paul Broyles. The conference approved a resolution calling on the governor to request the legislature to outlaw the CP.

Republicans across the state once more scented an opportunity to stir the red issue. Fred M. Alger, Jr, a candidate for the Republican gubernatorial nomination, pointed to the current problems in Detroit, and argued that by outlawing the CP, 'fringe groups and the wavering organizations' would be deprived of 'the excuse that the Communist Party is a legal entity in Michigan'. State Chairman Owen J. Clearly enthusiastically endorsed the proposal to outlaw the CP. Meanwhile, the Republican State Central Committee adopted a resolution to bar Communists from the ballot, and party leaders contemplated a possible referendum to prohibit 'any party dominated by a foreign power'. As the Republicans were declaring war on the CP, a strike in a state agency prompted Republican state Senator Colin L. Smith to urge the creation of a state loyalty board to screen the loyalties of state employees. The Detroit model was to be extended to the whole of Michigan. Even before the outbreak of the Korean War, the Republicans were positioning themselves to blast the Democrats in the 1950 campaigns with the heavy artillery of anticommunism.[27]

The primacy of party

The amplification of the Communist issue in Michigan politics was testimony not only to the pressures of Cold War but also to the persistence of the class war being waged in the state and to the revitalization of the two-party system. Many conservatives had not accepted the economic and political revolutions of the 1930s, and they continued to fight for 'the right to manage' through the 1940s, from time to time resorting to red scare tactics in attempts to turn back the clock. In its political dimension, anticommunism was primarily a Republican weapon, for it was the Republicans who spoke for the business classes and the Democrats who spoke for the organized labour which so affronted them. But in being channelled through the Republican party, the anticommunist cause was now being driven by political partisanship as well as class resentment, and the Democratic party too was obeying the laws of political survival in disavowing the CP. These anticommunist strategies were fashioned by party chieftains after careful calculation; they were not the products of populist rage, though they were meant to align the parties with popular sentiments. The state's workers had learned to be class conscious and to develop an antipathy for the corporations, but church, ethnic and even economic influences rendered them suspicious of Marxist doctrine. And their anticommunism was a temptation to the business classes. One reason for the Republicans' use of red scare tactics during election campaigns was their need to reach into labour constituencies; they hoped that Catholic, AFL and even UAW workers might be won over.[28]

Nonetheless by the late 1940s the class conflict which had sundered the old political order in Michigan in the New Deal years had grown a little less virulent. Management and industrial unions were accommodating to one another. The Taft–Hartley Act of 1947 had tipped the balance in industrial relations back towards management, while the bureaucratization of the industrial unions had rendered them less susceptible to shop-floor disruption. As industrial relations became characterized by a regular bargaining process between corporate and union leaders, the bitter warfare of the 1930s receded into the past. An important milestone was the GM–UAW contract of 1950, which set a five-year term and provided a pension system, and marked what William Serrin has called the 'civilized relationship' between labour and management. The steady work, high wages and fringe benefits that workers experienced in the postwar years enhanced their sense of security and admitted them more fully to the culture of the consumer society. The typical middle-class consumer, according to *Fortune* magazine in 1954, was 'the machinist in Detroit'. Politically, working-class Americanism was mediated primarily through the Democratic party. If class conflict had eased, urban nativism had not and party competition was fiercer than ever, and together they guaranteed the survival of red scare politics.[29]

The Democrats may have distanced themselves from the CP, but a consensus on the Communist issue had not been achieved. The redbaited Democrats generally opposed pressures for controls on Communists, and in the 1940s Republican demands for such curbs were largely frustrated. The election of Mennen Williams to the governorship in 1948 afforded the state's radicals some relief, but the deterioration of the Cold War, and the federal prosecutions of Communists and others, meant that anticommunist lobbies were given encouragement and that red scare emotions remained powerful in city councils and the state legislature. In 1950 the state's Republicans signalled their intention to make the Communist issue a central one in the upcoming elections, although Governor Williams was equally determined to resist the pressures from Detroit officials, veterans and the Republican party to smother the CP. Although other state business obliged him to call a special meeting of the legislature in 1950, he expected to control its agenda and to mediate anticommunist passions. But in June the outbreak of the Korean War fatally weakened his position. The final triumph of the Republicans now seemed at hand.

6

THE TRIUMPH OF LIBERALISM?
1950–1954

When in the spring of 1950 Governor Mennen Williams convened a special session of the legislature, he had hoped to find a harmless way of diverting or channelling the mounting anticommunist passions. 'Ideas cannot be suppressed by force or killed with a club', he insisted, and in keeping with the advice he had given Mayor Van Antwerp, he proposed a 'blue-ribbon' study commission to 'explore the whole question' of legal curbs on Communist activity and asked for $15000 to pay for it.

Williams's response was more than a delaying tactic. As governor he had a predilection for study commissions and he possessed a liberal's respect for expertise. If communism was a problem it needed a sophisticated solution. The file of literature on communism compiled by Williams's office contained articles by leading scholars Zechariah Chafee Jr and Henry Steele Commager and from the *Stanford Law Review*, in contrast to Kim Sigler's file which had been filled with US Chamber of Commerce, American Legion, and Tenney Committee publications. To his 'blue-ribbon' commission Williams wanted to appoint the best legal and constitutional experts he could find, such as law professors and distinguished jurists, and to equip it with a research staff able to consult other state and federal authorities. He stressed the complexity of the problem, pointed out that in Canada and elsewhere an outlawed CP had simply reappeared in different guise, and reminded legislators that the Callahan Act had failed because it had not observed constitutional rights. If the

125

conservative and Republican answer was to smash the CP, the liberal and Democratic answer was to trust in the experts.[1]

In 1950 many American liberals were championing this kind of solution to the problem of communism. In the US Senate liberal senators Hubert Humphrey, Herbert Lehman, Harley Kilgore and others introduced the Emergency Detention Act, authorizing the detention in an emergency of any person thought likely to engage in espionage or sabotage. This was an attempt to head off the McCarran bill's proposals to register Communists and Communist-front organizations, and to put the control of communism outside the reach of McCarthyite congressional committees. It sought to place responsibility for internal security on the Attorney General and the FBI, which would be charged with mounting surveillance on potential subversives. As Hubert Humphrey explained to the Senate, congressmen did not know how to catch Communists: 'This is a job that must be done by experts.' J. Edgar Hoover himself had opposed the registration proposals, and liberals of this time were much enamoured of the FBI. In July the ACLU's Patrick Malin had commended Hoover for the 'fine balance' he had shown on the 'intricate problem of national security in relation to civil liberties'. Ever since Franklin Roosevelt's administration, liberals had been attempting to centralize internal security matters in the FBI, to pre-empt vigilante and demagogic excesses, and they remained eager to remove the Communist issue from politics and make it a matter of administrative routine. Such was to be Mennen Williams's strategy in Michigan in the 1950s, and although the red scare emotions stirred up by the Republicans seemed awesome at times, at the end of the day he could claim a significant measure of success.[2]

Mennen Williams and liberal resistance

In the early summer of 1950 a stand-off obtained between the governor and the Republican-dominated legislature. The legislature declined to fund a blue-ribbon commission and the governor refused to contemplate more drastic action against the CP. The situation was transformed by the outbreak of the Korean War at the end of June. American boys were to give their lives in fighting communism and a Third World War seemed imminent.

The war emergency arrayed an impatient legislature against a civil libertarian governor, and over the summer the two fought for control over the state's response to the renewed red spectre.

Mennen Williams, unlike Earl Warren of California who called for a loyalty oath, stood his ground and appointed his own 'blue-ribbon' panel of 'outstanding lawyers' prepared to serve without pay. This was not enough to satisfy his Republican critics, chief among them Senator Colin L. Smith of Big Rapids who had replaced Senator Callahan as the state senate's most vehement anticommunist. Smith had already secured from the senate his own interim committee to consider the case for a state loyalty board, and with the Korean War the Smith committee escalated its demands, as a 'first step' calling for the establishment of a state subversive or red squad. The Smith proposal differed little from the Phillips–Hoxie bill of 1948 and Williams objected that, with its provision for civilian 'stool pigeons', it could 'transform the state police into a "Gestapo"'. He proposed instead an increased appropriation to allow the police to extend their investigative capacities within the existing framework. Emphasizing this course of police legitimacy, Williams instructed State Police Commissioner Donald S. Leonard to organize a security squad designed to 'guard against industrial espionage', investigate 'violations of laws against criminal syndicalism', and cooperate with the FBI 'in its drive against communistic and subversive activities'. Williams spoke of the squad as a 'little FBI', and in due course it would develop apposite professional attributes, under-taking surveillance of potentially disruptive groups, conducting security checks on prospective state employees, compiling statistics and submitting annual reports.[3]

Such an expansion of professional police activities, however, did not constitute the red squad wanted by the Republicans, and Senator Smith pressed for a broader programme to outlaw subversion. The restive veterans groups also called for stronger action. With the Korean War underway, Governor Williams met with the commanders of several such groups, who demanded the outlawing of the CP, the creation of a state subversive squad, and the use of veterans in security programmes. Williams resisted this offer of vigilante surveillance, but the Republicans kept up the pressure. Senator Smith introduced a proposal for a constitu-tional amendment against subversion and a bill to establish a

subversive squad. The governor wanted to await the recommendations of his blue-ribbon panel, but in the war-haunted high
summer of 1950 he was obliged to capitulate over the subversion
amendment. It was rushed through the legislature by both
Republicans and Democrats, the only public opposition coming
from the isolated CP and the suspect Civil Rights Congress, an
organization on the US Attorney General's notorious list. The
amendment defined subversion as an act intended to overthrow
the government by force and a crime against which the state's
constitutional rights provided no defence. It passed both houses
without a single dissenting vote, the Democrats having fallen into
line with the Republicans, and it was believed that it would in
effect 'outlaw the Communist Party in this State'. An unenthusiastic governor signed it into law. The Korean crisis had produced
consensus of a kind in Michigan politics.[4]

But the consensus did not extend much beyond the constitutional amendment, which without enabling legislation would
remain a symbolic gesture. Battle was joined again over the
substance of the communist-control programme. Advised by his
blue-ribbon panel, Williams wanted a strictly constructed law
protecting academic freedom and 'the good faith laborer' and a
security squad with limited powers under the control of the
attorney general. The Republicans, including Police
Commissioner Leonard, favoured vaguer criminal syndicalism
prohibitions and a police-controlled squad free to employ secret
informants. Legislative Democrats directed cries of 'Gestapo' at
the Republican proposal. Eventually an uneasy compromise was
achieved, albeit one which leaned to the Republican model. A
'little Smith Act' strengthened the law against subversion, and a
security squad was established under the direction of the Police
Commissioner with the power to employ spies, but labour
disputes were excluded from its jurisdiction. The attorney
general was given not control but access to its confidential files.
The police squad was soon at work and Williams began to press
for increased funding for its training and recruitment. The
governor was determined that it should develop as a professional
unit, not an old-style red squad.[5]

Mennen Williams's desire for an accountable security squad
reflected not only a respect for expertise and for civil liberties but
also an acknowledgement of some kind of Communist threat. As

a liberal he shared the suspicions of Americans for Democratic Action (ADA) of the Stalinist left, and was close both to the Reutherite UAW and to ACTU, of which his press secretary, Paul Weber, had been president. If libertarian in his instincts, Williams, a devout Episcopalian and a veteran, distrusted if he did not greatly fear the CP. In August 1950, while wrestling with legislative Republicans over the communist-control programme, he repudiated former state Senator Stanley Nowak, then a congressional candidate, insisting that the Democratic State Committee offered Nowak 'no support', since Nowak had been associated with the Progressive party in 1948–9 (and thus opposing Democratic candidates). At a time 'when American soldiers are dying in battle against Communist aggression', said Williams, 'it is imperative that any one seeking to represent the Democratic Party be a person of unquestioned loyalty to the American and Democratic principles of our party'. Nowak was subsequently defeated. Williams was seeking to limit the advances the Republicans had made in the summer of 1950 in defining the state's stance towards domestic communism.[6]

Korean War tensions
As Williams attempted to lead Michigan toward a moderate and constitutional anticommunism, the Korean War precipitated a variety of expressions of patriotism across the state, among both workers and professionals. Pro- and anticommunist factions were still slugging it out in certain UAW locals, particularly the mammoth Ford Local 600, where attempts to impose a non-Communist pledge won headlines. When the Detroit chapter of the liberal National Lawyers Guild declined to adopt a loyalty oath for members, three prominent Circuit Court judges resigned from it, insisting that the Soviet-controlled CP had to be repudiated at a time when American citizens were being killed by Soviet weapons. Media reports of local boys dying in action contributed to an atmosphere in which factory labourers thought to be Communists were at times physically assaulted by their fellows, stripped of their union badges, or ejected from the plant.[7]

   As usual it was the city of Detroit which bubbled most fiercely with patriotic impulses. The city's vaunted Loyalty Investigating Committee had been stalled by court order, but the Korean War jerked it to life and it began seeking the local red squad's files on city employees. The common council cited American casualties in the Korean War as a reason for closing down news-stands which sold the *Daily Worker*, and police duly hauled away Izzy Berenson's 'treasonable' stall. Ethnic and racial emotions jostled with the patriotic. The American-Polish Central Democratic Club, deeply antagonistic to the Soviet Union, applauded the ban on the *Daily Worker*. Among the suspect groups kept under surveillance by the red squad was the NAACP, its liberal views at odds with the strictly limited housing integrationism with which the Cobo regime attempted to keep racial peace in the city. Later in the year an angry crowd gathered after reports that a black youth had been shot by police. 'The first rumors were those that always come out of a thing like this', complained a senior police official. 'Then came the organized effort to make something of it. That came from the Communists.' There had long been Detroiters who shared the southern view that civil rights activists were reds. Mingling with the economic, ethnic and racial anxieties of metropolitan Detroit were occasional gender strains. Betty Friedan was later to speak of the 'nameless, aching dissatisfaction' with their lives felt by many suburban women, but some women gave their life meaning by attaching themselves to causes. Among them in Detroit were the fiery members of the Women's Crusade Against Socialism, which believed that the male sex was soft on communism, despaired of the pinkish composition of the Loyalty Investigating Committee (it contained a labour official), and looked to the day when 'Male Shisters' [sic] like Mayor Cobo would be swept from power and replaced by 'Women real Women'. [8]

The Loyalty Investigating Committee was finally prodded to action, and in September 1950 it levelled the awesome charge of 'Disloyalty to the United States of America' against a black garbage collector, Thomas J. Coleman, citing his membership of the CP and his office in the United Public Workers. The drama soon turned into high farce as Coleman, who had formally been on leave of absence as a union organizer, was successively fired, reinstated, recalled from leave, and suspended. The case dragged on through the winter, and the Loyalty Commission was eventually obliged to clear him, regretfully concluding that the evidence did not sustain the charges. (A police informant at one point had unhelpfully pointed to the wrong person when claiming to have seen Coleman with a radical.) The garbage collector celebrated his victory by quitting his job. The city's loyalty programme suffered another blow when it was determined that its jurisdiction did not extend to one of the city's largest employers, the board of education. Whatever animosities were agitating the urban polity, Detroit's conservative politicos were unable to direct them effectively.[9]

But patriotic emotions were there to be used for the elections of 1950, in Detroit and elsewhere. The Republicans once again paraded their anticommunist convictions, their gubernatorial candidate in particular concentrating on urban areas in the hope of winning over anti-Soviet and right-wing elements among the working class. The political potential of the Communist issue was advertised by convulsions within the state Democratic party, some of whose traditional constituents were uneasy over the party's reform ethos. Factional struggles aligned Governor Williams, CIO and AFL elements against the influence of Jimmy Hoffa, who was allied to some old-line Democrats. The leading Hoffa spokesman, George S. Fitzgerald, stalked out of one Wayne County Democratic convention in the summer with the announcement, 'I have just seen Socialism take over the Democratic Party of Michigan by communistic processes', words that were soon put lovingly to use by Republicans.[10]

Nationally the Republicans were making the Communists-in-government charge a central issue of their campaign, following the outbreak of the Korean War and Joe McCarthy's disruptive attacks on the State Department, though Michigan Republicans hardly needed prompting. In September the state Republican party met in convention and called for the outlawing of the CP throughout the United States. Michigan Republicans identified the ADA, of which Mennen Williams had been a founder member, as the Democrats' Achilles heel. Republican gubernatorial candidate Harry F. Kelly lashed out at the 'socialistic principles' and 'Communist processes' which he said activated the ADA in capturing the Democratic party. He identified certain of Williams's aides as ADA members and former 'Socialists'. Kelly, a Roman Catholic, seemed intent on nudging the antisocialist sentiments among industrial labourers. In Detroit he argued that the governor had permitted the 'socialist' ADA to take over the

Democratic party. 'It is a short jump', he asserted, 'from the methods used by the Americans for Democratic Action to capture control of the Democratic Party to the teaching of un-American philosophies in our schools.' Others also dwelt on the suspect pasts of Williams's assistants. Secretary of State Fred M. Alger Jr described Williams 'as truly a socialist as any one you've ever seen'. A Republican campaign advertisement was simply headed 'FIGHT SOCIALISM! FIGHT COMMUNISM!'[11]

Rural Democratic voters seem to have been relatively unmoved by the charge that their party had been taken over by socialist splinter groups, and Kelly increasingly targeted Catholic workers. In Flint, where he attracted a large crowd, Kelly attacked state CIO leaders Walter Reuther and Gus Scholle and called for the help of union members in 'halting the spread of socialism, as they stopped the inroads of communism in their own ranks'. In Detroit Kelly claimed that Williams was the prisoner of CIO leaders Reuther and Scholle and large crowds cheered his charges of 'Socialism'. In Pontiac he argued that 'The King and the king-makers are getting ready to turn loose 5000 paid workers to try to stampede Michigan into Socialism.' The Republican strategy of wooing antisocialist Catholics, however, was jolted when a prominent Catholic priest, Father William J. Flanagan, announced that he himself was a member of the ADA and that there was nothing communistic about it.[12]

Mennen Williams nonetheless was forced on the defensive, disturbed by rumblings within his own party as well as by Kelly's bare-knuckle punches. He gamely announced that he would welcome ADA support but was soon playing down his associations with the body (ironically, since liberals had explicitly founded it in order to repudiate communism), and he cautiously avoided sharing a platform with a Democratic congressional candidate who had once signed a CP-inspired petition. Williams counterat-tacked by representing Kelly as the agent of 'big moneyed interests', but he could not stem all the Democratic losses. There were old-line Democrats who were antipathetic towards him, elements which in some local party caucuses were being edged aside by ADA and CIO groups. In Wayne County some veteran Democrats broke away to form a Democrats for Kelly Club, complaining of 'Socialist influences' and charging that the Democratic party had been captured by the 'CIO and Americans for Democratic Action'. Another group of Detroit Democrats endorsed the rest of the party ticket but withheld support from Williams. Meanwhile the union trial of five left-wingers in Ford Local 600 was broadcasting evidence of the Communist penetration of labour groups. The constitutional amendment on subversion, then reaching the voters, also helped sustain red scare sentiments. The Democrats discreetly endorsed the amendment, although the ADA as well as civil libertarian and radical groups opposed it.[13]

In this atmosphere the Republicans expected to sweep the board in the elections, and they did increase their majorities in the legislature once more. At first they appeared also to have won the gubernatorial election, but after a recount stretching over an agonizing ten days Williams was declared the winner by a mere 1154 votes. All other state offices contested were won by the Republicans, who thus composed the governor's 'official cabinet'. The fact that the subversion amendment was endorsed by the major party leaders, in contrast to the Callahan Act two years before, seems to have made little difference to the voters, who upheld it by a similar three-fifths margin. The Republicans may have been denied the governorship, but the 1950 elections left Mennen Williams dangerously isolated as a defender of civil liberties. Perhaps the Republicans could press their advantage further.[14]

The red scare peaks

In the early 1950s not only was the Democratic governor surrounded by Republican officeholders and confronted by a hostile legislature. Additionally, the relentless conflict in Korea revived talk of Michigan being the 'arsenal of democracy', and raised both local and federal fears of industrial sabotage. In Congress the war gave new authority to HUAC, which put the nation's defences on its agenda, and the committee's interest in Michigan made demands for a stringent communist-control programme all but irresistible.

Republican legislators fashioned a bill in 1951 designed to implement the subversion amendment, primarily by fixing legal penalties for the crime. The only opposition came from branches of the ACLU and the Civil Rights Congress; within governing and

legislative circles there was no dissent. The bill passed the two
houses without a single negative vote and Governor Williams
obediently signed it into law. The modest Korean-induced
consensus achieved within the professional political community
still held, and for the moment the Republicans in the legislature
did not press their advantage further. Elsewhere in the state
patriots resumed their watch. Detroit reconstituted its discredited
communist-control programme, granting its investigators
subpoena powers. And in September 1951 the State Bar became
the first state lawyers group in the country to follow the recommendations of the American Bar Association to adopt procedures
for the disbarment of Communists.[15]

The relative calm in political circles did not survive the early
months of 1952, when the state was again invaded by the congressional gun-slingers of HUAC. Patrolling the home front during
the Korean War, HUAC had turned its attention to defence
plants. HUAC's natural interest in the 'arsenal of democracy' was
further encouraged by its Michigan member, Republican Charles
E. Potter, who was nurturing ambitions to higher office.
'Michigan has a very active Communist Party', explained Potter in
January. 'It is the most active state group next to New York and
California.' He predicted some 'shocking' revelations. Another
HUAC member, California Republican Donald Jackson, observed
that 'the Communists concentrated on Detroit to a much greater
extent than other manufacturing centers because of the massive
industrial potential'. The Detroit hearings, opening in February,
proved to be one of HUAC's major outings of the 1950s. Friendly
witnesses who had acted as undercover agents for the FBI named
some 350 Detroiters as somehow implicated in the Communist
conspiracy. A star turn was contributed by a 'slight, gray-haired
grandmother', Bereneice Baldwin, who had served as a local CP
official and who told of party cells at various auto plants and
campuses. The hearings focused particularly on Ford Local 600,
allowing representatives of the anticommunist faction to savage
their rivals. Unfriendly witnesses remained suspiciously silent.
Playing a prominent part in the interrogation was Charles Potter,
his sights on the Republican nomination for US Senator. When
the committee adjourned Potter obscurely charged that 'someone
high in the Democratic Party in Michigan' might be trying to stop
it returning. Governor Williams qualified his polite approval of
the hearings with the hope that 'the good effects will not be

spoiled by any further political mud-slinging such as Rep. Potter has engaged in'. The real target of the hearings, some suspected, was the UAW–Mennen Williams nexus in the Democratic party.[16]

The repercussions of the Detroit hearings were extensive, red scare emotions searing the state as never before in the Cold War era. HUAC had apparently established the presence of hundreds of Communists in the state's industrial and educational institutions even as Communists were mowing down American boys in Korea. Governor Williams conceded the necessity of responsible action, promising that anything that needed to be done by government 'is done promptly'. Even more prompt was the private sector, as employers fired or suspended workers implicated in the hearings or as outraged fellow workers forced them out of the plants. Blacks who had been named as Communists were particularly vulnerable to this purge, as the old prejudices of southern white workers resurfaced. Detroit public agencies were no more tolerant. The housing commission ordered the eviction from public housing of two of those named (and their unfortunate families), and the board of education fired a teacher. Wayne University expelled a student who had remained obdurately silent before HUAC – 'prima facie admission of criminal intent' – and her unsympathetic fellow students impatiently silenced speakers who tried to put her case. Within days of the HUAC hearings ending, UAW leaders named a board of administrators to take over Local 600 and purge its Communist leaders, and the awkward process of removing them kept the local in the headlines. Michigan's redbaiters had been empowered by HUAC's visitation.[17]

Mennen Williams's instinctive response as usual was to study the problem. He called a conference of appropriate authorities, notably the state and Detroit police chiefs, the director of the state Civil Service Commission, and the chairman of the city's Loyalty Investigating Committee. The police chiefs complained once more of the lack of a statute under which Communists could be prosecuted, for even the subversion amendment had not explicitly outlawed the CP. 'The biggest club we could have to fight these subversives would be a law to outlaw both the party, and the principles the Communists stand for', said Detroit Police Superintendent Edwin Morgan. A bill to this effect had been put to the legislature and the meeting apparently agreed to endorse it. The governor was no doubt happier to accede to State Police

Commissioner Leonard's request to augment the state security squad from 12 to 15 officers. These officials did stress that the HUAC hearings had not seriously touched the state government; only a 'paltry handful' of state employees had been implicated. Mennen Williams's staff assured worried constituents that CP activity 'is virtually nonexistent in Michigan', thanks to existing control measures like the security squad. The measured response of the administration to the Detroit hearings exposed it to Republican sniping. Republican State Chairman Owen J. Cleary delivered a blistering radio attack accusing Williams of heading an administration of 'commie-coddlers', citing Williams's history of circumspection on the need for communist control.[18]

The police were also encountering mounting public criticism. The state had adopted a communist-control programme in the summer of 1950, embracing the security squad and the little Smith Act, and the subversion amendment had been implemented in July 1951, yet by March 1952 no arrests had followed. In the wake of the HUAC hearings, which seemed to reveal the state to be liberally infested with Communists, the press and local patriotic groups were asking why no one had been prosecuted for subversion. Commissioner Leonard testily pointed out that the crime had to involve force or violence, and 'So far, we have never been able to prove that any person, even an admitted Communist taught or advocated overthrow of the Government by that means.' Police undercover agents attended Communist meetings, but at such meetings, it seemed, Communists perversely spoke of reform without violence. Leonard also pointed out that state investigators lacked subpoena powers. His solution was to convene a special grand jury to investigate Communists in Michigan; several former CP members were said to be ready to testify before it. The state attorney general reluctantly agreed to this form of inquiry, doubting that there was sufficient existing evidence to sustain a criminal prosecution. The Circuit Court, presided over by liberal jurist Ira W. Jayne, received the request coolly, suspecting a political motive, and eventually refused it on the grounds that grand jury probes were granted only on the 'breakdown' of the law enforcement agencies. As the court considered his proposal, Police Commissioner Leonard resigned his office to run for the Republican nomination for the US Senate.[19]

An opportunity for the security squad to demonstrate its utility did occur in the aftermath of the HUAC visitation, because Buick Local 599 at Flint, locked in the UAW's protracted internal battle, requested another HUAC visit to purge it of Communists. Local 599 was the largest in Flint and had been alternately friendly with and hostile to Walter Reuther. HUAC was unable to oblige, but the state attorney general sent in the security squad. Assistant Attorney General Maurice Moule actually conducted the investigation, showing that despite the legislature's attempts to make subversion a police matter, the attorney general's office retained much responsibility as Williams had intended. Nonetheless the state found it difficult to bring charges under the 1950 legislation and none arose out of the Flint probe.[20]

The prudence of the executive branch in responding to the red exposures of early 1952 contrasted with the vehemence of many legislators. Senator Carleton H. Morris, Republican of Kalamazoo, introduced a bill to make the Communist conspiracy punishable by death, though it failed to re-emerge from committee. But the HUAC visitation had generated expectations of some action. In January, Republican assemblyman Kenneth O. Trucks had introduced a bill based in part on the McCarran Act and designed primarily to require the registration of Communists and Communist front members, to bar the CP from the ballot and to exclude 'probable communists' from public jobs. A similar wide-ranging measure had failed in 1951, but the HUAC sensations transformed the bill's chances. 'Those hearings in Detroit by the House Un-American Activities Committee gave citizens some idea of the Communist menace in Michigan', said Trucks. 'This bill ... will give the State a tool it can use against them.' The senate added to the measure, which in its final form was the most drastic piece of communist-control legislation yet conceived in Michigan, retaining not only its registration provisions and ballot ban, but also empowering public agencies to fire Communists and denying public employees the use of the Fifth Amendment before official bodies. It passed both houses without a single dissenting vote, even CIO members in the legislature voting for it, although one Democratic senator attempted in vain to extend the proscription to sometime members of the Ku Klux Klan and the Black Legion. Again the only protests came from outside the arena of conventional politics, notably from the Civil Rights Congress, which complained that the bill would 'complete the pattern of repression begun in Michigan with the "little Smith Act", the "subversion" amendment to the Constitution and the establishment of the State Police Subversion Squad'. The Michigan ACLU seemed unable to mobilize the kind of opposition that its counterpart in Chicago had used to defeat the Broyles bills. Governor Williams's signing of the Trucks bill, despite reminders that he had 'sailed into office under the colors of a Roosevelt and a Murphy', only underlined the isolation of the radicals. Liberal Democrats like the governor had bowed to a yet more repressive consensus.[21]

The repressive potential of the Trucks Act was demonstrated on the day after it became law when the Republican Secretary of State invoked it to ban the Socialist Workers Party from the ballot. But this victory was quickly proved a Pyrrhic one. Within a few days the CP obtained a court injunction suspending the Trucks Act, disputing its constitutionality and pointing out that by registering as Communists its members could expose themselves to prosecution under the laws of 1950 and 1951. The ban on the SWP was lifted and Michigan's anticommunist legislation was again immobilized as it was scrutinized by the courts.[22]

But Michigan's aroused legislators did not intend to rest content with the Trucks Act. The firing of a Detroit schoolteacher named before HUAC and Mrs Baldwin's talk of Communist cells on the campuses had focused attention on education. Citing the Detroit hearings, Republican state Senators Charles R. Feenstra and James M. Teahen Jr (a former FBI agent), introduced a resolution to create a special committee 'to investigate allegations of communist influences in the educational system of the state'. Fortuitously advancing their cause was the US Supreme Court's decision in early March upholding New York's Feinberg law, a widely publicized ruling seen by other states as legitimizing the purging of school systems. The senate agreed to the committee and asked it to report to the 1953 session. The Detroit hearings and the Feinberg decision also helped persuade responsible bodies outside the legislature of the reality of the red menace. The Michigan Education Association and the Michigan Congress of Parents and Teachers supported bans on the employment of teachers associated with subversive groups. The University of Michigan adopted a rule virtually banning suspect speakers. As the educational establishment acceded to the anticommunist consensus, reports appeared in the press of a number of teachers being scrutinized for their affiliations, presumably by the Michigan and Detroit security squads.[23]

The Detroit hearings naturally enough evoked the strongest responses in the city in which they were held. The Detroit city council withdrew tax exempt privileges from a few local clubs which had apparently opened their facilities to Communists. The Detroit City Loyalty Commission pressed for extra resources. 'We have become "popular" since the hearings of the House Un-American Activities Committee', its chairman explained. 'Our work now is doubled.' James Sweinhart and the *Detroit News* tried to repeat their 1948 coup with a series of articles entitled 'The New Red Threat'. Sweinhart spoke of the 'emergency' created by CP penetration of 'the nation's basic industries' in readiness for 'Take-Over Day' or 'TOD'. [24]

Yet the new series triggered few alarms. The articles contained little new information, and in contrast to the 1948 publications were more the product than the cause of red scare emotions. By the time they appeared in May the impact of the February–March visitation by HUAC was fading. The HUAC foray had had serious consequences for Michigan, with the fashioning of new legislative and bureaucratic controls on communism and a number of job losses. But in the event the red scare of early 1952 was curiously short-lived, and its architects soon found their anticommunist programme failing. Their most substantive accomplishment, the Trucks Act, was stalemated within a few days of its becoming law. Even in Detroit the local communist-control programme failed to win the rehabilitation it sought. Questions were being asked about its cost, and there was a touch of desperation about the Loyalty Investigating Committee's announcement later in the year that it had smashed a CP plot to cripple the city's transport system; maintenance men had allegedly been conspiring to sabotage the bus fleet, but had quietly resigned when the committee had begun to investigate them. The lack of public scalps hardly enhanced the committee's credibility. The Korean War and the HUAC visitation had injured the political vision that Mennen Williams was protecting, but by summer of 1952 he could hope for some respite.[25]

The waning of red scare politics

In Michigan's political culture, however, the red scare was primarily an electoral phenomenon, and whenever it showed signs of flagging an election season arrived to resuscitate it. The campaigns of the fall of 1952 once again witnessed Republicans trying to redbait Democrats. The Republican gubernatorial candidate was Fred M. Alger, who told Detroit audiences with tolerable accuracy that anticommunist legislation in Michigan had been sponsored by Republicans and resisted by Democrats. Indulging the Communists, he alleged, was Governor Williams, 'who has connections with left-wingers, whose names appear in the files of the FBI'. He cited Williams's failure to support the 1949 proposal of Mayor Van Antwerp to bar the CP from the ballot, his similar response to the American Legion proposal of 1950, Williams's alternative of a study group which simply meant 'coddling' the disloyal, and attempts by legislative Democrats to destroy the Trucks Act with crippling amendments. The Alger campaign paralleled that of the national Republican leadership against the Truman administration for allegedly tolerating Communists in government. There was more redbaiting in the election for the US Senate. Charles E. Potter, the HUAC graduate who had played a prominent part in the Detroit hearings, had won the Republican nomination, and was pitted against Blair Moody, named by Williams to serve out the balance of the late Arthur Vandenberg's term. Potter accused Moody of favouring 'appeasement of Communism, which is an anti-God philosophy and, hence, immoral', and argued that Moody was a 'captive' of the CIO–PAC, the ADA, and Walter Reuther.[26]

The Republican campaign strategy revealed the limits of Michigan's anticommunist consensus. The Democrats' acquiescence in a communist-control programme had not bought immunity to red scare charges, and intense party competition continued to characterize the political culture of the state. Mennen Williams in his own campaign ran on his programme and repeated the old Democratic charge that the Republican organization had been 'completely captured by big business'. Class politics had not disappeared in Michigan, despite labour's patriotic Americanism. Before the Knights of Columbus Williams credited the leaders of the churches and the labour movement with being the first to awaken and react to the Communist conspiracy. In Michigan, he explained, 'the chief agency to combat subversion is the subversives squad of the State Police – the "little FBI" which daily keeps tab on red activities'. He castigated the Republicans who raised the Communist issue for refusing sufficient appropriations to strengthen the state security squad. The FBI commanded considerable respect from liberals in the 1950s and Williams, as usual, was placing his faith in professionalism rather than in hastily conceived legislation or prosecutions.[27]

In the event the Republicans swept the board in the November elections – with the exception of the governorship. In the presidential race Eisenhower carried the state by a handsome 300 000 votes, Potter displaced Moody in the Senate, and the Republicans maintained their large majorities in the Michigan house and senate. But Mennen Williams defied the Republican tide in a virtual reprise of the 1950 race. Again a recount had to be held and again Williams emerged as the eventual winner. But Williams's solitary victory bore an important political message. Red scare tactics had repeatedly failed against him and never again were the Republicans to employ them extensively. Anticommunist politics did not die overnight, but after 1952 they ceased to play a major role in Michigan history.[28]

Just as the intensive red scare triggered by the HUAC invasion early in 1952 had proved short-lived, the red scare emotions released by the election campaigns in the fall also quickly faded. They did not disappear, and anticommunist sentiments on occasion bubbled to the surface in such political arenas as the state legislature or the Detroit city council, but they lacked political force and direction. In part perhaps the weakening of the crusading spirit reflected some confidence in the network of anticommunist controls which now stretched across Michigan; from time to time individuals lost their jobs or otherwise fell victim to these institutional safeguards. But the flagging of anticommunist zeal also created opportunities for disabling the most objectionable of the Republican-inspired measures and for remoulding the state's communist-control programme in a way acceptable to liberal Democrats. Governor Mennen Williams wanted to replace the Republican model with a 'practical and effective anti-Communism', and in some measure he succeeded.

The weakening of red scare emotions became evident when the Republican-dominated legislature met in 1953. HUAC had issued its report on the Detroit hearings in December 1952, primarily berating Local 600 as Communist-led, and early in 1953 the

Senate Internal Security Subcommittee published a report on reds in the nation's schools as rumours surfaced about subversive Detroit schoolteachers. But these findings had little visible impact on the state legislature. The little HUAC created by the senate in 1952 failed to report, and a motion by a house Republican to create a Fact-Finding Committee on Un-American Activities died in committee. The one important piece of unfinished business was the Trucks Act, bottled up in the courts, which Kenneth Trucks tried to free by submitting a modified version to the legislature. The senate took the occasion to reduce the powers initially given to the state police, vesting them instead in the attorney general, thus edging the state's communist-control programme closer to the professional model once proposed by Mennen Williams.[29]

The state's politicos made these concessions because a considerable opposition to the Trucks Act had after all emerged outside the legislature if not in it. Apart from the CP, the Trucks Act was being criticized by the CIO, the ACLU, the ACTU, the Detroit Annual Conference of Methodist Churches, and even the Michigan Federation of Labor. This opposition had not been mobilized in the disturbed days following the Detroit hearings when the Trucks bill had been sped into law, but the success of the CP in stalling it had given time for resistance to grow. The use of the Trucks Act against the SWP had also upset several of these groups, for it had shown that CP members were not the only ones at risk. A Citizens' Committee Against the Trucks Law coordinated the opposition, holding protest meetings as court hearings approached. But the courts took their time with both the Trucks Act and its amended version, state and federal courts passing responsibility to and fro, and it was not until 1956 that a final decision was reached. By that time the American judiciary had entered a more relaxed phase, the *Nelson* decision had undermined state sedition laws, and the Trucks Act was struck down. It thus joined the Callahan Act as another Michigan anticommunist law which never went into effect. Conservative Republicans could sometimes secure such legislation; its enforcement forever eluded them.[30]

If the Communist issue was losing its urgency for Michigan lawmakers, the genie could not be firmly put back into the bottle, particularly when both local passions and national influences gave it some succour. The earlier red scares in any case had left an institutional legacy. Detroit remained an arena in which Communists and other radicals ran some risk, particularly when they fell foul of increasingly institutionalized loyalty programmes. Images of a sinister red underworld in Detroit were again deployed in the Smith Act trial held in the city in the fall of 1953, when six Michigan residents were prosecuted and convicted. This was followed by reports of renewed HUAC interest in Michigan educators, and in January 1954 a cautious Detroit board of education adopted a policy of suspending any teachers authoritatively accused of being subversives. In May, HUAC did visit Detroit to probe the schools, and three uncooperative teachers subsequently lost their jobs, as did two Wayne University instructors. The rules of most public and many private institutions in the United States by this date were such that Fifth Amendment witnesses could not normally keep their jobs. But while the Smith Act trial and the HUAC visitation provided some evidence of a 'subversive' presence in Detroit, and while a few more victims were sacrificed on a previously constructed altar, they did not precipitate a new round of anticommunist hysteria. At most they gave the city's official redhunters some legitimacy at a time when their reputation was beginning to suffer.[31]

In other respects too Detroit anticommunism was becoming institutionalized. The red squad re-established by Harry Toy kept up its surveillance and readily cooperated with the state security squad and the HUAC investigations. The Loyalty Investigating Committee also seemed to be straining to justify itself, its surveillance extending beyond the city employees who were its formal responsibility. During a well-publicized strike in 1954 the committee demonstrated its utility to its political masters by passing on data from its files on the strike leaders. The committee had evolved into a kind of local FBI, maintaining surveillance of CP, Communist front and other protest activities, and cooperating with J. Edgar Hoover's FBI. A more public role was denied it. Questions about its cost were periodically raised, and its image was not helped in 1953 when its chairman was obliged to resign following his admission of negligent homicide in a traffic accident. By the spring of 1954 the committee had never formally brought about the discharge of a single worker, although it claimed that its probes had led to a number of resignations. Attacks on the

expense of the committee and the easing of the red scare atmosphere led to some reduction in its personnel in the mid-1950s,
but it rather surreptitiously survived as an arm of the city
government, checking the loyalties of prospective city employees
and watching the activities of protest groups. The police red
squad was also reduced in size in the late 1950s but not abolished;
it supplied reports to the mayor's office until 1962. The red scare
had left its bureaucratic residue.[32]

An institutional anticommunism also survived in the state's
educational system. This was vividly illustrated by the 1954 HUAC
probe, which claimed victims both in Detroit and at the University
of Michigan. Like many other American universities, as congressional suspicions of higher education had grown the university
had simplified its procedures for divesting itself of members who
did not cooperate with official loyalty investigations. In May a
HUAC subcommittee met in Lansing, under the aegis of Lansing
Congressman Kit Clardy (who was running for re-election that
year), and three University of Michigan academics refused to
answer its questions. The university then subjected them to the
disciplinary procedures designed for such cases, and two of them
were dismissed after they had failed adequately to disavow the CP.
(One, Chandler Davis, was to go to prison in 1960 for contempt of
Congress.) Like the hearings in Detroit, however, the Lansing
hearings failed to ignite another scare. Perhaps because the
university was judged to have put its house in order, the legislature
was not deluged with new anticommunist bills. Indeed, while the
university again revealed its usual timidity on the Communist
issue, its actions on this occasion had little directly to do with state
politics. Governor Williams was not calling for the heads of red
professors, and the university was responding to the prods of a
federal rather than a state agency. It was also applying procedures
formulated earlier during the darker days of McCarthyism. In
contrast to that of 1952, the HUAC visitation to Michigan in 1954
left some victims but little excitement in its wake.[33]

Liberal anticommunism

The weakening of Republican partisanship as a force behind red
scare politics allowed the Democrats to complete the fashioning of
the state's communist-control programme. The New Deal

political order, in effecting an alliance between organized labour and the Democratic party, had promoted the values of liberal anticommunism through Michigan. Exemplary in this respect was ACTU, strongly entrenched in the state and influential within both the labour movement and the Democratic party. It had played a critical role in supporting Walter Reuther's successful drive against Communists in the UAW, and by the 1950s it was preaching a sophisticated version of anticommunism. Early in 1953 ACTU sponsored in Detroit a series of panel discussions, featuring Catholic priests, on 'a SANE, SOLID, DOWN TO EARTH CHRISTIAN AND AMERICAN explanation and understanding of Communism'. In the same spirit Governor Mennen Williams himself began to promote what he called 'practical and effective anti-Communism'. He had already had some success in shifting supervision of security squad probes to the attorney general from the police commissioner, as well as impressing bureaucratic standards on the squad. Williams thus resumed his attempts to invest the state's communist-control programme with professional attributes. It was Williams's practice to appoint nonpartisan 'study commissions' to help formulate policy, and he appointed one to advise him on a 'practical and effective' anticommunist programme. These eminently respectable citizens consulted community leaders and studied a number of proposals, such as closing the Polish Consulate in Detroit. The idea which eventually found greatest favour was a law to prohibit the transfer of funds from estates in Michigan to heirs behind the Iron Curtain. It was enacted in 1954.[34]

Williams's admirers boasted that this legislation prevented the 'looting of the estates of Michigan citizens' by Iron Curtain governments, though it seemed rather a modest monument to his campaign for 'practical and effective anti-Communism'. Nonetheless it had its political merits. It served as testimony to Williams's own distaste for communism, it harmonized with the anti-Soviet sentiments of many of Michigan's ethnic residents and, as a complicated legal measure, it advertised Williams's faith in expertise as a solution to public problems. Further, by the mid-1950s Williams could claim to have won the long war with the Republicans over the shape of the state's communist-control programme. The draconian Republican-inspired measures, most notably the Trucks Act, lay in tatters. Instead, with responsibility for enforcement effectively concentrated in the attorney general's office, records on subversive groups centralized with the state police, and the security squad functioning as a 'little FBI', the communist-control programme was close to Williams's recommendations of 1950. A biographer of Williams has spoken of his 'single-minded wearing down of the resistance' and of his 'drumming away, session after session', and such persistence enabled him to replace the Republican model for combating communism with one more respectful of Democratic sensibilities. As red scare politics ebbed, Michigan was left with Williams's 'little FBI' and his 'practical and effective anti-Communism'. The politician had been replaced by the professional, the partisan legislator by the bureaucrat. Williams's liberal elitism was better preserved in the state's programme than was Republican demagoguery.[35]

The passing of anticommunist passions became evident in the elections of 1954. Williams was the Democratic gubernatorial candidate yet again, this time opposed by that zealous but legalistic Donald S. Leonard who had been police chief of both the state and the city of Detroit. Despite his well-known anticommunist record, however, Leonard did not resort to redbaiting in this campaign. If the tactic had worked against Frank Murphy in 1938, it had failed against Williams in 1948, 1950 and 1952. In other races too the Communist issue was generally circumvented. *The Detroit Free Press* commented that among the issues sedulously avoided by the politicians were 'McCarthyism, bingo, business in government and urban-rural rivalry', although the voters were said to be thinking about them. 'Anyone who talks to varied groups knows that many Republicans and Democrats are violently split for and against McCarthyism ... ', said the columnist. 'Yet the only place in the state where McCarthyism is an open issue is in the Sixth Congressional District, where pro-McCarthy Rep. Kit Clardy, Republican, faces a political liberal Democrat Don Hayworth.' In the event Williams at last demonstrated his political dominance by winning by over a quarter-million votes. Other Democrats too won office in this Democratic sweep. Kit Clardy, alone running a McCarthyite campaign, lost his race.[36]

Anticommunist politics in Michigan had been failing since 1952, and the elections of 1954 can be said to mark their demise, a relatively early one, for in some states the Communist issue flickered on into the 1960s. More than in most states, red scare politics in Michigan had been a function of the two-party system and had characteristically been introduced during election campaigns. The repeated failure of redbaiting tactics to work against Mennen Williams, however, eventually discredited them, while the purge of the labour movement also removed Communists as tempting targets. Further, the more draconian anticommunist measures had been Republican-inspired, but Michigan was increasingly becoming a Democratic state. Mennen Williams retained his dominance in Michigan politics for the rest of the decade, and the Democratic vote was broadening with increased industrialization. Yet the Cold War red scare had left its mark. It did bequeath Michigan with a communist-control programme, and whatever constitutional and professional values Mennen Williams attempted to build into it, the state and city red squads remained in existence, to be deployed once more to combat the radicalism of the 1960s.

Conclusion

The course of red scare politics in Michigan between the 1930s and 1950s illustrates the complexity of McCarthyism. Through these years Republican politicians determinedly used the Communist issue as a weapon against the linked phenomena of industrial unionism, the Democratic party and New Deal reform. They often seemed to be speaking for an anguished business world slow to reconcile itself to its lost hegemony. But the Republican offensive was not the only source of the anticommunist animus. Anticommunism existed at popular level too, particularly among many of the Catholic, southern white and eastern European workers in the state's cities, and Republican candidates for statewide office were eager to make inroads into these normally Democratic constituencies. Because the state's party system had come to reflect its economic structure, McCarthyite tactics became an unusually strong feature of electoral politics, with the Republicans seeking to exploit the CP presence among the Democratic party's labour and academic allies and the Democrats dissociating themselves from the radical left, which was thus subject to victimization. The dynamics of party politics better explain Michigan anticommunism than any populist insurgency, although to some the rise of the New Deal order was itself a form of insurgency. This is not to deny that both Democrats and Republicans wished to harness grassroots sentiments, and both sought to benefit from the convulsions in the labour movement. As Walter Reuther understood, many of the state's industrial workers combined a class-conscious hostility to management with a fiercely patriotic Americanism, and Reuther himself was not prepared to compromise labour's integrity or jeopardize reform by allowing Communists any place in the New Deal order.

A red scare could ignite when such local configurations were subjected to outside pressures, as when the outbreak of the Korean War precipitated an unhappy consensus among the political classes, or when the HUAC visitations of 1938 and 1952 legitimized and reinforced the patriotic right. Prior to the Cold War, nativist and right-wing anticommunism had enjoyed only limited success, but in the early 1950s unnerving international tensions and the example of federal agencies allowed McCarthyism a brief season. Yet the repressive designs of conservative Republicans soon fell apart. They could claim a number of scalps, but it was to be a form of liberal anticommunism which was to prevail in Michigan, one which sought to remove the Communist issue from politics by vesting responsibility for internal security in the hands of experts. The price of peace was the enhancement of the national security state.

PART III

RED SCARE POLITICS IN MASSACHUSETTS

New England has been spared an extravagant reputation for red scare politics. Any anticommunist choir in the United States at large might expect to be stocked with lusty singers from southern California or the Republican Midwest. Yankees, perhaps, would not expect often to be found in such company. Among Senator McCarthy's most eloquent critics in the Senate were William B. Benton of Connecticut and Margaret Chase Smith of Maine. But of course New Englanders are capable of being superpatriots too, and McCarthy was to find some of his most loyal supporters in Boston. The political culture of Massachusetts has nourished vital libertarian traditions, yet more than in any other New England state the anticommunist persuasion has also fed on that culture. The Communist issue, indeed, effectively polarized political society. For a large part of the twentieth century the energetic anticommunist forces which emerged in the state were balanced by unusually strong interests fiercely protecting civil liberties. More than in most states, Massachusetts witnessed epic battles over the appropriate response to the challenge of domestic communism. In critical respects, the sustained fears of red subversion owed something to populist anxieties, once seen by scholars as a major source of McCarthyism.[1]

Because of the vitality of certain brands of patriotism, Massachusetts indeed was something of a pioneer in red scare politics. Governor Calvin Coolidge's behaviour during the 1919–20 Red Scare helped to make him vice-president of the United States, and a few years later Nicola Sacco and Bartolomeo Vanzetti became the most celebrated victims of the reaction of both state and decade. During the New Deal years the state was the first to employ a 'little HUAC' to stalk subversives, before the more notorious Dies or Rapp–Coudert Committees had even been founded. In 1949 the state adopted a loyalty oath for public employees, a year ahead of California, and in 1951 again made history by becoming the first state to outlaw the Communist party; not even the federal government had attempted to do that. In the mid-1950s, as red scare politics were dying in other parts of the Union, Massachusetts garnered notoriety for the energetic activities of its Bowker Commission, another little HUAC which was being egged on by both governor and legislature. By the time it disappeared in the early 1960s the John Birch Society had made its headquarters in the state. The Commonwealth of

Massachusetts has had its own distinctive contribution to make to the history of American anticommunism.

Like other states subject to strong red scares, Massachusetts did not possess a homogeneous political culture. Descriptions of Massachusetts politics have tended to emphasize the co-mingling of nationalities and ethnic groups, the uneasy mix of Yankee, French Canadian, Irish, Italians, Portuguese and others. One commentator speaks of the 'cauldron bubble' of Massachusetts politics; another writes that 'the ethnic and religious complexion' is 'the fundamental factor that shapes politics in the Bay State'. Regional forces have added to the fragmentation, reflected in particular in divisions between the Boston area and the western part of the state. Massachusetts has been characterized as a 'two-party' state, one moreover in which interest groups have to defer to party structures, yet party discipline has remained weak and commitment to a party ideology relatively low. 'The most striking feature' of the state's political scene, according to one of its alumnae, Elliot Richardson, 'is the subordination of programs and principles to personal relationships.' This observation is echoed by Murray Levin, a veteran academic specialist in Massachusetts politics: 'Massachusetts is governed not by organized or disciplined political parties but by shifting coalitions of prominent individuals for whom personal loyalties and commitments mean more than party unity and party platforms.'[2]

The 'feudal' nature of the Democratic party in particular, its segmentation into personal factions, is in large part a reflection of the variety of ethnic and religious groups, each often geographically distinct, of which it is composed. Dominated by the Irish nonetheless, the Massachusetts Democratic party has been heavily Catholic. It is something of a myth that party policy in the past was determined by the Roman Catholic church, if only because the church was selective in its interests, but the influence of the church cannot be denied. The Republican party, although more unified, also has a particular ethnocultural identity, with its strong Yankee and Protestant membership. Indeed, more than in most states, the Anglo-Saxon upper class retained an influence in politics, providing a significant part of the Republican leadership. In Massachusetts, as in other parts of New England but unlike much of the United States, electoral appeals have often been based less on policy issues and more on 'one's emotional identification with one's culture'. Overlapping the ethnocentric and regional identifications are those of economics and class. The Republicans tend to be the party of business and property, the Democrats the party of labour and the lower-middle class; the former are disproportionately rural and suburban, the latter predominantly urban. This was a political culture in which anticommunist politics could, for a time at least, win some momentum. If in the industrial Midwest class was initially the mainspring of the anticommunist cause, in Massachusetts it was religion.[3]

7

THE CONTOURS OF RED SCARE POLITICS, 1935–1945

The conspicuous roles in the Bay State's history of evangelical reformers and civil libertarians, of Radical Republicans and Progressives, and, more recently, of liberal Democrats and Republicans, have sometimes perhaps served to obscure the antiradical actors who have also strutted across its stage. In the late nineteenth and early twentieth centuries, indeed, a rather conservative brand of Republicanism dominated the politics of the state, although as the Democratic party began to win statewide elections more moderate Republicans came to displace the diehards. In Massachusetts though, Democrats could be conservatives too, and a reactionary patriotism could seize the state whichever party was in the ascendancy. Massachusetts participated in the Red Scare alarms of 1919, but it was in the 1930s that the contours of the state's anticommunism were fully revealed. In these years some of the lasting tensions in the state's political culture were exposed by the Communist issue; loose alliances were precipitated that were to re-emerge during the Cold War era, and the anticommunists fashioned weapons that they nursed for decades to come. Massachusetts could even be said to have been in the vanguard of red scare politics, because it proposed an elaborate communist-control programme even before Congress moved into the area with the Smith Act.

As a highly urbanized state, and one brimming with European immigrants, Massachusetts was no stranger to antiradical passions. Race-conscious members of the Boston intelligentsia

had invested nativism with a veneer of sophistication, local industrialists had used the Americanization programme of the 1910s as
a cover to spy on labour organizers, and the state had been
seriously burned by the Red Scare of 1919–20. Governor Calvin
Coolidge secured national celebrity with his pungent condemnation of the 1919 Boston police strike, and he subsequently won
re-election with a campaign directed against 'reds'. Not trusting
the federal government to take decisive action against such
radicals, the state protected itself in 1919 with an anti-anarchy law
making it a criminal offence to encourage the forcible overthrow
of government. In the event little use was found for this in the
1920s, but it was to be resurrected in the renewed red hunt of the
1950s. In January 1920 the Palmer raids netted hundreds of
suspects in Boston and other Massachusetts towns. This image of
industrial communities liberally infested with Communists and
anarchists set the backdrop for the state's prosecution of Nicola
Sacco and Bartolomeo Vanzetti, heartily sustained by public
opinion; 80 per cent of citizens, on one estimate, favoured the
execution of the two Italian anarchists. A political system
dominated by conservative old-stock Republicans, and shared
with Democrats informed by a Roman Catholic hostility to
'atheistic communism', could afford little protection to 'those
anarchistic bastards'.[1]

　While these antecedents hardly boded well for the state's
radicals, it was in the 1930s that Massachusetts anticommunism
assumed its distinctive shape, one which owed little to conservative Republicanism. In the middle of the decade a battle royal
was waged in the Commonwealth over a teachers' loyalty oath,
and in the later part of it those thought to be Communists were
not infrequently harassed by both official and vigilante bodies.
Massachusetts established a little HUAC before even there was a
national HUAC to ape, and it was soon preying on dissidents and
elaborating extensive communist-control legislation. The battle-
lines that formed during these contests were to re-emerge in their
essential outline after the Second World War. On the one side
tended to be ranged Roman Catholics, Democrats, veteran and
patriotic groups, and Irish politicos from Boston; the other
recruited from Protestants, Jews, Republicans, Yankees, the Ivy
League colleges and educators in general. These confrontations
were not primarily precipitated by electoral contests, as in
Michigan; rather, they tended to have a populistic dimension,

most acutely expressed in a mutual suspicion between demagogic Irish politicians and Harvard professors. The lines were never sharp, of course – there were Catholics who repudiated their redbaiting colleagues and Republicans who urged them on – but broadly these were the fissures exposed by the Communist issue for a generation.

The ethnic and social bases of Massachusetts politics help to explain these configurations. The Yankees, of course, as descendants of the original settlers, had long regarded themselves as the custodians of the Commonwealth's finer traditions. Over the generations many had acquired wealth and status, and the arrival of the Irish in the mid-nineteenth century had sharpened their own sense of identity. The alien invasion helped Yankees of different backgrounds to consolidate, the Brahmins of Boston establishing bonds with the poorer and often highly conservative 'swamp' Yankees. The closing of ranks against the uncouth outsiders, however, gave Yankees a reputation for arrogance, one of the bases for the politics of mistrust and revenge that are said to characterize the state. Unlike their peers in some other northern states, the Yankees fought hard to retain their political pre-eminence, and the Republican party became their vehicle. Even by 1940, some 84 per cent of the Yankee electorate of Boston was Republican. As the Yankees lost their political ascendancy to the Irish, they remained well represented on the governing bodies of the state's leading business, educational, and civic institutions. Often Anglophile, sometimes Progressive, sometimes standfast conservative, the Yankees remained an important component of the state's political culture. There were xenophobic and business-oriented Yankees, as the Sacco–Vanzetti case had shown, but as fears of class insurrection faded their cultural traditions imparted to many some sensitivity to civil liberties.[2]

The Irish too developed a sense of ethnic exclusiveness, in part because of the slights early accorded them by the Yankees. In time other immigrants, like the Italians, Jews and Poles, in turn rebuffed by the Irish, would evolve their own group identities. Their churches, schools, newspapers and fraternal societies helped each group to preserve and cherish its cultural inheritance, a process aided by the tendency to settle in particular city neighbourhoods. By 1920 over two-thirds of Massachusetts residents were either foreign-born or were of foreign parentage, and even by 1950 this category constituted some 40 per cent or more of the population, a higher proportion than obtained in most states. Although these groups generally aligned themselves with the Democratic party, their inherited political and social values were rather conservative. Irish and European peasants, having had impressed on them a respect for authority and hierarchy, if anything grew yet more conservative in their strange new land, searching for security in familiar cultural forms. 'They dreaded political change because that might loosen the whole social order, disrupt the family, pull God from His throne', Oscar Handlin has written of them.

Most were members of the Roman Catholic church, which encouraged such values. Catholics conceived politics, according to one authority, 'in essentially conservative terms – as a device for taking the risk and uncertainty out of urban life'. The antiradical dicta of ecclesiastical authorities interacted with the conservative impulses often found in Catholic communities. Papal encyclicals had made it clear that communism was a mortal enemy of Catholicism; the destruction of churches and the murders of priests and nuns during the socialist Mexican Revolution of 1911 had particularly horrified American Catholics. As workers Catholics entered the trade unions, but only a few were drawn to socialist ideologies, and church leaders, fearful of rival ideologies, worked hard to retain their loyalty. In the words of Boston's William Cardinal O'Connell, 'there cannot be a Catholic socialist'. For the Irish and other Catholics in Massachusetts, the Spanish Civil War in the 1930s was a compelling issue, since most identified strongly with the Church (and Franco) rather than with irreligion (and the republicans and Communists). The long reign of Cardinal O'Connell over the state's Catholic community, marked as it was by a combative conservatism and a reciprocated suspicion of such institutions as Harvard, helped to sustain traditional values. The great majority of Bay State Catholics were Democrats, but they were 'Al Smith Democrats' rather than 'New Deal Democrats', and by the end of the 1930s there were signs of disenchantment among them with Franklin Roosevelt's novel experiments. The intensely patriotic values of Americanism held a powerful appeal to many members of the Catholic community, anxious to demonstrate that not even the Yankees were more committed to American forms.[3]

The loyalty oath war

The first major issue to array supercharged patriots against libertarians and radicals was the teacher loyalty oath, a controversy
which greatly agitated the Commonwealth between 1935 and
1937. The Hearst press in particular was campaigning across the
country for the introduction of loyalty oaths for teachers. Some
states proved immune to the campaign; others acceded with little
resistance. What was unusual about Massachusetts was the
strength of the passions aroused and the protracted fight that
ensued. The issue touched some sensitive nerve ends in the tribal
politics of the state. By now the Irish had become well entrenched
in political office, but the old animosities between Irish and
Yankee had not abated, in part because of Cardinal O'Connell's
insistence that Catholics maintain a separate culture, and because
of the parallel strategy of exploiting the politics of ethnicity
developed by political leader James Michael Curley.[4]

In the country at large patriotic groups had been calling for
oaths of loyalty to state and national constitutions for schoolteachers since the Red Scare of 1919–20, and a handful of states
had dutifully responded. The cause gained renewed momentum
in 1934 when it was taken up by the Hearst press at the behest of
its owner, and when the annual convention of the American
Legion also endorsed it, although the less-than-united Legion left
it to each state department to act as it saw fit.[5]

The Massachusetts department did actively embrace the loyalty
oath, and was soon joined by other veteran and patriotic organizations, most notably the Veterans of Foreign Wars (VFW) and
the Daughters of the American Revolution (DAR). Roman
Catholic local radio broadcasts underlined the dangers of
communism, and the church's paper, *The Pilot*, endorsed suspicions of college reds. At this point the loyalty oath cause was being
promoted mainly by the patriotic lobbies and the press, although
it found a redoubtable legislative spokesman in Thomas A.
Dorgan, a Boston Democrat, Catholic and Legionnaire. A
distinctive feature of the Massachusetts proposal was that the oath
would be required of teachers in private schools and colleges as
well as public; even Harvard professors would have to take it.
Every organized teachers' group in the state resisted the measure,
as did the Massachusetts Federation of Labor and many
academics. The Civil Liberties Committee of Massachusetts was at

first disposed to remain rather aloof, anticipating that the issue would become 'a religious fight' between Protestants and Catholics, a strategy which was probably mistaken since in the event the resistance was led by educators, who were no match for the patriots. The presidents of Harvard, MIT and several other colleges were hissed and booed when they sought to testify on the bill, while American Legion officials were cheered. In the summer of 1935 the loyalty oath bill became law, when ill-tempered legislators overrode the recommendations of a prudent committee on education. In the debate, Thomas Dorgan named the presidents of Mount Holyoke and Smith Colleges and of Boston University as 'reds'; when challenged to name one teacher who had taught subversive doctrines he cried 'I'm not ashamed of myself'. The Hearst press and the Legion in particular were credited with the bill's passage.[6]

When first joined, the battle was largely fought between the rival lobbies trying to operate on the legislature. The American Legion believed that the Commonwealth was being undermined by 'the insidious forces of Communism', that 'Children and adolescent minds are ready prey for these destructive forces'. They contemptuously dismissed the 'highly organized lobby of college presidents and professors, aided and abetted by members of the Socialist and Communistic parties'. An eloquent opponent of the law was Boston University president Daniel L. Marsh, who conceded that the mandated simple oath of allegiance to the constitution was of itself a minor matter, but insisted that it 'points the way to despotism' and was part of 'a nation-wide program of regimentation' covertly promoted by 'the Fascist element in America'. Another college president called it 'a picturesque and somewhat flamboyant bill of the "Heil Hitler" type'. The momentous events in Europe, of course, were conjuring visions of a world divided between Communism and Fascism, and Massachusetts's own John McCormack was currently chairing a congressional committee charged with investigating both Nazi and Communist subversion in the United States. In Boston's Catholic community, the great issue of the day was often presented as a showdown between 'Communism and Christianity'.[7]

The reaction of the legislature to the issue that was thrust upon it was informed by its perceptions of the competing lobbies. There were more veterans than professors in the electorate, and in

Massachusetts's political culture – where neither Irish nor Yankee was prepared to concede the palm of patriotism to the other – it was doubtful whether there were many votes to be won by opposing loyalty legislation. The presiding officer of the senate, James G. Moran, was sufficiently moved to step down from his chair and address his colleagues, pointedly observing that school-teachers and college professors were only being asked to take the same oath of allegiance as legislators and other public officials, and ridiculing 'how intellectual it sounds for prominent educators to talk in glittering terms about freedom'. While arguing that the oath was needed to protect the 'youth of this Commonwealth' from 'anti-American propaganda', his true ire was directed at 'the intelligentsia', whose 'way of illogical reasoning ... is beyond the average mind to comprehend'. He derided the academic's 'segregated scheme of life' which enabled him to ignore 'the opinions of the rest of society'. After this populist outburst, Moran's colleagues supported the bill with substantial majorities. An analysis of roll calls in 1935 and 1936 (when there was a similar battle) established that it was Democratic votes that were most responsible for the legislation. The loyalty oath was supported by 17 Democratic senators and only one was opposed; some 101 lower house Democrats were supporters and 14 were opponents. Most Republican senators also supported the legislation, but less overwhelmingly (13 to 8), while the majority of Republican representatives were classified as opponents (81, with 43 supporters). These patterns – the professional politician's distaste for academic pretensions and the strong Democratic support for anticommunist measures – were long to endure in Massachusetts.[8]

The enactment of the loyalty oath law in 1935 was but the beginning of the battle. At first it was thought that the weak wording of the law might make its enforcement impossible, at least against private colleges. But the governor, the fabled James M. Curley, took a robust view of professors who refused to take an oath similar to that sworn by the highest public officials, and insisted that the law be enforced against those who 'hold themselves out as superior to the President and superior to the laws of the land'. His attorney general, Paul A. Dever, who was thought privately to be against the law, was forced to threaten the revocation of the charters of any colleges that did not cooperate. While there were doubts that this could be done, Harvard and other universities decided on a dignified compliance with the law coupled with an attempt to repeal it. Statehouse politicians at least had the satisfaction of obliging ivory tower professors to take loyalty oaths.[9]

But faculty cooperation had been won by the prospect of repeal, and teaching and civil liberties groups made this their early objective. To spearhead the movement, early in 1936 professors and schoolteachers formed the Massachusetts Society for Freedom in Teaching, which also won the support of the Massachusetts PTA, the AFL, and the Congregational, Methodist and Episcopalian churches. It was chaired by Harvard professor Samuel Eliot Morison, who had been visiting Rice University when the oath law was passed and had had to put up with Texan jibes about Massachusetts succumbing to the Ku Klux Klan or to Monkey Trials (or so he said in statements which won more headlines than legislative votes). Although Morison provided a historical account of test oaths, and eloquently distinguished between a public officer who exercises a portion of the sovereign power and a teacher, it may be doubted whether his widely reprinted testimony impressed many politicians. 'Education is the one thing in which Massachusetts has always excelled, from the days of the Puritans to the present', he instructed. 'Our teachers and our schools have done more honor to the name of Massachusetts, and carried her fame even farther, than her ships, her industries, her soldiers, or her statesmen.' Presidents Conant of Harvard and Neilson of Smith added their weight at legislative hearings which were jammed by 1200 spectators, who this year seemed to favour the educators. Conant saw the oath as an entering wedge towards the fascistic regimentation of teachers. Others, like the League of Women Voters (LWV), also perceived an incipient fascism surreptitiously eroding liberty by liberty. Taking a similar view were two Tufts professors, who resigned when they were not permitted to insert their own construction into the oaths they were taking.[10]

The protests from the academic community seemed only to convince the supporters of the loyalty oath that its repeal had to be resisted if the republic was to be saved from a creeping communism. The American Legion, the DAR and other professional patriots, and the Hearst press (though not most other newspapers) united to protect their legislation, and won some clerical and political champions. Such advocates dwelt on the subversive potential of schooling, focusing initially on the public schools and then – as professorial criticism mounted – on colleges. 'Educators', charged the Rev. Royal Hayes, 'refuse to stand up for this law because they use their professorships as a smoke screen to hide their malicious Communism.' A Boston College professor, Father Corrigan SJ, invoked the flames in Europe and persecution in Mexico to illuminate his claim that 'The nuclei of Communism have been planted in the ranks of labor, in the schools and colleges.' Smears directed at Harvard professor Felix Frankfurter (a Jew and a friend of Franklin Roosevelt), revealed some of the sentiments animating the debate, as did the freighted remark of a Legionnaire who exclaimed: 'You know as well as I do that these long-haired men and short-haired women are a menace to the country.' Thomas Dorgan charged that many professorial critics belonged to bodies subject to Soviet control. Another legislator angrily blurted out that 'We are after the college professors, not the public school teachers', before his embarrassed colleagues hastily dissociated themselves from the remark. But clearly some politicos deeply resented the lobbying professors, of whom Thomas Dillon of Cambridge said: 'Why, they treated the members of the committee as if they were so much dirt; and down deep in their hearts they really think we are that much dirt.'[11]

The repeal campaign foundered on such emotions in 1936, the lower house decisively rejecting the move by 133 votes to 88. Supporters of repeal vowed to campaign against their legislative foes in the forthcoming elections, and drew some comfort in November when Tom Dorgan was decisively defeated, freeing him to embark on a long lobbying career as 'the Father of the Loyalty Oath'. For the remainder of the decade such bodies as the LWV, the Civil Liberties Committee of Massachusetts, the Massachusetts Teachers Federation, and the state Council of Teachers' Unions, vainly pressed for the repeal of the loyalty oath. A low profile approach in fact almost succeeded in 1937, when a repeal bill was pushed through both houses, but it was aggressively vetoed by Governor Charles F. Hurley. Elected in 1936, Hurley, a conservative Democrat, Roman Catholic and Legionnaire, shared the perspective that Communists were poisoning the springs of liberty, as they had already done in other lands. Calling opponents of the loyalty oath a 'vicious minority', he insisted that this was 'no time to make it appear that we are withdrawing any of our supports for the authority of our State and Nation'. Hurley was to make this veto a cornerstone of the anticommunist reputation that he so assiduously cultivated.[12]

Hurleyism and Coughlinism

As the apocalyptic note invading the rhetoric over the loyalty oath betrayed, the distemper afflicting the Massachusetts body politic in the mid-to-late 1930s owed something to the course of world events. The rise of the European dictatorships raised the spectre of an Armageddon between Fascism and Communism, and Communist activities in Mexico and Spain in particular distressed Bay State Catholics. The Spanish Civil War, which broke out in July 1936, divided Massachusetts more than most states. Radicals in the academic, student and labour communities were to make their contribution to the Abraham Lincoln Brigade, but for many Catholics the Spanish Republic was the embodiment of anticlericalism, and the Catholic press blamed Communists for every outrage suffered by the church. Many Irish Catholics of Massachusetts, Democrats though they were, were dismayed by Franklin Roosevelt's growing coolness towards General Franco. On occasion local authorities in the state tried to ban pro-Loyalist demonstrations as communistic, as when Tom Dorgan prevailed on the mayor of Boston to disallow a Labor Day meeting on Boston Common on behalf of American trade unionists fighting in Spain, saying it was 'too controversial'. The anticommunist and nativist humours which flickered across the state in these years were kindled by external as well as internal stimuli.[13]

Charles F. Hurley was the leading politician to exploit and exacerbate these sentiments. He frequently exulted in his veto of the bill to repeal the teachers' oath, claiming that unspecified 'public happenings' had vindicated him (apparently 'red' advances in Mexico and Spain). 'Recent events have made it very plain that un-American agencies will stop at nothing to force their deadly doctrines into the lifestream of the nation', he told the Springfield Elks in April 1938, a month in which Boston newspapers had been reporting the furore over the appointment to Harvard of Granville Hicks, the prominent Marxist intellectual and CP member. 'It is easy to delude ourselves into the belief that our educational system is safe from the inroads of Communism and atheism, and that it will stand forever as a bulwark against the forces which assail it.' He told the Knights of Columbus of his impatience with the 'un-American agencies' which were under-mining the patriotic heritage, and insisted that 'Academic freedom is sometimes another name for academic license'. He disturbed liberals by advocating 'legal enactments' to preserve American liberty, and contrasted the 'birthright of American citizenship' with 'the unnatural practices of red Russia, red Mexico, or red Spain'. In Hurley's perspective, 'Modern liber-alism' had originated with the atheism of the French Revolution and remained fiercely anti-religious, which explained why it was sanguine about starvation in Russia, the 'killing of thousands of priests and nuns in Spain', and the 'destruction of the faith in Mexico'. He told a Catholic audience that 'It may yet be our destiny to save the America we love'.[14]

The growing anticommunist animus in Massachusetts during the late New Deal years was sometimes attributed to Hurley, at least by those he assailed. 'Hurleyism breeds Hagueism', complained a CP official referring to the notorious and antiradical machine politics of Jersey City: 'Another two years of Governor Hurley's regime will unquestionably give rise to Hagueism of a special kind in Massachusetts with a strong clerical fascist coloration of the Quebec type.' Academics too did not care for Hurley's aspersions on their patriotism and good sense. The Cambridge Union of University Teachers branded the governor 'a reactionary, red-baiting politician' for his attacks on the Hicks appointment, for his support of the loyalty oath, and for his proposal to censor school textbooks. Such episodes as the discovery of CP propaganda in Harvard dormitories in the spring of 1938 did nothing to improve relations between town and gown.[15]

Charles F. Hurley was hardly alone in stirring red scare emotions in these years. American Catholics generally were troubled both by the course of events abroad and by the popular front associations of some New Dealers, the 'outstretched hand' of 'atheistic communism' being an object of revulsion to many. Hurley's rhetoric was encouraged by and served to encourage other patriotic palpitations in the state. His campaign for the

governorship and the outbreak of the Spanish Civil War in 1936
coincided with the formation of Father Charles Coughlin's Union
party, and its anticommunist preachings attracted some support
from Irish and German Catholics in urban Massachusetts. In
1935 Coughlin had visited Boston and been well received by the
city council and state legislature. James M. Curley called Boston
the 'strongest Coughlin city in the world', and from it Coughlin
reputedly raised a large part of his income, and also selected local
lawyer (and Democrat) Thomas C. O'Brien as the Union party's
vice-presidential candidate. The Union ticket was a pitiful failure
as a national phenomenon, but it fared better in Boston than in
any other major city, winning between 10 and 16 per cent of all
the Irish votes cast for president. Coughlin remained solicitous of
his Massachusetts constituency through the rest of the decade, as
he used his National Union for Social Justice and subsequent
Christian Front to promote what seemed like an American variant
of fascism. The Christian Front pumped out antisemitic and
anticommunist propaganda from its Boston headquarters; its
New England leader, Francis P. Moran, called Franklin Roosevelt
a Jew and railed against the 'communist-riddled government of
the United States'. But even murkier elements than the
Coughlinites also stirred in Massachusetts. Small but active was
the German American Bund, which welcomed to its meetings 'All
Aryan (White Gentile) Americans'. Also circulating antisemitic
and antiradical propaganda in the late 1930s was the Industrial
Defense Association of Boston. It was in this atmosphere that the
state authorities determined on their own assault on domestic
communism.[16]

The first little HUAC and world war

Massachusetts was not the only state in which the apparition of
Nazism was glimpsed, and in Congress in January 1937 the New
York Democrat Samuel Dickstein, a Jew of Russian stock, called
for an investigation of all organizations disseminating 'un-
American propaganda'. That resolution failed, but Dickstein then
joined forces with the anti-labour Texan Martin Dies, and in 1938
HUAC was finally constituted. Ironically, however, Dickstein was
excluded from it and it quickly became a vehicle for the anticommunist right. This familiar story was paralleled and even antici-

pated in Massachusetts. There, a Jewish member of the legislature had called for a committee to investigate subversion, apparently in order to demonstrate that there were no Jews in the Communist party. Such a committee was established early in 1937, a good year ahead of HUAC, and it too rapidly became a weapon for harassing the left. It consisted of eight legislators and three others appointed by Governor Charles F. Hurley, then in his most anticommunist phase.[17]

The Special Commission to Investigate the Activities within this Commonwealth of Communistic, Fascist, Nazi and Other Subversive Organizations was chaired by Sybil H. Holmes, a lawyer and Republican state senator who, although said to be anti-labour, had a good record on civil liberties and had fought for the repeal of the teachers' oath law. Civil libertarians initially were not overly alarmed at the appearance of the commission, hoping that Nazi and Coughlinite groups would be subjected to at least as much exposure as the CP. Anticipating that Sybil Holmes would steer a moderate course, they helpfully supplied her with lists of fascist organizations. But their promptings were to little avail, and the commission was soon interrogating prominent Communists such as Earl Browder and Philip Frankfeld. Renewed in December 1937, the commission sought another extension in April 1938 after the commotion occasioned by the appointment of Granville Hicks, 'in view of the fact that Harvard College has given a position to an avowed Communist'. Its true character was finally revealed in May 1938 by its 599-page report, eight pages of which were devoted to 'Fascistic Activity', another eight to 'Nazi Activity', and almost all the rest to the various manifestations of the red menace. This imbalance was even greater than in the American Legion's newly published patriotic hit list, *Review of Alien Isms*.[18]

The commission's conclusion that the American CP was a revolutionary instrument of Moscow was hardly novel; nor was its vagueness about the boundaries of the Communist conspiracy, for it managed to implicate the ACLU and local campaigners such as the progressive labour activist Florence Luscomb. More distinctive was the commission's preoccupation with religion. Its members worried at hearings about whether Communists as atheists could be expected to tell the truth under oath, and they were particularly disturbed by the protest activities of the Rev.

Donald G. Lothrop, pastor of the progressive Community Church of Boston. The commission rehashed a 1935–36 news story of promiscuous sex at an Arkansas labour school as if to impugn the moral values of all Communists. The most vociferous member was the Irish Democrat Senator Thomas M. Burke of Boston, said to represent the Vatican, who rode witnesses hard and championed the Catholic church (though unlike the Coughlinites he was respectful of his Jewish constituents). Massachusetts Communists tried to persuade the commission that they were not anti-religious, but the report triumphantly refuted them, reprinting Langston Hughes's poem 'Goodbye Christ' and concluding that Communists were 'implacable enemies of all organized religion, whether of the Old or New Testaments'.[19]

Sybil Holmes, apparently placed on the commission to restrain headstrong members like Burke, at first conducted proceedings fairly judiciously, but was converted by the experience into a committed anticommunist, a fate which sometimes overtook those who assumed such a role. Determined to arrest the rapid spread of communism, her commission dutifully fashioned a series of communist-control bills, some of them fairly innocuous but two did alarm civil libertarians. One, seen as 'the heart and meat' of the Holmes programme, urged the establishment of 'a division of citizenship' for the purpose of 'eliminating' the activities of persons seeking to overthrow the American form of government, in short a sort of permanent commission to hunt subversives. The other sought to prohibit the advocacy of force or violence 'to effect political or economic changes', which some saw as impeding freedom of expression.[20]

Battle was now joined over the Holmes bills. The Roman Catholic church was credited by some observers with inspiring these measures. 'The Catholic Church, dominant political pressure group in the state', according to the *New Republic*'s reporter, 'is behind the bills and there is a serious possibility that during the summer session, when public vigilance is somewhat relaxed, they may become law.' More conspicuous were the veterans and patriotic groups rallying to their support. Senator Thomas Burke entertained the VFW by identifying 15 persons 'definitely linked to the Communist Party', including several professors from Harvard and other leading colleges, such as Kirtley Mather, and certain religious leaders, notably Donald Lothrop. He advocated putting all the Communists in a barge and dynamiting it. Sybil Holmes appeared before the DAR and the Boston city council, as well as the legislature, on behalf of her bills. The measures were speedily and favourably reported out of committee and civil libertarians scrambled to mobilize their forces against what one called the 'Irish-Catholic-Italian machine'. The Civil Liberties Committee of Massachusetts and the state CP held protest meetings and lobbied legislators, eventually securing deferral of the bills until the 1939 session, when battle was again joined. Holmes's favourite proposal for a division of citizenship was likened to Stalin's OGPU or Hitler's Gestapo, 'a permanent inquisition to smell out political heresy, independent of the ordinary police'. The campaign finally had its effect, a legislative committee reporting unfavourably on this bill, which was defeated in the lower house by 65 votes to 24; the other bills too failed to pass. The recent purges in the Soviet Union and Nazi Germany had not given political surveillance a good name.[21]

The legislators may also have been emboldened to reject the programme by the fact that Sybil Holmes and another member of the commission had been defeated in their re-election bids in November 1938. The Civil Liberties Committee had 'no doubt' that it was Holmes's anticommunist campaign that was primarily responsible for her defeat. As Tom Dorgan had previously discovered, redbaiting did not necessarily guarantee political success in Massachusetts. But the rebuff of some of the commission's members and of its proposals did not mean that it was without impact. It had injected the idea of a division of citizenship and a stronger sedition law into public debate, prescriptions which were to recur when red scare politics returned. Further, the Holmes Report itself had named names. As a result the International Workers Order, a CP-led insurance society, briefly lost its licence to operate in Massachusetts. Individuals who were cited, such as Florence Luscomb and Donald Lothrop, were to endure decades of redbaiting. The campaign for the Holmes bills had also become entwined with reports of left-wing activities in Boston high schools, and although Republican city councillor Henry L. Shattuck wither-ingly pointed out that the CP had polled only 0.2 per cent in the recent gubernatorial election, an investigation of this dangerous red invasion was launched. Little was uncovered beyond the odd piece of Communist literature in school locker rooms and the scare died away, but it left teacher George B. Faxon named as a dangerous radical, a charge that was to be revived in the Cold War years. As was to happen in New York with the Rapp–Coudert probe, an arrested red scare could be rekindled at a later date to claim more victims.[22]

By the close of the decade red scare emotions appear to have been abating in the state. The Nazi–Soviet Pact and the outbreak of war in Europe in 1939, which prompted a further burst of anticommunist measures in some states, left the Commonwealth relatively unscathed. An attempt to bar the CP from the ballot was rebuffed, as was Thomas Burke's demand that the local CP leader be arrested. Father Coughlin's strident antisemitism was tending to limit his appeal. By 1939 too Franco was winning the Civil War in Spain and there at least Communist anticlericalism was being punished, to the relief of many Massachusetts Catholics. While isolationism was stronger among the Boston Irish than in most other American communities, their patriotism remained as strong as ever and they shared with other Americans the perception that Nazi Germany had become the greatest foreign threat to the United States. When the Soviet Union after all became an ally, there was even less reason to harass Communists in Massachusetts.[23]

Yet if anticommunist sentiment eased, religious and ethnic anxieties survived to disfigure Massachusetts in the war and immediate postwar years. Nativist zeal now seemed to be directed more at Jews than Communists. The Christian Front retained some vitality in and around Boston, and antisemitic incidents occasionally occurred, usually associated with Catholic elements that the church leaders were anxious to disown. In 1944 there was an outbreak of Jew-baiting in some Boston suburbs, where, according to one account, 'Jewish boys and girls were set upon and severely beaten by "patriotic" bums glowing with Coughlinite "Christianity"', and with the ending of the war returning veterans sometimes organized vigilante groups. This was a period when it was rare for a priest and a rabbi to share a platform in Boston, and there were some who believed that the Catholic hierarchy was not cracking down hard enough on Coughlinite clerics.[24]

But Roman Catholics too could be the victims of prejudice, and the relationship between Catholics on the one hand and Jews and liberal Protestants on the other was an uneasy one in the 1940s. The extension of Soviet power over a large part of Catholic

Europe naturally distressed American Catholics, and in Massachusetts the imprisoned Archbishop Stepinac of Yugoslavia in particular became a popular martyr figure, occasioning a dispute in 1947 between Archbishop Cushing and a group of local Protestant clergymen who returned from a visit to Yugoslavia with favourable reports. Such Protestants sometimes suspected the Roman Catholic church of harbouring fascist instincts, a perception encouraged by its magnificent parades. In 1948 Dr Harold J. Ockenga, pastor of the Park Street Church, thought a parade of 80 000 Catholic youth organization members reminiscent of the marches of children in Nazi Germany and fascist Italy. In the same year the Unitarian lawyer Paul Blanshard began his attacks on Catholic power in the United States. Cushing and other church dignitaries complained of a wave of anticlericalism. Some civil libertarians undoubtedly were wary of Catholic influence, partly because of the prewar redbaiting but also because of the church hierarchy's position on issues such as censorship and birth control. In a state in which roughly half the population was Roman Catholic, 57 per cent of the voters in 1948 stood by the hierarchy in upholding a law prohibiting the distribution of birth-control information. Anticommunist passions may have been diverted by the international and domestic political configurations associated with the Second World War, but religious and ethnic loyalties and tensions remained as strong as ever and continued to inform the political process in Massachusetts.[25]

The divided polity
If the Holmes Commission had been rebuffed in 1939, so had another attempt to repeal the teachers' oath law, which survived as the principal legislative landmark of the anticommunist spasms of the 1930s. During the New Deal years the key features of red scare politics in Massachusetts had been exposed. There was a popular or populistic dimension, as in the case of the loyalty oath which had been thrust on the legislature by patriotic lobbies and local politicos, although political leaders leaped to join the cause when their instincts were aroused. Those politicians who made war on communism most stridently tended to be Democrats with Boston Irish (and other urban) constituencies, and in the legis-

lature Democrats were more likely to vote for communist-control measures than Republicans. But, in contrast to Michigan, these battles were not products of conventional party competition. What sometimes inflamed a politician was the perceived arrogance of academics who seemed to be claiming special privileges for themselves. In no small degree, red scare politics in Massachusetts were another manifestation of that old discord between the lower-middle and working-class Boston Irish on the one hand and on the other the Yankee Brahmins who clustered in the state's celebrated universities. But these Brahmins and their academic friends were a power in the land too. They nurtured a strong respect for civil liberties, and groups like the Civil Liberties Committee and the League of Women Voters, sometimes led by Harvard professors, were active and effective lobbies, while even the local CP was not without resources. With access to high political councils themselves, sometimes to gentlemanly Republicans who might be graduates of the Ivy League colleges, civil libertarians and educators were capable of turning back an anticommunist assault. The outbreak of the Second World War may have helped dissipate red scare politics for the moment, but the social and political configurations responsible for them remained as resilient as ever.[26]

8

THE POPULIST ASSAULT, 1945–1952

A Roman Catholic suspicion of radicalism and a populist distrust of Harvard and other universities had enlivened red scare politics in Massachusetts in the 1930s. While the victories of the anticommunists had been limited, they had displayed disturbing depths both of emotion and of potential. A governor had joined their cause, state legislators had followed suit, and an elaborate communist-control programme had been devised and debated, including the establishment of a pre-Dies little HUAC. While anticommunist proposals invariably drew the wrath of the academic community, elected politicians were all too aware of the voting power of the state's veterans and Roman Catholics, and were loath to take the unpatriotic side of any argument. If the political context changed in such a way as to give advantage to the anticommunist nexus, it was possible that the state could experience a full-blown red scare.

The onset of the Cold War in the late 1940s did tilt the political axis in Massachusetts and render its radicals highly vulnerable. The well-publicized Soviet brutalities in Catholic Europe caused as much torment to local Catholics as had the Spanish Civil War, and the detention of prominent clerics seemed vindication enough of the old Catholic claim that communism was incompatible with Christianity. To a significant degree the growth of the anticommunist animus in Massachusetts, at least when it took the form of an assault on domestic radicalism, welled up from below. For the most part, the initiative came not from within the political hierarchy but from local politicians and veterans and patriotic groups. The state's political leadership, wrestling with the insistent demands of government, usually tried to contain anticommunist ardour, and only deferred to it when that seemed the best means of reducing tension. Recent scholarship has tended to emphasize the role of elites in fashioning McCarthyite politics, but the case of Massachusetts suggests that populist pressures should not be discounted too readily. While the word 'populist' is problematic when applied to veterans and clerical lobbies, it seems a more appropriate description of this phase of the state's anticommunism than the word 'elitist'. Particularistic and parochial interests, in Massachusetts as elsewhere, found that the legislature (especially the lower house) afforded 'the best opportunity to maintain the values of the status quo'.[1]

A new anticommunist offensive rebuffed

By 1947 signs of a new anticommunist offensive were emerging. In February Monsignor John J. Wright, secretary to Archbishop Cushing, addressed the League of Catholic Women in Boston on 'How To Spot a Communist', offering such rules as 'If one objects to Franco and not to Tito, he is a Communist'; the overuse of such terms as 'liberal' and 'friend of Democracy' also betrayed the subversive. Perhaps this expertise had been learned from Louis F. Budenz, the former CP official whose reconversion to Catholicism had ensured a packed hall a few months before when he spoke in Boston. The archdiocesan newspaper, *The Pilot*, was giving prominent coverage early in 1947 to fearsome warnings of Communist subversion by such authorities as Budenz and J. Edgar Hoover. That spring, four Boston Democrats introduced two new communist-control bills into the legislature, one to establish a 'little Dies' committee and the other requiring the promulgation of a list of subversive organizations. These imitations of federal initiatives were ill-prepared and failed to pass the legislature, where the predictable civic, labour and educational critics were joined even by local commercial and bar groups. As yet there was no anticommunist stampede. But by 1948 the Cold War had deepened further, and the legislature was confronted by eight anticommunist bills, all introduced into the lower house. These overlapping measures broadly sought to exclude Communists and their sympathizers from educational and public employment, and one, 'the little Dies bill', was a better-drawn version of the 1947 measure. Seven of the bills were the work of Boston Democrats; the remaining bill, which struck at both public and private colleges by denying them the right to hire Communists, was a Republican measure, drawn up by Attorney General Clarence A. Barnes. Three of the bills specifically targeted education, a perennial worry of Bay State anticommunists. The Civil Liberties Union dubbed these legislative proposals the 'thought control bills' and quickly mobilized against them.[2]

The battle came to concentrate on the little Dies bill and the Barnes bill. A principal sponsor of the legislation, John B. Wenzler, set the tone for the hearings by explaining that Communist was 'another word for anarchist' and that even murderers 'are better than Communists, because murderers are punished for their crimes'. The advocates of the little Dies bill – held to be the 'most dangerous' of the measures by the Civil Liberties Union – urged the need to unmask Communist front organizations, then a favourite preoccupation of the FBI. Veterans' groups paraded their support for the bill, as did J. Ralph Granara of the Boston Civic League, who told of a local YWCA function that had been 'run by Communists'. Its most outspoken legislative supporters were Democrats, such as Edmond J. Donlan of Boston, who complained that the work of legislative committees was being obstructed by people 'who come in and lie and lie and lie on orders from Moscow'. When Donlan and other Boston Democrats faced such protesters at public hearings, Catholics were being arrayed against (mainly) Protestants, Jews and agnostics. Within the house the Boston Republican Gordon D. Boynton led the resistance, arguing that a little Dies committee would hinder the work of the FBI and inevitably smear its targets. When the bill finally reached the house floor, it lost by 110 votes to 53, an outcome which reflected the large Republican majority. Of the 53 supporters of a Dies committee, 50 were Democrats and 3 were Republicans; the 110 negative votes comprised 92 Republicans and 18 Democrats. The measure had been initiated by low-level Irish and Italian Democrats from Boston, and of the 25 Boston Democrats who cast votes, all but two favoured it.[3]

Even more controversial than the little Dies bill was the Barnes bill, which had the authority of the attorney general behind it, although it was a personal and not an administration measure. It

sought to ban the employment of subversives by any university or
school and, since it sweepingly embraced private as well as public
institutions, it threatened the grand Ivy League colleges. This was
an unlikely bill to emanate from a Massachusetts Republican,
though Clarence Barnes was anti-labour by reputation and a New
Yorker by birth and not one of the Harvard alumnae who graced
the Republican party. Governor Robert F. Bradford (also a
Republican) took no position on the Barnes bill and quietly
sought its amendment; it was reported that 'he would be embarrassed if it were offered to him for signature'. Barnes denied that
the bill was aimed at Ivy League professors, dismissing their
criticism with the comment 'Methinks they do protest too much',
but his own words betrayed him. 'We have just begun to fight', he
reportedly shouted at a Harvard professor as the bill ran into
difficulties: 'You can tell *that* to your friends in Boston and tell
them they better come out of their ivory tower.' His temper may
have been frayed by his inability to mobilize his party colleagues.
Within the legislature the bill's most tireless advocate was
Republican Kendall Sanderson, but its most vociferous critics
were also Republicans. Brookline Republican Samuel Atkinson
assailed the 'lack of a definition' of a Communist; Henry L.
Shattuck, former Harvard treasurer from Boston's fashionable
Back Bay, characterized the bill as a dishonest measure, and John
W. Vaughan of Belmont recalled the futile Holmes Commission
and asked 'Are you going to keep on hunting goblins which
nobody ever finds?' Barnes must also have been disappointed by
the lobbies which materialized to support his bill, notably the
Arminian Club of Massachusetts, 400 petitioners from
Springfield, and Tom Dorgan, Father of the Loyalty Oath.[4]

More impressive were the lobbies which crowded into the
hearing rooms to oppose the bill, among them the Civil Liberties
Union, the Massachusetts AFL, the League of Women Voters
(LWV) and various student groups. 'They're all Communists',
snarled one legislator, but this hardly disposed of the presidents
and other senior officers of Harvard, Clark, MIT, Wellesley,
Boston University, Simmons and Williams Colleges, who also
appeared to testify. Leading the parade was Harvard's James B.
Conant, itself an event which attracted much publicity, sometimes
front-page headlines. He cautioned against allowing the worrying
international situation to precipitate a self-destructive hysteria,
and queried the wisdom of the Barnes bill because it would

undermine the local control of education, and because there were no advocates of armed revolt on the campuses anyway. He reassured legislators that he would dispense with any teacher who used his position to advocate the forcible overthrow of government, which he likened to the 'advocacy of criminal action'. The high but tactful profile assumed by the college presidents had its desired effect. House members backed away from the attorney general's bill, a hostile committee report disparaging the hunting of 'mice in your pantry with a blunderbuss'. A milder measure was substituted to bar from teaching anyone convicted under the existing sedition law, a politicians' compromise which enraged partisans on both sides but which prevailed. Since no one had ever been convicted under the state's sedition law, civil libertarians persuaded themselves that its amendment was a piece of empty symbolism.[5]

The 'thought control' bills had been defeated, and for the moment the opposition could feel pleased. The Civil Liberties Union of Massachusetts (CLUM) in particular had played a critical role in articulating and coordinating resistance, in contrast to its caution over the loyalty oath bill in 1935. In addition to the civic, educational and labour groups cited above, protests were also lodged by the NAACP, the Massachusetts Council of Churches, the American Jewish Congress, the Progressive Citizens of America, the Community Church of Boston, and the CP. While business and legal groups were less in evidence than had been the case in the 1947 fight against the little Dies bill, this array of forces was enough to give legislators pause. Further, CLUM had not only forged something like a community of interest with these groups, but had also established valuable links with sympathetic members of the legislature, most notably Republican representatives Gordon D. Boynton, Henry L. Shattuck, and John W. Vaughan. This was an alliance that might be mobilized again when a red scare threatened.[6]

The civil libertarian alliance under strain

The course of international and national affairs in the late 1940s meant that this libertarian common front would be subject to extraordinary strain. The Communist coup in Czechoslovakia in March 1948 stunned many Americans and helped to increase support for the Marshall Plan to save 'democratic' Europe, not least in Massachusetts where the fate of Catholic Europe (particularly Italy) was being carefully watched. Communist advances in China were hardly less disturbing, and the federal government's decision to prosecute the top CP leaders under the Smith Act broadcast its perception that there were subversives at home. Harry Truman's increasingly anti-Soviet foreign policy seemed to enhance his standing with the Al Smith Democrats of Massachusetts. Campaigning in Boston during the presidential campaign, Truman lavished praise on Al Smith, cried out 'I hate communism', and pledged himself to resist it abroad and at home. His 'hate communism' line brought three loud cheers from the crowd. Analysing the results, Samuel Lubell concluded that Truman carried Boston heavily in 1948 because he was credited with saving Italy from communism. Truman's success in Massachusetts was paralleled by the state Democratic party. Paul Dever won the governorship and the Democrats won a modest majority in the house and tied with the Republicans in the senate.[7]

In some states a Democratic victory would have strengthened the barriers against an antiradical crusade, but the reverse obtained in Massachusetts. Anticommunists may also have been encouraged by the support that a few Democrats gave to Henry Wallace's Progressive candidacy, whose poor performance in the state meant that mainstream Democrats had less reason to defer to civil libertarian sensibilities on their left. In the winter of 1948–9 anticommunist bills poured into the General Court, which opened its new session with more such proposals than ever. Journalist W. E. Mullins attributed this surge to the 'public vehemence' which had followed 'the exposure of Communist-inspired prying into top drawer secrets in the State Department', by which he presumably meant Whittaker Chambers's accusations against Alger Hiss. The attempts by the shambling Chambers and the self-made Richard Nixon to establish that this Harvard Law School graduate was a Communist spy perhaps touched a populist nerve in Massachusetts.[8]

These bills were not being handed down by the administration. They were being introduced into the lower house by Democratic representatives or even by outside lobbies. One was sponsored by the mayor of Cambridge (a Democrat), one by the American Legion, and several by the energetic chairman of the Boston Civic League, J. Ralph Granara. The Legion and the VFW regularly attended hearings in support of such measures. The tone of the

1949 legislative session was set by an 'emergency law' that passed with little comment. It designated May 1st as Loyalty Day that 'we ... may be ever vigilant against subversive movements calculated to undermine our American form of government, and may embrace this occasion to strengthen our sentiments of faith and loyalty to our country'. The supporters of the anticommunist bills argued that they did just that. After the dust had settled attention focused on three bills. For once the Democrats were not pushing their favourite device of a little HUAC; the thrust of the latest proposals was to keep Communists out of the public service and the schools.[9]

Colleges unsurprisingly remained a major target, and a bill submitted by Ralph W. Sullivan, Democrat from Boston's Dorchester suburb, proposed the prohibition of 'the teaching of atheistic communism'; the sting for private institutions was the threatened cancellation of their tax exempt status or even revocation of their charters. Tom Dorgan turned up at the hearings to warn that certain college professors who were 'playing around with Communist fronts' were 'stooges for the Communists' and likely to influence 'kids with impressionable minds'. Republican and Harvard corporation member Henry L. Shattuck, no longer a legislator but leading the opposition at the hearings, was probably closer to the truth when he pointed out that 'no one ever heard of anyone doing such a thing' as teaching communism. The politicians themselves proceeded with great caution, both houses contriving to deal with the measure without a single vote being recorded against it. An amended form of the bill passed the house without dissent (testimony to the legislators' respect for public opinion) and the senate killed it with a voice vote. One house member confided that most of his colleagues were privately against the Sullivan bill but were 'afraid to voice opposition to it because they themselves might be open to accusations of sympathizing with Communists'. The executive secretary of CLUM privately recorded her opinion that 'the most effective' opposition had come from 'the Unitarian Church, the Rabbinical Association and our own members'. As had been noted in the 1930s, these confrontations in Massachusetts could almost be cast in religious terms.

Another assault on the academic community was triggered by a bill (proposed by two Cambridge Democrats) calling for a constitutional amendment to deny Communists the right to vote or hold office. The celebrated Dr J. B. Matthews, sometime HUAC employee and frequent 'expert witness' at hearings on communism, was produced to testify for the measure, a manoeuvre which guaranteed extensive publicity. He gripped his audience and the headlines by naming Harvard as one of the three educational institutions whose professors had 'the most significant record of supporting Communist fronts', and for good measure named several of these offenders, including Kirtley Mather (president of CLUM), F. O. Matthiessen, Ralph B. Perry, Harlow Shapley and Wendell Furry. Also accused was MIT's Dirk Struik, whose notoriety that week was being enormously magnified by the Smith Act trial in New York, at which he was named by Herbert A. Philbrick as a Communist. Matthews's inflammatory language in implicating thousands of professors across the country in 'this diabolical conspiracy' proved counter-productive, and the proposal was unfavourably reported out of committee and dropped. The General Court's managers were evidently less than enthusiastic about this and the Sullivan bill.[10]

But the patriotic lobby had its reward. The aborted constitutional amendment was replaced by a more carefully-worded loyalty oath bill, requiring public employees to disavow revolutionary intentions; CP members and others advocating the violent overthrow of government would be denied public jobs. This bill again passed the house with little difficulty, and the opposing lobbies concentrated on the senate, which had generally been more sensitive to civil liberties. But senators were also sensitive to public opinion; one told a reporter that the bill would fail unless a roll call were forced, in which case it would pass. The prediction proved accurate. A vote was called and the bill passed by 22 votes to 16. (In favour were 17 Democrats and 5 Republicans, against 3 Democrats and 13 Republicans.) Governor Dever signed the bill into law and for the first time in the postwar period the anticommunist forces had won a significant victory. The Democratic successes at the polls in 1948, together with Cold War terrors, had had their effect.[11]

Yet although the civil libertarian defences had been breached they had not been demolished. The spring anticommunist offensive had seemed to be directed largely at Harvard and its sister institutions, but the final legislation, in focusing on public employment, had left them untouched. Further, politicians were often disposed to regard loyalty oaths as modest measures which did not seriously impair American freedoms. The pressure on the colleges did not dissipate. The spotlight was trained on them again in the summer of 1949 when Frank B. Ober, a Harvard graduate and architect of Maryland's celebrated Ober Law, caused a stir with an attack on Harvard for employing professors involved in what he regarded as Soviet-inspired movements. Harvard declined to move against the offending professors and insisted that it would not screen faculty members for their political views, although President Conant in another context endorsed the view that Communists should not be employed as teachers (a variation on his 1948 position disowning those who advocated forcible overthrow of government). MIT announced in the fall that it would not admit CP members to its teaching staff, their doctrines being 'inconsistent with the principles of freedom on which American education depends'.[12]

The opposition to the anticommunist agenda, while still substantial, was not quite as resilient as it had been. Joining CLUM in lobbying against the 1949 bills had been the NAACP, the American Jewish Congress, Americans for Democratic Action (ADA), the Progressive party, and the American Veterans Committee (AVC), as well as several individual academics and clerics. The last two bodies at least were widely regarded as being infested with Communists, and labour groups were no longer conspicuous among the opposition. Towards the end of the year, disturbed by the piercing of its defences and fearing further assaults, CLUM called meetings of some 24 sympathetic organizations at which it was agreed to establish a Coordinating Committee to work in the legislative field and resist infringements of rights and liberties. Involved in these deliberations were representatives of such bodies as the AVC, the Civil Rights Congress, the Fellowship of Reconciliation, the International Fur and Leather Workers Union, the Massachusetts Council of Church Women, the NAACP, the Progressive party, the War Resisters League, and the Young Progressives. Some of these organizations were Communist fronts or Communist-led (the Fur Workers were about to be expelled from the CIO), and the pacifist groups and the AVC were perceived by many Americans to be dangerously radical. The loose civil liberties coalition was not as broadly based as when the AFL and local bar associations had endorsed its protests, and its pinkish tint was as likely to provoke as to give pause to the Bay State's anticommunists.[13]

Banning communism

As the new decade opened the anticommunist lobby found circumstances moving in its favour. The convictions of Alger Hiss and Klaus Fuchs early in 1950 further vindicated those who had claimed that American interests were being betrayed by Communists operating deep within the society. Cold War anxieties continued to intensify, particularly after the outbreak of the Korean War in the summer, invoking in many minds the terrifying spectre of nuclear annihilation. Of significance to the Commonwealth of Massachusetts was the evolution of the Truman administration's Smith Act case against the CP leadership. In April 1949 Herbert A. Philbrick, who for years had served the FBI as an undercover agent in the Massachusetts CP, had dramatically cited Dirk Struik of MIT as a Communist. Struik became a favourite whipping boy for local anticommunists, and pressure on MIT increased when the Supreme Court upheld the Smith Act convictions in the summer of 1951. Philbrick was now free to enjoy a hero's welcome in his own state, where he was pressed to elaborate on his story of life among local reds, not least by HUAC. Philbrick obliged with several names, among them Struik, who was summoned to testify but chose to plead the Fifth Amendment before HUAC. The state's newspapers in these years were thus relaying not only the unnerving events of the Cold War but also stories seeming to confirm that the prestigious ivory towers had indeed been harbouring Communists.[14]

The opening of the 1950 legislative session witnessed another raft of anticommunist bills. One, submitted by Somerville's Democratic representative Paul A. McCarthy, required college presidents to purge their staffs of Communists on pain of the revocation of college charters. Another urged the creation of a division of citizenship (as recommended in 1938 by the Holmes Commission) to collect information on subversive persons and groups. After the outbreak of the Korean War, Boston Democrat Edward J. Mulligan submitted a bill to outlaw the CP. In fact these bills did not make much headway, largely because the great symbolic issue of this session was a legislative order filed by

another Boston Democrat, Edmond J. Donlan, for the establishment of a joint Committee to Curb Communism, in short, a
'baby Dies Committee'. 'A vote for another Communist investigation is a "safe" vote', explained the *Boston Herald*, 'one sure to
go down well with constituents who are too busy to read between
the lines.'[15]

The proposed little HUAC, however, did not 'go down well' with
the party leaders, who reportedly attempted to block its passage.
Perhaps reflecting their influence, the rules committee reported
against the Donlan Order. The eruption in Korea, however,
allowed house Democrats to regain the initiative, and when forced
to a vote the house supported the Donlan Order by 190 votes to
19, figures which reflected an unusually low abstention rate in a
membership of 240. The Democrats as usual overwhelmingly
voted with the anticommunist side, with 122 ayes and 6 nays. More
novel was the Republican vote, which also strongly favoured the
measure by 84 to 12. Under the pressures of war and public
opinion the parties were beginning to close ranks on the
Communist issue. A little HUAC had finally been created, but the
party leaders were not yet prepared to surrender to populist
pressures. When the committee came to be organized, they
contrived to deny the chairmanship to Edmond Donlan, giving it
instead to Senator Philip G. Bowker of Brookline; the vice-chair-
manship went to a Democrat who had opposed the establishment
of the committee, Michael J. Batal. Further, the committee was
afforded an appropriation of only $10000, a far cry from the
$100000 once mooted. A political correspondent was to recall of
these events that Edmond Donlan had 'fought with his party
leadership on the ground that it sought to sabotage a genuine
probe'. Donlan's disgust was doubtless further deepened when the
committee failed to hold any hearings for the rest of 1950.[16]

The slowness with which the Donlan Order was implemented
and the lack of enthusiasm for it high in the polity gave
opponents some hope of undoing it before it went into effect.
CLUM again attempted to coordinate the opposition, and in
October it was empowered to organise 'an ad hoc watch-dog
committee' to initiate action. Reflecting the widespread revulsion
which redbaiting committees evoked, the Ad Hoc Committee was
substantially less pinkish in inspiration than the Coordinating
Committee of the previous year. The meeting authorizing it

contained representatives of five Jewish groups (such as the American Jewish Congress), five Protestant church groups (including Quakers), the LWV, and a scattering of political, community, and protest groups, including the ADA and local YWCAs. In November a CLUM-led 'group of 200 clergymen, educators and lawyers' filed a petition calling for the abolition of the little HUAC; leading Protestant and Jewish churchmen and prominent academics (including Samuel Eliot Morison) were present. Little HUAC chairman Philip Bowker observed of the petitioners that they were 'blind to the dangers of the international Communist conspiracy'.

Less restrained was the *Boston Post*, which directed its ire at the 'Harvard professors' and others who sponsored the petition: 'Apparently these people believe that this Commonwealth should be controlled by a minority of the so-called intelligentsia instead of by a majority of the citizens.' The quarrel continued into 1951. Former CLUM chair, Harvard professor Kirtley Mather, argued that the task of investigation was constitutionally the function of the executive branch, provoking Donlan's riposte that the legislature reflected the wishes of the people. CLUM itself was 'conceived, born and nurtured' in an 'atmosphere of disloyalty and conspiracy', according to Donlan. He conceded the loyalty of most of its members, but argued that 'its thinking has been dominated by men who can truthfully be dubbed Moscow Mystics or Bolshevistic Brahmins'. Thomas Dorgan introduced an even sourer note when he accused civil liberties activists of being motivated by anti-Catholicism, saying of one unnamed minister: 'I have never in my 17 consecutive years of fighting Communism heard a good word from him about the fight the Catholic Church is putting up against Communism.' It remained true that much of the resistance to anticommunist measures was located in an array of Protestant and Jewish groups (and also that groups like the League of Catholic Women regularly sponsored lectures on the dangers of communism).[17]

More muted was the resistance of those party leaders who sought to hamper the progress of anticommunist measures. Thomas N. Brown has posited the existence of two distinctive styles in the Irish community, that of the politician who functions as an 'organization man' accommodating differences in the 'ancient houses of power', and that of the 'rebel' who finds his support in the streets. Red scare politics were characteristically pressed by 'rebels' like Tom Dorgan, and resisted by the 'organization men' in party or state office. The Democratic governor struggling to contain the controversy over the little HUAC was Paul Dever, who sought to assume a statesmanlike pose on the Communist issue. He confirmed that 'the paramount issue of our day is that which is presented by international Communism', but the emphasis here was on the foreign threat, and his message was that domestic communism was best averted by social reform. But as a centrist politico he could not resist a few asides to 'the most addlepated of our fellow Americans who style themselves liberals'; the danger of communism was 'the intellectual appeal' it held for 'certain people'. Still, he doubted that many came to communism via this route.[18]

The elections of November 1950 did not change the political complexion of the legislature very much, but the delay in the production of the report of the little HUAC allowed further anticommunist bills to be introduced in 1951. Among them were a pair offered by Representative Paul A. McCarthy and the tireless Tom Dorgan, one seeking to ban the CP in Massachusetts and the other to instruct college presidents to rid their staffs of Communists and their sympathizers. The latter, as CLUM member Kenneth B. Murdoch observed, appeared to be 'the product not only of a desire to capitalize politically on popular fear of communist Russia, but also of a wish on the part of some politicians to interfere with what is taught and how in colleges, quite apart from politics'. But at the end of March consideration of these bills was overtaken by the report of the Bowker Committee, as the little HUAC was now known. To the disappointment of the more ardent anticommunists, the committee had held no public hearings and engaged in no redbaiting histrionics. As the legislative leadership had intended, it had conducted its studies behind closed doors, and its procedures won the tacit gratitude of some civil liberties groups. Its report too was unsensational. It named only avowed Communists, and while it cited a number of Communist fronts it did not enrage liberals by implicating their groups. It offered the familiar view that the Massachusetts CP was part of a well-disciplined conspiracy directed from Moscow, dwelt on the contemporary '"peace" front movement' occasioned by the Korean War, and drew attention to the elite character of the Communists' Professional Club of Boston, composed of 'doctors, lawyers, scientists, clergymen, college and university professors, businessmen and high labor union officials'. The number of CP members in the state was put at 900, and the committee urged the attorney general to cite four of them for contempt for refusing to testify before it.[19]

'The outcries against the pallid findings of the Massachusetts Committee to Curb Communism are somewhat comical', noted the *Boston Traveler*. 'From beginning to end it was obvious that many strident boosters for the committee wanted a slam-bang foray against Reds and fellow travelers, and if innocent liberals and dissenters got hurt, who cares.' One of the strident boosters was the *Traveler*'s own columnist Cornelius Dalton, who characterized the report as the work of 'eight frightened men' and 'a great victory for the letterhead liberals and their friends'. The committee's moderation was achieved at the expense of convulsions within it. Its only ardently anticommunist members appear to have been Donlan himself and Republican Senator Sumner G. Whittier, both of whom filed qualifying reports. Whittier's stance was a partisan one, implausibly linking the Dever administration to left-wing radicals, although he did make the most of the Democratic establishment's lack of enthusiasm for the committee: 'All the left wing groups, many so-called "liberal" and "progressive" organizations, the Governor's office, the top echelon of the Democratic leadership in the House, and many sincere citizens, along with some less sincere, actively and energetically opposed the creation of this investigation.' He had wanted public hearings and the naming of 'names, dates and places'. Vice-chair Michael Batal, intended as a restraining influence on the committee, bitterly denounced Whittier's dissent as 'sheer politics'. The Democrat Donlan could not associate himself with Whittier's partisan pose, but he too complained that the committee had not gone far enough.[20]

But the low-key proceedings and bland report of the committee belied the nature of its recommended legislation, which on inspection proved to be quite far-reaching. According to one report, members who had been put into place to check the ardent anticommunists had 'become convinced of the need for a real investigation of the Communist fronts'. Something similar had been experienced by the chair of the Holmes Commission in the 1930s, and Chairman Bowker in turn seems to have been given pause by his investigation of American Communists in the context of the Korean War. He was now convinced of the need for curbs, warning that local Communists had been instructed by national office to 'slow down' production in war industry plants. The proposals largely followed Maryland's Ober Law, which sought to ban subversive organizations, including the CP, and required a loyalty oath of public employees. The committee also wanted loyalty oaths for lawyers, which would make it even more difficult for radicals to secure legal representation.[21]

While the Bowker Committee's members had been persuaded that a communist-control law was necessary, party leaders remained sceptical and disinclined to facilitate legislative passage. For much of 1951, Massachusetts politicians bickered and plotted over the Communist issue. The American Legion, the VFW, and the Massachusetts Federation of Women's Clubs lobbied for the proposal, which as usual found favour with several urban Democrats, such as Roxbury's Charles Iannello, who recommended hanging Communists and himself volunteered to 'pull them out of bed and lynch them'. Opposing it were CLUM and the LWV, as well as several other civic and civil rights groups, and an impressive array of religious and ethnic groups, representing in particular Protestant and Jewish denominations. A large proportion of the several hundred individuals who lent their names to the protests were ministers or professors. An articulate opponent inside the legislature was the Needham Republican Harold Putnam, who saw the proposal as an invitation to 'witch hunts'. For the moment the civil libertarian alliance faced the patriots down, aided by the legislative leadership. Chaired by Republican Senator Silvio O. Conte, the senate committee on constitutional law recommended that action on all anticommunist bills, including the McCarthy–Dorgan bill to ban the CP, be deferred until the next session to allow for further study. This resolution, smacking of connivance between the civil libertarians and the party leaderships, enraged in particular the advocates of the McCarthy–Dorgan bill, which had been given a measure of legitimacy by the Bowker Report. Among those to protest at the shelving action was Archbishop Richard J. Cushing. 'I believe in fighting the Red enemy right out in the open and making it impossible for them to function in our midst', said the prelate. 'To delay is dangerous, very dangerous.'[22]

The General Court met in protracted session through the summer and fall of 1951 and the wrangling continued. At one point Democrat John F. Collins pulled the bill to ban the CP out of the package earmarked for recess study and won preliminary senate approval for it over the objections of Republican floor leader Charles J. Innes and committee chairman Silvio Conte. (Democratic senators favoured the measure by 16 to one, and Republican senators resisted it by 11 to 9.) But subsequently the leadership had its way and the bill was returned to the Conte committee for further study. The house proved even more recalcitrant. It had never endorsed the senate initiative for a recess study, and in August it substituted its own measure based on the Bowker Committee's 'Ober bill'. It later defied a committee recommendation to defer consideration of the McCarthy–Dorgan bill aimed at higher education, although the senate again rescued the colleges. The house also adopted its version of the Ober bill, and again the senate interceded, pre-empting it with a bill prepared by Republican leaders Conte and Innes which offered some protection to civil liberties (it introduced a court procedure to determine whether or not an organization was subversive). Finally a compromise had to be worked out between the Democratic house and the Republican-led senate, and the latter at least had the satisfaction of retaining a judicial hearing for any organization charged with being subversive. Governor Paul Dever somewhat unexpectedly signed the bill into law in the last hour of the legislative session.[23]

A major piece of communist-control legislation had finally been enacted. In a sense it represented the consummation of the drive begun in 1947 for a little HUAC. No permanent HUAC was established, and an attempt by Edmond Donlan to keep the Bowker Committee alive was defeated in the fall of 1951, but an Ober-style law, placing responsibility for investigating subversion in the attorney general's department, had long been intended as an alternative to an investigating committee. (In Michigan Governor Mennen Williams was also trying to soften a communist-control programme by locating responsibility with the attorney general.) The 1951 law, if less draconian than some house Democrats wished, was nonetheless a historic piece of legislation. It expressly declared the CP to be a subversive and unlawful organization, barred it from the ballot and made membership of it a punishable offence; those convicted under the law were disqualified from holding public office (including teaching). For the first time an American government had simply outlawed the Communist party. To a degree, Massachusetts had anticipated Congress's Communist Control Act of 1954 – by putting Communists beyond the pale, liberals might hope to protect themselves.[24]

Yet again Harvard and her sister institutions had escaped direct injury, although their suspect members might now be vulnerable to prosecution as subversives. This seemed an increasingly likely possibility. In the spring of 1951 a Cambridge city councilman, John D. Lynch, had won some celebrity with a resolution calling for a purge of alleged Communists at Harvard and MIT and had helpfully named some fifty suspects (including James B. Conant and the ADA's Arthur Schlesinger Jr). In the summer, as noted earlier, the upholding of the Smith Act released Herbert Philbrick to resume his naming of Boston and Cambridge Communists, an exercise further facilitated by HUAC. An eager district attorney took up the cause and secured a grand jury investigation, before which Philbrick again testified, and as a consequence Dirk Struik and two other local activists were indicted in September under the 1919 sedition law, the first time it had been used. The Commonwealth had – almost – bagged its first reds since Sacco and Vanzetti.[25]

Herbert Philbrick had become a celebrity. He had helped to put American Communists behind bars, and, perhaps equally important in Massachusetts, he was assisting zealous anticommunists to penetrate the hallowed ivory towers. The American Legion arranged a testimonial dinner for Philbrick in November and Governor Paul Dever proclaimed 27 November to be 'Herbert A. Philbrick Day' in Massachusetts. 'The free world is menaced today by the greatest threat it has ever faced – international Communism', explained Dever. It sought 'to destroy us from within through a gigantic conspiracy of subversion', resisted by men like Philbrick, 'a symbol of patriotic service and personal sacrifice'. A few days before Herbert A. Philbrick Day, the governor had signed into law the bill outlawing the C.P. The populist and patriotic impulse had finally forced an accommodation from the state's political leadership.[26]

Civil libertarian hopes

Since the 1930s an inchoate coalition of civil libertarians, educators, churchmen and prominent Republicans had generally been successful in rebuffing or restraining red scare politics in Massachusetts. The modest sedition measure of 1948 and even the loyalty oath of 1949 could be seen as minor setbacks, even as modest victories in so far as they were alternatives to more repressive legislation. The law of 1951 too was less than the ardent anticommunists had wanted, but there could be no denying that they had scored over the 'letterhead liberals' they despised. From one perspective, the civil libertarian fortifications had been overwhelmed when an ivory tower professor had been implicated in the Communist conspiracy; the grandest institutions in the Commonwealth had been rendered suspect. From another, red scare legislation had been enacted when powerful federal influences – the Smith Act trial, the HUAC probe – had interacted with local pressures. What does seem clear is that the anticommunist cause had been given little encouragement by the political leadership in the state. Not only Republican Yankees (and Italians) but also Democratic chieftains had sought to obstruct or divert red scare pressures. For years anticommunist passions had bubbled up mainly from below, often directed at the academic community, and had been given political expression by rank-and-file Democrats, sometimes Italian but mostly Boston Irish representatives in the lower house, vigorously abetted by a number of patriotic interest groups. They had failed to break through at the height of the Korean War scare in 1950, but in 1951 the vindication of the Smith Act prosecutions, the Philbrick testimony and the Struik affair had apparently demonstrated that the Commonwealth too was vulnerable to subversion.

The passage of the anti-CP law at the end of 1951 seems to have helped legislative leaders to ward off further anticommunist legislation for a time, although the public atmosphere was hardly comforting to radicals. In 1952 Boston Democrats promoted measures in the lower house to establish a new little HUAC, to revive the Bowker Committee, and to drive Communists from the campuses, but the legislators contrived not to act on them. Outside the General Court anticommunist patriots paraded their enhanced legitimacy. The feting of Herbert Philbrick continued, and Boston citizens were treated first to a newspaper serialization of his memoir, *I Led Three Lives*, and then to a television version. The *Boston Post*, a newspaper read largely by Catholics and possessed of a strongly anticommunist proprietor, generated a stir in the fall of 1952 after a copy of *The Communist Manifesto* had been found in the Boston Public Library, but even Herbert Philbrick was moved to discount this as evidence of red subversion. Another local furore broke out when Thomas Dorgan charged CP leader Otis A. Hood with conducting toymaking classes in his cellar – a Communist technique to 'spread their pernicious propaganda' – and the fire department obligingly quieted local patriots by declaring the workshop a fire hazard. Meanwhile, the authorities continued to pursue the sedition case against Dirk Struik. If the 1951 law had seemed like the consummation of a long-standing anticommunist campaign, and if its sponsors were unable to add to the state's communist-control machinery, nonetheless the proscription of Communists had left them even more exposed to harassment.[27]

But 1952 was an election year and civil libertarians could hope that new political configurations would serve to deflect anticommunist passions. The major candidates avoided crude red scare tactics. In the gubernatorial campaign the Republican candidate, Christian Herter, focused primarily on Democratic bossism and corruption, although he did manage to suggest that Democratic legislation had been in the tradition of Karl Marx and was 'leading us down the road to Socialism!', invoking Archbishop Cushing in support of this view. Such rhetoric was par for the Republican course in 1952, and for the most part Herter's alignment with anticommunism was presented in more subtle terms, his publicists in particular using Catholic newspapers to stress his role in securing the Marshall Plan and thus saving 'millions of Europeans' (or millions of Catholics) from 'Communist domination'. As a Republican, Herter needed to reach for independent, Catholic and Jewish votes. The Communist issue emerged more crudely in Cambridge, the scene of the redbaiting of academics. In one Cambridge district the Democratic candidates campaigned against incumbent Republican legislators on the grounds that they had obstructed little HUAC or other anticommunist bills and called on the voters to 'Aid In The Fight Against Communism' (a Democrat did win one of the contested seats).[28]

But local reverses apart, the Republicans fared well in the 1952 elections, winning the governorship and control of both houses of the General Court. Since Republicans in Massachusetts had tradi- tionally been more sensitive to civil liberties than Democrats, there was some prospect of the anticommunist advances of 1951 being rolled back. This at any rate was the hope of a number of groups, which now mobilized to secure repeal of anticommunist legislation. The Massachusetts Council of Churches, representing all the Protestant denominations in the state, approved a statewide education project to counter-attack threats to civil liberties. The ADA state convention determined to lobby for the repeal of the 1951 'Ober' law. And CLUM filed bills for the repeal of both the 1951 law and the 1919 sedition law. The anticommu- nists had breached the defences of the loose alliance of civil liber- tarians, clerics, academics and gentlemanly Republicans, but members of that alliance now saw an opportunity to regain the high ground.[29]

9

RED SCARE AND RESOLUTION, 1952–1962

In the fall of 1952, civil libertarians believed that McCarthyism in Massachusetts had peaked. But their hopes were to be brutally dashed. Within two years Massachusetts was in the grips of the most severe red scare it had yet sustained. As anticommunist passions were subsiding in most states, particularly after the ending of the Korean War, in Massachusetts they were increasing, and in the mid-1950s executive, legislative and judicial authorities alike were participating in the onslaught against red subversives. A potent little HUAC was stalking the Commonwealth, radicals were being indicted, and anticommunist bills were being enacted with unaccustomed ease. In the second half of the decade red scare passions did abate, but the instruments that had been fashioned to protect the Commonwealth from the red menace lingered on into the 1960s.

Congressional inquisitions and local patriots
The fond hopes that civil libertarians were nurturing in the winter of 1952–3 could not survive the ominous twist of events in the New Year. No fewer than three congressional committees were readying themselves for probes into higher education in Massachusetts. In January it was learned that HUAC had begun an investigation of Communist influence in American higher education, and that Harvard, MIT and other top universities could expect to be scrutinized. In the same month Senator Joe

191

McCarthy finally assumed chairmanship of a Senate committee, and a probe of the education system was promised. The Senate counterpart to HUAC, the SISS, was already investigating education, particularly in New York, where Bella Dodd had cited a number of Massachusetts institutions, including Harvard, for housing CP cells. The baleful attention of these congressional inquisitors was welcomed by some local patriots. Democratic representative Joseph D. Ward introduced a resolution into the house inviting SISS 'to come to this state to investigate relative to communism and communists in the universities of the Commonwealth'. The resolution was deflected, but not before Ward had urged an investigation of Harvard's President Conant himself. Edmond J. Donlan joined the attack, accusing Conant of 'giving aid and comfort to the common enemy when he leaves the impression that Communism is just an "unpopular political opinion"'. Some Irish patriots saw the congressional scrutiny of the ivory towers as an opportunity to breach them.[1]

HUAC began the process in February, when it listened to Smith College professor Robert Gorham Davis name ten people who had been in a Communist cell with him at Harvard in the late 1930s; two of those named, Daniel Boorstin and Granville Hicks, also offered such memories as they could. In effect they were corroborating Herbert Philbrick's charges of a red cell in Cambridge, and one of those named, Wendell Furry, was still there, a Harvard associate professor. Furry's own refusal to answer questions by invoking the Fifth did nothing to dispel suspicions that reds were still haunting Harvard Yard. One Boston businessman sponsored a plan for an 'alumni watchdog committee to investigate collectivist professors'. The academic community sustained even greater damage in March, when SISS came to Boston and subpoenaed a number of Harvard teachers and students, four of whom took the Fifth. Schoolteachers too were caught up in this probe, and two of those who refused to testify, Max Weitzman and George F. Faxon (a target of the prewar Holmes Commission) were suspended and subsequently dismissed. Those local patriots who had been inveighing for years against the elite colleges and their pinkish ways were rejuvenated by these new federal allies and the evidence they were extracting. As the storms broke some professors were suspended and one resigned, but no one was sacked. The suspensions served to confirm that the universities were indeed harbouring Communists, while the absence of dismissals lent credibility to the charge that they were incapable of putting their own houses in order. The sadder fates of the schoolteachers could only enhance the perception that professors were a privileged class. Archbishop Cushing complained that Harvard, Boston and Northeastern universities had too many professors who were destroying the faith and Americanism of Catholic students: 'It is American education which has supplied communism in the past with its opportunity.'[2]

The congressional probes fortified the usual anticommunist bills before the General Court and triggered yet others. Some called for another little HUAC, and Somerville's Paul A. McCarthy and Tom Dorgan revived their proposal to require college presidents to dismiss Communists. It was the familiar McCarthy–Dorgan bill which was given an unfamiliar buoyancy by the 1953 alarums. A legislative committee had recommended against the bill before the congressional hearings, but after them it was revived. A fairly draconian measure which threatened the colleges with the revocation of charters unless they purged themselves, the bill was at first resisted by many Republican representatives, but they gradually succumbed to pressure and enough joined the Democrats to pass it by 159 votes to 64. This in itself was disturbing, one CLUM officer writing to the governor that 'The real purpose of this bill ... is to vest control of our educational institutions in the hands of our professional political representatives.' The senate as usual played a more judicious role and extensively amended the bill, to the effect that institutions would be required to dismiss subversive teachers only on conviction in the courts. This would hardly have changed the existing situation, and the house, exhorted by Paul McCarthy, refused to concur. A confrontation between the two houses was resolved by a compromise, under which McCarthy and his allies agreed to accept a little HUAC in place of the McCarthy–Dorgan bill. Even so legislative leaders evinced little enthusiasm for an investigative commission, which was reported only to enjoy 'substantial support ... among rank and file members'. The commission was approved only in the dying hours of the session and received the meagre appropriation of $10000. A direct attack on the campuses had been averted yet again, but at the cost of the creation of a little HUAC, one which promised to be more permanent than the temporary Bowker Committee of 1950–1.[3]

The congressional inquisitors had left their mark, but they were not quite through. Senator Joe McCarthy himself had set his sights on Harvard, of which his old Wisconsin critic Nathan Pusey became president during this troubled year. In the course of his celebrated probe into Fort Monmouth in the fall of 1953 McCarthy subpoenaed Wendell Furry, questioned him in executive session, referred to 'the smelly mess' at Harvard, and queried whether anyone would send 'their children anywhere where they might be open to indoctrination by Communist professors'. Cambridge academics might shrug off these unwelcome attentions, but McCarthy was popular in Boston (as is illustrated by the political discretion of members of the Kennedy family towards him). In the winter of 1953–4 a poll of a middle-class ward in Boston indicated that some 90 per cent of respondents were sympathetic to McCarthy and regarded domestic communism as a serious threat. A Boston *Pilot* columnist suggested that the vehemence of McCarthy's critics owed something to 'his race and his religion'. It is little wonder that the state's political leaders were unhappy about having conceded the state's own version of a McCarthy committee, the Special Commission Established To Make An Investigation and Study of Communism and Subversive Activities, soon known more succinctly as the Bowker Commission.[4]

The Bowker Commission

Massachusetts's new weapon in its anticommunist armoury was ready for action in November 1953. Republican Senator Philip G. Bowker again became chairman. Joining him from the senate was the Democratic floorleader John E. Powers, a pro-labour politician, sometime campaign manager for both Governor Paul Dever and Senator John F. Kennedy, and once characterized as 'South Boston personified'. One of the house members was the vehemently anticommunist Democrat Paul A. McCarthy of Somerville, whose long-standing suspicions of Ivy League Communists had helped to bring the body into existence. As it happened McCarthy was mortally ill, and control of the Commission remained in the hands of its seasoned leadership,

Bowker and Powers. They certainly bore some responsibility for steering it away from a confrontation with the campuses, a process in which Senator Joe McCarthy was destined to play a role.[5]

Founded in the aftermath of the storm over 'red professors', the Bowker Commission began its deliberations by listening in private to the presidents of Harvard, MIT, Boston College and Wellesley, who could only tell their interlocutors that there were no Communists on their staffs. The presidents were treated with some deference by the Commission, appearing by invitation rather than by summons. But no sooner had the Commission heard their reassurances than it was involving itself in a labour dispute. Senator McCarthy's Fort Monmouth investigation had led him on to a scrutiny of General Electric (GE) plants, and an undercover FBI agent, William H. Teto, testified to Communist infiltration into the United Electrical union (UE) in a number of them, including those at Lynn and Fitchburg. This evidence of CP activity in the Commonwealth proved irresistible to the Bowker Commission (whose leaders in any case were probably looking for an excuse to cease tilting at the academies), and within days of telling his tale to McCarthy, Teto was retailing it to Bowker, naming 'about 50' suspect names. Teto's implication of UE officials also interested James B. Carey, the deeply anticommunist CIO leader who had organized a rival union to UE, the International Union of Electrical Workers (IUE), and who was currently engaged in a ferocious war with the UE for the loyalties of the nation's operatives in the electricity industry. He enjoyed strong support from the Catholic church, concerned about the many Catholic workers in UE. Carey duly presented himself to the Bowker Commission and obligingly told it that there were over 200 Communists in the ranks of UE officials, and that 45 of them were currently in Lynn for National Labor Relations Board (NLRB) elections. Carey's charges were a 'lie', according to the Lynn UE president, but his names were taken seriously by the Bowker Commission, as were those that the Commission found arriving daily in the mail. Philip Bowker asked Governor Herter to assign additional police to check on the 600 and more names he had to date. 'I've got writer's cramp from signing so many summonses', he joked on 9 December; on the same day GE, bowing to McCarthy's demands, announced that it would fire all admitted Communists and suspend all employees who took the Fifth.[6]

On the following day the last act in this little drama was played out. The NLRB election in Lynn, held five days after Carey's explosive testimony before Bowker, was one in which UE was seeking to regain bargaining rights in the Lynn and Everett plants that had previously been lost to the IUE. Whether or not because of the attempt to paint local UE officials red, the IUE narrowly won. In short, the Bowker Commission was evidently colluding with both Senator McCarthy and the IUE in an assault on the UE, a rather easy target as the largest of the Communist-led unions to have been expelled from the CIO. It was demonstrating that it had a constructive role to play in the rooting out of subversives.[7]

The Bowker Commission continued to cultivate the Wisconsin senator. In December 1953 its member George W. Cashman was said to be in Washington 'working out a plan for closer liaison with the FBI and the Jenner, McCarthy and Velde committees'. In January 1954 McCarthy brought his investigative subcommittee to Boston to resume his probe of GE plants and the defence industry, invited the Bowker Commission to attend both the public and private hearings, and furnished it with files. He was reported as saying that 'he wanted to work closely with the Massachusetts Commission, and ... was turning over data in some of his files relating to Communism in this state'. McCarthy was not the only patriot eager to help Bowker. The American Legion also handed over to the Commission what it considered to be documented evidence of Communist infiltration, complete with dossiers, pamphlets and books, including case histories of 412 alleged Communists. (Tom Dorgan was an active member of the Legion's Anti-Subversive Committee.)[8]

By the start of 1954 the Bowker Commission was enjoying an authority that had never been accorded to its predecessors. This was made clear by the approbation given it by Governor Christian Herter. The governor, a Harvard overseer, was precisely the kind of Republican who had traditionally protected the Ivy League colleges from redhunting Boston Irishmen. His 1954 annual message, however, was delivered in the wake of McCarthy's well-publicized clash with Harvard, and Herter used the occasion to denounce those witnesses who took the Fifth. He held it 'a sound proposition' that anyone taking this refuge in subversion cases 'makes himself suspect to the point where his usefulness as a State or municipal official, a teacher, or as a worker in the field of key public contracts, State or Federal, is at an end'. It was this part of

Herter's message that provoked the loudest applause; he seemed to be referring both to professors who had taken the Fifth and to GE employees, and he subsequently confirmed that he had Harvard in mind. Republican Congressman John W. Heseltine assured Herter that 'your blast about holding the "fifth amendment" people at Harvard was both common sense and timely'. Herter concluded his address by commending 'the impartial, careful, quiet and fair work' of the Bowker Commission and looked forward to it producing 'a truly constructive report'. A few weeks later Herter again praised the work of the Commission and asked the legislature to increase its appropriation by $18 000 (from a modest $10 000), a request which was speedily met. Most unusually, a Massachusetts redhunting agency was being spurred on by both executive and legislature and by the highest authorities in the state.[9]

In January 1954 Philip Bowker announced that the Commission was on the verge of 'breaking and destroying the Communist conspiracy in this commonwealth'. This seemed now to be located more in the labour movement than on the campuses. In February the Commission did question eight prominent educators, either formerly or currently connected with Harvard or MIT, including Kirtley F. Mather and Harlow Shapley, but it soon moved on. The scrutiny of GE plants had opened a number of lines of inquiry, some of which were obstructed by recalcitrant witnesses who refused to testify. One such was the former head of the state CP, Otis A. Hood, and another was Nathaniel Mills, suspended from the Lynn plant after refusing to testify before McCarthy. The frustrated Bowker Commission turned from private to public hearings in order to expose Communist groups and see they were 'put out of business'. At one public hearing an enraged legislator, the populist Roxbury Democrat Charles Iannello, slapped Nat Mills before being hustled away by police. The Commission's success in disrupting UE seems to have emboldened it to move against another union, the Distributive, Processing and Office Workers, CIO. The union had called a strike at the Boston Mutual Insurance Company after the company seemed obstructive about renewing a contract. Mutual's chairman allegedly interceded with John E. Powers, seeking a Commission probe of the union. On the eve of the strike, the Commission obligingly subpoenaed the local union leaders, including its president Frank Siegel, who took the Fifth when asked about the CP. Cooperative witnesses testified to Communist 'influence' in the union. The besieged union called off the strike, the company withdrew recognition of the local and forced a pay cut, and eventually the rival AFL union won the right to represent the workers concerned. Powers's pro-labour reputation was being used to strengthen anticommunist unionism.[10]

The Commission's preoccupation with labour was confirmed in its first full report, published May 1954, which expressed concern that the CP (outlawed in 1951) was still active, noted that some teachers had once been attracted to Communism but implied that education no longer gave grounds for concern, and concluded that: 'There is some evidence that during the last few years the chief effort of the leadership of the Communist Party has been directed to the infiltration of the ranks of labor.' Even the AFL took exception to the indiscriminate linking of communism with labour. But the Commission was not deterred and it threw itself into a major investigation of the International Fur and Leather Workers Union (IFLWU), which had been expelled from the CIO in 1950 as Communist-led and was thought to have 10 000 members in Massachusetts. The recent conviction of its president Ben Gold for perjury added to its appeal as a target. Factional struggles within the IFLWU between pro- and anti- Gold factions, particularly in the large Local 21 at Peabody, doubtless contributed to the Commission's interest. True to form, the Bowker Commission contrived to release testimony charging Communist domination of Local 21 at a time when another Peabody local was suffering an AFL offensive. A few months later Walt Rostow of MIT, serving as an authority on the Soviet Union, testified that recent IFLWU policy statements showed 'unmis-takable indications' of 'political lines' laid down by Moscow, and also reassured the Commission that it was 'making an absolutely essential contribution to the maintenance of our form of society'. It was a singular experience for the Commission to bask in the approval of a luminary of the ivory towers. After several Local 21 members had invoked their constitutional rights, and others had testified against them, the Commission duly concluded that there had been 'a ruthless crushing of those in this Commonwealth who opposed the Communist domination'. Local 21 seceded from the union and others followed suit. The IFLWU was melting away, under fire from all quarters, and the Bowker Commission claimed some credit, arguing that it had shown how 'a legislative body can powerfully assist in removing Communist control over unions without in any way violating the proper rules of a democratic society'.[11]

The harassment of labour continued into 1955. UE remained an easy target. In March the Commission subpoenaed several UE staff members at a time when the union was engaged in contract discussions with a number of New England firms and when UE members were on strike at a machine company in Peabody. UE again accused the Commission of disrupting contract negotiations and engaging in strikebreaking, but the Commission was unperturbed and happily named those UE officials it believed to have been CP members. It claimed that by training its spotlight on the Communist leaders it could arouse a previously indifferent rank-and-file against them; 'once rid of Communism', it hoped that a union's members would 'never again permit it to be recaptured'.[12]

The esteem in which the Bowker Commission was held was reflected in the favourable treatment accorded to its legislative proposals. The intensification of red scare pressures in the state had resulted in another rash of anticommunist bills in the General Court, mainly in the house, but the political leadership was discouraging those not emanating from the Commission. A bill requiring candidates for political office to swear that they had not been CP members for ten years did pass the house when a roll call was forced, but the senate shelved it. Petitions thanking William H. Teto, Senators McCarthy and Jenner and Congressman Velde for their services in exposing the Communist conspiracy in the state similarly failed to re-emerge from committee, although the house did adopt a resolution commending Tom Dorgan for his 'tireless efforts ... in combatting the menace presented by the communists of every kind and hue'. The Bowker Commission bills in contrast enjoyed an easy passage; every proposal in its 1954 report quickly became law over little opposition. For the most part they tidied existing legislation, such as by strengthening the authorities' power to issue search warrants for subversive documents. One measure, rebuffed in some other states, made it a criminal offence to refuse to testify before legislative committees. More far-reaching was an act to create a division of subversive activities within the department of public safety, prompted by the discovery that since 1949 the police had been reporting evidence of subversion only to the FBI, and lacked their own monitoring facilities. Similar to the Holmes Commission proposal of 1938, this was an idea whose time had finally come. By the fall of 1954 the state police had established a division of subversive activities and were offering assistance to the Bowker Commission. The Bay State was embarking on a mission of political surveillance.[13]

Anticommunism triumphant

In the summer of 1954 a CIO poll established Massachusetts as the most McCarthyite of the ten states surveyed, and the only one in which there were more Catholics supporting than opposing a McCarthy-endorsed candidate. Anticommunist rhetoric was spurting out from almost every quarter in the mid-1950s, even as it was dying in many other states. The traditional conservatism of the state's Catholics, their anxieties about their place in the polity, the unsettling committee probes, and the verification of the red menace by the state authorities, were interacting to provide Massachusetts anticommunism with an Indian summer. The American Legion held a major Anti-Communism Seminar in the spring of 1954, featuring such celebrated speakers as Victor Lasky, Bella Dodd, Alfred Kohlberg and Boston's Tom Dorgan. The Legion, the VFW, the Disabled American Veterans, and the AMVETs, together constituted a kind of united anticommunist front, campaigning for curbs on subversion and maintaining pressure on the General Court. Archbishop Cushing was becoming more outspoken on the Communist issue, telling one group that 'The Reds have taken on so many colors that it is sometimes difficult to spot them', and another that 'If Senator McCarthy is the answer to Communism then I am for him'. In 1955 he urged *The Pilot*, the diocese's weekly newspaper, to add Louis Budenz's anticommunist column to its pages, although the editor demurred. New anticommunist bills continued to be introduced into the legislature – the proposal to require college presidents to rid their staffs of Communists made its annual appearance – although the existence of the Bowker Commission meant that they could now simply be referred to it for consideration.[14]

The executive branch of government was also joining the legislature in the war on domestic communism. The 1951 law outlawing the CP was finally invoked in the spring of 1954 against Otis A. Hood, and the case began to wend its slow way through the courts, where Hood received the assistance of the communistic

Civil Rights Congress. The state also made use of the 1919 sedition law, charging seven leaders of the Massachusetts CP with its violation. The attorney general, Republican George Fingold, was running for re-election that year, a consideration which may have informed his decision to prosecute, and in the fall he pledged that there would be no let-up in his 'relentless fight to rid the Commonwealth of Communists'. In the electoral race his Democratic opponent was state Senator John F. Collins, who charged Fingold with bungling the state's fight against communism. Eventually the state was obliged to admit defeat, for after the Supreme Court's April 1956 decision in the *Nelson* case, reserving internal security matters for the federal authorities, the state prosecutions of Otis Hood and other CP leaders had to be abandoned. But within the state the anticommunist temper of the mid-1950s was deeply discouraging to those trying to keep alive libertarian sensibilities. The Boston chapter of the League of Women Voters found that each year it lost ten or more members when it lobbied against anticommunist measures in the legislature; by January 1955 its representative on the state LWV board was arguing that: 'It would be easier for the Boston League to work in the Legislature if we soft-pedalled the Civil Liberties Bills.'[15]

But not everyone despaired. It was the Bowker Commission even more than the anti-CP prosecutions which occasioned greatest concern, and its centrality was underlined by the General Court's routine referral to it of new anticommunist proposals. In January 1955 a challenge to it was launched by the redoubtable Florence Luscomb, the feminist and labour activist who had been pilloried a generation earlier by the Holmes Commission. Summonsed as a witness, Luscomb refused to testify, but she did so not by invoking the familiar Fifth Amendment but by invoking the First and turning the occasion into a defence of civil liberties. She denied the right of the Commission to probe into 'matters of my conscience and opinions, speech, writings, associations and political views'. (The Supreme Court's decision in the Emspak case on the legitimacy of the First Amendment defence was still awaited.) Luscomb's spirited stand won her much notice and the acclaim of other civil libertarians, encouraged defiant stances from other witnesses, and formed the basis for a campaign against the Bowker Commission. It was to be some years before the Commission was free of the tiresome attentions of Florence Luscomb.[16]

The redhunters in retreat

But as it seemed to be at the height of its power, the Bowker Commission overreached itself. There had been pressure in the legislature, particularly from house Democrats, for the Commission to identify CP members more clearly in future (the vague references in the 1954 report to Communists in the labour movement had caused resentment). Accordingly, the law renewing the Commission required it to publish the names of those about whom there was 'creditable evidence' regarding membership of the CP or of other subversive groups. This amendment disturbed civil libertarians, but it also gave them an opportunity to discredit the communist-control programme: with CP membership already a felony in Massachusetts, the publication of names could constitute a bill of attainder, that is an arbitrary declaration of guilt by the legislature, something barred by the state constitution. The highly questionable constitutionality of the provision enabled CLUM to mobilize some formidable opposition, particularly as the Commission was preparing its 1955 report. Five leading lawyers, including a former Massachusetts house speaker and a former president of the state bar association, sought a writ of mandamus prohibiting the Commission from naming names in any report. The move failed on the technical ground that these lawyers themselves were not named in the anticipated report, but the decision left open the way for further action should individuals be named. The report itself was published in June.[17]

The biographical details of 85 persons thought on 'creditable evidence' to be CP members were published. Senator John E. Powers dramatically read the names of the Bay State's enemies out to the senate. Most were Bowker Commission witnesses who had invoked their constitutional rights and refused to testify, several of them members of the Peabody branch of the IFLWU. The event occasioned a furore of more than local dimensions. 'To the best of our knowledge', thundered *The Nation*, 'no investigating committee has previously attempted to promulgate a list of this kind which is tantamount to a mediaeval judgment of outlawry.' CLUM denounced the list as 'a deplorable usurpation of the judicial function and punishment by blacklist without due process'. The listed persons themselves held a protest meeting in Boston at which they charged the Bowker Commission with pursuing a 'witch hunt' for anti-labour and repressive purposes.[18]

Florence Luscomb led the counter-attack. The legal challenge had to be made in the name of one (or more) of those listed, and already something of a heroine for her recent stand against the Commission, Luscomb was the obvious candidate. She instituted a suit to have the blacklisting power declared unconstitutional. The campaign against the Commission gained momentum from reports that some of those listed had lost their jobs or lost business, and the civil liberties groups won new allies, such as the Liberal Citizens of Massachusetts. Initially rebuffed by the courts, in July 1956 Florence Luscomb won a signal victory when the Massachusetts Supreme Court granted her the right to proceed with her case, costly and slow-moving though it was to prove. The *Nelson* decision that year encouraged her to broaden her suit, challenging not merely blacklisting but also the Commission's authority to conduct any inquiries into subversion.[19]

As attacks on the Bowker Commission mounted it became somewhat more circumspect in its activities, and its lower profile may have been encouraged by some weakening of anticommunist passions in the state in the second half of the 1950s. When Commission member John E. Powers ran for mayor of Boston in the fall of 1955 there were fears that he might precipitate a renewed witch hunt. Walter A. O'Brien Jr called on civil libertarians to oppose Powers's candidacy, describing him as the 'leading pro-McCarthy politician in Boston' and the 'most zealous member' of the Bowker Commission. But such fears proved to be misplaced. Powers did not run an aggressively anticommunist campaign, and his Republican opponent, incumbent mayor John B. Hynes, won after concentrating his fire on Powers's machine and unsavoury associations rather than on his redbaiting. (Powers, a popular South Bostonian, was to lose the mayoral race again in 1959 to a 'non-political' bureaucrat; the politics of ethnicity, which had helped to sustain the anticommunist persuasion, seem to have been fading.) If Powers's attacks on Communist trade unionists had been prompted by electoral considerations, they had failed in their objective.[20]

After 1955 the Bowker Commission abandoned its strike-breaking activities and confined its attentions to the CP or to those associated with groups thought to be Communist fronts. Its main activity in 1956 was to try to appraise the significance of the local CP by listening to the friendly testimony of Herbert A. Philbrick and the cool testimony of Dirk Struik. Supreme Court decisions were narrowing the functions of bodies like the Bowker Commission, leaving them with little more than the weapon of exposure. This power could lose people their jobs, but when a commission could not even get someone fired its pitiable condition was exposed. Considerations of this sort underlay the decision to go after Struik. The MIT professor had been named frequently before official bodies as a Communist, his criticism of the Korean War added to his offences, and in 1951 he had been indicted under the 1919 sedition law, but after the *Nelson* decision the state abandoned its case and his fate was left to his employer. MIT investigated the charges, decided that there was insufficient evidence to proceed against Struik as a Communist, and while deploring his attitude, reinstated him fully. This infuriated the Bowker Commission, which thought preposterous the claim that there was no conclusive proof of disloyalty. Tenaciously, it launched its own investigation, with the help of Philbrick, an FBI agent and some of Struik's colleagues. The Commission confidently concluded that Struik had been 'an active member of the Communist Party in Massachusetts' and called on MIT to reopen the case against him. MIT, however, chose to leave Struik undisturbed. In 1957 the Commission turned its sights on another familiar target, Donald G. Lothrop of the Community Church, which was also accorded a central role in the Communist conspiracy.[21]

But the Bowker Commission was being pushed into irrelevance. The furore over its blacklisting capacity had dented its credibility and broadened its range of critics. Florence Luscomb's court challenge to its powers perhaps encouraged it to restrict its attention to well-attested radicals like Struik and Lothrop, but in so doing it could only rehash ancient charges, hardly the best way to enhance its investigative reputation. Lothrop had first been named as a 'red' by the Holmes Commission way back in 1938. The survival of Struik and Lothrop in their positions further underlined the Bowker Commission's weakness. The *Nelson* decision also made it seem redundant, as its members themselves recognized, for some of them travelled to Washington to try in vain to persuade Congress so to amend the Smith Act as to give states some authority in subversion matters. The Commission was being undermined too by its earlier success; the legislation it had procured in 1954 had placed the function of political surveillance in the new police division of subversive activies. In 1957 the Commission lost the services of three investigators from the Boston police department, although it retained some state police officers.[22]

Sensing the Commission's weakness, from 1956 CLUM and other groups mounted annual campaigns for its abolition. Florence Luscomb too persisted with her legal challenge, and in 1957 she was raising funds to enable her to continue the fight. In the spring of 1958 she heard that the Supreme Judicial Court was unlikely to hear the case before October, but by that date she had won at least a moral victory. During that year the Commission's terms of reference were changed, so that it was no longer required to publish the names of those it believed to be Communists, although it could do so if it wished (an invitation that was to be withdrawn in 1961). Florence Luscomb, presumably satisfied that the Commission was moribund and with other campaigns requiring her services, ceased to press her suit.[23]

Yet the Commission lingered on. It was performing one function, and that was as a safe receptacle for the anticommunist bills that were still being introduced into the legislature. Boston Democrats like Charles Iannello and Edmond J. Donlan were loath to abandon the patriotic cause and annually revived their favourite measures, which were then routinely referred to the Bowker Commission, 'where we expect they will die', as a CLUM report accurately put it. The Commission had become a convenient dustbin for the anti-Harvard and other proposals which so embarrassed the political leadership, and it was finally reverting to the kind of purpose that party leaders had initially intended for it.[24]

It thus survived into the 1960s. CLUM and other groups regularly called for its abolition in the late 1950s. Prominent in the campaign were Harvard professors such as Zechariah Chafee and Samuel Eliot Morison, two episcopal bishops and other top churchmen, and several distinguished lawyers, as well as groups such as the Massachusetts Baptist Convention, the Massachusetts Council of Churches, committees of the Boston and Massachusetts bar associations, and the state ADA. The libertarian common front was once more reaching the breadth that it had possessed in the early days of the Cold War. But every assault on the Bowker Commission also brought out its champions.

Lobbying to sustain it were the VFW and other veterans' organizations, and, more revealingly, the Archdiocesan Councils of Catholic Men and Women, the Catholic Daughters of America, the Holy Name Society, Roman Catholic lay leader Thomas H. Buckley, and, inevitably, the veteran Father of the Teacher Oath, Thomas Dorgan. Archbishop Cushing himself was recorded by one Catholic spokesman as favouring the continuance of the Commission, and another explained that it would be 'foolish to spend millions in Europe and the Middle East, to say nothing of our armed forces, and then let down the guard at home'. While Catholic notables as individuals had previously spoken out for communist-control measures, and Catholic politicians and newspapers had strongly supported them, Catholic groups had never before been so conspicuous in the legislative lobbies. The Communist issue was now being contested on what had become virtually a religious battlefield, with Protestant groups arrayed on the one side and Roman Catholic on the other. With the growing secularization of the political culture and the subsiding of red scare passions, perhaps, these were the groups to whom the symbolism of the issue still mattered.[25]

If anything, Catholic groups seemed more tenaciously anticommunist than they had ever been, locked into a Cold War mentality in which the battle between a Christian civilization and a godless communism was still reaching its height. The 1957 Congress of the League of Catholic Women of Boston took 'Christianity Embattled' as its theme, and featured local hero Herbert Philbrick, who assured the 1500 assembled women that they were 'in the front line trenches of this struggle' between communism and Christianity. Richard Cardinal Cushing was himself taking a high profile anticommunist stand by the late 1950s. A large proportion of his surviving pastoral letters and publications employing the word 'communism' in the title date from this period. In 1959 Cushing led the movement in Massachusetts to protest at the visit of Nikita Khrushchev to the United States and presided over a prayer meeting of 20 000 Catholics at Bunker Hill Monument. In the same year the Cardinal Cushing Commandos were formed from a local teenage group (previously designed to combat juvenile delinquency) to counteract a perceived Communist drive among youth, whose susceptibility to propaganda particularly troubled Cushing. One of his correspondents cited John Birch Society leader Robert Welch as saying that 'the

Catholic Church was the last remaining stronghold in the world against Communism', and for a time Cushing adopted a friendly attitude towards Welch and the Birchers, but distanced himself when their notoriety grew. Catholic groups like the Daughters of St Paul and the Knights of Columbus distributed Cushing's anticommunist addresses, such as his 1960 publication, *Questions and Answers on Communism*, which deplored the 'abject appeasement' of both government and media towards the Soviet Union and felt that 'the Kremlin has too often dominated the American mind through the Communist line'. The repeated message was that this was not the time to lower defences against Communist subversion.[26]

While the ritual annual contest in the legislature over the little HUAC continued to be resolved in favour of the veterans and Catholic groups, by the summer of 1960 the Commission – now the Caples Commission after its new chairman Democratic Senator Richard R. Caples of Boston – had been inactive for at least two years. Its life was again extended, but civil libertarians were commenting on the welcome 'dearth' of anticommunist bills before the legislature. In 1961 the Commission burst unexpectedly into action, and even revealed a new grasp of subversive behaviour. In January a disturbance had followed a protest in Boston organized by American Nazi party leader George Lincoln Rockwell. So alerted, the Commission summoned eight witnesses to testify in executive session on Rockwell and the Nazis; its subsequent (and last) report informed the public that it was active 'in an investigation of the spread of Fascism and Naziism in the Commonwealth, as well as the activities of the Communist Party'. The body which had been founded to deflect an attack on Harvard and campus Communists had come a long way. Its life was extended again in 1962 but, unusually, no time limit was placed on it, probably a contrivance of the political leadership. Without the annual contest over its renewal to bring out the patriots, the Commission could die quietly in its sleep. It never stirred again.[27]

The institutional residue

One reason for the increasing irrelevance of the Special Commission on Communism was that the function of political surveillance was being assumed by the police. The 1954 legislation had provided for a division of subversive activities, and by 1956 it had established a depository in which it was accumulating information on the CP and other suspect organizations, had conducted over 300 interrogations, and was assisting the Bowker Commission. Over the next few years it had little to do for the Commission, although it did assist the attorney general's office in enforcing such sedition legislation as had survived the *Nelson* and other court judgments.[28]

Attorney General George Fingold, who had had to discontinue the state prosecutions of Dirk Struik and the CP leaders, had not entirely abandoned hope of claiming a few red scalps. In February 1958 he asked the division of subversive activities to investigate two faculty members of Lowell Technological Institute, Elies Snitzer and David Murray Fein. Soon after HUAC arrived in Boston, intent on exposing New England Communists, and the star witness at its proceedings was Armando Penha, who, inspired by the examples of Herbert Philbrick and Matt Cvetic, had in 1950 become an undercover member of the CP for the FBI and had risen to responsible CP offices. Penha named over 200 CP members and insisted that 'the Communist conspiracy ... is much stronger than it has ever been', on the implausible ground that its weak links had been removed. Several of those identified, mainly those already named by the Bowker Commission, were hauled before HUAC, where they generally invoked the Fifth, as did the Lowell teachers Fein and Snitzer. The Lowell Technological Institute subsequently held its own hearings on these two faculty members and terminated their employment. The state's communist-control programme, through the instrumentality of the division of subversive activities and with the help of HUAC, had claimed victims of a kind. Others of a different political complexion followed in 1961, when the Commission on Communism's encounter with the Nazi party led the police division to arrest Rockwell and two others. They were found guilty and fined under the True Name Law. A rough justice had perhaps been served.[29]

The division of subversive activities was evolving as a unit for political surveillance, collecting information on politically suspect groups, investigating complaints of subversion, and screening candidates for employment. In the late 1950s it was attending CP meetings and undertaking perhaps 300 investigations of individuals and organizations each year. By the mid-1960s it was monitoring the activities of peace, civil rights and other protest groups which, 'due to their enthusiasm', might be tempted to unlawful deeds. Its files had long been used for security checks not only by the state government but also by other agencies, such as the FBI, the Immigration and Naturalization Service, and the armed forces. Industrial plants and other employers in Massachusetts seem also to have been allowed to clear prospective employees with the division. Its screening services came to be widely deployed. In the year ending June 1965 it conducted over 2000 security name checks, and observed that queries from police departments in the South had grown with the civil rights movement. The division also liaised more generally on subversion matters with the FBI, HUAC, and similar police units in other states.[30]

The red scare of the mid-1950s had thus left an institutional residue. The populist passions against Harvard and the intellectual elite had contributed to the creation of a bureaucratic and police apparatus which had acquired a life of its own and which generally served to protect the political status quo from its critics. A visceral hatred of Communists had been used by political leaders, wittingly or not, to further the expansion of the national security state. Ironically, if not altogether unfittingly, the only arrests reported by the division of subversive activities in the first ten years of its life were those of the three Nazis.

Surviving too for a while was the loyalty oath in its various versions, most notably that of 1935 which was expected of all teachers, whether in public or private institutions. Resentment towards loyalty oaths was growing in the libertarian 1960s, when John F. Kennedy himself was quoted as being against such 'harassment' of teachers, and in 1966 an embarrassing case flared up at Harvard, which had ordered the dismissal of economics instructor Samuel B. Bowles (son of New Dealer Chester Bowles) for refusing to take the oath. To Bowles, echoing S. E. Morison's complaint from the 1930s, the oath meant 'a politically inspired interference with the independence of the university'. But the oath was already being challenged in the courts, which instructed Harvard to retain Bowles until its constitutionality had been resolved, and in 1967 Tom Dorgan's celebrated handiwork was finally struck down. If Dorgan had intended it as a thrust at the liberal and elitist tendencies of the New Deal, it had succumbed to a fitting nemesis.[31]

Conclusion

By the 1960s red scare politics in Massachusetts were disappearing. Anticommunist bills were no longer being pressed on the legislature, the little HUAC had ceased to function, and bureaucratic surveillance had replaced populistic alarums. There were patriots who continued to inveigh against wicked Communist machinations but they had lost their leverage with the political community. Studies made in the mid-1950s suggested that New England was somewhat less tolerant of political deviants than other American regions outside the South, and Joe McCarthy, as previously noted, was particularly popular in the Boston area. By the early 1960s a more relaxed political culture had taken shape, and a fairly tolerant attitude was displayed towards such unconventional figures as 'peace candidate' H. Stuart Hughes, a radical Harvard professor who ran for the US senate on a platform proposing unilateral disarmament for the United States. The issue of domestic communism was no longer agitating regular politicians, although the Democrats had assumed substantial majorities in the legislature. Massachusetts had possessed a political culture which was polarized by the Communist issue, one in which both the anticommunist and the libertarian persuasions were unusually strong. By the 1960s the libertarian and liberal persuasion was becoming pervasive, and the state was acquiring its modern reputation for political liberalism.[32]

The history of Massachusetts anticommunism, as with red scare politics in the United States more generally, suggests the inadequacy of any monocausationist explanation. More than in some states, there was a strong populist dimension to it; for at least a generation the most vehement demands for Communist controls stemmed largely from the lower and middle-class communities of urban Massachusetts, mediated by Irish and Italian politicians whose constituents were mainly Democrats and Catholics. (The later anti-busing movement in Boston, described by Ronald P. Formisano as a form of 'reactionary populism', had similar roots.) Legislation was typically introduced by minor or middling politicos into the lower house, often to the embarrassment of party leaders. Much of it reflected the old Boston Irish suspicion of the Ivy League colleges and the Yankee gentry associated with them. It is little wonder that much of the early academic literature to analyse McCarthyism emphasized its populist character, for the residents of those ivory towers could hardly have been unaware of the shafts directed at them. But few of these shafts hit their targets, or at least effected the kind of damage intended. The civil libertarians could claim many victories, and the unusual strength of civil liberties groups in Massachusetts meant that anticommunist pressures were for the most part successfully contained until relatively late in the Cold War period. Further, it required the anxieties associated with international crises to give anticommunism much purchase. And when the pressures proved irresistible, the particular programmes put into place were as much the work of party leaders as of South Boston patriots. The political managers were notably successful in diverting attacks on Harvard and her sister institutions, and a number of the measures introduced, however offensive they may have been to civil libertarians, were intended as much to direct anticommunist passions along safe channels as to expose reds. To some degree, as Sigmund Diamond has shown, Harvard sought to protect itself from the attention of legislative committees by some discreet cooperation with the FBI; it also sensibly used its friends in the political community to derail legislation aimed at it. The price of thwarting the impulses of reactionary populism was anticommunist controls which bore mainly on others.[33]

Yet it is also important to acknowledge the elitist dimension to Massachusetts anticommunism. Red scares were at their most intense in the late 1930s and especially in 1953–5 when the state executives decided to join the crusade. Without the endorsement of the governors, the Holmes and Bowker Commissions could not have inflicted the damage they did. Red scares in state as in nation were at their most effective when executive, legislative and judicial authorities acted together. The role of leadership can also be discerned in the way in which anticommunist politics in Massachusetts evolved. The Bowker Commission was established after years of pressure from urban Democrats and veterans' groups, but it quickly became a device for harassing CP-led unions, a strategy on which both moderate Democrats and Republicans could agree. At this stage, an agency close to the ruling authorities of the state was preying on those low in the polity. Political leaders, it could be said, were bending red scare impulses to their own purposes.

Perhaps the most distinctive characteristic of Massachusetts anticommunism was its association with the Democratic party. There were anti-labour Republicans who joined the cause, but

civil libertarians could usually count on some sympathetic assistance from Republican Yankees, while the patriotic groups looked
for champions to Boston and other city Democrats. This configu-
ration reflected the religious and ethnic loyalties and rivalries
which had long given shape to the state's politics. The lower
house's almost knee-jerk obeisance when a roll call was forced on
a Communist issue reflected a healthy respect for a substantially
Roman Catholic electorate, with its network of newspapers,
church and social groups perpetuating largely conservative values
on moral and political issues.

During the first half of the twentieth century Massachusetts
Catholics had established themselves confidently in political
offices. 'The Puritan has passed, the Catholic remains', boasted
the ambitious Cardinal O'Connell on one occasion. But
O'Connell's hard-won order was fading. In Boston, it has been
argued, the 'traditional world of the urban ethnic', bounded by
neighbourhood, church and family, was being prised apart by the
1960s, when a more pluralistic, managerial and coalitional style of
politics came to characterize the city. As Cardinal Cushing recognized, the triumphalist and separatist spirit of O'Connell was ill-
suited to the modern world, and the new prelate sought to
establish better relationships with the variety of ethnic and
religious groups that inhabited his diocese. Distinctively ethnic
localities were eroding, and the urban electorate was proportion-
ately declining. A younger generation of ambitious Catholic
politicians, seeking city-wide or statewide offices, were less
inclined to exploit their ethnicity, recognizing the need for larger
political alliances (as when at presidential level John Kennedy
made it clear that he would not be beholden to the Catholic
church). On the city council and in the lower house of the legislature, however, a more traditional style of politics survived
among those with local perspectives, and many Catholics,
including on occasion Cushing himself, sought to cling to ancient
certainties. As red scare sentiments died in Massachusetts, it was
Catholic bodies which remained most conspicuously stranded on
the shore, still calling for controls on domestic communism, an
issue perhaps which could unite many Catholics. Imbedded in
red scare politics was a last anxious hurrah for an old order.[34]

PART IV

RED SCARE POLITICS
IN GEORGIA

The Deep South in the first half of the twentieth century constituted the core of the Solid South, a region noted for its
dominance by the Democratic party, its commitment to white
supremacy, and its abiding poverty. Progressive strains could take
hold in the South, but for the most part the local white oligarchies
which exercised power cleaved to conservative political and social
ideologies designed to protect their status and interests.
Inheriting a sectional identity shaped by slavery and the traumas
of Civil War and Reconstruction, the guardians of the Solid South
characteristically combined a suspicion of outside influences with
a veneration for local traditions. Such a mentality militated
against economic growth or indeed change of any kind. The
parochial elites of the South, intent on the preservation of racial
and economic privilege, presided over a traditionalist political
culture in which radicalism seemed indistinguishable from
subversion. From the Russian Revolution onward every labour
organizer or civil libertarian in the Deep South risked being
labelled a red, an alien 'other' to whom the normal constitutional
protections need not apply. The South has often been neglected
as a source of McCarthyite politics, although contemporary
scholars have begun to appreciate its significance.[1]

Yet for the duration of the Solid South the resort to red scare
politics remained limited. While a red scare was scorching parts
of the Midwest in the late 1930s, and while redhunting
committees were on the loose on the West Coast in the late 1940s,
the South remained relatively unmoved by the prospect of
Communist subversion. Even as late as 1955 Nathan Glazer and
Seymour Martin Lipset concluded from a poll analysis that the
South was 'the most anti-McCarthy section in the country'.
Although the political order had long denied legitimacy to
Communists and other radicals, it was not until the Solid South
was crumbling that a full-scale anticommunist crusade was
launched in the region.

The old political order, sometimes known as the 'classic' period
of southern politics, was characterized by a one-party political
system and by the disfranchisement of virtually all African
Americans and of many poor whites. Power had come to rest with
propertied local interests – plantation owners and farmers, town
bankers and merchants, county lawyers and editors, landlords
and low-wage industrialists – who could often afford to ignore the

claims of the 'have nots' as they cultivated their own fortunes. The Democratic party was both their vehicle and their symbol, the political manifestation of southern rights. Their uniform and passionate attachment to the party provided southern leaders with a first line of defence against unwelcome national pressures, but also meant that within each state, politics became an ill-defined jumble of factions. General elections were meaningless and the key elections were Democratic primaries, a feature which encouraged folksy campaigns and demagogic candidates. The absence of ideological cleavages between rival Democrats put a premium on personality, and while the electorate was narrow it did contain many small farmers and other low-income whites, whose support had to be recruited without threatening the local elites. Whipping-boys had their value to such campaigning politicos, whether Washington bureaucrats, interfering Yankees, uppity blacks – or Communists. The somewhat insular ruling classes of the Deep South saw little need for a sustained red scare, but sighting the occasional Communist subversive helped them to sustain their political order. The CP's conspicuous championing of the cause of African Americans after 1928 reinforced the anticommunism of the white supremacists.[2]

The state of Georgia typified politics in the Deep South. Its substantial population of African Americans (42 per cent in 1920 and 31 per cent in 1950) were effectively excluded from political life, even after the Supreme Court had ruled against the all-white primary in 1944, Georgia perpetuating their debarment by use of a literacy test. The state was overwhelmingly rural, nearly two-thirds of the population living in rural areas in 1940, and, as elsewhere in the South, its politics were dominated by the economic elites of its villages and small towns. A counterpoint – and irritant – to rural Georgia was the burgeoning city of Atlanta, a somewhat worldly community with its new-found businesses, civic groups, educational institutions, rather grand newspapers, trade unions, clusters of white liberals and even African American voters. The state's many farmers and textile mill owners wanted to keep wages low, and Georgia's Democrats continued to peddle brands of Jeffersonian and Jacksonian philosophy, with their emphasis on limited government. In some respects the political culture of Georgia seemed not too distant from that of the Jacksonian era, as local Democratic chieftains staked out their positions in their own crudely hewn newspapers, and as a countrified style of politics – folksy, individualistic, racist and anti-urban – drowned out the emerging metropolitan culture of Atlanta. The hold of local elites was reinforced by Georgia's celebrated county-unit system, a unique electoral arrangement that gave the rural counties an excessive influence in primary elections and which exacerbated rural-urban tensions. And quite apart from the county-unit system, malapportionment magnified the strength of rural areas in statewide elections.[3]

The loosely knit Democratic party tended to polarize into two rival factions in statewide campaigns. The dominant faction for many years was led by Eugene Talmadge, governor in the mid-1930s and early 1940s, the so-called 'Wild Man from Sugar Creek', who combined an identification with plain folks with a highly conservative political philosophy. A powerful stump speaker, he was able to harness the class and racial fears of his small-town and farming constituents. His anti-labour and anti-government views also captivated the many businessmen who helped to finance him. Resisting the Talmadge phenomenon were ill-organized and somewhat more liberal (though not integrationist) elements which tended to be associated with urban and with northern Georgia.[4]

Georgia's traditions meant that Ku Klux Klansmen were more likely to be found within its borders than Communists. This was one reason for the almost casual approach to domestic communism which characterized much of the state's history. Anticommunist measures could be adopted with little controversy and little publicity because no one – or almost no one – in the state was threatened by them. Redbaiting tactics were sometimes deployed in election campaigns in the 1930s and 1940s against liberal candidates, but full-scale red scares did not ensue. The one-party system meant that the Communist issue was not used systematically as a party weapon, as in Michigan, and it took pressure from outside the state to intensify the anticommunist cause. Loyalty oaths were adopted in 1935 and 1949, but they were prompted more by examples set in other parts of the Union than by any fear of disloyalty in Georgia. It was not until 1953 that Georgia politicians seriously discussed a communist-control programme, and not until the second half of that decade that red scare politics were fully embraced. This was the work of political elites, less subject to populist pressures than were the governing authorities in Massachusetts, but prepared to use populist rhetoric to mobilize support for a traditional regime. As the anticommunist persuasion was fading in other parts of the union, in Georgia it seemed to be gaining momentum. It remained strong into the 1960s, although by then it had assumed some unexpected forms. Georgia had her own distinctive contribution to make to the course of anticommunist politics in the United States. In other parts of the union red scares could be fuelled by such phenomena as class antagonisms, religious ideology and party politics; in Georgia, as elsewhere in the Deep South, race was the underlying issue.

10

DEFENDING THE OLD ORDER, 1935–1948

In 1935, when Georgia adopted its first formal anticommunist measure, the governor of the state was Eugene Talmadge, the fiercely anti-labour champion of the 'wool hat boys' and critic of Franklin Roosevelt, whose New Deal he denounced as communistic. In 1949, when the state adopted an anticommunist loyalty oath, the governor was Eugene's son Herman Talmadge, rather more progressive than his father in social and economic policy but soon to express himself a warm admirer of Senator Joe McCarthy. The Talmadge faction did not reign unchallenged through these years, but it was the most resilient faction and the one most identified with the old order. The Talmadges were 'good ole boys' who vigorously upheld white supremacy, fought to retain the county-unit system, and drew their support from rural Georgia and from some working-class whites in the cities. Public opinion polls suggested that most Georgians actually favoured liberal and New Deal philosophies in these years, but many such liberal-minded respondents (African Americans and poor whites) could not vote, and in other ways too the Talmadges were able to insulate themselves from public opinion. Committed to preserving the status quo in a political system that encouraged demagoguery, they used whatever weapons came to hand in defence of the old order, and one such weapon was the red scare. Anticommunist passions never really convulsed the state in these years, if only because there were few radicals in Georgia, but anticommunist rhetoric was regularly deployed whenever cracks appeared in the traditional political edifice, primarily during election campaigns.[1]

The Wild Man from Sugar Creek

Nurturing the timeless values of the Old South, the conservative political leaders of Georgia were less disturbed by threats of insurrection from below than by threats of intrusion from the outside. There had probably been no more traumatic experience in the state's history than General William Tecumseh Sherman's infamous 'march through Georgia' in 1864, and since then any phenomenon which tended to question the political order was likely to be attributed to a malign external force. Of course, social and economic change was subtly if rather slowly transforming the bases on which the political system was built, but any innovation that was unwelcome to the traditional guardians could be discredited as alien and unnatural. To many Georgians, the 'enemy within' was indistinguishable from the 'enemy without'. In the decade which opened with the adoption of an unusually sentimental loyalty oath in 1935, anticommunist and xenophobic sentiments were mobilized from time to time to ward off disturbing influences.

Political and social repression was hardly a novelty in Georgia, where the 'reincarnated' Ku Klux Klan had made its appearance in 1915. In the early 1920s the Klan was briefly an influential presence in Georgia politics, sternly upholding a traditional moral code and preying on ethnic and religious minorities. When the shattering economic conditions of the early 1930s unnerved local elites and ejected many poor whites from their farms and jobs, urban areas simmered with class and racial resentments. As the largest city, Atlanta experienced some of the earliest manifestations of anticommunist sentiment. A local group known as the Black Shirts was formed by Atlanta salesman Holt J. Gewinner and others 'to combat the Communist Party and to discourage the teachings of Communism and foster white supremacy'. It appealed to unemployed white youths eager to drive blacks from jobs, and although its violence was to lead to its early demise, some of its members such as Gewinner himself were to reappear in similar organizations, and another member, Eugene Talmadge, was soon to be governor. Crude and unlawful tactics in fact were hardly necessary given the mindset of the local political and police authorities. The Communist organizers of an integrated meeting in 1930 were arrested for insurrection. In 1932 Angelo Herndon, a teenage African American Communist, was arrested in Atlanta for inciting insurrection after helping to organize a hunger march; he was brutally sentenced to 20 years in a chain gang. More fortunate were two sisters arrested in 1934 for distributing 'Communist literature' among striking mill workers but released when it was conceded that they had committed no crime.[2]

If the city fathers of Atlanta, with their reputed liberal tendencies, could equate protest and integrationist activity with insurrection, there was little hope of a more generous understanding among the rural-oriented incumbents of the county seats and state capitol. The views of these classes were probably best articulated by Eugene Talmadge, elected governor in 1932. Representing himself as a populistic champion of the farmer, Talmadge put his trust in the work ethic and his distrust in government, and his cuts in taxes and utility rates were welcomed by large landowners and business interests, as well as small farmers. His fierce belief in individual self-sufficiency put collectivist solutions beyond the pale, and he came into increasing conflict with the New Deal, not for its philosophy alone but also because it threatened to force up wages in the state, and undermined his control of political patronage.The raising of wages in depression-hit Georgia was anathema not only to the planters and struggling cotton mill-owners, but also to the small white farmers who periodically dipped into the pool of surplus black labour. Talmadge developed a strong hostility to labour, perceiving strikes and unions as un-American, and used the National Guard for strike duty, on one well-publicized occasion in 1934 holding the pickets in a detention camp without trial. He claimed to have 'personally broken the back of the Unions in Georgia'. Talmadge's anti-New Deal views won him some right-wing admirers outside the state and by 1935 he was developing presidential ambitions. He even embarked on a national speaking tour, inveighing against Roosevelt and the 'communist' attributes of his administration. With the backing of elements of northern business, Talmadge, Gerald L. K. Smith and other southern racists held an anti-New Deal 'Grass Roots Convention' of disaffected Democrats at Macon early in 1936. However, a disappointing turnout of those 'united to oppose Negroes, the New Deal and ... Karl Marx', killed any thoughts Talmadge may have had of winning the White House.[3]

As the embarrassment over the Grass Roots Convention suggested, Talmadge's conservatism was not altogether typical of Georgia, where Franklin Roosevelt was popular and the New Deal was credited with filling bellies. Its modest liberals may not have been very radical but some were happy to account themselves New Dealers; the New Deal did not strike directly at race relations. Richard B. Russell ran successfully for the US Senate against Talmadge on a pro-New Deal platform, and in the legislature a reform group coalesced around the speaker, E. D. (Ed) Rivers.[4]

Yet it was the New Dealer Rivers who introduced a teacher loyalty oath bill in 1935, and saw it through the lower house with 113 votes in favour and two against, and through the senate without dissent. 'It is a shot at Reds, Pinks and Communists and radical doctrines and isms', explained Rivers of the measure, which required teachers and state employees to swear allegiance to the national and state constitutions. Indeed, the oath went further than most with an extraordinary pledge 'to refrain from directly or indirectly subscribing to or teaching any theory which is inconsistent with the fundamental principles of patriotism and high ideals of Americanism'. In some states much milder loyalty oaths precipitated great controversy, and it is a comment on Georgia's political culture that her sweeping declaration attracted little opposition or press attention. Also revealing was the perceived source of the threat, for the state was said to have been 'flooded with propaganda' from the outside, and to combat this patriotic ideals had to be 'cultivated in the minds of our children'. It was actually the oath which had been inspired from the outside, for it arose not from any controversy within Georgia but from the campaigns of the Hearst press and the Daughters of the American Revolution. It was a speaker from the knavish city of Washington who had most eloquently warned the state DAR convention of the 'unseen force' threatening the republic. The state's legislators were happy to display their patriotism, as they similarly endorsed the American Legion's bills to bar the CP from the ballot and to punish sedition. Governor Talmadge unexpectedly vetoed these latter bills in the name of free speech; his bemused critics speculated that given his venomous assault on the New Deal, he could be vulnerable to a sedition prosecution himself![5]

These measures prompted little debate in Georgia because they were not thought to be directed at indigenous groups. Since the convulsions of the Civil War era, Georgia's political leaders had consistently identified agitators or subversives as being directed by hostile forces external to the South. This suspicion of outsiders was reflected in a law of 1938, which barred aliens from public employment except where there were no qualified American citizens available. The antipathy towards interfering 'furriners' was triggered even more vigorously that year when Franklin Roosevelt attempted to use his connection with the state to purge Georgia's conservative Senator Walter George. The tactic backfired as indignant Georgians expressed their support for George, who invoked memories of Reconstruction, called on 'white Democrats' to resist this 'Second March Through Georgia', and characterized Roosevelt's advisers as 'CIO Communists and sit down strikers'. Eugene Talmadge, whose own candidacy was ruined by the popular sympathy unleashed for George, explained that Roosevelt had made himself a 'furriner', that is 'anyone who attempts to impose ideas that are counter to the established traditions of Georgia'. Or as a tobacco farmer commented on the affair, 'We Georgians are Georgian as hell!' This defiant local patriotism was also illustrated in 1938 by the 'Georgian's Creed', adopted by the legislature at the prompting of veterans and patriotic groups. Designed for use in schools and public meetings, it enabled a Georgian to 'strive to be a pure upright Citizen' and 'feel a sense of pride in the history and heroic deeds accomplished by my forebears'. The old political order took strength from this cherishment of the past, and Georgia would continue to turn to its history to rebuff ideas of alien pedigree.[6]

The political classes' pride in their state's distinctive heritage was linked to their determination to maintain their political culture, most vitally the system of race relations. In some other states the heightened nativism at the end of the decade helped to fuel a 'little red scare'; in Georgia such sentiments were directed towards preserving segregation. The NAACP's success in chipping away at the 'separate but equal' doctrine (in the Missouri *Gaines* case) had not gone unnoticed in the Deep South. It was Eugene Talmadge who rode this nativist wave, having again been elected governor in 1940, subsequently embarking on a campaign 'to keep the education of the races separate'. He suspected the state's campuses of harbouring integrationists, and promised to remove 'any person in the university system advocating communism or racial equality'. Talmadge's attempts to expel two professors escalated into major confrontations in 1941, which saw the dismissal of ten university employees and the banning of 'subversive' textbooks from the libraries. Thus might Georgia's cherished way of life be preserved from outside saboteurs. As Talmadge expressed it, he was not going to have 'foreign professors trying to destroy the sacred traditions of the South'. Since there were over 700 'foreign' (not Georgian) professors and instructors in the university system, the potential mischief was enormous. As criticism mounted, Talmadge reasserted his intention 'to stamp out Communism in our educational system', but it was Talmadge who was inflicting perceptible harm on the state's institutions, and professional bodies began removing accreditation from the colleges. He was also inflicting damage on himself, and while he campaigned in 1942 'very glad to be called the Champion of White Supremacy in Georgia', he was defeated in the primary by the young Ellis G. Arnall, campaigning as a friend of education if not of integration.[7]

The new governor headed a reformist administration during the booming war years, but the Talmadge faction remained a powerful force in the state, if an increasingly reactionary one. The 1942 campaign had intensified racial tensions, as Talmadge officials encouraged the brutal harassment of blacks, and a mutiny of black soldiers at Camp Stewart in 1943 only aggravated white fears. The faction's newspaper, *The Statesman*, stood ever more starkly for the old Georgia, a vehicle for anti-northern, anti-integrationist and anti-red propaganda. A typical article in 1945 spoke of Moscow's plan to 'subvert' the republic 'by EDUCATING TEACHERS in SOCIALISM, or "Collectivism" ...'. Another piece warned that the Federal Council of Churches was propagating communism 'under the guise of the Church of Jesus Christ'. Meanwhile the Arnall administration, with its identification with urban and suburban elites, tried to promote economic growth and good government.[8]

The fortunes of the Talmadge faction were boosted in the mid-1940s by evidence that Georgia was indeed being threatened by sinister external forces. The national Democratic party itself seemed an increasingly unreliable custodian of southern interests, with its heritage of New Deal reform, urban bosses, labour activists and African American groups. In a Texan case, *Smith* v. *Allwright*, the US Supreme Court in 1944 invalidated the white primary, and Governor Arnall's acceptance of that decision gave Eugene Talmadge a powerfully emotive issue in the 1946 gubernatorial campaign. Blacks would be able to vote in the primary, and the prospect that Arnall would be able to forge a progressive political alliance greatly disturbed Talmadge. 'I shall see', he said, 'that the people of this state have a Democratic white primary unfettered and unhampered by radical, Communist, and alien influences.' Yankee troops, he suggested, again invoking the spectre of Reconstruction, would enforce black voting in the South: 'The people of Georgia must declare whether or not they will continue to run the state or whether they are willing to turn it over to Moscow-Harlem zoot-suiters.' Even more incontrovertible evidence of a northern plot to subvert the South, however, was provided by the CIO's decision to launch Operation Dixie. The combination of labour organization and northern inspiration could only make conservatives of the Talmadge stripe see red, particularly since an ill-concealed motive in the CIO offensive was to sever the roots of reaction.[9]

With the ending of the war northern companies were decamping to the South to take advantage of the low wages and non-union conditions, particularly in the textile and furniture industries, and the CIO determined on a major unionizing drive in the region. In May 1946 trade union activists directed from Atlanta were deployed across 12 southern states. The AFL, worried by this initiative, launched its own southern organizing drive, and, for good measure, sought to discredit the CIO's leaders as 'the devoted followers of Moscow'. The AFL's redbaiting of the CIO campaign was scarcely more sophisticated than that of right-wing extremist Joseph P. Kamp, whose message was conveyed in his pamphlet, *Communist Carpetbaggers in Operation Dixie*. Such intimations merely confirmed the expectations of the guardians of the Deep South. Operation Dixie's main target was North Carolina, but Georgia's textile workers were also to be encompassed, and the campaign's headquarters in Atlanta heightened its visibility to Georgians. 'Parson Jack' Johnston in his Columbus newspaper equated Operation Dixie with integration and miscegenation and with a Communist plan for 'a revolution in America'. To a minister in the mill town of Clarksville the CIO organizers were 'intruders', 'Communists', and 'parasites living off the common laboring people'. Operation Dixie did raise the race issue, for both CIO and AFL spokesmen declared themselves for the participation of African Americans in southern primaries. But it could not overcome southern suspicions, and by the end of 1946 the CIO was winding Operation Dixie down. In 1947 Georgia – like other southern states – increased its barriers against labour organization with a right-to-work law.[10]

Operation Dixie did not precipitate a major red scare in Georgia, but it deepened the perception that any threat to the state's traditional political, social, and economic arrangements came from the outside and it once more enabled integrationists, labour organizers and Communists to be depicted as inseparable. Politically its greatest immediate impact was to put weapons into the hands of Talmadge faction candidates eager to discredit the state's liberals in the 1946 elections.

Progressive hopes and racial fears

The immediate postwar period was a confused one, particularly in Atlanta. As with other American cities, Atlanta's wartime experiences had tended both to raise reformist hopes and to deepen racial and economic friction. White and black labourers had surged into the city, and the local unions were seeking to organize them and were itching for pay increases after the wartime constraints. Returning black veterans looked forward to a recognition of their democratic rights. Political and industrial democracy was also the goal of the Southern Conference for Human Welfare (SCHW), which for the moment was the South's leading liberal group and which enjoyed some support in Atlanta. The quickening of the labour movement, the growing aspirations of African Americans, the unprecedented access of the latter to the Democratic primary, together with the reputed liberalism of some middle-class Atlantans, raised the prospect of progressive gains during 1946. But also growing in the city were tensions that the white supremacists could exploit.

Some insecure white workers, often schooled in the fundamentalist values of the southern countryside, were as hostile to unions and African Americans as was Eugene Talmadge, seeing the labour movement as a vehicle for black aspirations. The national campaign for a FEPC law did nothing to ease this disquiet, which was exacerbated by the appearance of Operation Dixie and the drive to register black voters in Atlanta. Residential overcrowding and job insecurity also helped to spawn a number of racial or hate groups. One was the West End Cooperative Corporation, formed in 1946 by whites resentful of black encroachment on previously white neighbourhoods. More formidable were the Columbians (legally chartered in August 1946 with the aid of partisans of leading Democrat James C. Davis), whose aim was to expand the 'noble tradition of the Whiteman of the Southland'. Sporting a Nazi-like lightning emblem, the brown-shirted Columbians roamed the poorer districts trying to arouse whites against the 'nigger bloc vote' and held meetings bewailing the housing shortage and denouncing Communists, Jews and blacks. Their leader was former Klansman Emory Burke, and associated with them was Holt Gewinner, a Davis aide who had been a member of the earlier Order of Black Shirts. At a meeting in September 1946, attended by two or three hundred mill workers, Gewinner concentrated a range of demons in his line that 'a Communistic Jewish Block is regimenting the Negro vote'. The workers applauded the antisemitic and anti-black sentiments expressed on this occasion, although only a few signed up with the Columbians.[11]

Also working the meaner streets of Atlanta was the Ku Klux Klan. The Knights of the Ku Klux Klan had formally disbanded in 1944, but the postwar labour and racial disquiet proved irresistible, and the reconstituted Knights, aroused in particular by Operation Dixie, registered themselves with the Secretary of State early in 1946. In May a great bonfire, burning crosses and a massive rally at Stone Mountain, Atlanta, spectacularly announced the reappearance of the Klan, which some attributed to Talmadge's racist demagoguery. Dr Samuel Green was the Klan leader, organizing marches against the invasion of the CIO and AFL unions. The spectre of the Klan, however, jarred Ellis Arnall's vision of a more civilized Georgia, and the antics of the Columbians were no more welcome to him. No doubt the governor was aware too that these groups were closer to the Talmadge wing of the Democratic party than to his own. He decided to go after them, appointing the young assistant attorney general Daniel Duke to spearhead the operation. Duke filed a suit to revoke the Klan's charter, which in time it voluntarily surrendered. His investigation of the Columbians uncovered a cache of dynamite, and in December 1946 their leaders were charged with conspiring to overthrow the government, and Emory Burke was sentenced to three years with the Georgia chain gang. This action broke the Columbians, but the Klan was more resilient. While it abandoned its claims to a charter, it re-emerged as the Association of Georgia Klans, feeding on the fears of communism intensified by the deepening Cold War. Samuel Green told a Klavern congregation in May 1947 that there were 50 Communist meetings a week in Atlanta, often in private homes, and he called on his members to identify these meeting places so that he could report them to HUAC. In June 1947 he claimed that 20 new Klans had been added in the year and urged his members to 'help in the great fight to uphold WHITE SUPREMACY and to stop COMMUNISM'. Whether or not there were tangible connections between political leaders such as Gene Talmadge and James C. Davis and the Ku Klux Klan, they were using the Communist issue for the same white supremacist purpose.[12]

Such were the sentiments surging through Atlanta as the 1946 elections were conducted, although the progressive forces remained optimistic. The most fearless liberal Democratic politician was the remarkable Helen Douglas Mankin, an anti-Talmadge Atlantan allied to Governor Ellis Arnall. In February 1946 she stood in a special election (in which the county unit did not apply) in Georgia's fifth congressional district. Her opponent Tom Camp was of the Talmadge faction. The CIO and its Political Action Committee (CIO–PAC), readying itself for Operation Dixie, embarked on a registration drive to recruit new black and white voters and endorsed Mankin. The Camp response was at once antisemitic and anticommunist: 'Sidney Hillman and the East Side Communists of New York are attempting to dictate our political affairs here in the 5th Georgia district.' With the help of black voters from the Ashby Street precinct Helen Mankin won a narrow victory, a stunning outcome for a Deep South election. The upset commanded headlines across the country. Eugene Talmadge, disturbed by this breach of the old order, dubbed Mankin 'the Belle of Ashby Street' and sniped endlessly at her success with the 'Darktown votes'.[13]

Helen Mankin's troubles were only just beginning. To keep her seat she had to surmount a Democratic primary in July, and in the meantime her conscientiously liberal votes in Congress gave ammunition to her enemies. A Supreme Court decision confirmed the right of blacks to vote in Georgia's primary elections, raising the unnerving prospect of their mass enfranchisement, and when Georgia house speaker Roy Harris lost his seat in the Augusta primary, in which some blacks had voted, the cause of white supremacy seemed at stake. Eugene Talmadge was running once more for governor, and although his principal formal rival in the primary was James V. Carmichael, Talmadge directed much of his attention to Mankin, the symbol of a slowly emerging new Georgia built on African American votes. (Carmichael, like Arnall, believed in reform but not integration.) On her first day in Congress Mankin voted against an appropriation for HUAC and was commended for so doing by the *Daily Worker*, a vote and an imprimatur which she was never to be allowed to forget. Talmadge ruthlessly pilloried 'that woman from the wicked city of Atlanta' and contrived to extend the county-unit system in the congressional primary to the fifth district, tipping the advantage to the rural areas. 'Once firmly entrenched as voters, the Moscow-Harlem-Zootsuiters with the aid of local quislings will strike the death blow at our segregation laws', warned Talmadge in Savannah. Mankin's official opponent was sometime Klan member James C. Davis, and while he won fewer popular votes than Mankin the county-unit system did its job and delivered him the prize. Talmadge similarly trailed Carmichael in the popular vote in the gubernatorial primary only to be accorded victory by the county-unit system. Talmadge also benefited from Arnall's recent abolition of the poll tax, for this enfranchised many poor whites.[14]

The rent in the traditional order was thus closed once more by these gerrymandering devices, but Mankin refused to play dead. The November election, usually a formality in southern politics, was still to be held, and Mankin determined to get on the ballot. She also filed suit against the county-unit system. Because that system in any case did not operate in a general election Mankin was well placed to defeat Davis, and the desperate guardians of the Solid South resorted to even nastier tactics in the fall campaign than they had in the summer. The Ku Klux Klan's revival was well under way. More clearly linked to the Davis camp were the Columbians, who prowled the poorer districts of the city seeking to intimidate the African American vote. In his own campaign James C. Davis made great play of Mankin's 'endorsement' by the *Daily Worker* and by the 'Communistic' CIO–PAC, then much reviled in the South for its association with Operation Dixie and its support of a national FEPC bill. Mankin, Davis insisted, was the candidate of 'the communist party, and its motley crew of red and pink followers' who wanted to place 'American men and women, boys and girls, churches and schools under their filthy, indecent, communistic, un-American doctrines'. The worried Talmadge forces eventually succeeded in having Mankin's name removed from the ballot, whereupon she launched a write-in vote campaign. Despite further fraud and intimidation Mankin won an impressive official total of 19527 votes, but Davis was declared the winner with 31444 votes. The old order had successfully used traditional tactics and the red scare to see off a challenge.[15]

Liberal anticommunism and the election of 1948

For several years the guardians of white supremacy were to use anticommunist prejudices to discredit the proponents of change. As the Cold War intensified, anticommunist rhetoric came to be more extensively deployed, but was largely restricted to electoral purposes and through the 1940s Georgia escaped the serious red scares that disfigured some states. Perhaps this was because a surprising degree of consensus prevailed in the state on the Communist issue. It was not only the old guard which repudiated the CP but liberals too. On the whole, foreign crises triggered fewer alarms in the state than examples of unwelcome Yankee interference.

Eugene Talmadge's anti-black and anti-red campaign, aided by the county-unit system, took him to victory in the election of 1946, but death precluded his return to the governor's chair. It also interrupted the restoration of the old regime, for after an unseemly squabble between the Arnall and Talmadge factions the courts vested the governorship in the incoming lieutenant governor, Melvin E. Thompson, an Arnall man. The Talmadge mantle fell on Eugene's son Herman, who thus took over the responsibility for repairing the defences of white supremacy. The threat of Operation Dixie had receded, but in the early years of the Truman administration a national civil rights campaign was gaining momentum, centred on the FEPC bill, and later on the President's Committee on Civil Rights. No more reassuring to the guardians of the Solid South was the radical insurgency among some northern Democrats, which was to lead to the creation of the Progressive party under the leadership of Henry Wallace. *The Statesman*, voice of the Talmadge faction, recorded the reactions of the traditionalists. The CP was the author of the FEPC bill, it revealed, and further it was 'invading the solid South' and attempting to defeat the bill's congressional opponents. 'They are in Atlanta!' it warned, echoing the Klan's claims about sighting Communists, and added that many CP members were black. When Henry Wallace attempted to speak to integrated meetings in the South the paper drew attention to their sponsorship by the 'Communist-aligned' SCHW. Herman Talmadge himself in November 1947 attacked Wallace as 'the Number One Communist fellow-traveler in America'. As well as revealing the apprehensions of his class, Talmadge was positioning himself for a run for the governorship in 1948.[16]

The Communists that Talmadge perceived in Atlanta were not entirely figments of his imagination. There were a few, perhaps a few dozen, and before the election of 1948 they were reinforced by the arrival of organizer Homer Chase, who as a New Hampshire citizen was as damned a Yankee as any southern mind could conceive. A Progressive party also emerged in Georgia, and in January 1948 the state's modest CP confirmed local suspicions with its statement that it would 'not be denied the privilege of helping the new party'. The reaction of the Talmadge forces to this surfacing of radical politics was predictable, an attitude which served to encourage local abuses of Progressive party activists, as when five of them were abducted in Augusta, an affair dismissed by the police since the five had been 'openly associating with the colored race in that locality'. But what sealed the fate of the radicals was the reaction of those constituencies usually accounted moderate or liberal.[17]

The outspoken foe of segregation, Lillian Smith, had already resigned from the SCHW, in part in protest at those members 'who follow the Communist line'. The CIO Industrial Councils of both city and state expelled a Progressive party official in May 1948, and in the same month the University of Georgia terminated the contract of an assistant professor nominated as the Progressive candidate for governor, on the grounds that his 'extensive' political activities were interfering with his work. The Progressive party, of course, was being widely redbaited through the country, but it was not yet the Communist front that it was to become. Perhaps more revealing was the determined campaign conducted by the *Atlanta Constitution* against Don West, a Wallace activist, poet, and minister who had been associated with radical causes in the 1930s. The *Constitution*'s Ralph McGill was gaining a reputation as a southern moderate, but like many liberals of his era he was convinced that 'Communists owe their loyalty first to Soviet Russia', leaving West, McGill privately explained, as 'an enemy to this country'. To prove West's disloyalty McGill even had Congressman James C. Davis procure material from HUAC's files, and soon after receiving it, he exposed West's left-wing activities in the *Constitution*, losing him his position at Oglethorpe University. The exposé precipitated a few worried letters from Georgia communities in which Don West had resided, including one from the Lula postmaster, who enclosed a report he had prepared distancing himself from West in case the new federal loyalty programme uncovered the association. 'The question with me and MANY of us now is', said this country postmaster, 'Do I or do we have to Hollar NIGGER NIGGER not to be called a communist???' It was a good question, again reflecting the southern tendency to equate communism with African American rights. In 1949 the *Constitution* conducted a similar campaign against Homer Chase. A vicious circle was being closed; with the likes of Talmadge and Davis smearing critics of segregation as Communists, liberals had even more reason to repudiate the C.P.[18]

In some other parts of the Union civil liberties groups might have been mobilized to defend at least the Progressive party activists. Liberal civic, civil liberties and labour groups, however, were weak in the South. The redbaited SCHW disbanded in 1948. A chapter of the American Civil Liberties Union appeared belatedly in Atlanta in 1947, and this did concern itself with physical attacks on CIO organizers and the more vicious forms of racial discrimination, but it was small and poorly funded, and anticommunism as such was hardly a top priority. In Georgia it was Klan activities that most concerned civil libertarians, and other red scare tactics often went unrebuked. The southern liberals' fierce rejection of the CP meant that the state's few radicals were isolated and vulnerable.[19]

Herman Talmadge, having been denied the governorship in 1947, was determined to win it in his own right in 1948 and reassert traditionalist authority. He ran against the civil rights programme of the Truman administration and the mild reformist stance of Governor Thompson, and behind both he espied subversive influences. He even blamed the acting governor for tolerating the presence of Homer Chase: 'I do not believe Mr. Chase would have come to Georgia if I had been Governor.' If elected he promised to resist the Truman civil rights programme, 'this oppressive, communistic, anti-Southern legislation', and told horror stories of a New York FEPC law which had led to white women taking orders from black foremen. The company that Melvin Thompson kept was no better. Talmadge accused him of cooperating with his liberal predecessor Ellis Arnall and with a 'Communist and Socialist crowd' in Atlanta bent on destroying the hallowed county-unit system and hence undermining 'individual liberty and freedom in this country'. Talmadge's press partisans loyally identified Thompson with Arnall, and Arnall with Henry Wallace, the 'well known American Traitor'; Talmadge, in contrast, would steadfastly protect Georgia 'from the foreign invader, Communism'. Talmadge won the election decisively; he was to recall the episode as 'the restoration'. The old guard even triumphed over the 'Communist crowd' in Atlanta. Helen Mankin had decided to contest James C. Davis again for the congressional seat, and Davis again pilloried her for her *Daily Worker* 'endorsement', her support among African American voters, and her association with the CIO–PAC and 'Reds'. On this occasion Davis won an easy victory, as some white workers apparently switched to him as the candidate of white supremacy and as disillusioned blacks stayed away from the polls. The Solid South had reasserted itself in Georgia.[20]

An anticommunist consensus

The old guard could feel well pleased with its 'restoration' in 1948. It had carried the legislature as well as the governorship and its critics had been seen off. The one independent candidate in the gubernatorial campaign who had objected to Talmadge's use of the race issue had won only 0.5 per cent of the popular vote. The Progressive ticket in the presidential campaign had fared even worse with 0.39 per cent of the vote, even less than in Alabama (where the city of Birmingham could supply a few radical votes). That nascent progressive coalition of African Americans, trade unionists and urban and suburban liberals, which Helen Mankin's initial 1946 victory had seemed to promise, had been shattered, in part by the remorseless redbaiting of the Talmadge camp. The white supremacists had equated any questioning of the state's system of race relations with communism, and while moderates of the stripe of Ralph McGill may have had a more subtle understanding of civil rights claims, they too saw the CP as the subversive agent of a hostile power. The anticommunist consensus in the state seemed to be even more solid in 1948 than it had been in 1935. Indeed, Georgia's reputation for red scare politics was unusually strong, largely because of the exuberant rhetoric of the Talmadges. Their bemusing invocation of Marxist-inspired zootsuiters left its mark. Georgia was the only southern state to play a significant part in the Interstate Legislative Conference on Un-American Activities in Los Angeles in September 1948, the legislature sending four delegates, including the presiding officers of both house and senate.[21]

Underlying this consensus was the successful identification of communism with the African American cause; race, in Georgia as elsewhere in the Deep South, remained the key to understanding the dominant political postures. The identification was made the easier by the state's almost pathological distrust of outside influences and its proud faith in its own traditions. The international Communist movement, after all, was nourished by the Soviet Union, and all too often the advocates of both desegregation and radical political reform seemed to be sustained by obscure Yankee forces. The materialization of Operation Dixie, the Progressive party, and CP leader Homer Chase in Georgia owed little to homebred sources; they were alien invasions, bent on dismantling the existing sociopolitical order. And for the moment at least the state of Georgia had closed ranks against them.

11

CONTROLLING COMMUNIST SUBVERSION, 1948–1956

For years the political leaders of Georgia had been shrugging off the threat of red subversion, other than in election campaigns. Where party chieftains systematically pressed the Communist issue for political advantage in Michigan, it did not divide major factions in Georgia. Red scare rhetoric was most likely to be deployed when cracks appeared in the old order, but the cracks for the most part were soon cemented over and the political classes relaxed again. Serious internal convulsions had been avoided too because there were few radicals and relatively few integrationists in Georgia, that is to say little in the way of political enemies against whom red scare emotions might usefully be mobilized. Civil liberties bodies were weak, and the state's liberals were eager to avow their own anticommunism. In these circumstances symbolic anticommunist measures might be adopted with little comment, as they equally ensnared no victims. The patriotic consensus within the state was protection of a kind against red scare pressures. But as the Cold War deepened, patriotic lobbies intensified their demands for action and the state authorities were obliged to address the Communist issue.

The old guard had used the Communist issue to repair its defences, but the election of Herman Talmadge in 1948 (together with a friendly legislature) did not mean the unleashing of a red scare on Georgia. It was one thing to invoke the red menace during a hyperbolic election campaign and quite another to introduce a communist-control programme, and in the latter the new Talmadge administration evinced little interest. Even the outbreak of the Korean War in 1950 did not precipitate the patriotic convulsions that it did in some states. Indeed, the state's political leaders could be held to be governing responsibly; in 1951, when anticommunist measures were being hastily introduced elsewhere in the Union, Georgia was enacting a law to curb the Ku Klux Klan. As late as February 1953 an Atlanta ACLU official held that 'aside from the race question', the position of the South 'on civil liberties is better than that of other sections'. It was only as the Korean War was ending that Georgia began seriously to secure itself against Communist subversion, which characteristically was seen as a form of external harassment, a foreign ideology forcing its impertinent way into the state.[1]

A red scare fails to ignite

Because the 1948 gubernatorial election had been a special one, and because Herman Talmadge was re-elected in 1950, he served the unusual term of six years. His populistic style and unyielding white supremacism embarrassed the advocates of modernization, as did the warm support that he offered to Senator Joe McCarthy. But Talmadge himself was more a pragmatist than an ideologue. His superpatriotic rhetoric helped him to retain the support of the small farmers and many white urban workers, but he also saw a need to make some accommodation to the growing business interests of urban Georgia. He adopted a somewhat more progressive stance than had his father on economic and educational policy and took few initiatives to strengthen the communist-control programme. But given the anticommunist consensus in Georgia and the menacing nature of the Cold War, there could be no guarantee that his administration would not embrace a red scare if it was to its advantage to do so. And in Georgia the governor usually enjoyed considerable power over the legislature.

As always, much of the redbaiting of the 1948 campaign had been directed against national or outside bodies. If Helen Mankin had once been viciously hounded, then the ripe rhetoric directed at Arnall and Thompson had probably fallen within the accepted bounds of southern oratory. There was little political need to continue the witch-hunt. In 1949 the words 'Herman wants it' were enough to speed most bills through the legislature, but the administration did not show much inclination to abet the anti-red bills that patriots had introduced, such as a proposal to designate as a public nuisance any building in which 'subversive organizations' met. But if not willing to launch a crusade, the Talmadge group did want to reinforce their citadel of white supremacy. A measure close to Herman Talmadge's heart was a constitutional amendment to extend the county-unit system to the general election, since the need for further curbs on urban and African American votes had been highlighted by the outlawing of the all-white primary, and by the Mankin affair. The legislature duly endorsed the proposal, Clinch County's redoubtable representative Iris Blitch describing it as another weapon to resist the 'communistic' trend which threatened American life. As it happened, Talmadge failed to persuade the voters to ratify the amendment in the subsequent referendum. The Talmadge faction may have controlled the levers of power, but the popular bases of its support were relatively narrow.[2]

There were patriots in Georgia who wanted more than the county-unit system as a shield against communism. The local branches of the American Legion and other veterans' groups were lobbying for a loyalty oath, and the Talmadge administration was willing enough to endorse a symbolic measure of this kind. Senator Spence Grayson of Savannah gladly took charge of a bill requiring a loyalty oath and an explicit disclaimer of CP membership or sympathy from all public employees, and with the support of the Talmadge forces it passed both houses of the legislature with no votes recorded against it. It would have been fiercely resisted in many states. The 'people of Georgia and the real Anglo-Saxon' of the state, explained Grayson, 'believe there is no room in this country for Communism or any other ism'. Herman Talmadge proudly became the first citizen to sign the oath and promptly directed all state employees to do likewise or leave the payroll. Unfortunately the wording required takers to be citizens of the state, and not all public employees were. Quite apart from residents of adjacent states, there were four foreign doctors at the Battery State Hospital whose services were needed for several hundred tubercular patients. Talmadge resolved the embarrassment rather arbitrarily by directing changes in the wording of the law that had already passed. However messily, Georgia had added to her protection against the red menace, although the casualness of the episode was also illustrated a few years later when it was discovered that the new version had been widely overlooked when officials took the oath of office. What was revealing was the absence of perceptible opposition to the loyalty oath, even less than there had been for the 1935 teachers' oath. Even the Atlanta Civil Liberties Committee contented itself with issuing a statement against loyalty oaths rather than challenging the Georgia oath in the courts. A University of Georgia professor later commented that there was 'no tradition of protest in this sort of matter'. The anticommunist consensus in Georgia, to which the liberal community had recently been demonstrating its commitment, left little purchase for dissent.[3]

The weak civil liberties groups in the state were more disturbed by physical attacks on African Americans and by the revitalization of the Klan than by the loyalty oath. A recent Klan parade outside Atlanta which included several uniformed policemen had occasioned particular outrage. Klan opponents called for an 'anti-mask' bill, that is a law prohibiting the use of masks and hoods in public, but the Talmadge ascendancy in the legislature ensured that the bill was buried. In 1949 the US Attorney General added the Association of Georgia Klans to his List of Subversive Organizations, and even in states like Alabama, Virginia and Florida the governors spoke out against the Klan. Governor Talmadge remained silent, and Samuel Green boasted of the multiplication of Klaverns. Talmadge represented communism as the greater threat. 'We in Georgia', he told a gathering of farm boys and girls in the summer, 'as well as the right-thinking people of our whole country are engaged in a real fight to prevent the infiltration of evil and Communistic doctrines, which have as their aim the destruction of our American way of life.' This was becoming a favourite Talmadge theme. On another occasion he called for 'an aggressive fight against the dissemination of communist doctrines into the schools and colleges of the country'.[4]

Outside the governor's office the fight for an anti-mask law continued, and was joined by several church groups and such respectable organizations as the Georgia Junior Chamber of Commerce and the American Legion. When the legislature convened again early in 1950 the issue was stormily debated, but for the first time a majority of house members voted in favour of the anti-mask bill. The required two-thirds majority, however, proved elusive without the support of the Talmadge forces. Even as veterans and businessmen denounced the Klan, the governor preferred to take refuge in anticommunist rhetoric.[5]

But rhetoric it was. A red scare was not on the administration's agenda, at least not before the outbreak of the Korean War in the summer of 1950 intensified pressures throughout the country for a prohibition of the CP. In the Deep South it was the city of Birmingham, Alabama, which responded most spectacularly, as Police Commissioner Eugene 'Bull' Connor ordered his men to arrest local Communists. Two CP officials were sent to gaol for vagrancy, the weeping judge explaining that he had just been told that 'the first Birmingham boy has been killed in Korea', and soon after the city council legitimized Bull Connor's crusade with an ordinance requiring CP members to leave town. The publicity accorded the Birmingham example sparked demands for similar programmes in other southern cities. The Atlanta council considered but retreated from a Birmingham-style prohibition, which seemed unconstitutional and impracticable, and – over some protests – settled for a resolution condemning communism, and advising citizens and the police to report any disloyal behaviour to the FBI. Macon followed the Birmingham example of ordering Communists out of town, despite its mayor's constitutional reservations.[6]

Pressures on the state's political leadership to do something about domestic communism were increasing. James C. Davis, for example, was bombarded with letters from constituents urging draconian action against Communists as 'traitors to our Country'. The American Legion called for state legislation to outlaw the CP, and representative Luther Alverson of Fulton County promised such a bill at the next session, believing that 'a special measure is needed to smoke out the Red influence that we see around us'. The State Democratic Convention endorsed the proposal. At first the Talmadge administration seemed only too eager to oblige. 'I hope we can run every Communist out of Georgia', said Herman Talmadge while explaining that state action was necessary because the recent federal Internal Security Act did not go far enough. 'If we can't run them out of the state I want to run them in the penitentiary.' As it prepared for the new legislative session the governor's office sought a copy of the Australian law against the CP, thinking it looked 'rather severe and stronger' than the McCarran Act.[7]

Yet once again a red scare failed to ignite in Georgia. The governor's office lost interest in a communist-control programme and, while Herman Talmadge's annual address to the legislature paid tribute to the young men in Korea 'pitted in battle against Communistic forces who know no God', it proposed no specific action for Georgia beyond improvement to the educational system. Like other states, Georgia acceded to the presidential request to strengthen its civil defences, but otherwise there was no attempt to curb Communists. CP activity in the state was in fact declining. The FBI reported only 83 CP members, and in 1950 Homer Chase left the state; by 1951 there was little formal CP activity left in Atlanta. Perhaps too the administration's attention was being distracted by the continued civil liberties campaign against the Ku Klux Klan, for the Talmadge forces finally threw their weight behind the anti-mask bill. It sailed through the legislature with but one negative vote, a victory, as the *Atlanta Journal* expressed it, for 'the religious and civic groups, the newspapers, and, in general, the thousands of respectable citizens who for years have been waging a relentless fight against the Klan'. While other states were enacting communist-control programmes, Georgia was legislating against the Klan, arguably a testimony to the rationality of her political leaders.[8]

There was one politician whose impetuosity over the red menace could not be restrained; he was not a member of the administration but chair of a legislative committee. In 1951 the legislature created a committee to investigate the state welfare department, which, among other things, was suspected of the crime of 'bureaucracy'. It was chaired by Miller County's Bush Mims, who was greatly disturbed to find that the child welfare chief, Loretto Chappell, had once signed a petition favouring the FEPC. Mims's suspicions deepened when he discovered that the welfare department's library contained such books as the *New Russian Primer* and worse, John Dollard's *Class and Caste in a Southern Town*. Summoning Miss Chappell before his committee, Mims suddenly asked 'Are you a Communist?' Chappell, the 55-year-old daughter of a women's college president, consistently denied being a Communist or fellow traveller, explained that she had signed the FEPC petition as 'a private citizen', and charged Mims with trying to destroy the department's merit system. But Mims was not to be quieted. The 'fundamental purpose' of the CP in the South, he insisted, was to break down the race barriers and

'She is going along with this plan'. He could only question her
loyalty 'to the state in which she lives, to the ideals of the section
in which she lives, and to the traditions of the section in which she
lives'. Mims's attack on Loretto Chappell suited the State Welfare
Director, who thought her uncooperative and tried to fire her,
though she eventually resigned. Mims for his part called for a
state loyalty oath for employees to pledge loyalty to racial segregation. His committee reported on the deplorable 'bureaucracy'
of the welfare department, found other employees 'afflicted with
ideas not exactly in keeping with democratic and Southern
principles', and urged the establishment of a 'watchdog'
committee that would further investigate 'the "pink-minded"
persons employed in the state government'. Mims's intemperate
campaign, however, drew criticism from civic bodies and responsible newspapers, and the legislative leadership quashed his
request to renew the committee and buried its recommendations.
For the moment the state's rulers did not want a little McCarthy
on the loose. In the early 1950s they were behaving with
admirable restraint.[9]

As the Korean War was being waged, the state of Georgia
proved more resistant than many to red scare pressures. Georgia
newspapers faithfully reported on the course of the war and on
national Communist controversies such as the federal Smith Act
prosecutions, but these were not matters that greatly agitated the
state's political waters. Veterans and patriots might call for
displays of chauvinism, but alarmists like Bush Mims failed to
secure the influence that, say, Jack Tenney had once won in
California. In 1952 the legislature did accede to a DAR request to
encourage high schools to strengthen the teaching of American
history, so that children would be 'indoctrinated with the ideals of
democracy' in order to frustrate the 'subversive ideas ... being
conveyed ... through our educational system'. This was a period
when there was a significant lobby for educational reform (though
not integration), and one of the accomplishments of the Talmadge
administration was better funding for the schools. A fusing of
anticommunist with educational objectives, rather than chartering
a red hunt, seemed a sign of responsible government.[10]

Communist controls enacted

The mood began to change in 1953. In that year, lagging distinctly behind such states as Maryland, California, New York, Michigan, and Kansas, the reputedly reactionary state of Georgia finally adopted a fairly comprehensive communist-control programme. Somewhat unusually too the programme had its critics, largely because it did threaten citizens of Georgia, and a few of them were to fall early victims of it.

Early in the year two anticommunist measures were introduced into the lower house of the legislature, one, by Marson J. Dunaway Jr, calling for a little HUAC, the other, by James H. ('Sloppy') Floyd, aiming to outlaw subversive activities and to provide for the screening of all state employees. The two were seen as rival measures but the Dunaway proposal incurred the greater unease. The minority (or anti-Talmadge) leader in the house, John Greer, warned against 'abridging free speech', adding 'We don't want to do any witch-hunting'. Herman Talmadge and the legislative leaders put their weight behind the Floyd proposal and Dunaway withdrew his resolution. After some years of official complacency about the red menace in Georgia the state authorities were addressing the issue. Little had happened inside the state to account for this change of attitude, but it was known that the US Supreme Court was considering moving against segregation in the *Brown* case.[11]

The Floyd bill was quite far-ranging. Patterned initially after Maryland's Ober Law, it sought to make it a crime to be a member of any subversive group and directed the governor to appoint a special attorney general to investigate subversion. Floyd believed that this would deliver on the Democratic convention's 1950 promise to outlaw the CP. Less disturbing than the Dunaway proposal for a little HUAC, the Floyd bill nonetheless did trigger some apprehensions. For the first time in the state, an anticommunist measure stimulated extensive debate, both inside and outside the legislature, although, in keeping with the anticommunist consensus, no one denied the need for some kind of communist-control law. One of the groups most critical of the Floyd bill was the United Church Women of Atlanta (evangelical

Protestants who worked 'across denominational lines for Christianity'), which wanted it amended rather than defeated, a line also taken by the *Atlanta Journal* and other newspapers. The Mayor of Atlanta, the Junior Chamber of Commerce and the League of Women Voters were also said to be 'not publicly but nonetheless surely' expressing their unhappiness in political circles. Inside the legislature the chief critic was Atlanta's Senator G. Everett Millican, although he too eventually voted for the bill. The fractious debate in Georgia was conducted within a broad consensus.[12]

One fear expressed about the Floyd bill, by no less a patriotic body than the American Legion, was that it duplicated existing legislation. Others feared that it could be used indiscriminately against political adversaries. The ACLU's Atlanta correspondent believed that the bill 'could be a vehicle protecting an unscrupulous governor or attorney general in character assassination against political enemies'. The United Church Women agreed that the bill was 'extremely dangerous' in its vulnerability to abuse, and the Active Voters League, an Atlanta civic group, thought it a 'dangerous bill' giving the state government 'the power to smear good Georgia citizens and their political opponents'. Millican pointed to the vagueness of a clause which would make 'other unlawful acts' punishable and to the lack of an adequate definition of a subversive organization. One answer to the last point would be to list the proscribed organizations, perhaps by adopting the US Attorney General's celebrated list, an idea which met with a cool reception in Georgia because that list included the Ku Klux Klan. The state's leaders had reluctantly bowed to the pressures for an anti-mask law but they were not prepared to ban the Klan outright. (One supporter of the Floyd bill, Iris Blitch, when asked whether the Klan should be listed as a subversive organization, explained that she did not know what the Klan stood for since no one in her family had ever been a member. The same logic, apparently, did not apply to the C.P.)[13]

Senator Iris Blitch was one of those responsible for deepening the unease over the bill. She identified the chief opposition with the Active Voters League, which included some 'misled' people, whom she proceeded to name, charging them with having been members of organizations exposed by HUAC as subversive. Her hit list included the president and professors of Atlanta

University; their chief offence was to have been associated with SCHW. She further charged that Communists had infiltrated civic and church groups in Georgia (including the controversial Methodist Federation for Social Action). 'We send our boys abroad to shed their blood in a fight against communism', she said, 'while we should wake up at home.' This McCarthyite outburst attracted wide attention.[14]

The bill's sponsors sought to allay the fears of its critics. Some modifications were made and the former chairman of HUAC, Georgia's respected John S. Wood, was called on to testify that the bill did not conflict with federal agencies and that it would 'serve to strengthen the common defense against communism'. The Talmadge faction tried to make clear its own commitment to responsible government. 'I, as governor, will not advocate the harassment of any individual with this new legislation', promised Talmadge. 'If I have anything to do with it', said Attorney General Eugene Cook, 'there will be no witch-hunts.' In the event, the bill passed both the senate and the house without a single negative vote, although Senator Millican indicated his intention to try to amend it in the next session. As was the case in many states with such bills, what eased the passage of the Floyd bill was the reluctance of lawmakers to be seen to be opposing it. A *Macon News* columnist revealed that a legislator had told him 'It is a damn fool stunt but I am going to vote for it', explaining that 'I'm afraid to vote against it. I'm afraid to even question it. I'm afraid to even be quoted about it.' Governor Talmadge quickly signed Sloppy Floyd's bill into law: 'If other states will follow suit now, we'll clean up this mess.' He argued that 'when we are fighting a war against communism abroad it is vitally necessary that our local governments ... weed out those who would undermine our lawful institutions at home.'[15]

The assurances of the political leadership that there would be no witch-hunt carried some plausibility because a claim of the Ober model was that it allowed little scope for demagoguery and put responsibility in the hands of professional lawyers. The young Lamar W. Sizemore was appointed as the special assistant attorney general to investigate subversion. The state authorities appear to have left Sizemore to his own devices, but he took his duties seriously, assuming office with the promise to confer with the FBI and with similar state programmes elsewhere, and hiring a former FBI agent to assist him. About six months later he produced a report which conceded that there was no widespread activity in the state, but which did speak of 'fellow travelers, Communist sympathizers and some former Communists', 'some of whom are in positions of high authority'. This disturbing intelligence prompted Herman Talmadge to call for a state un-American activities committee, and he seemed on the point of launching a red hunt in Georgia. But cooler counsels prevailed. He drew back, scrapped his proposal for a little HUAC, and explained that he had just learned that a congressional committee was to conduct hearings in the South and that there was little point in duplicating the process. This was ironic given that the Talmadge faction had earlier argued for the Floyd bill in terms of the need to preserve state over federal prerogatives, and the real reason for Talmadge's hesitation was probably the way Sizemore's investigation was taking him into the university system. The files on four professors had been forwarded to the state board of regents, evoking complaints from academics and memories of the ruinous confrontation with educators that had cost the elder Talmadge the governorship. By this date too the Talmadge circle was making contingency plans for the anticipated Supreme Court *Brown* decision, and it was no time to make enemies unnecessarily. One professor did resign, albeit protesting his innocence.[16]

Talmadge acknowledged that Sizemore's findings were 'disturbing', and he assured the legislature that the state had been making 'earnest effort' to free the public payroll of 'any Communists, fellow-travelers, or disloyal persons'. But because of the recent 'revelations' in the university system he thought it vital that the state introduce 'a sane and constructive loyalty program' to guarantee that all state employees were '100% loyal Americans'. No probe was necessary, he now reassured his fellow Georgians, and he recommended the simpler alternative of an amendment to the Floyd Act requiring the execution under oath of a question-naire similar to that required of federal employees. In order to defuse a sensitive situation, Talmadge was prepared to follow a federal example.[17]

The legislative leadership moved swiftly on the proposal, stirred by the scent of red professors. In the senate both Iris Blitch and Everett Millican complained about the laxity of the university system and strongly endorsed the call for tighter

Communist controls. Mrs Blitch, evidently assuming that no true Georgian could possibly be a subversive, assured her colleagues that persons 'found suspect' would soon be leaving the state. House floor leader Frank Twitty also cited Sizemore's findings that there were at least four persons on the campuses with 'Communist leanings' as a reason for action. The principal suspect campus was the black Atlanta University, as Mrs Blitch's outburst earlier in the year had made clear, but the University of Georgia was also giving legislators concern, particularly when the student newspaper the *Red and Black* expressed some sympathy for desegregation. The arch-segregationist Roy V. Harris – a power in the state and an influential member of the board of regents – used his newspaper to rage against 'those little sissy boys' who should be 'made to play football'. He insisted that 'the time has come to clean out all of these institutions of all Communist influences and the crazy idea of mixing and mingling of the races which was sponsored in this country by the Communist Party'. Harris's intemperance caught the attention of the national press, but the harried student editors resigned. The legislature meanwhile amended the law as requested, without a dissenting vote. The centrepiece of the legislation was a lengthy questionnaire about activities and affiliations to be filled out under oath by all public employees, including teachers. The real reason for it, in the mind of one University of Georgia academic, was 'to hound' dissenters from the state: 'the present administration ... and other powerful groups are out to get all honest liberals who deviate from the "Talmadge Party Line".'[18]

Teachers in particular were uneasy about the revised law, voicing greater concern than they had over the original Floyd Act. The Georgia Education Association led the attack and won the support of some major newspapers, objecting to two features, first, the so-called 'informer' provision requiring the subject to say whether any family member had been in a subversive organization (something not in the federal loyalty programme), and second, the proposal to set up centralized files of completed questionnaires to which high-placed politicians might have access. (In Michigan a centralized file in the attorney general's office had been seen as protective of civil liberties, at least as opposed to a system under police control.) The security questionnaire was certainly an intrusive and rather impracticable document, requiring employees to list 'all' groups they had ever joined and to name any family members who had ever belonged to an organization on a given list, a list which included the Progressive party, the SCHW, and, for balance, the Ku Klux Klan. The moderate *Atlanta Journal*, drawing attention to the witch-hunting potential, recalled that the state loyalty programme had originally been devised as an alternative to a little HUAC. Governor Talmadge, ever pragmatic, bowed to the pressure and ordered the 'informer' clause removed from the questionnaire, an instruction that was later found to have been only imperfectly executed. Assistant Attorney General Sizemore defended the questionnaire and claimed that 'one man in the university system' had been 'a party organizer for years', arguing that the best way to fight Communists was to keep them off the public payroll. It was later reported that a professor who lost his job because of the questionnaire did so because he had falsely claimed to be married once rather than four times.[19]

By the end of the Korean War the state had finally equipped itself with a communist-control programme. The loyalties of public employees were to be interrogated via the questionnaire and the assistant attorney general was to investigate suspected cases of subversion. Yet this officer failed to unearth much, and the questionnaire appears to have been introduced at least in part in order to make active probes redundant. Little more was heard from the assistant attorney general's office. By the winter of 1953–4 the Talmadge administration was readying another weapon for the fight against communism.

Preserving segregation
Dominating the minds of Georgia's politicians towards the end of 1953 was the impending Supreme Court decision in the *Brown* case. In the summer the Court had asked for further argument about the compatibility of segregation with the Constitution, which, set against earlier decisions, clearly signalled the direction it was taking. Alarm bells rang across the South, and a number of states contemplated preventive action, Georgia being one of the first to act. Talmadge reconvened the legislature and it was this session that tightened the communist-control law, part of the larger strategy to build a barrier against outside influences. The political elite's first priority was to preserve segregated schooling,

and to this end it advanced a two-pronged plan. One proposal was for a constitutional amendment to allow the state to abolish the public school system and replace it with grants for education in private schools. The other established the Georgia Commission on Education (GCE), comprising some of the state's weightiest figures, and instructed it to study ways of preserving separate schooling. Piloted by Talmadge's floor managers, the two measures sped through both houses with little opposition. The Talmadge newspaper, *The Statesman*, bracketed the creation of the GCE with the strengthening of the Floyd Anti-Subversion Act as the main accomplishments of the second legislative session of 1953. More symbolic was a resolution designating May 1st as 'Loyalty Day' in order to rebuff the 'godless hordes of socialism'. To the guardians of the Solid South these various measures cohered, for resisting integration meant resisting subversion and the GCE soon began to function as the state's own un-American activities agency. It was to become central to Georgia's developing strategy of massive resistance. In the 1940s anticommunism had been used against radicals and black activists; it was now to be deployed more generally against white and black dissenters from the state's segregationist policies.[20]

As the state's political leaders contemplated ways of preserving school segregation, well-publicized congressional episodes early in 1954 brought reminders of the threat of red subversion. In March Senator James Eastland of the Senate Internal Security Subcommittee led a one-man visitation to New Orleans to investigate the Southern Conference Educational Fund, and the hearings implicated a number of prominent southern liberals in the Communist conspiracy. The incompetence of the probe limited its damage, but once again the loyalty of southerners sympathetic to integration had been impugned. But increasingly commanding the headlines in the spring of 1954 were the Army–McCarthy hearings. Georgia's segregationists identified with the now-beleaguered Wisconsin senator. Roy Harris warned that if Americans 'crucify' McCarthy as they had done Martin Dies then the 'ghost of Communism will rise to haunt Eisenhower and all these peanut officials in Washington who are joining up with the howling mob today'. Governor Talmadge justified McCarthy's methods by arguing that they were the only ones being applied against communism. 'In the vacuum left by inactivity, the controversial McCarthy has stood almost alone in a constant, active fight against the menace', he said, suggesting that the inactive were diverting attention from their negligence by attacking the heroic senator. Even after Vice President Nixon had publicly repudiated McCarthy, Talmadge refrained from doing so. Talmadge and McCarthy had common enemies in the defenders of civil liberties, whose remonstrations they could always dismiss as Communist-inspired.[21]

If segregationists were looking for evidence that the Communist conspiracy had penetrated Washington, proof for many came with the Supreme Court's *Brown* decision. Politicians and the press throughout Georgia vehemently denounced the ruling. An extreme reaction was offered by the *Morgan County News*, which proposed that it would be best for 'the personal safety and liberty' of both races if 'a strong and well armed' Ku Klux Klan were organized, a strategy that had worked when 'the Yankees invaded the South before'. Civil rights bodies that welcomed the Court's decision were subjected to intensified racist pressure. Roy Harris's *Augusta Courier* launched a furious assault on the Southern Regional Council, a reformist organization centred on Atlanta. After 'a thorough and searching study', it concluded that the council was 'a haven for known communist fronters and could well become the Communist Party apparatus in the South'. Segregationist papers obligingly repeated the charges, and the SRC was forced to express its opposition to 'all that Communism stands for'. White grassroots sentiment on *Brown* for the most part echoed that of the political elite. When liberal groups like the United Church Women saw some virtue in integration, other citizens exploded. One wrote to ask the GCE 'Isn't the break down of the white race the treasured goal of the communist?' Another predicted that desegregation would be followed by the legalization of miscegenation: 'It is my honest opinion that the Communists are working to destroy our churches, and schools, then they will have America.' Grady Fowler of Lagrange announced the launching of a Citizens Crusade to persuade the Christian churches to become petitioners in counter suits against school integration. 'In crusading, I will remain conscious of being only two jumps ahead of State Communism for the future of our country', he promised; '... this move to amalgamate the races of God is designed to prepare social ground for the deadly system hated by God.' The political leadership's attempts to identify integration with atheistic communism was touching a vibrant chord in a state in which fundamentalist religion remained strong.[22]

The administration was determined to find a way of preserving segregated schooling. The GCE, under executive director Durwood T. Pye, an Atlanta attorney, canvassed parents and teachers' groups and others for ideas on how best to effect this. 'The Communists and their dupes are on the march', Pye told one correspondent: 'It is their purpose to destroy all standards set by the present organization of our society and all standards set by laws such as those providing for separate education.' The Commission joined in the Talmadge campaign to persuade the voters to approve the constitutional amendment privatizing the schools, reportedly sending out some 90 000 pieces of literature. In November 1954 the electorate duly approved the amendment, albeit by rather a narrow vote, the rural counties supporting it most strongly.[23]

The electorate more clearly endorsed segregation in the gubernatorial campaign. Herman Talmadge was unable to succeed himself, and he gave his unofficial blessing to Lieutenant Governor Marvin Griffin, who ran against the 'meddlers, demagogues, race baiters and Communists' who were out to destroy states' rights. But Talmadge's personal popularity and the widespread fury over *Brown* had established the clear dominance of the Talmadge faction, from which a number of eager candidates emerged to claim the crown. The wilting anti-Talmadge camp was also divided, and in a campaign dominated by the segregation issue the only pro-*Brown* stand was taken by a Sunday school teacher. She finished last in a field of nine, while Griffin finished an easy first, with nearly 75 per cent of the county-unit ballots. For the rest of the decade Georgia politics remained a scene of confusing rivalry between segregationist politicians, divided more by personality than policy.[24]

The fusion of segregationism and anticommunism was symbolized when Marvin Griffin took the oath of office, pledging himself to 'the fundamental principles of patriotism'; a paragraph explicitly disavowing CP membership had been added to the oath taken by all officials, a feature required by the act of 1949 but widely overlooked until rediscovered during the anticommunist zeal of 1953. In his inaugural address Griffin defined one of the challenges before him as preserving 'our Georgia way of life' and promised to 'cooperate with veterans and other patriotic groups to make sure at all times there is no Communist infiltration in Georgia'. Communism was 'materialistic and atheistic' while Democracy was based on 'the humane teachings of the Christian tradition'. These musings were followed by a denunciation of the *Brown* decision, a 'tyranny' which 'must be resisted with every resource at our command'. Soon after Griffin urged the legis- lature to enact the measures recommended in the GCE report of December 1954, which had laid out draft laws designed to prohibit integrated public education and to underwrite private segregated schools. At Griffin's suggestion, the Commission's terms of reference were amended to require it to submit reports and drafts of legislation to every legislative session. The GCE was being turned into a major agency of the state government, and its remit was fundamentally to preserve white supremacy and Georgia's cherished traditions.[25]

The propaganda offensive

While the GCE canvassed opinion and framed laws designed to protect segregation, the state's political leaders determined on a propaganda campaign of unusual ferocity. In a political culture in which oratory held a respected position, propaganda seemed an appropriate weapon. Furthermore, in the absence of a large number of domestic dissidents (who might be subject to legal action), the power of persuasion remained one of the few resources of the leadership. By this date reformers such as Ellis Arnall and James V. Carmichael had effectively left the political stage, which was now dominated by aggressive racists such as Herman Talmadge (seeking election as US Senator in the upcoming 1956 race), his protégé Governor Marvin Griffin, Attorney General Eugene Cook, Atlanta Congressman James C. Davis, and the fabled intriguer Roy V. Harris. This was the group that put its considerable wits to the twin causes of resisting integration and exposing red subversion in Georgia in the mid- 1950s. Harris, Talmadge and Griffin also cooperated in September 1955 in founding the States' Rights Council of Georgia, the state's version of the citizens' councils that were spreading across the South.[26]

The first round in the propaganda war waged by these politicos had been launched by Roy Harris soon after the *Brown* judgment, when he used his newspaper to savage the Southern Regional Council, making much of its inheritance of functions from the suspect SCHW and of the 'fact' that it 'has consistently followed the Communist Party line as laid down for the South'. In 1955 Herman Talmadge contributed his two bits' worth, a short book entitled *You and Segregation*, which represented integration as a precursor of miscegenation and communism. Attorney General Eugene Cook decided to take on no less a body than the NAACP. By the fall of 1955 the state's senior law officer was engaged in an extraordinary confrontation with the country's leading civil rights organization.[27]

The NAACP had been the body to press the *Brown* case before the courts, and if it could be shown to be Moscow-directed, the process of desegregation would be wrecked. The Supreme Court itself in May 1955 virtually invited southern racists to obstruct integration with its signal to the states that implemention of the *Brown* decision might proceed cautiously. In July Eugene Cook proposed that public school teachers in Georgia be prohibited from membership of the NAACP. The state board of education demurred, but agreed that the teachers' loyalty oath should pledge them to refrain from 'indirectly subscribing to' any theory of 'social relations' contrary to state law. This did not satisfy Cook, whose suspicions of the NAACP were encouraged by the prominent black educator Dr J. W. Holley, a college president and advocate of separate development for African Americans and a one-time ally of Gene Talmadge. Holley wrote to Cook in August 1955 saying that the Rosenwald Foundation was 'spearheading' a drive to do away with segregation throughout the South, working through the National Council of Churches, the CIO, and the NAACP, which were 'putting into effect the seven points promulgated by the Communist Party in 1929'. He urged denying the NAACP any recognition, since nearly all its leaders had been 'given "citations" by communist front people and they are known to be putting into effect the seven points of Communism heretofore outlined'.[28]

So prompted, Cook spent 'many weeks' gathering information on the NAACP, with the assistance of the staffs of Congressman James C. Davis and of Senator James O. Eastland of Mississippi. The investigation left him in no doubt that 'the issue involved is not one of race but rather of subversion'. He shared this insight in

October with the Peace Officers Association of Georgia in an address subsequently published as *The Ugly Truth About The NAACP.* The 'ugly truth' that Cook had stumbled upon was that, wittingly or not, the NAACP was 'part and parcel of the Communist conspiracy to overthrow the democratic governments of this nation and its sovereign states'. In a manner reminiscent of Joe McCarthy and the congressional redhunting committees, Cook put on a display of research, offering 'authenticated details' and 'facts' which had been 'uncovered, checked, assembled and correlated'. Many of these 'facts', apparently culled in part from HUAC files, consisted of the suspect associations of the NAACP's founders and especially its current officers, presented to prove their 'Communist, Communist-front, fellow-traveling or subversive' sympathies. Cook further charged that the NAACP was being assisted in the South by three 'front' organizations, the Southern Conference Educational Fund, the SRC, and the Georgia Committee on Interracial Cooperation (a SCEF affiliate). All three were being currently investigated, he revealed, and he warned Georgia citizens to keep clear of them. 'On the basis of the evidence now in hand – a minute portion of which I have related to you this afternoon –' Cook told the law officers, 'no other conclusion can be drawn but that the NAACP is being used as a front and tool by subversive elements in this country.' Cook was soon elaborating on his charge against the NAACP, citing the Tenney Committee's notorious 1948 report as documenting the 'records of membership in or identification with known Communist Front organizations' of 30 of its leading officials, and obligingly cited their names and alleged suspect associations.[29]

Having created a sensation with his attack on the NAACP, Cook moved on to other bodies. He wanted to show that the SRC and the Georgia Committee on Interracial Cooperation were also Communist-led, and Congressman James C. Davis cooperatively obtained for him data from HUAC files on Dr George S. Mitchell and other officers of these groups. When redbaiting charges against the SRC were duly publicized in 1956, it felt obliged to secure a statement from the HUAC chairman attesting that it had never officially been cited as subversive. Jimmy Davis also helped the cause in other ways. He inserted into the *Congressional Record* a subsequently reprinted speech by Hugh G. Grant, vice president of the States' Rights Council of Georgia. This offered a variation on Cook's diatribe against the NAACP, 'the most powerful political pressure group in the United States'; a 1928 *Daily Worker* article was cited as proof that behind the NAACP 'are Communists and Communist-fronters, who see in this plot a means of destroying the American Republic from within'.[30]

Davis was also making speeches of his own. In 1956 the Supreme Court offended southern states' rights sensibilities even more with its *Nelson* decision, and in an address to the States' Rights Council of Georgia Davis called for resistance to the 'judicial dictatorship' to which the country was being subjected. 'The left-wing press ... together with all the left-wing organizations in the country', he said, including the Communists, were engaged in 'a massive campaign of super-brainwashing' to deify the Supreme Court. He told horror stories of incidents in integrated schools, and insisted that integration was but a step towards the NAACP's goal of 'intermarriage and complete mongrelization of the American people'. To Davis, the 'fact that this is also the identical aim of the Communist Party of the United States is more than just coincidental'. At the prompting of Governor Marvin Griffin, the GCE published this address in pamphlet form for wide distribution.[31]

Massive resistance

By 1956 the political elite's strategy of massive resistance was in place. Legislation had been enacted providing for the closing of public schools and their replacement by private schools should desegregation proceed, the anti-subversion programme had been strengthened, the well-staffed GCE was formulating plans and publishing analyses identifying integration as a Communist plot, and the state's leading politicians were urging their fellow citizens to stand fast against federal interference. In this atmosphere the Ku Klux Klan experienced a new surge of support. A cross-burning ritual at Stone Mountain in 1956 was celebrated by some 3500 Klansmen. In that year Herman Talmadge ran for the US Senate, for which he was opposed by his old moderate rival Melvin E. Thompson, but as Talmadge recalled, 'I carried every county in the state and ended his career.' One hostile newspaper predicted that with Talmadge in the Senate 'Talmadgeism and McCarthyism will appear somewhat synonymous'. The Talmadge forces for the moment seemed unstoppable, and Georgia was finally to experience its version of a red scare.[32]

12

THE RED SCARE AS LAST HURRAH, 1956–1966

Ostensibly at least the traditional political order stood fast in Georgia in the mid-1950s. The monopoly of the Democratic party had not been questioned, the legacy of white supremacy had not been dented by the few African Americans who had secured the vote, and the offices of state were commanded by conservative racists in the tradition of Eugene Talmadge. In some respects this citadel of the Deep South seemed even more solid than ten years earlier, for the reform element which had emerged with the New Deal had all but disappeared, while additional barriers had been erected against political change. Even the state's few bona fide Communists had vanished, while civil rights organizations could barely function.

But while the old guard had successfully fortified its redoubt in the decade after the Second World War, the society that it sought to defend was nonethelesss being eroded by changes from both within and without. Old Gene Talmadge's popular support had come largely from the 'wool hat boys' of the Georgia countryside, but the proportion of the population living in urban areas rose from just over a third in 1940 to over 55 per cent in 1960. This growing urbanization reflected an expansive economy, as low wages and anti-union laws attracted new businesses to the state and as federal military expenditures contributed to a consumer boom which magnified the service industries. The proportion of African Americans gradually declined as many left the state, while the number of skilled whites increased with economic diversification. The businessmen and middle-class professionals who were assuming strategic roles in Georgia's economy were not necessarily liberal on political issues, and many of them supported segregation, but they were not always entranced by the crude and folksy racism still deployed by the likes of Marvin Griffin, and they were sensitive to the image Georgia presented to the world. Entrepreneurial values were slowly displacing traditionalist values in Georgia's growing urban and metropolitan communities. Political styles were also changing. The vast crowds that had attended political rallies in the earlier part of the century were disappearing, as radio and television reached even into remote rural areas, and as campaigners adjusted their techniques to better educated and more urban voters.[1]

For years, the political establishment in Georgia was able to resist these demographic, economic and technological changes. The all-white primary, the county-unit system, and malapportionment of the legislature, had enabled a narrow and unrepresentative political elite to survive, and the racism and anticommunism of the postwar years had even served to solidify that elite. But the oratorical skills of the state's political leaders were not matched by organizational prowess. The Talmadge faction practised the politics of personality rather than of party machinery, and it had been personality – initially that of Gene Talmadge – that had been largely responsible for polarizing the state's Democrats. When that bifactionalism disintegrated in the mid-1950s, as a host of segregationists jockeyed for position, the party was left without an effective command structure. The GCE was perhaps intended to provide unified leadership, but as we shall see, it dissipated its authority. Further, the political structure sustaining the old guard was under attack from without. Southern Democrats did not enjoy quite the privileged position they once had in the national Democratic party, identified with northern and western cities and the labour and black votes within them. The all-white primary had been struck down by the Supreme Court in 1944, and the *Brown* decision of 1954 was imparting growing confidence to the national civil rights movement. Herman Talmadge and Marvin Griffin might, for the moment, cherish the 'Georgia way of life' and display a massive resistance to change, but the old political order was more vulnerable than its rhetoric allowed.

The old guard enjoyed its last hurrah in the second half of the 1950s. Using the linked causes of racism and anticommunism, the state's principal political leaders launched a massive crusade to discredit the instruments of change. The 'Georgia way of life' was projected as a sacred cause, and those bodies which pressed for integration – from the NAACP to the US Supreme Court – were mercilessly redbaited. These years witnessed Georgia's most vigorous resort to red scare politics. Yet, as always in the minds of southerners, subversion was essentially identified as the work of outsiders, and anticommunist passions were only rarely directed at persons within the state. The red scare in Georgia was more an exercise in propaganda than in persecution. By the early 1960s it had run its course. In part because of demographic, economic and other internal changes, as well as outside pressures, a more moderate variety of segregationist was coming to the fore, one less inclined to use red scare tactics to preserve an antiquated political order. Anticommunism had not disappeared, but its more crusading champions had been pushed to the fringes. Yet an emphasis on the powers of persuasion remained. Communism was to be combated in the classroom, although even there professional educators rather than politicians won control of the agenda. By the mid-1960s, anticommunist passions were more likely to erupt in Georgia than in most states, but only as ephemeral phenomena.

The Georgia Commission on Education
The Georgia Commission on Education was increasingly becoming the forum in which the state's conservative leadership conducted its propaganda campaign against integration – or 'subversion'. As the vanguard of the state's political fleet, the GCE was manned accordingly. Its ex officio membership included the governor, the lieutenant governor, the speaker of the house, and the attorney general (all stalwart segregationists) and such other prominent citizens as Roy Harris, the acknowledged master of the county-unit system.

At the beginning of 1957 Governor Marvin Griffin again asked the legislature for the enactment of bills drawn up by the GCE to further the design to maintain segregated schooling, but his most important proposal was aimed at strengthening the GCE itself.

This was to be done in two ways. First, the GCE was to be given the power to employ investigators, to hold hearings, and (vitally) to subpoena witnesses: it was being turned into a little HUAC. House floor leader W. Colbert Hawkins told the chamber that the GCE should have the power to ask such 'laudable' questions as whether a witness was a Communist or belonged to the NAACP. This invasion into 'private beliefs', as James A. Mackay put it, proved too much for four legislators from urban counties, who voted against the proposal, but it swept through. The second thrust of Griffin's plan was to extend the GCE's propaganda functions. It was to be empowered to take the 'Georgia story' to 'the people of the entire nation' by publishing its findings, so that 'the distorted views which have been presented by certain segments of the Northern press and other periodicals may be combatted'. One legislator, Arthur K. Bolton, resisted this proposal, not because of its objective but because it gave 'unlimited appropriations for printing'. This no doubt was the intention, and the GCE was duly accorded its licence to print propaganda.[2]

It was propaganda rather than serious investigation which interested the GCE, now directed by executive secretary T. V. Williams Jr, the young and ambitious son of Governor Griffin's fiercely segregationist state revenue director, T. V. Williams. Although the legislation of early 1957 empowered the GCE to conduct formal public inquiries, a hearings committee was not established until 1958 and it seems never to have met or issued a subpoena. But the GCE lost no time in vigorously promoting its Deep Southern views and in establishing contacts with other segregationist and anticommunist bodies. It did employ investigators to dig up information on bodies it wanted discredited, but through 1957 and the first half of 1958 the GCE functioned as the propaganda arm of Georgia's old guard, issuing a series of widely distributed pamphlets advancing the line that civil rights activity was synonymous with communism. The same argument was being peddled by the parallel private organization, the States' Rights Council of Georgia, which also published pamphlets (although it failed to distribute them effectively).[3]

The GCE did not need to do much investigating to mount a case against the NAACP, since Eugene Cook's office had already gathered the necessary material, which was mined to compile a list of the Communist fronts, so called, of which NAACP directors had been members. This exercise coincided with the hearings of the Louisiana Joint Legislative Committee in March, which Cook attended as Georgia's representative and at which he introduced this material. The GCE rushed it into print as *Ten Directors of the NAACP*, putting on public display the alleged Communist associations of such figures as Channing H. Tobias, Benjamin E. Mays, and Eleanor Roosevelt.[4]

Other publications followed. The legislative session which had extended the powers of the GCE had also called for impeachment proceedings against Chief Justice Earl Warren and Associate Justices Black, Reed, Frankfurter, Douglas and Clark, who were said to be 'carrying on a pro-communist racial-integration policy in violation of the Constitution of the United States, and usurping the powers and rights of the individual States'. By the summer of 1957 the GCE had produced a booklet publicizing this resolution and mailed it to newspapers throughout the country. As T. V. Williams Jr explained, 'instances of action on the part of the Supreme Court aiding subversive activities should be brought to the attention of the American people'. By the fall the GCE had also published pamphlets on race, the dangers of mixed schools, the evils attending school integration in Washington DC, and most famously, Tennessee's Highlander Folk School. It had also contemplated making a film on the 'Georgia Way of Life', though this was not effected. The literature was sent, often in bulk, to public figures and interested parties throughout the Union, the greatest demand coming from the South. At the end of 1957 it was reported that the GCE had mailed some 515 000 pieces of propaganda and was compiling a mailing list of 2 million opinion leaders. It was making the most of its blank cheque.[5]

It was the Highlander Folk School folder which attracted the greatest attention to the GCE. In the course of its suspicious surveillance of civil rights groups in Georgia, the GCE had remarked on the influence of the Highlander Folk School in Monteagle, Tennessee, a celebrated adult education centre with which many civil rights projects through the South had connections. Highlander was to hold its 25th anniversary celebrations during the 1957 Labor Day weekend, and the GCE despatched photographer Edwin Friend to register as a participant. This was an extraordinary act, a state legislative committee spying on an affair in a sister state. Friend returned with photographs featuring leading civil rights figures such as Martin Luther King Jr, Bayard Rustin, Aubrey Williams, Pete Seeger and others, as well as Georgia's notorious Don West, and also of another infiltrator, Abner Berry, who turned out to be a *Daily Worker* correspondent. The GCE rapidly produced a publication designed to look like a newspaper bearing the damning photographs and critical articles. The 'Communist Front Records' of the Highlander participants were cited at length, and several civil rights leaders were reported to have been trained at this 'Communist Training School'. Apart from the photographs of major civil rights activists with 'Communists' West and Berry, there were pictures of whites and blacks swimming and dancing together, the caption of one suggestively reading 'Both the day and night life at Highlander Folk School Labor Day Weekend Seminar were integrated in all respects'. This publication was dignified with the signature of the governor of Georgia as the GCE chairman.[6]

The state's segregationist elite believed that it had clinched the argument it had been vociferously advancing for the last few years. 'It behooves each of us to learn more of Communist infiltration and the direction of Communist movements', the GCE editorialized. Other organizations were invited to reproduce any part of the publication, and for years segregationists recycled the photographs, particularly one displaying the 'four horsemen' of racial agitation, namely Abner Berry, Martin Luther King Jr, Aubrey Williams and Highlander's co-founder Myles Horton. T. V. Williams Jr explained to the press that a Georgia agency had investigated a Tennessee group because it believed 'that racial strife and tensions are part of a Communist plan to subvert America'.[7]

The GCE was soon mailing out large numbers of the Highlander folder. Copies were sent to every daily and weekly newspaper in the United States, to other federal and state investigating committees, and to veterans' posts, patriotic groups, citizens' councils, and businessmen. The Commission was flooded with requests for more copies, sometimes for a thousand or more at a time, particularly after the magazine *Human Events* reported the Highlander affair on 26 October. Interest was strongest in other southern states and in California, although among those requesting copies were the American Legion of Illinois, the Conference of American Small Business Organizations, the New York ex-CP witness Bella Dodd, and the China Lobby's Alfred Kohlberg. The chairman of the Pasadena Anti-Communist League also asked for copies, and in return offered a receptive T. V. Williams Jr confidential information from police files relating to a morals charge against Bayard Rustin. So the anticommunist cause was furthered.[8]

The furore over Highlander stirred the *Atlanta Constitution* to make its own investigation, and it sent newsmen to attend a Thanksgiving Weekend workshop and reporter Jack Nelson to interview Myles Horton. The Nelson series of articles was much more restrained than the GCE exposé, relating both the old charges against Highlander and Horton's denials, but as the series progressed it became less friendly to the school, which was reported to have 'glorified' those African American students who had succeeded in enrolling in white schools, to have lost its tax exempt status because the Internal Revenue Service judged it to be 'a propaganda and political organization', and to have trained '40 or 50' Georgians for civil rights work in the preceding two years, many of them black and some students from Georgia Tech and Emory University. While the Nelson series did not substantiate the charge of communism, the GCE was sufficiently pleased to want to reprint and distribute it, though ultimately it failed to do so. At Roy Harris's insistence it did order a reprinting of another 300000 copies of its own Highlander pamphlet in January 1958, instructing that it be sent to 'every postoffice box and rural boxholder in Georgia'.[9]

The publicity brought by the Highlander affair allowed the GCE to add to its already extensive connections with other anticommunist and segregationist agencies. The potency of such bodies rested in part on their capacity to tap into a larger network. During the summer of 1957 Senator Herman Talmadge formally requested HUAC to keep the GCE supplied with all its publications, said to be 'essential' to its 'program of research and study'. The GCE also exchanged reports and information with the Senate Internal Security Subcommittee, offering its files and assisting in the preparation of SISS hearings at Memphis in October on Communist influence in the South, at which Don West was a prominent hostile witness. Similar relationships were established in 1957 with the California Fact-Finding Committee on Un-American Activities and the Louisiana Joint Legislative Committee to Maintain Segregation, and in 1958 with the Florida Legislation Investigation Committee. The GCE further established a mutually supportive relationship with Billy James Hargis's Christian Crusade, and in June 1958 such figures as Herman Talmadge and James C. Davis joined Senator Jenner, Martin Dies and others in a great anticommunist 'Spectacular' on an Atlanta radio station, organized by Hargis. The GCE also drew on resources closer to home. It liaised with the Georgia Bureau of Investigation, which reported to Attorney General and GCE member Eugene Cook, who in turn urged close scrutiny of CP activities on the Bureau. The GCE liaised too with the Georgia States' Rights Council, of which Roy Harris was a prominent member, and the executive secretaries of the two bodies exchanged information and even money. 'In the final analysis', wrote one of them to the other, 'we are fighting communism: it is waging a relentless world-wide struggle for domination of the minds of men', and Moscow had chosen the race issue in the South as 'our soft spot as far as attacking us is concerned'.[10]

These connections helped to supply the GCE with information for its great propaganda blitzkrieg, though from time to time it did launch its own investigations. In March 1957 the Louisiana Joint Legislative Committee held hearings designed to demonstrate that racial unrest was a Communist creation, and a principal witness was the ex-CP member Manning Johnson, who implicated the SRC as well as the NAACP in the red conspiracy. This prompted the SRC's old foe Eugene Cook to propose the circulation of transcripts of Johnson's testimony, since 'several Georgia groups' were involved, and Congressman James C. Davis in turn again procured information from HUAC files on SRC directors. The most damaging exposé of the SRC as it happened was published by the American Legion's *Firing Line*, using Johnson's dubious evidence, but the GCE republished and widely disseminated it. Also attracting the attention of the GCE was the Methodist church, which had a large following in Georgia but which was being embarrassed by the popular frontish activities of the unaffiliated Methodist Federation for Social Action. Could the Communists have found a way of seducing the God-fearing members of the Bible Belt? The GCE embarked on a remarkable scheme to compile a list of every Methodist minister in the country. T. V. Williams Jr was convinced of the 'magnitude' of the

'inroads of atheistic Communism in our churches'. He believed
the same of the nation's colleges, privately confiding to a
Congressman that the GCE was compiling a list of university
professors affiliated to Communist movements, which, he anticipated, would reach 5000 names. 'No greater access to the minds
of men exists than through the schools and churches', he mused,
observing that 'approximately 90%' of the membership of
Communist fronts had been educators and clergymen. One pair
of professors to catch the GCE's attention were Colus Johnson
and Carson Pritchard of West Georgia College, whose brainwashing techniques had included showing the film *The Ox Bow
Incident*, according to a local citizen who informed on them after
seeing the Highlander report. The success of the Highlander
investigation and the suspicion of liberal clergymen also
emboldened the GCE to send photographer Ed Friend to an
interracial meeting of the Georgia Council of Churches, from
which he emerged with yet further photographs. Marvin Griffin
promised that more such work would be found for Friend.[11]

Yet investigation remained less important to the GCE than
publicity and liaising with other anticommunist and segregationist bodies in a common front. As the GCE's propaganda
machine cranked up in 1957, the southern crisis deepened.
Georgia's political leaders were particularly disturbed by the
federal intervention in Little Rock, in which opinion had solid-
ified against integration after Marvin Griffin and Roy Harris had
visited the city to urge resistance. To Griffin the despatching of
paratroopers in late September was comparable to the military
rule of Reconstruction, and he blamed it on 'the Nixon–Adams
group' in the Republican party and the NAACP. Encouraged by
Griffin and Harris, the GCE explored ways of enhancing its
influence. Its officers were authorized to buy wiretapping
equipment and to extend their mailing lists, but after a row about
'gestapo' tactics Governor Griffin was obliged to disavow the
'overenthusiastic' wiretapping request. Early in 1958 the GCE
discussed at length the idea of placing advertisements in the
northern press to make clear Georgia's immovable stand on
segregation, though this was shelved on the advice of Senators
Talmadge and Russell, who feared its impact on the congressional
civil rights debate. Harris, however, kept returning to the idea,
especially after the Louisiana Joint Legislative Committee had

won widespread attention with a full-page notice in the *New York Herald Tribune*, ingeniously arguing that segregation was part of that pluralist tradition which had enabled liberty to flourish in the United States. As the GCE weighed such tactics, its facilities were used to reprint and distribute thousands of copies of racist diatribes by James C. Davis.[12]

The GCE's most important production of 1958 was a pamphlet entitled *Communism in the NAACP*, offering yet more material on the suspect connections of that organization's leaders and based largely on the testimony given by the celebrated 'authority' Dr J. B. Matthews to the Florida Legislation Investigation Committee. (At one point the GCE sent an agent to Florida to prompt the authorities there in their probe of the NAACP, apparently with the aid of funds from the States' Rights Council.) This publication triggered an enormous response. The demand for copies was comparable to that for the Highlander folder, and requests poured in from southern law offices, American Legion posts, church and business groups, and even the University of Illinois. The two-volume pamphlet marked the consummation of the state's war against the NAACP. Eugene Cook's sensational exposé in 1955 had been followed in 1956 by action by the state revenue commissioner, T. V. Williams (the father of the GCE's executive secretary), who had obtained a court order to force the NAACP to produce its records to see whether it was subject to state income tax. A refusal to produce such records had resulted in Judge Durwood T. Pye (former GCE executive secretary) holding the NAACP in contempt, imposing a fine of $25000, and giving the Atlanta chapter president a suspended prison sentence. Pye and his fellow judges obstructed the NAACP's attempt to appeal, and the matter was still unresolved by June 1959, when Eugene Cook declared that 'no institution in America is more un-American, defiant and ruthless than the NAACP' and vowed that as long as he remained attorney general the NAACP 'will be a prime legal target of mine'. While Georgia was not as successful as Alabama in putting the NAACP out of action, the state's political elite had coordinated a sustained and damaging campaign against it, and had been central to the endeavour to represent it as part of the Communist conspiracy.[13]

Outside the forum of the GCE too segregationist politicians seized every opportunity to broadcast warnings about Communist subversion. Eugene Cook arranged for New Hampshire's attorney general, Louis Wyman, noted for his redhunting activities in his own state, to address the Georgia legislature in 1958. Wyman had previously been selected by Cook (president of the National Association of Attorneys General) to argue the *Nelson* case before the US Supreme Court. He obligingly told the Georgia legislators that the *Nelson* decision was 'Perhaps the most grievous invasion of States' Rights in this decade', and deplored the Court's weak stand against communism. Also addressing the lawmakers that year was Georgia Congressman Tic Forrester, prominent in the congressional fight against the 1957 civil rights bill, who told them that the destruction of states' rights had been the work of the CP, led by Jews from New York, where law had already crumbled to the point where 'the favorite indoor sport in the Brooklyn schools is the rape of 13- and 14-year old white girls by members of the negro race, occasioned by the wild-eyed left-wingers mixing the schools'. The former president of the States' Rights Council, R. Carter Pittman, offered a more sophisticated message to a university club, analysing the voting records of Supreme Court judges to show their partiality to Communist litigants; Justices Warren, Black and Douglas, he reported, voted 'for the Communists and against America' in each case. The segregationist press duly popularized this interpretation. *The Southern American* argued that 'No one who has studied recent decisions of the Supreme Court can doubt for a moment that far-reaching influence of Communism upon its members.'[14]

The sustained campaign against outside influences at least meant that there was little in the public discourse in Georgia to focus concern on possible subversion inside the state. By July 1958 no one had been prosecuted under the Anti-Subversion Act of 1953, and probes were no longer conducted by an assistant attorney general, although the Georgia police maintained their security division. Ironically it was federal inquisitors who showed most interest in the state's subversive residents, HUAC itself, a rare federal agency with which the state authorities were prepared to cooperate. In the summer of 1958 HUAC was investigating communism in the South, and it stopped at Atlanta as a convenient regional headquarters. Governor Griffin welcomed the subcommittee and offered it any assistance, which presumably meant access to the state's own files on suspected subversives. An important witness at the hearings was the Massachusetts former

FBI undercover agent Armando Penha, who told the subcommittee that the CP had sent 'colonizers' into the textile industry in
the South. SCEF official Carl Braden and anti-HUAC activist
Frank Wilkinson were summoned to testify, and their refusal to
do so led to their indictment by an Atlanta grand jury and subsequent imprisonment. The subcommittee chairman, Edwin Willis
of Louisiana, closed the hearings with the warning that as
elsewhere in the country a 'pattern of Communist activities and
techniques' existed in the South. But the testimony did not clearly
identify a nest of local reds and the visitation did not trigger a
witch-hunt in the state. Georgia's guardians remained more
troubled by the prospect of external pressure than internal
subversion; the US Supreme Court was more likely to be harassed
as treasonably communistic than were local professors or trade
unionists.[15]

Massive resistance undermined

By 1958 fissures were beginning to appear in Georgia's defences
against communism and integration. The energetic propaganda
activities of the GCE and its partisans had for the last few years
served as a kind of patriotic smokescreen behind which the
staunch segregationists had hidden. But the absence of party discipline meant that there was little restraint on personal rivalries,
some leaders began to wonder whether the federal authorities
could be defied indefinitely, and the growing forces of modernization served to accentuate the anachronism of the old guard.

The extravagances of the GCE had not won universal applause,
even in Georgia, and the 1958 gubernatorial campaign was to
prove its undoing. The furore over its attempt to secure
wiretapping equipment in the fall of 1957 had weakened it, for it
became clear that this was an initiative of T. V. Williams Jr of
which most Commission members knew nothing, and Lieutenant
Governor S. Ernest Vandiver had warned against allowing the
GCE to become 'a state gestapo where intrigue and dangerous
tactics are substituted for sincerity, sound thinking and legal
procedure'. Vandiver was breaking with the Griffin administration, the honesty and competence of which became a major
issue in the 1958 campaign. Marvin Griffin could not succeed
himself, and more than one candidate emerged from the loose
Talmadge–Griffin camp. The favourite was Vandiver, who won

the support of Senators Talmadge and Russell and of Roy Harris, while Griffin remained formally neutral. Vandiver was a firm segregationist, but he and Griffin were at odds and some arch racists backed the candidacy of William T. Bodenhamer, a Baptist minister, legislator and former secretary of the States' Rights Council.

Throwing in their lot with Bodenhamer were the T. V. Williamses, father and son. T. V. Williams Jr had earlier been criticized by Vandiver for mismanaging the GCE, and Williams's segregationist zeal in any case probably took him naturally enough into the Bodenhamer camp. Governor Griffin directed that no departmental heads were to appear on platforms with gubernatorial candidates, but the visibility of the two Williamses in the Bodenhamer campaign led to charges that they were using their state offices for political purposes. Revenue Commissioner T. V. Williams was credited with masterminding Bodenhamer's highly racist campaign, and reportedly called Vandiver a 'weakling on segregation'. (Vandiver was obliged to commit himself to closing the schools to see Bodenhamer off.) T. V. Williams Jr's own aides complained that the GCE was being used to promote Bodenhamer's election (it distributed a campaign document with a fake picture of Vandiver posing between two African Americans), and two of them resigned in protest. The publicity produced outraged calls from the State Auditor and others for the abolition of the GCE, described by the *Atlanta Constitution* as having become 'merely a political arm of the governor and of the revenue commissioner', and forced the resignation of T. V. Williams Jr as executive secretary. A similar scandal soon overtook his father, whose employees in the revenue commission complained of being forced to contribute to Bodenhamer's campaign fund, and the senior Williams's resignation followed. The controversy over the GCE drew attention to its size, Governor Griffin expressing astonishment that it had as many as 11 employees – almost as many as his own office – and ordering their reduction to 5. T. V. Williams Jr was replaced as executive secretary with a Griffin aide, Paul Stevenson, who announced that he was going to bar political activity and return the GCE to its original function of preserving school segregation. He gave notice that he was abandoning the national propaganda campaigns favoured by his predecessor and that he would not place advertisements in northern newspapers: 'I don't think we ought to just pour money down a snake hole'.[16]

Vandiver's election – by an overwhelming margin – sealed the fate of the GCE. The exposure of its activities during the campaign had revealed that the full Commission had rarely met in the previous year and had raised questions about what it had accomplished, apart from disseminating vast amounts of segregationist propaganda. Vandiver was a conservative and a segregationist, but not a racist of the Bodenhamer stripe. He decided to abolish the 'ill-fated and battle-scarred' GCE and replace it with a Commission on Constitutional Government, designed to cooperate with similar agencies in other states. The legislature readily agreed, floor leader Senator Carl Sanders dismissing the GCE's work as 'gumshoeing, spying'. The new commission was charged with providing for 'the clear delineation between the general sovereignty of the States and the limited sovereignty of the Federal Government', a prescription which moved the issue from segregation to states' rights. Governor Vandiver did try to avert integration but, despite his campaign promise, was not prepared to go to the lengths of closing the schools. The Commission on Constitutional Government remained passive, and by the early 1960s the Vandiver administration was easing back from massive resistance.[17]

No less a figure than Herman Talmadge signalled that the old guard was accommodating itself to the modern world. In January 1959 he conceded to the US Senate that the *Brown* decision was 'an accomplished fact', and, however much he reviled it, only the Court itself or Congress or 'the people' could change it. In Atlanta and other large cities in particular there was a growing demand that education not be disrupted and that federal court rulings be respected. Former Governor Ellis Arnall insisted that the schools be kept open. Governor Vandiver searched for ways to preserve segregation, but he made no use of the old anticommunist rhetoric. In 1960 the legislature agreed to the creation of a new committee to study the school issue, which in due course recommended that the state abandon massive resistance and allow each local community to determine its own policy. The legislature accepted these recommendations in 1961 and token desegregation began.[18]

The painful retreat from massive resistance was a mark of Georgia's changing political culture. Urbanization and industrialization were continuing apace, creating a more variegated society and larger numbers of Georgians to whom economic progress mattered more than ancient tradition. When Atlanta itself moved toward desegregation, state leaders were virtually powerless to resist the process. More African Americans were being registered to vote and the Republican party was growing in size. One sign of the changing times in Atlanta came in 1962 when well-to-do white voters joined with blacks to replace James C. Davis with a progressive candidate in the Democratic primary. Pressure from the federal courts was chipping away at Georgia's political institutions as well as its school system. The county-unit system was under assault and in 1962 the Democratic party decided to conduct its gubernatorial primary instead on a popular vote basis. The hold of rural conservatives on the legislature was being broken too by reapportionment, precipitated by the Supreme Court's 1962 *Baker* v. *Carr* decision. In that year the racial moderate Carl Sanders was elected governor, defeating the unrepentant Marvin Griffin. This was not quite the end of red scare politics in Georgia, since the celebrated segregationist Lester Maddox made use of such tactics when he ran for governor in 1966, but the 1970 election of Jimmy Carter returned the state to sober hands.[19]

Taking the fight to the classroom

Georgia's political elite may have been abandoning the use of red scare techniques by the early 1960s, but they still avowed a duty to preserve the state's proud traditions and to combat communism by other means. Subversive ideas could be fought by patriotic ideas, and if subversion infiltrated from the outside, patriotism could be strengthened from within. The South could not stop change, perhaps, but it could see that the rising generation was schooled in American values. The state of Florida pointed the way with a 1961 law requiring the teaching of a high school course entitled 'Americanism vs Communism'. In Georgia a group of legislators from Chatham County pressed a similar measure in 1962. 'Our youth today can't fight what they can't understand', explained Representative Crawford. 'They wouldn't recognize communism if they were confronted with it.' Eventually the legislature passed a resolution (SR 105) enjoining on the educational authorities the need for a course on 'the principals [sic], traditions, advantages and institutions of representative democracy and free capitalism' and on 'why Communism and Socialism are evil and vicious ... and why they are our implacable enemy'. Adopted in what one journalist called 'a flurry of anticommunist zeal', many academics and schoolteachers regarded SR 105 with apprehension. As another columnist put it, the legislators had in effect laid 'open the schoolteachers of Georgia to all the bitter pressures and prejudices of the know nothing fringe which has been snuffling at the school house doors without, until now, being admitted'.[20]

Yet victory of a kind eventually went to the educators. They were obliged to ensure that schoolchildren learned something of democracy and communism, but they introduced the programme on their own terms. The university system itself had anticipated the politicians, sponsoring a seminar on the problem of teaching about the Soviet Union in 1961, and early in 1962 West Georgia College held a series of academic lectures on 'Communism and the Changing World'. One of the organizers was J. Carson Pritchard, who had once aroused the suspicions of the GCE. The state board of education adopted this model. It resisted the idea of a separate course on Americanism vs Communism and argued that the essential instruction could best be conveyed in existing history, social science, geography and other courses. It was decided to extend the experiment being tried on the campuses with a view to providing appropriate training for teachers. A number of campuses were to hold summer institutes or courses for schoolteachers on Conflicting Ideologies in a Changing World, and a detailed syllabus to guide the programme was drawn up, entitled 'Social Science Bulletin S. R. 105'. 'The syllabus is an appeal to the intellect, not to the emotions', explained the president of the Georgia Council for Social Studies. Five summer institutes and some Saturday seminars were held in 1962, considering such themes as the dynamics of the American economy and international communism. 'It is working', reported one teacher. 'Some states are teaching communism as a course by itself, and they're making an issue of it. I think our way is better.'[21]

The Georgia approach to the teaching of communism went some way toward defusing the issue, although the summer institutes varied in quality and did not reach large numbers of teachers. Some were hardly detached academic exercises. An institute at Georgia Southern College in 1963 included lectures by such figures as Cartha D. DeLoach of the FBI and Princess Catherine Caradja of the Romanian royal family. This particular course attracted 54 schoolteachers and was one of seven held that summer. Some officials worried about the small numbers and the underfunding of the programme, and the Georgia Junior Chamber of Commerce tried to drum up support for it. A state educational report in September 1963 spoke reassuringly of the provision of a teacher's guide which outlined 'the teaching and learning of American democracy, free enterprise, and the difference between a country under the control of a dictator and one that the people govern for themselves'. Georgia's teaching on communism may not have been value-free, but the educators had succeeded in implementing the legislative will in their own way, one which they believed did not seriously compromise academic freedom; there was little resistance to the programme from either teachers or local communities. But its reach was limited. The menace of domestic communism had ceased to be a political issue in Georgia.[22]

The last flickers of red scare politics

While the political complexion of Georgia took on a more moderate colouring in the 1960s, the old-style politicos did not disappear overnight and a red threat was periodically sighted. In 1962 Marvin Griffin returned to contest Carl Sanders in the gubernatorial election, and fought a racist campaign which depicted Sanders as the tool of the NAACP. Sanders emphasized the role of economic development in promoting a more harmonious future and, unencumbered by the county-unit system, won the election handsomely, faring particularly well in the metropolitan and medium urban counties. A variant of the old guard fared better in 1966, when in a confused gubernatorial race no candidate won an overall majority and the Democratic legislature unenthusiastically chose its party's unexpected nominee, the populistic Lester Maddox. Maddox proved to be less reactionary than anticipated, though his explanation for civil rights activity rested on an unlikely alliance between the 'big capitalists', their foundations and the 'Communists'. The common element in this confused image was again that of outside influence.[23]

Fiercely anticommunist bills were still being submitted to the legislature in the early 1960s, but, denied administration support, they failed to become law. What was instructive was the level of support some of them received. In Columbus, where the John Birch Society was said to be active, the city council had required shopkeepers selling products from Communist countries to display a sign reading 'Communist Made Products Sold Here', and an attempt in 1963 to extend this to the whole state won 97 votes in the house, a majority but not enough to pass. In March the house debated a resolution condemning the visit of four Russian churchmen to the state, its sponsors arguing that all Russian priests were CP agents, and it was defeated by the narrow margin of 79 votes to 69. Patriotic fury also erupted outside the legislature, especially when provoked by civil rights demonstrations. Roy V. Harris, for example, was still fulminating against the agents of change in his newspaper. Martin Luther King was charged with belonging to more Communist front organizations 'than any Communist in the United States'. The campaign led by Hosea Williams to desegregate Savannah in the summer of 1963 was not only 'Communist-inspired, Communist-tinged, Communist-supported and Communist-directed', according to Harris, but was also the work of 'trained outsiders' from New York.[24]

For a brief moment in the mid-1960s this ancient perspective regained some vitality. Since reapportionment African Americans had begun to appear in the General Assembly, and the dissolution of the old order was made even more unnervingly apparent in November 1965 when an Atlanta district elected the young black activist Julian Bond, a veteran of the 1960 sit-ins, and a local official of the Student Non-Violent Coordinating Committee. Bond's election horrified the conservative representatives of rural Georgia. In January 1966, after the national SNCC office had issued a statement condemning the Vietnam War, Bond sparked an explosion in Georgia by agreeing and saying that he 'admired the courage' of the young men who were burning draft cards. Even liberal whites recoiled, and the house refused to seat Bond by the overwhelming vote of 184 to 12, spurred by the oratory of Sloppy Floyd and Jones Lane. The legislators' patriotic fury brought anticommunist sentiments once more to the fore. Senator James Wesberry proposed a new loyalty oath for public employees, accompanied by pointed references to 'draft-card burners'. More strikingly, Representative Jim Westlake proposed the creation of a new un-American activities committee, citing

Atlanta as 'the world headquarters of at least several subversive groups'. At first it was dismissed as 'another one of those super-patriot bills that are introduced each year', but a groundswell of support suddenly developed, particularly among rural legislators, and within a week Westlake had secured 72 co-sponsors. Old foes of the federal government, including some of Marvin Griffin's followers, rallied to the patriotic cause. Disturbed moderates bemusedly warned against the revival of a 1950s witch-hunt, and the *Atlanta Constitution* observed that the 'biggest single impression being left of the 1966 Georgia Legislature is that of a loyalty policeman on a binge'. But by the end of January the patriotic moment was over. Governor Sanders and the legislative leadership signalled their opposition to the bill and sponsors trickled away, and the cause was not helped by the endorsement of the Ku Klux Klan. Eventually the house leaders consigned the bill to a slow committee death, despite Westlake's attempts to link civil rights activities to the CP. The new leadership had prevailed in its attempt to protect Georgia's image.[25]

In the meantime the remaining props of the old order were being dismantled. In 1965 some 165 faculty members, from both public and private colleges, filed a suit challenging the constitutionality of the state's loyalty oath, complaining that it served to chill 'open-minded inquiry'. The challenge provoked a modest public furore, as senior state officials and some of the press backed the oath. In a TV debate, Senator Wesberry admitted that the oath was probably unconstitutional, but that now with 'our boys laying down their lives in Viet Nam, this is a poor time to bring such a suit'. Two professors in public colleges who refused to sign while the case was still pending were struck off the payroll. The Chief Justice of Georgia was determined to fire anyone 'who has thus revealed a will to gamble on American liberty', and the American Legion state commander pointed out that thousands of officials had happily complied with the law, while 'the only objection to this oath comes from a small group of professors'. Even Governor Carl Sanders, in the wake of the Watts riot, defended the state's loyalty programme against 'outside agitators'.[26]

As usual it was the federal rather than the state courts which brought relief to the petitioners – they were rescued, it could be said, by outside influence. State officials were embarrassed when it was shown that the 'informer' clause in the questionnaire was still in use, although the legislature had repealed it in 1956. The dissenting professors expressed themselves willing to take an unambiguous oath to uphold the constitution, but objected to vague oaths and the use of the invasive questionnaire. A federal court under Griffin Bell agreed, ruling the state's loyalty oath unconstitutional though conceding that more precise wording might be acceptable. The state authorities reworded it where they could, and Wesberry introduced a revised oath into the 1966 legislature, but it never reached the statute books. So the loyalty programme was abandoned, or at least almost, for this was Georgia, and the state had always experienced difficulty both in implementing and in divesting itself of loyalty measures. Several state agencies did discontinue the practice, but in the late 1960s a modified oath and questionnaire (including a question on associations) were still in use in some offices. In 1972 state employee Allison Kitfield, on moving departments, was asked to disavow CP membership and to answer questions on her affiliations. She appealed to a federal court, which instructed the state to desist. Georgia was finally coming into line with the rest of the country.[27]

Conclusion

As in any state, anticommunist politics in Georgia both shared some characteristics with the larger red scare and had a distinctive history of their own. Perhaps the most distinguishing feature of the anticommunist persuasion in Georgia was the extent to which it was directed at forces external to the state. In California red scare tactics were deployed against members of the old popular front groups, in Michigan at liberal Democrats and industrial unionism, and in Massachusetts at the Ivy League colleges. Civil rights activists and integrationists in Georgia were of course subjected to abuse and worse, but there were virtually no Communists and little sense of an indigenous constituency under attack. The harassed local members of the NAACP were seen as the agents of a larger subversive body located primarily in New York and Washington. Disposed since at least the Civil War to assume that the enemies of the state's peculiar institutions were located beyond its borders, Georgia's political leaders were quick to identify any questioning of the status quo with outside interference, and communism was tailor-made for demonization as an alien scapegoat. This impulse to externalize the agents of change may have protected the state from severe internal convulsions; the forays of SISS and HUAC into the South, for example, did not spark local scares. Colouring the attitudes of white southerners towards the Communist Party was its early identification with the cause of African Americans.

For much of the period between the 1930s and the 1950s the attitude of the political leadership to the red menace was almost casual; loyalty oaths were adopted in 1935 and 1949 with relatively little debate or opposition, and a number of measures were only imperfectly implemented. Formally, almost everyone in Georgia accepted the need for some controls on communism, although liberals resented attempts to implicate civil rights groups in the Communist conspiracy. Measures which seemed more symbolic than substantive were enacted with little resistance, in part because of the weakness of civil liberties and related groups in Georgia, in part because such groups preferred to invest their limited political capital in resisting the Ku Klux Klan and racist brutality. The anticommunist consensus which obtained itself militated against a destructive red scare. Thus HUAC-style investigations and state prosecutions of radicals were rare. The relative absence of such official harassment, however, hardly made life in Georgia safe for dissidents. Progressive party activists, such Communists as there were, and civil rights workers were probably more at risk from vigilante and Klan behaviour than from official indictments. During Operation Dixie, CIO organizers were sometimes kidnapped and beaten. In 1948 five Progressive party workers were abducted from the home of a party organizer, and others were threatened with lynching. Through this period those African Americans who dared to assert their rights risked being flogged by vigilantes and local police officers. When the atmosphere of massive resistance came to permeate the state in 1956, Koinonia Farm, an integrated Christian community which had been allowed to flourish unharmed since the early 1940s, suddenly became subject to dynamite attacks.[28]

The primary function of red scare rhetoric in Georgia was to sustain the old power structure, that in particular represented by the Talmadge faction. Anticommunism alone, of course, does not explain the Talmadge 'restoration' in 1948 or the dominance of the faction for much of the 1950s. The county-unit system, malapportionment, and the exclusion of the great majority of African Americans from the ballot all helped to insulate the old guard from the changes that were taking place in the state. A belief in the separate development of the races and a resentment of northern interference served to unite many white Georgians behind the Talmadge strategy, whether or not they were moved by red scare rhetoric. But this rhetoric was among the means deployed to prop up an antiquated political system, serving to camouflage and legitimize its racism. The election of Ellis Arnall to the governorship in 1942 and the initial election of Helen Mankin to Congress in 1946 suggested that there was some possibility of progressive political formations in Georgia, but the tactics employed by the traditionalists together with the pressures bearing in on the state ensured that progressive politics were deferred to a later day. The Cold War had a complex impact on Georgia. On the one hand, the US assumption of leadership of the 'free world' served to focus attention on the imperfections of American democracy, encouraging presidential administrations and the Supreme Court to exert more pressure on the South to move towards integration; many Georgians too, particularly in urban and suburban areas, were sensitive to the image that the state presented to the world. On the other hand, this attention offended many reared in the traditionalist culture of Georgia, and the old guard was able to mobilize anticommunist sentiments to close ranks against the outside world. It is arguable that without the Cold War and the rhetoric that it engendered, the old political order in Georgia would have disintegrated earlier.[29]

Red scare politics in Georgia cannot be neatly labelled as either populist or elitist. They were more the work of factions in which leaders and followers shared similar mentalities. There was a popular dimension in that men like Talmadge and Griffin were using such rhetoric to mobilize grassroots support, and it is clear that legislators did not care to be seen to be voting against anticommunist measures. But the elitist dimension was the stronger, since the old guard leaders were selective as to when they deployed anticommunist sentiments, and for some years they could claim that they restricted them to campaign oratory and did not allow them to affect the governance of the state. It

was only when they determined on a strategy of massive resistance to school integration that red scare emotions came to be
fully exploited, and then the leaders sought to turn populistic
sentiments against powerful outside institutions like the Supreme
Court.

More than was the case in some states, the anticommunist cause
in Georgia was a struggle for the minds of men and women. The
state's cherishment of its traditions helped to make symbolism
and oratory central to its political culture. Its politicos were
comfortable with such concepts as the 'Georgians' Creed' or the
'Georgia Way of Life'. Politicians first used anticommunist
rhetoric mainly to discredit campaign opponents, and only
belatedly introduced substantive communist-control measures.
When the state's racist leadership decided to intensify red scare
emotions after the *Brown* decision, their energy was put into an
extraordinary propaganda campaign, aimed both at fellow
Georgians and at the American people. This was the politics of
persuasion at its most ambitious and extravagant, an attempt both
to solidify support in Georgia for massive resistance and to
manipulate public opinion at large. When the propaganda
campaign failed in its objectives, Georgia's leaders turned to
moulding opinion within the state in another way, by requiring
the school system to impregnate children with the virtues of
American democracy and the evils of communism. So might the
Georgia Way of Life be preserved.

PART V

CONCLUSION

Domestic anticommunism, that American tendency to espy a red enemy within, had its roots deep in the nation's past. A cluster of ideological, sociological and political circumstances had co-existed to render nineteenth-century Americans both anxious about subversion and deeply suspicious of socialist doctrine. Most Americans, after all, were both propertied and Christian, so that both elites and citizens at large were likely to be allergic to 'atheistic communism'. One source of insecurity was the perceived frailty of republican government, forever vulnerable to corrosion or debasement, particularly among a people as diverse as those inhabiting the United States. Americans were united more by shared values than by an ancient heritage or powerful institutions, that is by a common patriotic faith which could only feel threatened by an alien ideology. Reinforcing this cultural unease were the insecurities inseparable from a capitalist economy and a democratic polity. No class or interest could be sure of permanently retaining power in this republic, with its weak tradition of deference and limited powers of coercion, and those in authority were constantly tempted to exaggerate any challenge to their position. The insecurities of elites were matched by the anxieties of the people. The relatively wide distri-bution of property and of political rights gave republicanism a popular basis, and many Americans, told that the republic was theirs to preserve, pressed the tradition of an active citizenry into the counter-subversive cause.

In a political culture thus disposed to search for and to magnify evidence of subversion, the process of industrialization gave firmer shape to red scare politics. In the late nineteenth and early twentieth centuries a racking class conflict supplemented by nativist apprehensions about immigration generated fears of violent insurrection. In this phase of domestic anticommunism, the red menace was located in an underclass, among foreign-born workers who had brought alien doctrines with them from the class-ridden Old World. In time extensive safeguards against insurrection were put into place, but the Russian Revolution together with the growth of government at home served to revive and redirect anticommunist pressures. Class war was being replaced by global struggle, and during the interwar period the red menace was redefined. The threat in this phase lay less in insurrection than in conspiracy, one directed from Moscow and using the methods of infiltration, manipulation, and ideological seduction. Such techniques could ensnare the highest in the land, and anyone was now a potential subversive. The New Deal's alliance with the labour movement even rendered those in power suspect, and red scare tactics came to be deployed against the privileged as well as the underprivileged. This image of an invisible red menace underlined the need for systems of surveillance, whether by government agencies or by groups of patriotic citizens, as it also rendered suspect the moulders of opinion, in education, the media, or even the churches. The sources as well as the targets of anticommunist politics were also tending to change. The class fears of propertied elites had not altogether disappeared, but with the Communist movement controlled by a hostile power, the issue increasingly became one of national security, and hence of compelling interest to those guardians of the state, politicians and bureaucrats. Intense party competition became a primary engine of red scare politics, as did the bureaucratic imperative.[1]

It is at this point that the history of American anticommunism merges with that of McCarthyism, itself the subject of extensive debate. McCarthyism's first generation of students, led by Daniel Bell and Richard Hofstadter, tended to emphasize its populistic or 'mass politics' roots; the status anxieties or grievances of various rising or declining groups were credited with sustaining Senator McCarthy in his attacks on the establishment. McCarthyism was something of an aberration, a popular insurgency against those in authority. In 1967 this approach was challenged by Michael Rogin, who demonstrated the strength of McCarthyism in traditional Republican constituencies and the responsibility of various elites. McCarthyism was more the product of those with political influence than a revolt against them. A little later, Robert Griffith extended this perception by locating McCarthyism in the dynamics of conventional party politics. Other scholars too have subordinated McCarthy himself to larger and fairly conventional political processes. Some have related the escalation of domestic anticommunism to the Truman administration's anti-Soviet rhetoric and policies, while others have emphasized the resurgence of Republican and conservative politics. Either perspective tends to direct attention to the formative role of the federal government, whether controlled by

Democrats or Republicans; a major government agency in which some scholars have located a pervasive anticommunist animus was J. Edgar Hoover's FBI. Ellen Schrecker has recently emphasized the power of the modern state to set the political agenda; anticommunists had long been present in American society, but it was the actions of the Truman and Eisenhower administrations in the pursuit of national security which legitimized and empowered the destructive creature known as McCarthyism. A somewhat different thrust in recent scholarship has been that which has stressed the seriousness of communism as both a foreign and a domestic threat, and while these scholars see the antics of Joe McCarthy as despicable and counter-productive, they tend to present moderate anticommunism as a rational response to a clear and present danger.[2]

13

McCarthyism in State and Nation

There was no single source of red scare politics. McCarthyism was clearly a protean creature; it assumed different shapes and changed over time. For this reason, a number of the interpretations that scholars have advanced have some validity. If status anxieties are difficult to identify, regime anxieties at least did play their part, or at least the anxieties of those who identified with power structures threatened by political and social change. The guardians of the white South, for example, whether chieftains like the Talmadges or the rednecks of the Ku Klux Klan, embraced anticommunism as well as segregation for reasons of this sort. The dynamics of party politics could also play a major role in generating a red scare, as illustrated in this study by the case of Michigan. In a number of states too the internal security issue served to further bureaucratic authority, with the assistance of those interested in fashioning little FBIs. It is clear also that the power of federal example had a major impact on the wider society; federal legislation such as the Smith and McCarran Acts and federal initiatives such as the loyalty-security programme were imitated in various ways at state and local levels. This study has also drawn attention to phenomena less often encountered in analyses of anticommunist politics, such as the potential of urban environments for reactionary populism. And there could be idiosyncrasies too, as when particular individuals had a distinctive role to play. One reason for the strength of New Hampshire's communist-control programme was simply the zeal of its attorney general.

In a large and heterogeneous country like the United States an analysis of state activity offers a means of appraising both the constituent elements of McCarthyism and their interaction. The state was the unit traditionally charged with countering subversion, and although the federal government had begun to encroach on this area, it was to be expected that there would be a significant state response to any sightings of the red menace within American society. And if it needs to be established whether McCarthyism was the product either of populist eruptions or of elitist machinations, the state, positioned between federal and local governments, is an appropriate unit for study. An identification of both the location and the timing of McCarthyite eruptions makes possible a fuller understanding of the scope, intensity and evolution of red scare politics in the United States.

Metropolitan discontents

Virtually all states were touched in some measure by anticommunist sentiments. However public opinion may have been formed, it was invariably and decisively (if not always overwhelmingly) anticommunist in stance, and politicians found it prudent to defer to such sensibilities, even if only by adopting measures of the most emptily symbolic sort. But it is possible to delineate the contours of state anticommunism a little more fully than this.

All but a handful of states adopted either loyalty oaths or communist-control laws or both. In the early 1950s Utah alone appears to have been free of such measures, but the roster of states to adopt only one of these devices (by 1953) is at least suggestive. There were Wyoming, Idaho and Nevada in the West; in the Midwest and Plains region there were Minnesota, Wisconsin, Iowa, North and South Dakota and Nebraska. In New England, Rhode Island and Maine exhibited this degree of restraint, as elsewhere did the states of Missouri and Delaware. Anticommunist measures were difficult to resist entirely, but it would seem that the farm and mountain states were somewhat more likely to resist them than most. Another indicator is that provided by the outcrops of little HUACs, which usually if not invariably signalled a red scare of some intensity. They occurred in the Cold War period in California and Washington in the Pacific West (and also in the territory of Hawaii), in Illinois, Ohio,

Michigan, and Indiana in the Midwest, in New Jersey, New Hampshire and Massachusetts in the Northeast, briefly in Oklahoma, and in Florida, South Carolina and Louisiana in the South. Leaving aside for the moment the peculiar traditions of the South, it would appear that active little HUACs were most likely to appear in the more urbanized and industrialized states. A few states, such as New York and Pennsylvania, which did not boast little HUACs in these years (New York's Rapp–Coudert Committee was deployed earlier), put into place other anticommunist programmes. Very broadly, this analysis suggests that red scare politics were least likely to be found in the more rural states and more likely to be found in the urban-industrial states. Michael Rogin long ago exploded the myth that McCarthyism had its roots in the rural Populist tradition; these findings not only reinforce Rogin but also suggest the possibility that it might be better to seek the roots of McCarthyism in metropolitan culture.[1]

One correlation is with Communist activity. Some recent scholars, as noted above, have emphasized the rationality of much of American anticommunism, pointing to the strategic positions held by many American Communists in both the economy and the polity and the degree to which the CP was subject to the will of Moscow. Whether the response was commensurate to the threat is doubtful, but it can be agreed that in the states red scares fed on a Communist presence. Of the ten states with a thousand or more Communists within their borders in 1950 (according to FBI estimates), seven sported little HUACs at some stage in these years, and another, New York, had done so earlier. Anticommunists co-existed with Communists, and although the latter were few in number their secretiveness and their well-publicized changes in party line had raised serious doubts about their loyalty in the Cold War. Moreover, their activities in many local communities had earned Communists much grassroots hostility over the years. Legislators, looking uneasily to the next election, doubtless found it difficult to dismiss the need for communist-control measures if Communists were demonstrably present in a state. The CP's natural habitat was in the more industrialized and urbanized states, which possessed relatively advanced welfare systems, labour organizations and educational institutions of the kind which conservatives had long eyed suspiciously and which did contain clusters of radicals and liberals. Further, the socioeconomic charac-

teristics of these states tended to give them polarized or competitive political systems, so that insecure politicians were presented
with a standing temptation to exploit the CP presence. In almost
all the non-southern states noted above as touched by red scares,
party competition was relatively close.[2]

It is impossible to divorce the most celebrated state red scares
from metropolitan politics, even if, ironically, it was often nativist
and particularist perspectives that seemed to flourish in the big
cities. As we have seen, anticommunist activity in Massachusetts
cannot be explained without reference to Boston and other
industrial cities; at its heart were the Irish (and Italian) Catholic
communities of urban Massachusetts. In Michigan too, anticommunist sentiments bubbled up most fiercely from Detroit, and
were to be found also in other motor cities. The bloodiest battles
in the Union were fought out in the state of New York, where the
1949 and 1951 legislation encouraged a purge of some four or
five hundred teachers and other public employees, mainly in New
York City. At the centre of these convulsions was the city's left-
wing Teachers Union. Competing for notoriety were the
headhunters of California, where, despite the furore at the
University of California at Berkeley, it was Los Angeles that
proved the epicentre of the earthquake. The city of Los Angeles
adopted a communist-control programme two years before
California followed suit, and it was Los Angeles politicians such as
Sam Yorty and Jack Tenney who were in the vanguard of the
state's red scare. Tenney was the sole state senator from Los
Angeles, at a time when Los Angeles County boasted about 40 per
cent of the population of the state, and his obsession with
communism, as with that of his fellow southern Californian
Ronald Reagan, owed something to a desire to settle old local
scores. The furore associated with the infamous Broyles bills in
Illinois had at first centred on the Chicago campuses of Roosevelt
College and the University of Chicago, against whose
obstreperous and arguably radical students a number of Cook
County politicos took particular exception. In the South the most
fiercely anticommunist city was Birmingham, a steel town and the
centre of southern CP activity in the 1930s. Long before the
police chief Bull Connor made headlines around the world in the
1960s by setting police dogs on civil rights demonstrators, he was
rousting the city's reds. Birmingham too adopted a communist-

control programme before the state did. 'There's not enough
room in town for Bull and the Commies', explained Connor in
1948 when he arrested the vice-presidential candidate of the
Progressive party after he set foot in the city. In Texas, Don E.
Carleton has graphically analysed the passions fuelling Houston's
red scare, which the state's 1951 Communist registration law
served to exacerbate. Red scare emotions also churned such
polities as Cincinnati and Pittsburgh.[3]

To suggest that the resort to red scare politics was usually
intimately linked to metropolitan discontents is not to deny the
role that rural areas played in promoting anticommunist
programmes. The state of Nebraska, for example, showed no
particular fondness for Communists, but in the absence of
plausible radical targets had little need for elaborate communist-
control measures. Better to ensure that the coming generation
was raised right, and a 1949 law required Nebraska schools to set
aside specified hours for memorizing 'The Star Spangled
Banner'; school boards were also to satisfy themselves about the
'character' of all teachers and their acceptance of the 'American
form of government'. (An old red flag law survived in Nebraska,
and in the early 1960s it was reportedly being used against cheer-
leaders at football games; one of the University of Nebraska's
colours was crimson!) In Michigan, the Republicans, responsible
for much of the communist-control legislation, relied for their
support largely on the farm and forest counties, and used red
scare tactics to prise extra votes away from the Democrats in the
industrial cities. In Maryland the Ober Law was upheld by a
referendum in which rural areas provided significantly higher
majorities for it than urban areas. In California too the Tenney
Committee was sustained in no small part by support from rural
and suburban areas. Red scares may not have scorched the
prairies or much of small town America, but their citizens (mostly)
were against communism much as bishops are against sin. In state
legislatures in which rural areas were over-represented, rural and
small-town support for communist-control programmes was
critical, although the role was a supporting one.[4]

A red scare was more likely to be triggered by a convulsion in
metropolitan than in rural America. The United States is
frequently said to have been characterized by consensus in the
1950s, but the big cities do not appear to have been particularly

harmonious. If the CP had succeeded in recruiting some members among the Jewish, African American and labour communities of urban America, its activities had also made enemies among these very groups. As Richard Gid Powers has shown, Jewish, Catholic, African American and socialist hostility to the CP can be traced back to the 1920s, and was related to the anguished experiences with communism of members of those communities in both the Old World and the New. To such 'popular' anticommunism might be added the nativist and fundamentalist Protestant antipathies to communism found in many cities by the 1940s. Urban ethnic constituencies of different sorts were susceptible to anti-radical appeals and localist perspectives. Scholars such as Arnold R. Hirsch and Thomas J. Sugrue have recently drawn attention to the often reactionary and distinctly non-consensual sentiments touching the white working class of the northern cities in the postwar era, sentiments which also moved some professionals and suburbanites. Pluralist and cosmopolitan values were not embraced by all members of these troubled societies. The tensions of class, ethnicity and race were agitating metropolitan polities, promoting forms of reactionary populism, and the presence of a few Communists or other radicals, as well as of highly conservative business and patriotic groups, always made a recourse to red scare politics all too likely. Such McCarthyism was exposing the fragility of the New Deal order.[5]

Urban tensions first became apparent before the end of the Second World War. The massive influx of labour into urban areas, on top of that which had already occurred in the Depression, created serious problems of overcrowding in cities throughout the country. In the industrial Midwest southern whites thronged to the cities in much greater numbers than southern blacks (through the period 1919–45); one observer blamed the Detroit riot of 1943 on Klan-like white southerners. But the disquiets in the cities were exceedingly complex. Labour unions were anxious to throw off wartime controls, even to expand their numbers, and the unprecedented strike activity which was underway by the end of 1945 disrupted many cities; a few experienced what were in effect general strikes. The fear of losing jobs and even housing with the ending of the war deepened working-class apprehensions; the Depression still harrowed many memories. The strike wave also reinforced the determination of many employers to regain 'the right to manage', a goal which was in some measure to be secured in the Taft–Hartley Act, with its anticommunist provision. The influx of African Americans and sometimes of Mexican Americans into the wartime cities exacerbated tensions of another kind, particularly as these newcomers began to encroach on traditionally white neighbourhoods. Public housing schemes were as likely to attract charges of Communist inspiration as were CIO-directed strikes. In cities in which workers sought security and spiritual nourishment in their churches, religious sentiments could gloss those of ethnicity and class. Evangelical storefront churches flourished in the Midwestern cities, propagating the values of southern fundamentalism, as the Roman Catholic church similarly promoted a traditional and anti-radical culture among its adherents throughout urban America. Nativist emotions surfaced in several wartime cities, not only in the Klan-like activity found in such cities as Atlanta and Detroit, but also in the antisemitism which emerged in New York and Boston. Such unhappy environments provided some purchase for red scare politics.[6]

The metropolitan discontents may have eased somewhat with the return of prosperity, but they did not disappear. A measure of affluence encouraged the encroachment of growing black neighbourhoods on white. By the 1950s many of the old industrial cities were suffering from the flight of manufacturing jobs to low-wage areas, and the mid-1950s witnessed renewed and extensive strike action. For much of the Cold War period urban passions continued to sustain red scare attitudes. This was partly because of urban sociology. The targets which attracted anticommunist attentions were themselves urban phenomena, such as those universities which aroused such wrath in California, Washington state, Illinois and Massachusetts. More important in perpetuating red scare activity was the concentration of organized labour in the cities, particularly those unions that had Communists among their leaders. The great convulsions in the labour movement in the late 1940s and early 1950s, as the CP-led unions were expelled from the CIO, again directed attention for the most part to urban areas, and incited right-wing patriots across the land to capitalize on the labour troubles. And racism continued to encourage the use of red scare tactics. Not only was anticommunism used in the South as a weapon to defend segregation, but in northern cities too white homeowners sometimes sought to protect their neighbourhoods from African American incursions by invoking the red menace. Not all urban Americans remained true to the New Deal ideal of a protective state and an integrated society; indeed, it is not clear that many white urban workers ever embraced the consensual vision with much enthusiasm, not to mention some members of the middle class. One function of McCarthyism was to keep alive a kind of reactionary populism which was later to receive pungent expression in the urban support for George Wallace. According to public opinion polls, about half of Americans believed that the Communist party was implicated in the race demonstrations and riots of the 1960s. McCarthyism cannot be characterized purely as an elitist phenomenon.[7]

The anticommunist cycle

If the phenomenon of red scare politics was most likely to be associated with the urban-industrial states, it was also subject to some change over time. The protean and variegated nature of the creature makes generalization hazardous, but it is sometimes possible to glimpse an imperfect cycle, one in which anticommunist sentiments first emerged on the fringes or relatively low in a polity, sometimes in opposition to a governing regime, and in the course of time came to be embraced by elites which used red scare tactics to preserve the status quo. By the 1950s communist-control programmes were generally being turned against the relatively powerless members of society. In short, those explanations of McCarthyism which assign responsibility to populistic or demagogic elements tend to be most plausible when applied to the early stages of a red scare; explanations emphasizing the role of the privileged classes become more persuasive as the cycle advances. But it needs to be remembered that the American polity as a whole was shifting to the right between the late 1930s and the early 1950s, assisted by the impact of foreign affairs, which reinforced the anticommunist stance of the federal government abroad and at home.

Like congressional anticommunism, red scare politics in the states preceded the Cold War era. In several states patriotic emotions appear to have deepened in the mid-1930s with the introduction of loyalty oaths, and little HUACs and other communist-control measures were introduced during the 'little red scare' of the late 1930s and early 1940s. While Cold War terrors were undoubtedly to strengthen the anticommunist persuasion, they were not the exclusive cause of it. Suspicions of the red menace, of course, had long been endemic in the United States, but the eruptions after about 1935 owed much to a conservative reaction against labour advances and New Deal reform. This was sometimes animated by a rather populist outrage at the pretensions of universities, as obtained in Massachusetts and Oklahoma. In the Bay State, in fact, an Irish Catholic governor urged the redbaiters on, but red scare politics could also be directed at a state regime. In Michigan, red scare politics were extensively deployed to destroy the New Deal administration of Governor Frank Murphy, and California's little HUAC was the creation of politicians who had broken with the reform regime of Governor Culbert Olson. It busied itself with hunting Communists in the state's welfare system, the proudest creation of the state's New Deal. A little later, the mild reform administration of Governor Ellis Arnall in Georgia was also subjected to demagogic red scare tactics.[8]

While the prewar red scares were usually of limited impact, the political configurations which they exposed anticipated those of the late 1940s and 1950s. In both Michigan and Massachusetts, for example, the patterns which took shape initially in the 1930s reappeared in the Cold War years. In the former state, unreconstructed business interests and conservative Republicans, flanked by nativist, some Catholic, and fundamentalist Protestant elements, together with right-wing trade unionists, pressed the anticommunist cause most ardently, as they did also after the war; in the latter state, red scare politics were resisted by an informal coalition of civil libertarians, academics, Protestant and Jewish churchmen, and patrician Republicans throughout these decades. In this sense, the McCarthyite activities of the Cold War era were no aberration; they were rooted in a traditional American political culture, albeit one with a populistic dimension, and rose to prominence through the normal operation of American politics. Even during the Second World War, when the Soviet Union was an ally of the United States, patriotic Catholics, fundamentalist Protestants, democratic Socialists, and much of organized labour, remained unrelenting in their hostility to both domestic and international communism. A function of the Cold War was to move government closer to such anticommunist constituencies.[9]

That domestic anticommunism was partly energized by an anti-New Deal animus was confirmed after the Second World War, when several states experienced a drive against the New Deal heritage or against popular front or progressive political configurations. Sometimes New Dealers themselves defended their heritage by turning vigorously against the Communist elements. As noted earlier, little HUACs were particularly active in the late 1940s, and while Cold War anxieties contributed to their buoyancy, so did credible New Deal-popular front targets. One reason for the strength of little HUACs in the Pacific West was the relatively strong popular front and labour traditions in California, Washington and Hawaii. Those Democrats and others who in the 1930s had embraced left-wing causes became highly vulnerable to attack at a time when even most liberals had assumed an anticommunist stance. Similar patterns can also be discerned elsewhere. In Minnesota a popular front coalition won control of the Democratic-Farmer-Labor party in 1946, and, as John Earl Haynes has shown, its attempt to ally with the third-party Wallace movement precipitated a war in the party, as liberal anticommunists such as Hubert Humphrey rebelled against the CP and Progressive elements. There the anticommunist offensive was largely conducted within the major party. In New York during the Second World War, Communists won ascendancy in the American Labor party, which nursed friendly relations with left-wing Democrats and served as the state's Progressive party, but in the late 1940s it was vigorously resisted by anticommunist liberals, right-wing Democrats and Republicans and was effectively routed by 1950. Even in Georgia the glimpses of a progressive style of politics provided by Ellis Arnall and Helen Douglas Mankin helped to provoke an anticommunist reaction. Progressive political configurations were not greatly in evidence in the industrial Midwest, but a major force behind red scare politics in the late 1940s were business-oriented Republicans anxious to discredit the New Deal order. The politics of exposure, legitimized by democratic and libertarian traditions, suited those who believed that their political enemies could be tainted by old radical associations.[10]

As the Cold War deepened, and as the Truman administration legitimized the domestic campaign against the revolutionary left, most states hastened to embrace the politics of patriotism by passing loyalty oath laws, and from 1949 more elaborate communist-control laws were enacted, designed to prohibit or regulate Communist activity. Government was becoming aligned with the traditional anticommunist constituencies. Maverick redhunters, detached from the state governing bodies, did not disappear – Senator Broyles kept up his lonely campaign in Illinois – but anticommunist activities were now more likely to emanate from the political elites than to be directed at them. Bending to Cold War pressures and the example of the federal government, the state elites were joining the cause. They sometimes did so with reluctance, and were prompted as much as anything by a desire to contain it, but in embracing it gave it considerable authority. Both national and state political elites, in enlisting in this new holy war, not only invigorated it but in some measure succeeded in redirecting red scare pressures downwards and outwards. An anticommunist consensus, if sometimes uneasily contrived, was uniting those in public life, and its victims were primarily men and women of relatively modest status.

The fates of the university campuses and of labour unions respectively illustrate the subtle redirection of emphasis, as red scare pressures came increasingly to exude from inside the political establishment. Left-wing unions, of course, had long been the subject of anticommunist attentions, but universities were often prominent in the early stages of a red scare. In the immediate postwar years, red scare fears had been particularly triggered in 1947 when J. Edgar Hoover and HUAC made much of the Communist connections of American Youth for Democracy. Though the FBI was a government agency, neither Hoover nor HUAC wished the Truman administration well, and their counterparts in the states were equally prepared to stoke populist suspicions of higher education, with its identification with liberal elites. In Michigan, Illinois and Wisconsin attention was drawn to the campuses, and in two cases major storms were to occur. In Massachusetts the academic havens across the Charles River were the favourite targets of Boston redhunters. In California the controversial measure of the university regents was in part designed to pre-empt legislative patriots such as Jack B. Tenney. In Oklahoma too it was the campuses that first attracted the attention of those politicians who were to fashion an anticom-munist programme. In the early 1950s pressure on the campuses increased as congressional bodies began to probe their activities.

Disruptive and disheartening though this experience was to the academies across the land, with the passage of time some state anticommunists tended to turn to other targets, notably to labour and sometimes to schoolteachers. Exemplary in this respect was the state of Massachusetts, where throughout this period the universities were the first and favoured targets of the ardent anticommunists. Yet on every occasion they emerged virtually unscathed. Radical professors may have been pilloried, but the threats of revocation of charters or other political controls on the campuses were always turned aside, often at the expense of some other communist-control measure. By the mid-1950s, apart from unfortunate individuals like Dirk Struik and Donald Lothrop, the principal targets of Bay State redhunters were left-wing unions. In the Midwest too labour was tending to be accorded a greater share of attention. The outbreak of the Korean War underlined the potential for sabotage of the industrial Midwest, as it also provided an excuse for probing those unions known to contain Communists. Detroit's anticommunists completed their war against the United Public Workers in the early 1950s, and Michigan authorities in 1952 launched a probe of a UAW local in Flint, one in which Walter Reuther had been contesting Communist influence. In Illinois Senator Broyles was less preoccupied with the campuses and more with labour, supported by the American Legion, which complained that eleven unions expelled by the CIO were still operating in the state and were 'in a mighty fine position to commit espionage and sabotage'. In Ohio too, while education was not neglected, anticommunists were paying considerable attention to the 'Communist-domination of industrial groups', especially in plants 'engaged in war work'.

Red scare pressures were deflected onto the public schools as well as onto the left-wing unions, unsurprisingly in that the school systems were the major public service for which state governments were responsible. But schoolteachers now seemed more vulnerable than college or university teachers. In New York the Rapp–Coudert probe of the early 1940s had resulted mainly in job losses in higher education, but in the 1950s it was the public schools that were most seriously hit. During the California loyalty oath controversy of 1950 hundreds of college employees refused to sign the state oath, though by 1952 it was the Los Angeles school system and the Los Angeles City Housing Authority that were being purged, and in 1955 the state's Senate Interim Committee on Education reported itself 'deeply gratified' at the progress made by school districts in firing teachers who had taken the Fifth Amendment. It would be a mistake to press the point too far, since prominent academics continued to be skewered by marauding redhunters, as Chandler Davis and others discovered, but by the 1950s, when many state governments had closed ranks with the anticommunist patriots, red scare pressures were often being directed downwards in the polity, and less at elite institutions.[11]

By this date, of course, the CP-led unions were the most vulnerable of targets, as were a variety of individuals scattered across the country who had refused to repudiate a Communist past. Regarded with suspicion and hostility by both federal and state governments, afforded little protection by the courts and even by civil liberties groups, the CP-led unions provided tempting targets for any elements wishing to demonstrate their anticommunist credentials. Further, as Ellen Schrecker and Sigmund Diamond have shown, many universities had bought themselves some protection by introducing their own communist-control programmes or by affording some discreet cooperation to the intelligence agencies.Whatever populist impulses had helped to bring about a red scare, in time the elites had learned to appropriate and use them.[12]

The enhanced identification between the political leadership and communist-control programmes is also illustrated by the increasing institutionalization of the latter. As has been shown, a high proportion of state anticommunist legislation was more symbolic than substantive, and much of it never went into effect, either because it was not implemented or because it was destroyed by the courts. But significant aspects of these communist-control initiatives did survive and came to be embedded in governmental structures. In a few states little HUACs evolved as surveillance agencies, monitoring radical and dissident activities on behalf of the authorities. A number of states established police anti-subversive divisions ('red squads'), performing a similar function, screening applicants for public (and sometimes private) office and keeping protest groups under surveillance. These 'little FBIs', as Governor Mennen Williams called them, varied considerably in competence and conscientiousness, sometimes decaying as in

Maryland and sometimes remaining vigilant as in Michigan. Often they were supplemented by city red squads in the metropolitan areas, and these did remain active. As Cold War pressures eased, these various agencies survived as institutional legacies of red scare politics, ready to protect the polity from the 'coming apart' of the 1960s.[13]

The South provided another kind of example of existing regimes assuming anticommunist functions in order to preserve themselves. As previously noted, red scare politics were relatively late in reaching the Deep South, at least in extending much beyond campaign rhetoric, and little HUACs and the like came only to be extensively deployed as part of the massive resistance to school integration that emerged in the mid-1950s. Characteristic was Louisiana's Joint Legislative Committee, whose chairman reasoned in 1957 that since 'Nowhere in the world' had whites and blacks lived in 'so much peace' as in the South, the growing unrest could have been caused only by an outside force, the international Communist conspiracy. Old 'communist experts' like Dr J. B. Matthews, their expertise no longer much wanted elsewhere, prolonged their working lives for a few years by testifying before such southern bodies.[14]

The Louisiana committee, like the Georgia Commission on Education with which it cooperated, saw propaganda as a principal weapon to be utilized in protecting the southern way of life. Proselytizing and educational campaigns were a feature of the region, and probably owed something to its evangelical traditions. In the South the religious revivalism of the 1950s continued to gain strength through the decade, and often displayed a strong anticommunist bias, as in Billy James Hargis's Christian Crusade, which zealously inundated the region with radio broadcasts and fundamentalist literature, and incessantly warned of the imminent Communist takeover. Dr George Benson's National Education Program, based at Harding College, Arkansas, produced television and radio broadcasts, textbooks, free newspaper columns and travelling experts to 'immunize our people to Communist infiltration and propaganda'. The military too on occasion became involved in such propaganda or educational programmes. Defense Secretary Charles E. Wilson in 1955 had promoted educational programmes on Soviet communism in the armed forces; in 1958 a National Security Council directive, responding to the 'brainwashing' of prisoners-of-war in Korea, admonished military officers to educate their troops and the general public on Cold War issues, and some southern commanders took this as an invitation to cooperate with local anticommunists. The Pensacola naval training station worked with Benson's National Education Program in establishing Florida's Project Alert, a community agency based at the naval station which disseminated anticommunist broadcasts and literature. In South Carolina too the state's little HUAC at first cooperated with South Carolina Alert, a private body of right-wing educators, in developing an educational programme to inform citizens 'of the threat of communism to the National security'.[15]

In the threatening Cold War years educators throughout the country were expected to play their part in instilling American values in the rising generation, and in many school systems the teaching of American history and allied topics was enhanced. The National Defense Education Administration sponsored institutes (or professional courses) for history teachers. But no region surpassed the South in the effort to combat communism by educating children in the virtues of patriotism. As in Georgia, as massive resistance gave way to a token integration strategy, a number of southern states turned to using schools to preserve traditional ways. A pioneer was Florida, which, encouraged by Project Alert, enacted a law in 1961 requiring the teaching of a high school course entitled 'Americanism vs Communism', emphasizing the virtues of the American 'free-enterprise-compet-itive economy', such as in producing 'higher wages, higher standards of living, greater personal freedom and liberty than any other system of economics on earth'. Teachers were forbidden to present communism as 'preferable' to the American system. The law proved extraordinarily resilient, an attempt to abolish it in 1983 encountering fierce resistance from the Cuban community. In South Carolina, after its little HUAC's connections with South Carolina Alert attracted criticism in 1962, the committee put its energies into encouraging educators 'to insure that a factual, reasonably full presentation is made in the public schools of the two contrasting systems – Democracy and Communism'. Arkansas's department of education in 1963 issued a booklet entitled *Strengthening America*, prepared by the Arkansas American Way of Life Committee. One teaching unit, 'Democracy v. Communism', was designed to illuminate the 'merits' of American democracy and the 'pitfalls' of the Soviet system;

J. Edgar Hoover's *Masters of Deceit* was among the recommended
reading for teachers. Louisiana too adopted a course intended 'to
alert the high school youth ... to the dangers of the Communist
conspiracy', while Virginia's future citizens were instructed in 'the
difference between the alluring promise and the enslaving
practice of communism'. This period also witnessed attempts in
southern states to ban 'subversive' textbooks from the schools. If
outside forces were prising apart the Solid South, its fundamental
principles might somehow survive if a One-Hundred-Percent
Americanism could be transmitted to future generations.[16]

Red scare ingredients

Expressions of red scare politics varied according to place and
over time. Populist or grassroots pressures might bubble up from
below, the media might magnify and sensationalize a radical
presence, well-resourced lobbies might mobilize their contacts
within governing circles, influential elites might embark on a
purging of the institutions they controlled. But this analysis of red
scare politics in the states suggests that certain elements needed
to be present for a red scare to enjoy any vitality. Communists,
patriots, anticommunist networks, political elites, and the power
of federal example – within the baleful context of the Cold War,
each had a role to play.

While anticommunist rhetoric and activities could be directed
at almost any body, they lacked plausibility unless Communists or
other radicals had been operating in the community. It is hardly
coincidental that some of the most ferocious red scares occurred
in states possessed of a popular front tradition, perhaps briefly
reinvigorated by the Wallace candidacy of 1948. In such areas
there were both renegade liberals anxious to establish their
anticommunist credentials and unrepentant liberals and radicals
against whom red scare tactics could be used. Similarly, those
states in which CP-led unions had been active were also prone to
red scares, and in the South civil rights groups came to serve as
surrogates for Communists. The generation of a red scare also
required the presence of patriotic lobbies, particularly those in a
position to reach state legislators. American Legion departments
tended to be conspicuous in such activities, not only because they
were relatively well resourced but also because many legislators
were legionnaires themselves. But other veterans' groups,

patriotic societies, business organizations, some Catholic societies and fundamentalist Protestant groups, and in the South white citizens' councils, were also often able to cultivate friendly relationships with state politicos. Such activists also frequently became part of larger informal networks from which they could draw strength. The little HUACs and other such bodies corresponded with one another and exchanged ideas and information; national and state probers sometimes coordinated their activities, as in Massachusetts; congressmen, like Jimmy Davis in Georgia, might secure information from FBI or HUAC files and feed it back to local activists. Such 'horizontal' and 'vertical' anticommunist networks could add potency to a state red scare.

Yet for a red scare to be both pervasive and effective, the highest authorities in the state needed also to be recruited to the cause. The loyalty oath fever swept California only after Governor Warren decided to pre-empt the patriots' demands, while Governor Stevenson limited the scope of red scare politics in Illinois by vetoing the Broyles bills. In Massachusetts, the red scare was at its most destructive when the executive added its weight to legislative forces. Georgia's distinctive version of a red scare gained momentum only when the state's political leaders made the cause their own. Such leaders, of course, were subject to influences arising from outside their states as well as inside them. Senior state officials were most likely to join the anticommunist patriots when Cold War pressures became irresistible. The governors of several states, among them California and Michigan, became unenthusiastic converts to the need for some kind of communist-control measures after the disturbing outbreak of the Korean War, when President Truman himself urged the states to strengthen their civil defences. Congressional committees fortified by the Cold War, like HUAC and SISS, might spark state action by initiating their own investigations of the suspect inhabitants of local communities, sometimes at the urging of local patriots. The greater interest by the authorities in anticommunist drives in Massachusetts and New Hampshire from 1953 owed something to the menacing scrutiny being accorded to higher education by congressional committees in that year. Cold War anxieties, of course, could beset anyone, not only political elites; the range and vigour of anticommunist lobbies generally strengthened with the deterioration of American-Soviet relations. The legitimization of communist-control programmes by the federal government and the growth of the national security state also served to encourage both public and private bodies across the land to engage in the varied forms of political surveillance.

Yet any analysis which seeks to identify the ingredients of a red scare risks oversimplifying the phenomenon. Most state communist-control programmes were compromises of sorts. In Michigan, Governor Williams engaged in a prolonged tug-of-war with the legislature over the state's stance towards the Communist menace, and the advantage shifted to and fro over the years; the machinery constructed in the early 1950s could claim no single architect. In Massachusetts the measures periodically adopted by the state were almost always put into place by the political leadership as weaker alternatives to the draconian proposals promoted by the lower house. Maryland's much-vaunted Ober Law was barely enforced by those charged with administering it. Thus the ultimate responsibility for a state's communist-control programme rested with the political leadership, often forced to pick its perilous way between warring patriotic and civil libertarian lobbies and fashioning remedies which promised the least political strife. A 'statist' interpretation of McCarthyism (of the kind that political scientists such as Theda Skocpol have advanced for other areas of American political history) holds some credibility. It was often a state's political class rather than specific interests within the community that determined the final shape of the anticommunist programme, in the process sometimes enhancing state power, as with the institutionalization of political surveillance. The strongly anticommunist nature of public opinion frequently demanded some kind of governmental disavowal of Communist legitimacy once the issue had been raised; in state after state legislators and governors fashioned or endorsed measures which they privately detested.

The case studies examined in this book also suggest that attempts to identify the direction taken by anticommunist currents – whether upwards or downwards in a polity – although instructive are ultimately of limited utility. In a political culture as open as that of the United States, in which Cold War images are conveyed to a variety of audiences by a variety of media, initiatives taken by, say, the federal government, do not neatly trip down an idealised political hierarchy from federal to state to local levels. Anticommunist currents in the 1940s and 1950s were swirling in all directions. What does seem to be the case is that those deploying red scare strategies at all points in the polity needed one another. HUAC and the little HUACs, like the FBI and the 'little FBIs', abetted one other and provided mutual corroboration. Whatever the power of federal example, a red scare also needed grassroots support, or at least the ardent engagement of local lobbies, and state officials were exposed to pressures reaching them from both above and below. Igniting a red scare was rather like activating an electrical circuit; once the switch was thrown – by whatever participant – the circuit was complete and the flow of the current immaterial.

Regime anxieties and the American political order

Red scares tended to be phenomena that appeared in areas subject to rapid change. It was in the urban-industrial states that anticommunist politics were most vigorously deployed, for the reasons previously discussed. The industrial Midwest had been wrenched from a Republican and business-oriented political order to one in which class-conscious workers had become a force in the land. The extraordinary flux and expansion of southern California in the Cold War years, when defence contracts were generously showered on the state, helped to make the region receptive to conservative anxieties. Don Carleton has related Houston's red scare to the 'confusion and fear' produced by 'rapid economic and population expansion'. Attention has earlier been drawn to the cauldrons of emotions in the nation's great cities. Crushed into these fluid urban environments, culturally diverse workers, worried about their jobs and housing, were prey to a host of class antagonisms, ethnic and religious tensions, and nativist and racist insecurities. And such populist emotions were hardly confined to workers; lawyers, businessmen, churchmen and even educators were often prominent in the patriotic, veterans' and other groups that warned that their communities were threatened by the red menace.[17]

Paradoxically, the increasingly pluralistic nature of American society was provoking something akin to a fundamentalist reaction, or rather a set of reactions. In each of the three states examined in detail in this book, an older political order was giving or had given way to a new and troubling one. In Michigan much of the energy behind red scare politics was imparted by those who yearned for a restoration of business hegemony. In Massachusetts a powerful and continuing impulse was that issuing from the Catholic community, which no longer enjoyed quite its old influence or at least security in an increasingly secular and pluralistic world. Red scare politics in Georgia were deployed most vigorously by the old guard, the white supremacist champions of a political order being subjected to intense pressure to change. It was not only in the South that 'localist' interests were reacting against outside influences and centralized authority. A fundamentalist fury with the changing times could also be detected in many others who joined the anticommunist cause. The Minute Women of Baltimore and Houston and elsewhere, committed to 'the traditional American way of life'; the Legionnaires who had fought for a world that they now seemed to be losing; the middle-class propertied Protestants of southern California, who saw themselves as the inheritors of the American Dream and seemed ready to strike at every encroachment on their autonomy: all seemed to possess a mindset that poised them against a pluralistic order and a secular, bureaucratizing state. It is not surprising that scholars once located the roots of McCarthyism in forms of status anxiety and a revolt against modernization, for anxieties of a sort played their part. There was nothing irrational or paranoid, however, in clinging to traditional ways; the CIO activists in the Midwest and civil rights agitators in the South were real threats to established orders. For many, McCarthyism was the last hurrah of an older style of politics.

In the larger, national arena a host of rather disparate cultural forces lent their energies to the anticommunist cause. Juxtaposed in uneasy array by the institutional structures of American politics, the representatives of some business, labour, Catholic, nativist, white racist and other constituencies tasted a moment of power by embracing McCarthyism. In congressional politics, as in the Midwest, Republican partisanship played a major role in creating the red scare atmosphere, though McCarthy and others were also sustained by the populist currents that bubbled up from cities like Boston and Detroit. In Congress too the support of the South was essential to the functioning of such committees as HUAC, SISS and Senator McCarthy's own subcommittee. If, as some scholars have cogently argued, the shape of the American national state cannot be understood without reference to the potent role of the white South in the system of politics between the 1930s and the 1960s, neither can the structure of McCarthyism. When the federal government, driven by the demands of Cold War and the national security state, enlisted in the cause, a fateful connection was effected between the old anticommunist constituencies and this powerful legitimizing force. In Congress and the national government, as in many states, liberal leaders allowed unreconstructed conservatives some purchase by denying the legitimacy of domestic communism, even as they attempted to moderate or defuse superpatriotic demands. And, in both state and nation, it needed some measure of cooperation between the executive and legislative branches and a compliant judiciary for a red scare to strike deep.[18]

In both state and nation, too, the reigning elites were adept at pre-empting anticommunist politics for their own purposes, paradoxically enhancing the cause while diverting its animus from establishment institutions. But by the end of the 1950s the imperatives of the national security state had driven the states out of the business of combating subversion, other than by the promotion of American values through education. Yet the fundamentalist impulses clinging to older political orders had not quite died; many of the tensions associated with the anticommunist persuasion helped to shape the politics of the future, as they simultaneously ate away at the foundations of the New Deal system of politics. The extraordinary burst of support for the presidential candidacy of George Wallace in the 1960s tapped the racist and economic discontents of the unreconstructed South and of the industrial cities, and by the end of the decade Richard Nixon was forging an alliance which drew strength from many of the old anticommunist constituencies, including conservative business interests, the white South, Catholic ethnics, and blue-collar workers. Red scare politics had played a part in the reshaping of the American political order.[19]

NOTES AND REFERENCES

1 The Politics of Exposure: Investigating Committees

1. Earl Latham, *The Communist Controversy in Washington: From the New Deal to McCarthy* (New York: Athenaeum, 1969).
2. Arthur M. Schlesinger Jr. and Roger Burns (eds), *Congress Investigates, 1792–1974* (New York: Chelsea House, 1975), pp.xii–xvi, 3–4; Telford Taylor, *Grand Inquest: The Story of Congressional Investigations* (New York: Simon & Schuster, 1955), pp.67–74.
3. State of New York, *Revolutionary Radicalism, Its History, Purpose and Tactics with an exposition and discussion of the steps being taken and required to curb it, being the Report of the Joint Legislative Committee Investigating Seditions Activities, Filed April 24, 1920, in the Senate of the State of New York* (Albany, 1920), ostensibly in 4 volumes, some of the volumes are published in two separate parts; M.J. Heale, *American Anticommunism: Combating the Enemy Within* (Baltimore: Johns Hopkins University Press, 1990), p.111; William H. Cobb, 'The State Legislature and the "Reds": Arkansas's General Assembly v. Commonwealth College, 1935–1937', *Arkansas Historical Quarterly*, 45 (Spring 1986), 3–18; REPORT ON STATE LEGISLATION, undated typescript carbon in vol.983, 1937, American Civil Liberties Union (ACLU) Records, Seeley G. Mudd Library, Princeton University.
4. Heale, *American Anticommunism*, p.124; ACLU, *Let Freedom Ring!* (New York, June 1937), p.56; 'Report of the Special Commission to Investigate the Activities within this Commonwealth of Communistic, Fascist, Nazi and Other Subversive Organizations', *Massachusetts Legislative Documents, House, 1938*, No. 2100, pp.56, 318, 460 and passim; Robert Morss Lovett, 'Witch-Hunting in Massachusetts', *New Republic*, 1 Dec.1937, pp.96–7; *Boston Sunday Post*, 26 June 1938; Lawrence H. Chamberlain, *Loyalty and Legislative Action: A Survey of Activity by the New York State Legislature, 1919–1949* (Ithaca: Cornell University Press, 1951), pp.68–79; M. J. Heale, 'Red Scare Politics: California's Campaign Against Un-American Activities, 1940–1970', *Journal of American Studies*, 20 (April 1986), 5–32; 'Attacks On The Communist Party', typescript in Vol.2203, 1940, ACLU Records; James A. Robinson, *Anti-Sedition Legislation and Loyalty Investigations in Oklahoma* (Norman: University of Oklahoma, 1956), pp. 23–31. In New York, a legislative committee established to investigate crime

diverted its attention to un-American activities in 1938: Chamberlain, *Loyalty and Legislative Action*, pp.58–60.

5. Ellen W. Schrecker, *No Ivory Tower: McCarthyism and the Universities* (New York: Oxford University Press, 1986), pp.76–83; Heale, 'Red Scare Politics', pp. 5–32. The Tenney Report was still being cited in the 1960s: State of Louisiana, Joint Legislative Committee on Un-American Activities, *Report No.1*, 8 May 1961 (Baton Rouge, 1961).

6. Clifford Forster to Robert E. Mathews, 15 April 1947, Box 1029, Folder 6, ACLU Records; Robert K. Carr, *The House of Committee on Un-American Activities, 1945–1950* (Ithaca: Cornell University Press, 1952); Joint Fact-Finding Committee on Un-American Activities in California [hereafter CUAC], *Third Report 1947* (Sacramento, 1947), *Fourth Report, 1948*, pp.91–393, *Fifth Report, 1949*, p.601; *Los Angeles Times*, 26 March 1948, 11, 19, 20 May 1949; *San Francisco Chronicle*, 22 June, 21 Oct., 1–9 Nov.1947, 24–27 May 1949; Sn. Cal. ACLU, *Open Forum* (Los Angeles), 10 July 1948, 2 Oct.1948; Washington Legislature, Joint Legislative Fact-Finding Committee on Un-American Activities [hereafter WUAC], *First Report, 1948*, pp.v–vii; Vern Countryman, *Un-American Activities in the State of Washington* (Ithaca: Cornell University Press, 1951); Jane Sanders, *Cold War on the Campus: Academic Freedom at the University of Washington, 1946–64* (Seattle: University of Washington Press, 1979), pp.21–86; *Journal of the Senate of the State of Michigan, 1948, Extra Session* (Lansing, 1948), 27 April 1948, p.208; State of Illinois, *Report of the Seditious Activities Investigation Commission* (1949), pp.5–7, 361–4; James Truett Selcraig, *The Red Scare in the Midwest, 1945–1955: A State and Local Study* (Ann Arbor: UMI Research Press, 1982), pp.6, 20–1, 23–4, 33–4; Herman Kogan, 'The Sucker State Sees Red', *New Republic*, 11 April 1949, pp.18–19; *Report of the Commission to Investigate Communistic and Un-American Teachings and Activities in the Public Schools and Tax-Supported Colleges and Universities in the State of New Jersey to Governor Alfred E. Driscoll* (1953); BAKER BILL, SB 238, and Milton L. Farber to Robert N. Gorman 23 April 1947, Box 1029, Folder 6, ACLU Records; ACLU, *The States and Subversion* (New York, 1953), p.6; Leo C. Graybill to Roger Baldwin, 18 Jan.1949, and Harlow Pease to Baldwin, 15 Feb.1949, Box 1033, Folder 5, ACLU Records; *The Harvard Crimson*, 26 May 1949; Florence H. Luscomb to Roger Baldwin, 29 Jan.1949, Box 1033, Folder 6, ACLU Records; *Manchester Union Leader*, 11 March 1949; Robinson, *Anti-Sedition Legislation*, p.32; *The Oklahoman*, 16 Feb.1949. 'Report of the Commission on Subversive Activities to the Legislature of the Territory of Hawaii, March 1951' [copy in Library of Congress], p.1; see also Thomas Michael Holmes, 'The Specter of Communism in Hawaii, 1947–53' (Ph.D diss., University of Hawaii, 1975), pp.6–12; *Journal of the House of Representatives of the Commonwealth of Massachusetts, 1950* (Boston 1950), pp.548, 1830, 1849, 1850, 1933; *Report of the Un-American Activities Commission, State of Ohio, 1951–52* [hereafter OUAC], *Report*, pp.5–8; Warren P. Hill, 'A Critique of Recent Ohio Anti-Subversive Legislation', *Ohio State Law Journal*, 14 (1953), 439–93.

7. 'Report of the Special Commission ...', p.579; Hoover quoted in Richard Gid Powers, *Secrecy and Power: The Life of J. Edgar Hoover* (New York: Free Press, 1987), p.289; *Communist Infiltration in the United States: Its Nature and How to Combat It* (Washington: US Chamber of Commerce, 1946), p.33; Richard B. Allen, 'Bar Association News', *American Bar Association Journal*, 34 (March 1948), 252; see also 'Shall We Outlaw the Communist Party?' *Plain Talk*, 1 (April 1947), 3–4.

8. CUAC, *Second Report, 1945*, p.212; *Detroit News*, 8 March 1948; WUAC, *First Report, 1948*, p.605.

9. The FBI list is reported in *Counterattack*, 1 Sept.1950.

10. Joseph R. Starobin, *American Communism in Crisis, 1943–1957* (Cambridge: Harvard University Press, 1972), pp.22–4, 100–3, 113; Harvey Klehr and John Earl Haynes, *The American Communist Movement: Storming Heaven Itself* (New York: Twayne Publishers, 1992), pp.73–5, 85–6, 100–1, 108–9; Austin Ranney, 'Parties in State Politics', in Herbert Jacob and Kenneth N. Vines (eds), *Politics in the American States: A Comparative Analysis* (Boston: Little, Brown, 1965), p.65.

11. Patrick Murphy Malin to Paul Feltus, 9 March 1953, Box 1042, Folder 12, ACLU Records; Jack B. Tenney, 'California Legislator' (Oral History Program, UCLA, 1969), pp.1303–6, 1345–8; CUAC, *Third Report, 1947*, p.46, *Fourth Report, 1948*, p.8, 91–393; *Los Angeles Times*, 26 March 1948; *San Francisco Chronicle*, 1, 2, 4–7 Nov.1947, 1 March 1949.

12. WUAC, *First Report 1948, Second Report 1948, Report January 1949*; Jack Hardy, 'Smoking Out the Reds in Washington State', *National Republic*, 35 (March 1948), 15–17, 32; Countryman, *Un-American Activities*, pp.33, 72–3, 80, 150–1, 185, 370; Schrecker, *No Ivory Tower*, pp.94–104; Kogan, 'The Sucker State Sees Red', pp.18–19; Howard Rushmore, 'Mr Anti-Communist', *American Mercury*, 76 (May 1953), 80; Seditious Activities Investigation Commission, State of Illinois, *Special Report: Investigation of the University of Chicago and Roosevelt College, 1949*; James O'Gara, 'What Price Anti-Sedition?' *The Commonweal*, 50 (8 July 1949), 312–15; *Detroit News*, 15, 23 April 1948.

13. Robert E. Burke, *Olson's New Deal for California* (Berkeley: University of California Press, 1953), pp.36–8; 119–23, 126–31; Fraser M. Ottanelli, *The Communist Party of the United States from the Depression to World War II* (New Brunswick: Rutgers University Press, 1991), pp.118–19, 206; John Earl Haynes, 'The New History of the Communist Party in State Politics: The Implications for Mainstream Political History', *Labor History*, 27 (Fall 1986), 559–60; Heale, 'Red Scare Politics', pp.7–13; Karl M. Schmidt, *Henry A. Wallace: Quixotic Crusade 1948* (Syracuse: Syracuse University Press, 1960), p.109; Countryman, *Un-American Activities*, pp.1–24, 35, 44–7; Melvin Rader, *False Witness* (Seattle: University of Washington Press, 1969), pp.31–2 (see ch.3 on popular front activities in Washington before the war); Harvey Klehr, *The Heyday of American Communism: The Depression Decade* (New York: Basic Books, 1984), pp.253–7, provides a good analysis of Washington popular front politics; Holmes, 'Specter of Communism

in Hawaii', pp.v–vi, 1–6, 13; Steve Woods, 'How To Capture An Island', *Plain Talk*, 3 (July 1949), 1–8; Victor Lasky, 'Red Wedge in Hawaii', *Plain Talk*, 2 (May 1948), 34–41; Roger Bell, *Last Among Equals: Hawaiian Statehood and American Politics* (Honolulu: University of Hawaii Press, 1984), pp.141–3, 150, 156–61.

14. John Earl Haynes, *Dubious Alliance: The Making of Minnesota's D F L Party* (Minneapolis: University of Minnesota Press, 1984); Chamberlain, *Loyalty and Legislative Action*; Schmidt, *Henry A. Wallace*, pp.139–43, 233, 236, 237; Michael Straight, 'The Midwest is Worried', *New Republic*, 4 April 1949; Selcraig, *Red Scare in Midwest*, chs 1 and 2; *Cincinnati Enquirer*, 5 March 1951; ACLU, *Report on Civil Liberties, January 1951–June 1953* (New York, 1953), p.52; Kogan, 'The Sucker State Sees Red', pp.18–19; James O. Monroe to Chicago ACLU, 1 July 1949, Box 1032, Folder 17, ACLU Records; *The Nation*, 173 (7 July 1951), 1.

15. WUAC, *First Report 1948*, p.v; Rader, *False Witness*, p.167; CUAC, *Third Report 1947*, pp.1–2, *Fifth Report 1949*, pp.129, 600–1, *Seventh Report 1953*, p.201; Sub-Committee Minutes, 27, 28 May 1948, in State of Illinois, *Report of the Seditious Activities Investigation Commission* (1949), pp.88–9; Tenney to Sigler, 29 Jan.1948, Sigler to Tenney, 16 Feb.1948, Sigler to Thomas E. Bienz, 27 Aug., 18 Oct.1948, in Communism, 1948 file, Kim Sigler Papers, Michigan State Archives, Lansing; Sigmund Diamond, *Compromised Campus: The Collaboration of Universities with the Intelligence Comunity, 1945–1955* (New York: Oxford University Press, 1992), pp.250, 267; Kenneth O'Reilly, *Hoover and the Un-Americans: The FBI, HUAC, and the Red Menace* (Philadelphia: Temple University Press, 1983), pp.191, 274, 309.

16. CUAC, *Fifth Report 1949*, pp. 599–650 (quotation on p.603); Sub-Committee Minutes in State of Illinois, *Report ... (1949)*, pp.88–9, 92, 100–3; Commission Minutes in ibid., p.106; 'Interstate Legislative Conference on Un-American Activities: Proceedings', in ibid., pp.294–382; *Los Angeles Times*, 18, 21, 22 Sept.1948. The ten participating states were California, Washington, Alabama, New Mexico, Arizona, Iowa, Illinois, Colorado, Montana and Georgia.

17. Tenney, 'California Legislator', pp.1395–6; *Counterattack*, 5 March 1948; *Los Angeles Times*, 26 March 1948, 11, 19, 20 May 1949; *Sacramento Bee*, 11, 12, 18, 25 Jan.1948, 10, 16–19, 24 May 1949; *San Francisco Chronicle*, 17–20, 24–7 May, 7 June 1949; *Open Forum*, 10 July 1948, 2 Oct.1948; Luther H. Lincoln, 'Young Turk to Speaker of the California Assembly, 1948–1958' (Oral History Office, Bancroft Library, 1980), p.14; Rader, *False Witness*, p.166; Countryman, *Un-American Activities*, pp.163, 181, 183; *The Nation*, 173 (7 July 1951), 1–2; Selcraig, *Red Scare in Midwest*, pp.25–8; *Collinsville Herald*, 8 July 1949; James O. Monroe to Chicago ACLU, 1 July 1949, Box 1032, Folder 17, ACLU Records; Robinson, *Anti-Sedition Legislation*, pp.31–5; *Michigan Senate Journal, 1948*, pp.208–11; Robert J. Mowitz, 'Michigan: State and Local Attacks on Subversion', in Walter Gellhorn (ed.), *The States and Subversion* (Ithaca: Cornell University Press, 1952), p.194n.; Gellhorn (ed.), *The States and Subversion*, p.389.

18. *Report of the Commission ... to Governor Alfred E. Driscoll*, pp. 4–16; Gellhorn (ed.), *The States and Subversion*, pp.371, 389; *The Harvard Crimson*, 26 May 1949; ACLU, *The States and Subversion*, p.6; *Massachusetts House Journal, 1950*, pp.1849–51, 1933; 'Anti-Communism and Civil Rights', *Boston City Reporter* (May 1951), p.1; *Boston Traveler*, 2 April 1951; Commonwealth of Massachusetts, *Report of the Committee to Curb Communism, March 30, 1951* (Boston, 1951); Holmes, 'Specter of Communism in Hawaii', pp. 6–12, 20–30; US House of Representatives, Committee on Un-American Activities, *Hearings Regarding Communist Activities in the Territory of Hawaii – Part 1* (Washington 1950), p.1353; US Senate Committee on Interior and Insular Affairs, *Statehood for Hawaii: Communist Penetration of the Hawaiian Islands* (Washington 1949), p.14; 'Report of the Commission on Subversive Activities to the Legislature of the Territory of Hawaii, March, 1951', p.1; 'Address by Dr Lyle G. Phillips, Past President, Hawaii Residents Association', in *All-American Conference Proceedings: Sixth Annual Meeting, Chicago, Nov. 4 and 5, 1955*, pp.23–5.

19. *Massachusetts Senate Journal, 1953*, pp.1220–1, 1344; *Boston Evening Globe*, 30 Nov.1953; Governor Christian A. Herter, *Addresses and Messages to the General Court, Proclamations, Public Addresses ...* (Boston, 1956), p.142; *Massachusetts House Journal, 1954*, pp.667–8, 833; *Boston Herald*, 21 Feb.1954; *Christian Science Monitor*, 19 May 1954; *New York Times*, 18 June 1953; 'McCarthyism in New Hampshire', *Christian Century*, 71 (28 July 1954), 908–9; 'The Sweezy Case', ECLC, *Rights* (Sept.1954), 7–9; Willard Uphaus, *Commitment* (New York, 1963), pp.131, 172; Louis C. Wyman, *Subversive Activities in New Hampshire: Report of the Attorney General to the New Hampshire General Court, Pursuant to Laws 1953, Chapter 307* (1955), pp.v, 257–63. The Indiana legislature possessed a Counter-Subversion Study Commission in 1957–8, but it could not find much to do and was allowed to expire: Dale R. Sorenson, 'The Anticommunist Consensus in Indiana, 1945–1958' (Ph.D diss., Indiana University, 1980), pp.194–200.

20. *California Senate Journal: Regular Session, 1970*, pp.1899–1901; Hugh M. Burns, 'Legislative and Political Concerns of the Senate Pro Tem, 1957–1970' (Regional Oral History Office, Bancroft Library, Berkeley), pp.iv, 60, and passim; CUAC, *Seventh Report 1953*, p.135 and *Fourteenth Report 1967*; Mary Ellen Leary, 'California's Lonely Secret Agent', *Los Angeles Times* 'West Magazine', 2 April 1967.

21. Leary, 'California's Lonely Secret Agent', pp.33–40; *California Senate Journal: Regular Session*, 1970, pp.4645–6; James R. Mills, 'Locking Up The Tenney Files', *The Nation*, 213 (5 July 1971), 10.

22. CUAC, *Seventh Report 1953*, pp.78, 121, 135, 141–9, 209–11, *Eighth Report 1955*, pp.75–7, 180–1, 396–418, *Ninth Report 1957*, p.158; *New York Post*, undated [1954?] clipping in National Emergency Civil Liberties Committee Papers, Box 2, Columbia University; Ralph S. Brown, Jr, *Loyalty and Security: Employment Tests in the United States* (New Haven: Yale University Press, 1958), pp.101, 104; ACLU, *Annual Report, 1953–54*, p.37; ACLU, *Annual Report, 1954–55*, p.43; Leary,

'California's Lonely Secret Agent', pp.33–40; *Los Angeles Times*, 21 March, G5, and 3 April, pt.2, p.10, 1971; Mills, 'Locking Up The Tenney Files', pp.10–11.

23. 'Report of the Commission on Subversive Activities to the Legislature of the State of Hawaii, February 25, 1961' [mimeograph vol., Library of Congress], p.53; OUAC, *Report of the Un-American Activities Committee, State of Ohio, 1953–1954* (Columbus, 1954), pp.9, 25–6, 31–7; *Boston Herald*, 9, 10 Oct.1953.

24. OUAC, *Report 1951–1952*, pp.11–13; *Boston Traveler*, 1 Dec.1953; *Boston Herald*, 7 Dec.1953; Wyman, *Subversive Activities*, p.114 and passim; 'Report of the Commission on Subversive Activities in the Legislature of the Territory of Hawaii, February 28, 1955' [in LC], p.65.

25. Nathan Glazer and Seymour Martin Lipset, 'The Polls on Communism and Conformity', in Daniel Bell (ed.), *The New American Right* (New York: Criterion, 1955), p.160; George G. Green, 'McCarthyism in Texas: the 1954 Campaign', *The Southern Quarterly*, 16 April 1978, p.261. Virginia Durr attributed the indifference of the South to McCarthyism to the face-to-face nature of southern communities – 'The idea of calling people Communists ... doesn't work so well when people know each other': Hollinger F. Barnard (ed.), *Outside the Magic Circle: The Autobiography of Virginia Foster Durr* (University: University of Alabama Press, 1985), p.154.

26. For southern activities, see e.g. Louisiana Joint Legislative Committee [JLC], *Subversion in Racial Unrest: An Outline of a Strategic Weapon to Destroy the Governments of Louisiana and the United States* (1957), and also Louisiana JLC on Un-American Activities,*Report No.1* (May 8, 1961), *Report No.2* (April 24, 1962), *Activities of the Southern Conference Educational Fund, Inc. in Louisiana* (Baton Rouge, 1963); Louisiana's first JLC was formed in 1954 and was known as the Joint Legislative Committee to Maintain Segregation or the Rainach Committee after its chair William M. Rainach, though in 1960 the legislature created the expressly entitled Joint Legislative Committee on Un-American Activities as well as a State Sovereignty Commission – see also Adam Fairclough, *Race & Democracy: The Civil Rights Struggle in Louisiana, 1915–1972* (Athens: University of Georgia Press, 1995), pp.170, 205–6, 223–4, 226–9, 323–4, 373; George B. Weaver, 'Liberation – Red Bait for Negroes', *American Mercury*, 87 (Nov.1958), p.37; Numan V. Bartley, *The Rise of Massive Resistance: Race and Politics in the South During the 1950s* (Baton Rouge: Louisiana State University Press, 1969), p.188; *Report of the Committee To Investigate Communist Activities in South Carolina, March 26, 1963* [n.p., n.d.]; *Report of the Committee ... South Carolina, April 8, 1964* [n.p.]; *Report of the Florida Legislative Investigation Committee, February, 1965*, pp.v, 48–58. In Alabama George Wallace endorsed such a committee in 1963, under the inspired title the Alabama Legislative Commission to Preserve the Peace; he also created an Alabama Sovereignty Commission: Dan T. Carter, *The Politics of Rage: George Wallace, the Origins of the New Conservatism, and the Transformation of American Politics* (New York: Simon & Schuster, 1995), pp.231–5.

2   The Politics of Patriotism: Loyalty Oaths

1. Joseph R. Gusfield, *Symbolic Crusade: Status Politics and the American Temperance Movement* (Urbana: University of Illinois Press, 1963).
2. ACLU, *Thirty-Fourth Annual Report, 1953–1954* (New York, 1954), p.35; ACLU, *Thirtieth Annual Report* (1951), p.23; ACLU, *Report, 1951–1953* (1953), p.53; E. Edmund Reutter, Jr, *The School Administrator and Subversive Activities* (New York: Teachers College, Columbia University, 1951), pp.6–48; Solomon Golat to ACLU, 16 Sept.1953, Box 1043, Folder 18, ACLU Records, Seeley G. Mudd Library, Princeton University; Ralph S. Brown, Jr, *Loyalty and Security: Employment Tests in the United States* (New Haven: Yale University Press, 1958), pp.95–9.
3. Harold M. Hyman, *To Try Men's Souls: Loyalty Tests in American History* (Berkeley: University of California Press, 1959), pp.15, 57–8, 85, 139–250, 259; State of New York, *Revolutionary Radicalism ...* (Albany, 1920), pt.1, vol.1, p.16; Robert K. Murray, *Red Scare: A Study in National Hysteria, 1919–1920* (Minneapolis: University of Minnesota Press, 1955), p.238.
4. M. J. Heale, *American Anticommunism: Combating the Enemy Within, 1850–1970* (Baltimore: Johns Hopkins University Press, 1990), pp.85–6, 111; *Boston American*, 29 March 1935; *New York New Leader*, 13 April 1935; Elizabeth Gilman to ACLU, 22 July 1935, Vol.807, 1935, ACLU Records; William Pencak, *For God and Country: The American Legion, 1919–1941* (Boston: Northeastern University Press, 1989), p.268; Diane Ravitch, *The Troubled Crusade: American Education, 1945–1980* (New York: Basic Books, 1983), p.90; American Legion, Department of Massachusetts, *Annual Proceedings, 1935, Seventeenth Annual Convention*, pp.85–6; ACLU, *The States and Subversion* (New York, 1953), p.9; Reutter, *The School Administrator*, pp.6–13; William B. Prendergast, 'State Legislatures and Communism: The Current Scene', *American Political Science Review*, 44 (Sept.1950), 557.
5. ACLU, *Twenty-Ninth Annual Report* (1949), pp.14, 20, 26; Prendergast, 'State Legislatures and Communism', pp.560–2; *Daily Texan*, 7, 26 April 1949; Clarence E. Ayres to Louis Joughin, 25 Aug.1951, Box 1038, Folder 23, ACLU Records; E. Houston Harsha, 'Illinois: The Broyles Commission', pp.88–9, 135 in Walter Gellhorn (ed.), *The States and Subversion* (Ithaca: Cornell University Press, 1952); *Collinsville Herald*, 8 July 1949. The five states adopting teacher loyalty oaths were Kansas, New Jersey, Maryland, Washington and Arkansas, and the seven extending oaths to all public employees were Massachusetts, New Hampshire, Maryland, Georgia, Florida, Texas, and Kansas.
6. Brown, *Security and Loyalty*, pp.95–6; Winthrop Wadleigh to Herbert M. Levy, 27 Sept.1949, Herbert M. Levy to Osmond K. Fraenkel, 13 Oct.1949, Box 1033, Folder 8, ACLU Records; ACLU, *The States and Subversion*, pp.11–12; M. J. Heale, 'Red Scare Politics: California's Campaign Against Un-American Activities, 1940–1970', *Journal of American Studies*, 20 (April 1986), 5–32; ACLU, 'Weekly Bulletin, #

1508', 24 Sept.1951; ACLU, *Thirty-Fifth Report, 1954–55* (1955), p.36. The nine states in 1951 were Washington, Arizona, Montana, Texas, Nebraska, Oklahoma, Alabama, Indiana, and Pennsylvania.

7. ACLU, *The States and Subversion*, pp.10–11; Brown, *Loyalty and Security*, p.92. Utah used a special oath only for the state police, and Idaho and Alabama restricted oaths to civil defence workers.

8. Massachusetts Council for Constitutional Rights, *We Hold These Truths* (n.p., 1953).

9. James A. Robinson, *Anti-Sedition Legislation and Loyalty Investigations in Oklahoma* (Norman: University of Oklahoma Press, 1956), pp.46–7, 96; Sn. Cal. ACLU, *Open Forum* (Los Angeles), 12 May 1951; ACLU, 'Weekly Bulletin #1486', 23 April 1951; Scott Keyes, 'Round Two on the Pechan Bill', *The Nation*, 173 (22 Sept.1951), 234. The federal civil defence oath, model for many state oaths, required first a promise to uphold the American Constitution and to discharge any official duties faithfully. Second, it insisted on what in that period constituted an anticommunist commitment: 'And I do further swear ...that I do not advocate ...the overthrow of the government of the United States by force or violence'; a similar denial had to be made of membership of any group with that objective.

10. *San Francisco Chronicle*, 22, 25 June 1949; Robinson, *Anti-Sedition Legislation*, pp.45–6; Jack B. Tenney, 'Address by the Honorable Jack B. Tenney, California State Senator', in *All-American Conference Proceedings, Hotel Astor, New York City, January 28–29, 1950* (in Library of Congress), pp.57, 60.

11. Samuel A. Stouffer, *Communism, Conformity, and Civil Liberties* (New York: Doubleday, 1955), pp.40, 44; Sn. Cal. ACLU, *Open Forum*, 30 Oct.1948; *San Francisco Chronicle*, 22 June 1949; Clark Byse, 'A Report on the Pennsylvania Loyalty Act', *University of Pennsylvania Law Review*, 101 (Jan.1953), 507–8; *Pittsburgh Post-Gazette*, 24 July 1994, p.B-1.

12. James Q. Wilson, 'A Guide to Reagan Country: The Political Culture of Southern California', *Commentary*, 43 (1967), 37–45. For other discussions of Californian political culture, see Michael P. Rogin and John L. Shover, *Political Change in California: Critical Elections and Social Movements, 1890–1966* (Westport: Greenwood Press, 1970); Gladwin Hill, *Dancing Bear: An Insider Look at California Politics* (Cleveland: World Publishing, 1968); Carey McWilliams (ed.), *The California Revolution* (New York: Grossman, 1968); Kevin Starr, *Inventing the Dream: California Through the Progressive Era* (New York: Oxford University Press, 1985).

13. Heale, 'Red Scare Politics', pp.12–14; Ingrid Winther Scobie, 'Jack B. Tenney and the "Parasitic Menace": Anti-Communist Legislation in California, 1940–1949', *Pacific Historical Review*, 43 (May 1974), 199, 200.

14. *Los Angeles Times*, 15 March 1947; Sn. Cal. ACLU, *Open Forum*, 6 Sept.1947, 21 Aug., 30 Oct.1948; CUAC, *Fifth Report 1949*, p.614.

15. Scobie, 'Jack B. Tenney', pp.206–7; Tenney, 'Address', *All-American Conference*, p.59; Heale, 'Red Scare Politics', pp.21–2; CUAC, *Seventh*

Report 1953, p.201; David P. Gardner, *The California Oath Controversy* (Berkeley: University of California Press, 1967), pp.14–22; *San Francisco Chronicle*, 12, 13, 14, 25, 26 June 1949; Ellen W. Schrecker, *No Ivory Tower:McCarthyism and the Universities* (New York: Oxford University Press,1986), pp.117–25.

16. Gordon Pates, 'California – The Oath Epidemic', *The Reporter*, 3 (26 Dec.1950), 29–31.
17. Edward R. Long, 'Earl Warren and the Politics of Anti-Communism', *Pacific Historical Review*, 51 (1982), 51–70; Sn. Cal. ACLU, *Open Forum*, 22 July 1950; A.A.Heist to Patrick Murphy Malin, 19 Sept.1950, Box 426, Folder 7, ACLU Records.
18. *Los Angeles Times*, 5 Aug.1950; *Sacramento Bee*, 21 Sept.1950.
19. *Sacramento Bee*, 21 Sept.1950; State of California, *1950 Third Extraordinary Session: Senate Journal*, pp.146–51; Federation for the Repeal of the Levering Act [FRLA], *California's New Loyalty* (San Francisco, n.d.); A. A. Heist to Patrick Murphy Malin, 24 Oct.1950, Box 1037, Folder 21, ACLU Records; Long, 'Earl Warren', p.67; Pates, 'California – The Oath Epidemic', pp.29, 31.
20. John D. Weaver, *Warren: The Man, The Court, The Era* (Boston, 1967), pp.95–6; *Baltimore Sun*, 2 Nov.1950; *Sacramento Bee*, 8 Jan.1951; Long, 'Earl Warren', pp.68–9.
21. *Sacramento Bee*, 8 Jan.1951; Sn. Cal. ACLU, *Open Forum*, 3 March, 18 Aug.1951.
22. *Sacramento Bee*, 4 Feb., 26 April, 2 May 1951; *Call-Bulletin* (San Francisco), 26 April, 6 June 1951; FRLA, *The Repeal Newsletter*, 23 March, 20 June, 2 Aug.1951, in ACLU Papers, California Historical Society, San Francisco. The lawyers' oath bill may have been defeated, but lawyers who represented alleged Communists were subjected to other pressures, not least loss of business. One Hollywood Ten defender, Bartley Crum, was to commit suicide.
23. Joint Action Council for the Repeal of the Levering Act, *Seek Not Loyalty with a Sword* (San Francisco, Dec.1950), in Bancroft Library; Ernest Besig to John H. Michener, 6 March 1951, in Levering Act Corr., ACLU Papers; Frank Rowe, *The Enemy Among Us: A Story of Witch-hunting in the McCarthy Era* (Sacramento: Cougar Books, 1980), pp.58, 78, 80; FRLA, *The Repeal Newsletter*, 28 Nov.1950, p.1.
24. FRLA, *The Repeal Newsletter*, 13 Dec.1950, p.2; Sn. Cal. ACLU, *Open Forum*, 2 Nov.1952; ACLU, *Report on Civil Liberties, January 1951–June 1953* (1953), p.57; State of California, *Senate Journal 1950*, p.147.
25. FRLA, *The Repeal Newsletter*, 11 April 1952; FRLA, 'Second Annual Report, January 23, 1953', pp.1, 4–6, and *Would You Take This Oath?* in ACLU Papers; Rowe, *The Enemy Among Us*, pp.91–3, 99, 104; Sn. Cal. ACLU, *Open Forum*, Sept., Nov.1952; *San Francisco Examiner*, 1 Nov.1952; Eason Monroe, 'Safeguarding Civil Liberties' (Oral History Program, 1974, Bancroft Library), p.92.
26. 'ACLU Legislative Bulletin' in Sn. Cal. ACLU, *Open Forum*, March–April 1953; CUAC, *Seventh Report 1953*, p.124; Robert H. Sollen, 'Do They Deserve To Be Free?' *Christian Century*, 75 (20 Aug.1958), 945–7.

27. Dean R. Cresap, *Party Politics in the Golden State* (Los Angeles, 1954); James Reichley, *States in Crisis: Politics in Ten American States* (Chapel Hill: University of North Carolina Press, 1963), ch.10; *Baltimore Sun*, 2 Nov.1950, p.6; Heale, 'Red Scare Politics', pp.29–30.

28. Robert W. Kenny, 'My First Forty Years in California Politics, 1922–1962' (Oral History Program, Bancroft Library), p.385; *Los Angeles Daily News*, 10 April 1954; State of California, *Statement of Vote: Direct Primary Election, June 8, 1954*, p.21; *Sacramento Bee*, 1 Jan., 29 March, 5 April 1954; Rogin and Shover, *Political Change in California*, p.139; *San Francisco Examiner*, 31 March 1954, 3 June 1955; *San Francisco Chronicle*, 20 May, 2 June, 17, 21 Oct.1955; Reichley, *States in Crisis*, p.180.

29. Rowe, *The Enemy Among Us*, p.113; *American Civil Liberties Union – News* (San Francisco), no.6, June 1953; ACLU, *Thirty-Fourth Report, 1953–54* (1954), p.35, *Thirty-Fifth Report, 1954–55* (1955), pp.32–3, *Thirty-Sixth Report* (1956), p.33; 'California Churches Balk at Oath Law', *Christian Century*, 71 (7 April 1954), 419–20; Emergency Civil Liberties Union, *Rights* (New York), March 1954, p.15, May 1955, pp.2–3; *San Francisco Chronicle*, 9, 10, 11 May, 26 Aug.1955; *San Francisco Examiner*, 10, 11 May 1955.

30. Sollen, 'Do They Deserve To Be Free?' pp.945–7; N. Cal. ACLU, Press Release, 13 Sept.1965, Box 182, Folder 8, ACLU Records; Rowe, *The Enemy Among Us*, pp.111–14, 124; Monroe, 'Safeguarding Civil Liberties', pp.314–15.

31. Thomas Michael Holmes, 'The Specter of Communism in Hawaii, 1947–53' (Ph.D diss., University of Hawaii, 1975), pp.6–12, 20–30, 268; US Senate, Committee on Interior and Insular Affairs, *Statehood for Hawaii: Communist Penetration of the Hawaiian Islands* (Washington, 1949), p.14; 'Report of the Commission on Subversive Activities to the Legislature of the Territory of Hawaii, March 1951', and 'Report of the Commission ... March 1953', bound typescripts in Library of Congress; Roger Bell, *Last Among Equals: Hawaiian Statehood and American Politics* (Honolulu: University of Hawaii Press, 1984), pp.170, 187; Louise S. Jessen to Patrick Murphy Malin, 24 May 1951, Gov. Oren E. Long to Malin, 8 June 1951, Allan F. Saunders to Malin and Herbert Monte Levy, 19 Nov. 1951, Box 578, Folder 14, ACLU Records; *The Nation*, 173 (14 July 1951), 21–2.

32. Robinson, *Anti-Sedition Legislation*, pp.23–35, 37–8, 41–8; Bruce Johnson and Jean Lomenick, 'Oklahoma's Loyalty Oath', *The Nation*, 173 (11 Aug.1951), 106–8.

33. Ibid., pp.106–8; Robinson, *Anti-Sedition Legislation*, pp.49–55; ACLU, *Report, 1951–1953* (1953), pp.60–1; Brown, *Loyalty and Security*, pp.96–7.

34. Keyes, 'Round Two', pp.234–6; Byse, 'Report on the Pennsylvania Loyalty Act', pp.480–508; *Philadelphia Bulletin*, 30, 31 July 1951; *Philadelphia Inquirer*, 1, 3 Aug.1951; ACLU, 'Weekly Bulletin, #1524', 14 Jan.1952. The state's loyalty oath required the signer not knowingly to be a member of an organization advocating violent overthrow, with 'the specific intent' of furthering its aims.

35. Byse, 'Report on the Pennsylvania Loyalty Act', pp.481–3, 487, 497–503.
36. Ibid., pp.482–3; ACLU, *Report, 1951–1953*, pp.57–8; ACLU, *Thirty-Fifth Report, 1954–1955*, p.33; Library of Congress Legislative Reference Service, *Internal Security and Subversion:Principal State Laws and Cases* ... (Washington: Government Printing Office, 1965), p.360; Thomas I. Emerson, David Haber, and Norman Dorsen, *Political and Civil Rights in the United States* (Boston: Little, Brown and Co., 1967), I, p.349; ECLC, *Rights* (New York), Nov.1954, p.15; *Pittsburgh Post-Gazette*, 24 July 1994, pp.B-1, 4. While the Pechan Act led to few direct job losses, HUAC visitations to Philadelphia in the early 1950s prompted the city's board of education to fire a score of uncooperative teachers: David Caute, *The Great Fear: The Anti-Communist Purge under Truman and Eisenhower* (New York: Simon and Schuster, 1978), pp.419–20.
37. Prendergast, 'State Legislatures and Communism', p.561; Pates, 'California – The Oath Epidemic', p.31.
38. ACLU, 'Bulletin #2256', 7 Feb.1966, 'Bulletin #2279', 31 Oct.1966, and 'Bulletin #2301', 5 June 1967; Emerson et al., *Political and Civil Rights*, I, pp.329–32, 336, 339, 340–7, 348n; Caughey, 'Farewell to California's Loyalty Oath', p.127; Rowe, *The Enemy Among Us*, pp.113–14. In the late 1960s loyalty oaths were struck down in California, Massachusetts, Nebraska, New Hampshire and Colorado.

3   The Politics of Regulation: Communist-Control Laws

1. *Counterattack*, 6 Jan.1950, p.2.
2. ACLU, *The States and Subversion* (New York, 1953), pp.8–9; James A. Robinson, *Anti-Sedition Legislation and Loyalty Investigations in Oklahoma* (Norman: University of Oklahoma, 1956), p.37.
3. Maurice Isserman, *Which Side Were You On? The American Communist Party During the Second World War* (Middletown: Wesleyan University Press, 1982), pp.69–71; *St. Cloud News*, 7 Nov.1940; *Daily Worker*, 24 Aug., 27 Dec.1940; Robert Justin Goldstein, *Political Repression in Modern America From 1870 to the Present* (Cambridge, MA: Schenckman, 1978), p.349; William B. Prendergast, 'State Legislatures and Communism: The Current Scene', *American Political Science Review*, 44 (Sept.1950), 556–7, 561–2; Walter Gellhorn, 'A General View', in Gellhorn (ed.), *The States and Subversion* (Ithaca: Cornell University Press, 1952), pp.373–4, 375.
4. Ralph S. Brown, *Loyalty and Security: Employment Tests in the United States* (New Haven: Yale University Press, 1958), p.106.
5. Ellen W. Schrecker, *No Ivory Tower: McCarthyism & the Universities* (New York: Oxford University Press, 1986), pp.75–83, 113–14; Kenneth Culp Davis, 'Standing, Ripeness and Civil Liberties: A Critique of *Adler* v. *Board of Education*', *American Bar Association Journal*, 38 (Nov.1952),

924–7; University of the State of New York, *Regents Rules on Subversive Activities* (Albany: University of the State of New York Press, 1953), pp.13–17; Brown, *Loyalty and Security*, pp.105–6; *Report of Special Committee to the Board of Regents in the Inquiry Relative to Subversive Organizations, September 24, 1953* (Albany: University of the State of New York Press, 1953), pp.4–12; Robert W. Iversen, *The Communists & the Schools* (New York: Harcourt, Brace, 1959), pp.263–7, 337; David Caute, *The Great Fear: The Anti-Communist Purge under Truman and Eisenhower* (New York: Simon and Schuster, 1978), pp.442, 445.

6. Brown, *Loyalty and Security*, pp.106–7; ACLU, News Release, 14 March 1951, Box 1038, Folder 16, ACLU Records, Seeley G. Mudd Library, Princeton University; *New York Times*, 22, 27 March 1951, 27 March 1955; 'New York Security Risk Law: An Analysis', *Civil Liberties in New York* (NY Civil Liberties Union, Nov.–Dec.1955), v.4, no.2, pp.7–10; ECLC, *Rights*, Feb.1956, pp.16–17, March 1956, p.15, March 1957, pp.11–12, April 1957, pp.11–12; Thomas I. Emerson et al., *Political and Civil Rights in the United States* (Boston: Little, Brown, 1967), I, pp.328–9.

7. Robert E. Stripling, *The Red Plot Against America* (Drexel Hill, PA.: Bell Publishing, 1949), p.13; Louis Francis Budenz, *Men Without Faces: The Communist Conspiracy in the USA* (New York: Harper, 1950), p.xii; *All-American Conference Proceedings, Hotel Astor, New York City, January 28–29, 1950* [mimeograph booklet in Library of Congress (LC)], pp.36, 42, 45, 99; M. J. Heale, *American Anticommunism: Combating the Enemy Within, 1830–1970* (Baltimore: Johns Hopkins University Press, 1990), p.156.

8. Goldstein, *Political Repression*, p.349.

9. Robin D. G. Kelley, *Hammer and Hoe: Alabama Communists during the Great Depression* (Chapel Hill: University of North Carolina Press, 1990), pp.224–5; A. J. Noble, *State Anti-Communist Legislation* (Montgomery: Alabama Legislative Reference Service, Sept. 1950 [mimeograph doc. in LC]), pp.1–2; Department of the Attorney-General of Kansas, 'Memorandum on Kansas Statutes and Judicial Opinions In Re Communism, Criminal Syndicalism and Subversive Activities' (Topeka, 1953 [mimeograph doc. in LC]), p.7; Prendergast, 'State Legislatures', p.564.

10. E. T. Baker, 'Maryland Betrays Its Past', *New Republic*, 120 (25 April 1949), 15–17; *Baltimore Sun*, 2 June 1935; Philip Frankfeld, 'A United Front Defeated the Ober Law', *Political Affairs*, 28 (Oct.1949), 85–6; Joshua B. Freeman and Steve Rosswurm, 'The Education of an Anti-Communist: Father John F. Cronin and the Baltimore Labor Movement', *Labor History*, 33 (Spring 1992), 217–47; Robert Griffith, *The Politics of Fear: Joseph R. McCarthy and the Senate* (Amherst: University of Massachusetts Press, 2nd edn, 1987), pp.126–31. A variety of issues probably contributed to Tydings's defeat, but anticommunist emotions in the state were certainly stirred vigorously.

11. *Journal of the Proceedings of the House of Delegates of Maryland, January Session, 1947* (Annapolis, 1947), pp.955, 1526, 2269–70 [hereinafter *Md House J* and corresponding for senate]; *Md Sen. J,1947*, pp.1542,

1647; *Baltimore Sun*, 26 April, 15 June, 11 Sept.1947, 19 June 1948; Baker, 'Maryland Betrays Its Past', p.17; *Md House J, May 25, 1948*, pp.136, 152–3.

12. Frank B. Ober, 'Communism vs the Constitution: The Power To Protect Our Free Institutions', *American Bar Association Journal*, 34 (Aug.1948), 645–8, 741–7; *Report of Commission on Subversive Activities to Governor Wm. Lane, Jr and the Maryland General Assembly, January, 1949*, p.1; Prendergast, 'Maryland: The Ober Anti-Communist Law', in Gellhorn (ed.), *States and Subversion*, p.143.

13. *'Operation Anti-Communism': A Report by the Maryland Committee Against Un-American Activities* (Baltimore, n.d.), pp.1–5; *Baltimore Sun*, 29 Oct., 4, 23 Nov. 1948, 6 Aug., 3 Sept. 1950; *All-American Conference Proceedings*, p.48; Frankfeld, 'A United Front', p.87; Edna R. Walls to Clifford Forster, 9 Nov. 1948, Box 566, Folder 7, ACLU Records; Prendergast, 'Maryland', p.157.

14. *Report of Commission on Subversive Activities*, pp.6–9, 13, 17, 56–8.

15. Ibid.; *Baltimore Sun*, 11 Feb.1949. The oath required takers to state that they neither belonged to subversive groups (defined in the act) nor advocated any act intended forcibly to overthrow government: Form 424, Certification of Applicant for Public Employment, Subversive Activities Vertical File (VF), Enoch Pratt Free Library, Baltimore.

16. *Report of Commission on Subversive Activities*, pp.6–7, 31–3, 56–65, 107–8. See also Warren P. Hill, 'A Critique of Recent Ohio Anti-Subversive Legislation', *Ohio State Law Journal*, 14 (1953), 439–93.

17. *Md House J, 1949*, pp.155, 558, 920–1, 1031–2; *Md Sen. J, 1949*, pp.89, 380, 722–3; Frankfeld, 'United Front', p.87; Edna D. Walls to Herbert M. Levy, 15 Feb.1949, Folder 2, and Carl Bassett to Levy, 8 March 1949, Folder 1, Box 1033, ACLU Records; Baker, 'Maryland Betrays', p.17; *Baltimore Sun*, 11 Feb., 1 April 1949; *Baltimore Evening Sun*, 14 April 1949.

18. *Baltimore Sun*, 1 April 1949; Baker, 'Maryland Betrays', p.17; *Counterattack*, 19 Aug.1949.

19. *Baltimore Evening Sun*, 14, 23 April, 4 May 1949; *Baltimore Sun*, 31 March 1950; Frankfeld, 'United Front', pp.85–94; Herbert M. Levy to John H. Skeen, 16 May 1949, and Skeen to Levy, 18 May 1949, Box 1033, Folder 1, ACLU Records; Carl Bassett, President of Maryland Civil Liberties Committee, to 'Friend', 12 Oct. 1950, Subversive Activities VF, Pratt Library; Circuit Court No.2 of Baltimore City (1949), *H. Carrington Lancaster, et al.*, v. *Hall Hammond ...*, *Opinion by Sherbow, J*; Court of Appeals of Maryland (Oct.Term, 1949), *Hall Hammond ...v. H. Carrington Lancaster, et al., Appellants.*

20. Ct of Appeals, Md., *Hammond* v. *Lancaster*, pp.2–3; see e.g. F. I. Linehard to Tydings, 5 May 1950, Series II, Millard E. Tydings Collection, McKeldin Library, University of Maryland, and other letters in this file; *Baltimore Evening Sun*, 19, 27 Sept., 2, 5 Oct., 6 Nov., 27 Dec.1950, 18 Jan.1951; *Baltimore Sun*, 22 Sept., 3, 9 Oct.1950; see also Don Edward Carleton, 'A Crisis of Rapid Change: The Red Scare in Houston, 1945–1955' (Ph. D diss., University of Houston, 1978), pp.102–24, on the Minute Women's effectiveness in Houston.

21. Joseph I. Paper to Herbert M. Levy, 8 Dec.1949, Box 1033, Folder 1, and Frances French to George E. Rundquist, 11 Oct.1950, Box 427, Folder 3, ACLU Records; Carl Bassett to Friend, 12 Oct.1950, Subversive Activities VF, and 'Protect Our Form of Government', 'Smash the Reds at Home!', and 'You Can't Straddle the Fence', leaflets in Md Committee Against Un-American Activities (Md CUAC) VF, Pratt Library; *Baltimore Evening Sun*, 1 July, 30 Aug.1950; *Baltimore Sun*, 23 July, 6 Aug., 3 Sept., 6, 9 Nov.1950; Md CUAC, *The Ober Law Explained* (Baltimore 1950); Prendergast, 'Maryland', p.161.
22. *Baltimore Sun*, 2 Aug.1949, 31 March 1950; 'One Absurd And Two Untrue Arguments Against The Ober Law', *Baltimore Sun*, 3 Nov.1950, p.16; C. P. Ives, 'The Phony Case Against the Ober Law', *Baltimore Sun*, 6 Nov.1950, p.12; League of Women Voters of Md, 'Constitutional Rights', April 1953, pp.3–5, memo in Subversive Activities VF, Pratt Library.
23. *Baltimore Sun*, 2 Aug.1949, 31 March, 27 April, 3 Nov.1950, 2, 9 Nov.1951, 1 April 1952, 11 May 1953; LWV, 'Constitutional Rights', pp.2–3, *Baltimore Evening Sun*, 12 April 1951.
24. *Baltimore Sun*, 11 May 1953, 19, 23 Jan.1955, 5 Jan.1964; *Baltimore Evening Sun*, 9 Dec.1954.
25. *Baltimore Sun*, 19 Jan.1955, 3 April 56, 5 Jan.1964, 31 Oct.1965; *Baltimore Evening Sun*, 3 April 1956, 15 Jan.1971; Frank Donner, *Protectors of Privilege: Red Squads and Police Repression in Urban America* (Berkeley: University of California Press, 1990), p.298.
26. *Baltimore Sun*, 2 June 1964, 23 Jan., 23, 24 Feb.1966, 20 Jan.1967; *US Reports*, v.389, pp.54–63; *Federal Supplement*, v.287, pp.60–5; *Baltimore Evening Sun*, 14 Feb.1967, 15 Jan.1971; *Baltimore News American*, 5 Dec.1967; *Washington Post*, 7 Feb.1970.
27. *New Republic*, 26 March 1951; Massachusetts Council for Constitutional Rights, *We Hold These Truths* (n.p., 1953), p.9; *Report of the Un-American Activities Commission, State of Ohio, 1953–1954*, pp.9, 33–35; ACLU, *Report for 1951–53*, p.52; Brian Usher, 'The Lausche Era, 1945–1957', p.36, in Alexander P. Lamis (ed.), *Ohio Politics* (Kent: Kent State University Press, 1994).
28. Elba Chase Nelson to Patrick Murphy Malin, 14 Nov.1951, Box 1038, Folder 13, ACLU Records; *Manchester Union Leader*, 23 May 1951; 'McCarthyism in New Hampshire', *Christian Century*, 71 (28 July 1954), 908–9; 'The Sweezy Case', ECLC, *Rights*, Sept.1954, pp.7–9; Willard Uphaus, *Commitment* (New York, 1963), pp.131, 172; Louis C. Wyman, *Subversive Activities in New Hampshire: Report of the Attorney General to the New Hampshire General Court, Pursuant to Laws 1953, Chapter 307* (1955), pp.v, 3–4, 57, 190–254, 257–63; Louis C. Wyman to Winthrop Wadleigh, 15 July 1953, Box 1043, Folder 17, ACLU Records; ECLC, *Rights*, May 1955, pp.5–6; ACLU, *Thirty-Sixth Annual Report, 1955–56* (New York, 1956), p.33; Brown, *Loyalty and Security*, p.17n; 'New Hampshire Jails Uphaus', *Christian Century*,76 (30 Dec.1959), 1517.
29. Brown, *Loyalty and Security*, p.103.
30. Dale R. Sorenson, 'The Anticommunist Consensus in Indiana, 1945–1958' (Ph.D diss., Indiana University, 1980), pp.133–4; 'New

Anti-Communist Law', *New Republic*, 125 (17 Dec.1951), 7; *Mass. House Journal, 1951*, pp.2451–4; *Mass. Sen. J., 1951*, p.1823; *Boston Globe*, 23 Nov.1951; *Boston Traveler*, 22 March 1954; *Boston Herald*, 25 May 1954; *Mass. Legislative Documents, House, 1958*, No.2626, p.6; ACLU, *Report for 1955–56*, p.25; ACLU, *States and Subversion*, p.4; *Detroit Free Press*, 29 March 1952; ECLC, *Rights*, March 1954, p.15; ACLU, *Report for 1953–54*, pp.34–5; *New York Herald Tribune*, 26 March 1954; Theodore H. White, 'Texas: Land of Wealth and Fear', pt. 2, *The Reporter*, 10 (8 June 1954), 32–3; George N. Green, 'McCarthyism in Texas: The 1954 Campaign', *Southern Quarterly*, 16 (April 1978), 259–61; Robinson, *Anti-Sedition Legislation*, p.55; Frederick K. Beutel to Alan Reitman, 25 Oct.1961, and Nebraska Laws 1961, Ch.124, Box 900, Folder 14, ACLU Records.

31. Herbert Monte Levy to George A. Dreyfous, 10 June 1952, Box 1040, Folder 5, ACLU Records.

32. M. J. Heale, 'The Triumph of Liberalism? Red Scare Politics in Michigan, 1938–1954', *Proceedings of the American Philosophical Society*, 139, no.1 (March 1995), 44–66; Emerson, *Political and Civil Rights*, I, p.194; ACLU, *Report for 1955–56*, p.32; Carroll H. Lemon to George Rundquist, 29 May 1951, Box 1038, Folder 11, and Henry Beitscher to Patrick Murphy Malin, 7 July 1953, Box 1043, Folder 9, ACLU Records; Wayne Addison Cole, 'An Analysis of the Relationship Between Anti-Communism and Segregationist Thought in the Deep South, 1948–1964' (Ph.D diss., University of North Carolina, 1976), pp.62, 76; Carleton, 'A Crisis of Rapid Change', pp.90–2.

33. *New Orleans Item*, 23 Sept.1952; ACLU, *Report for 1951–53*, p.51; Hunter O'Dell, 'The Political Scene in Louisiana', *Political Affairs*, 35 (Aug.1956), pp.13–23; Arthur Kinoy, *Rights on Trial: The Odyssey of a People's Lawyer* (Cambridge: Harvard University Press, 1983), pp.215–17, 283–85; Emerson, *Political and Civil Rights*, I, pp.205–10; Adam Fairclough, *Race & Democracy: The Civil Rights Struggle in Louisiana, 1915–1972* (Athens: University of Georgia Press, 1995), pp.323–5; Kelley, *Hammer and Hoe*, p.227; ACLU, *Report for 1954–55*, p.124; ECLC, *Rights*, Sept.1955, pp.11–13, July 1956, p.3. Bull Connor in July 1950 sought 'to pick up every known Communist in Birmingham', and even contrived to have one arrested in his own home on a charge of vagrancy: *Montgomery Advertiser*, 9 July 1950.

34. ACLU, *Report for 1948–49*, p.20, *Report for 1951–53*, pp.53–4, *Report for 1954–55*, p.31; ACLU, 'Weekly Bulletin, #1606', 10 Aug.1953; R. Will Burnett and Henrietta DeBoer, 'Resistance in Illinois: Is the Tide Turning?' *The Nation*, 177 (8 Aug.1953), 112–13; Hill, 'Critique of Anti-Subversive Legislation', p.449; Michael O'Brien, *McCarthy and McCarthyism in Wisconsin* (Columbia: University of Missouri Press, 1980), pp.188–93; Edward H. Meyerding to Alan Reitman, rec'd 14 July 1953, Box 1043, Folder 11, Robbins W. Barstow Jr. to ACLU, 13 July 1953, Box 1043, Folder 7, and 'A Summary of SF384 – Iowa Subversive Activities Bill of 1951', Box 1038, Folder 5, ACLU Records; *New Republic*, 26 March 1951; ECLC, *Rights*, Feb. 1956, pp. 2–3.

II Red Scare Politics in Michigan

1. Michael Paul Rogin, *The Intellectuals and McCarthy: The Radical Specter* (Cambridge: MIT Press, 1967); Robert Griffith, *The Politics of Fear: Joseph R. McCarthy and the Senate* (Lexington: University of Kentucky, 1970).
2. For general background see William Haber et al., *The Michigan Economy: Its Potentials and Its Problems* (Kalamazoo: Upjohn Institute, 1959); Willis F. Dunbar, *Michigan: A History of the Wolverine State* (Grand Rapids: Eerdmans Publishing, 1965); William P. Browne and Kenneth VerBurg, *Michigan Government and Politics* (Lincoln: University of Nebraska Press, 1995). For more specific data see Kenneth T. Jackson, *The Ku Klux Klan in the City, 1915–1930* (New York: Oxford University Press, 1967), pp.127–9; Ronald Edsforth, *Class Conflict and Cultural Consensus: The Making of a Mass Consumer Society in Flint, Michigan* (New Brunswick: Rutgers University Press, 1987), pp.18–20, 28–9, 79–80; Stephen B. and Vera Sarasohn, *Political Party Patterns in Michigan* (Detroit: Wayne State University Press, 1957), pp.1–4; John C. Leggett, *Working-Class Consciousness in Detroit* (New York: Oxford University Press, 1968), pp.43–7.
3. Edsforth, *Class Conflict*, pp.81,112; Roger Keeran, *The Communist Party and the Auto Workers' Unions* (New York: International Publishers, 1980), pp.43–5, 48; Lois Rankin, 'Detroit Nationality Groups', *Michigan History Magazine*, 23 (Spring 1939), 129–30, 134–40, 146–63, 175–84, 189–95; Sidney Fine, *Frank Murphy: The New Deal Years* (Chicago: University of Chicago Press, 1979), p.256; Robert J. Mowitz, 'Michigan: State and Local Attacks on Subversion', in Walter Gellhorn (ed.), *The States and Subversion* (Ithaca: Cornell University Press, 1952).
4. Ronald P. Formisano, *The Birth of Mass Political Parties: Michigan, 1827–1861* (Princeton: Princeton University Press, 1971), chs 2, 6, 8, 14; Dunbar, *Michigan*, pp. 469–663.

4 Class Conflict and Party Politics, 1933–1945

1. Joseph LaPalombara, *Guide to Michigan Politics* (East Lansing: Bureau of Political and Social Research, Michigan State University, 1960), p.104 and passim; see also Sarasohn, *Political Party Patterns*; Leggett, *Working Class Consciousness*, pp.47–52; Dudley W. Buffa, *Union Power and American Democracy: The UAW and the Democratic Party, 1935–72* (Ann Arbor: University of Michigan Press, 1984), pp.3–25.
2. Keeran, *The CP and AWUs*, pp.34–47, 50; Edsforth, *Class Conflict*, pp.83–100, 106–9, 114–22, 125–6; Jackson, *Ku Klux Klan in the City*, pp.129–39; B. J. Widick, *Detroit: City of Race and Class Violence* (Chicago: Quadrangle Books, 1972), p.3.

3. Harvey Klehr, *The Heyday of American Communism* (New York: Basic Books, 1984), p.50; Robert Lacey, *Ford: The Men and the Machine* (London: Heineman, 1986), pp.342–5; Edward P. Johanningsmeier, *Forging American Communism: The Life of William Z. Foster* (Princeton: Princeton University Press, 1994), p.262; Christopher H. Johnson, *Maurice Sugar: Law, Labor, and the Left in Detroit, 1912–1950* (Detroit: Wayne State University Press, 1988), pp.120–3; Robert Conot, *American Odyssey* (New York: William Morrow, 1976), pp.284–6.

4. Johnson, *Maurice Sugar*, pp.181–9; 'Red-Baiting', p.1, typescript in Civil Rights Congress of Michigan [hereafter CRC] Papers, Reuther Library, Detroit; Mowitz, 'Michigan', p.188; Widick, *Detroit*, p.66; State of Michigan, *Journal of the Senate, 1937* [hereafter *Mich. Sen. J.*] p.624; Michael C. Clinansmith, 'The Black Legion: Hooded Americanism in Michigan', *Michigan History*, 55 (Fall 1971), 243–62; David J. Maurer, 'The Black Legion: A Paramilitary Fascist Organization of the 1930s', in Frank Annunziata et al., *For the General Welfare: Essays in Honor of Robert H. Bremner* (New York: Peter Lang, 1989), pp.255–69.

5. Robert W. Iversen, *The Communists and the Schools* (New York: Harcourt, Brace, 1959), pp.130–2, 184–6; Clifford McVeagh, 'Academic Napoleons No.1: Ruthven of Michigan', pp.2, 4 in CRC Papers; State of Michigan, *Journal of the House of Representatives, 1935* [hereafter *Mich. House J.*], pp.908–9; Arthur Miller, *Timebends: A Life* (London: Methuen, 1987), pp.94, 97; *Detroit News*, 31 Oct.1950.

6. *Michigan Daily*, 24 April 1939; *Detroit Free Press*, 25 April 1935; *Mich. Sen. J, 1935*, pp.486–7, 531, 782, 835, 844, 1406; *Mich. Pub. Acts, 1935*, No.23, pp.34–5, No.168, p.266; *Mich. House J., 1935*, pp.908–9; H. P. Marley to Roger Baldwin, 3 June 1935, Vol. 842, 1935, ACLU Records, Seeley G. Mudd Library, Princeton University; McVeagh, 'Academic Napoleons', p.4; *Student News* (Ann Arbor), 27 Sept.1935.

7. Fine, *Murphy: New Deal Years*, pp.247–53; Edsforth, *Class Conflict*, pp.142–55, 188.

8. Keeran, *The CP and AWUs*, pp.29–32, 117–19, 185; Harvey A. Levenstein, *Communism, Anticommunism, and the CIO* (Westport, CT: Greenwood Press, 1981), pp.52–5.

9. Foster Rhea Dulles and Melvyn Dubofsky, *Labor in America*, 4th rev.edn. (Arlington Heights, Ill.: Harlan Davidson), pp.302–7; Keeran, *The CP and AWUs*, pp.184–5; Sidney Fine, *Sit-Down: The General Motors Strike of 1936-1937* (Ann Arbor: University of Michigan Press, 1969), pp.313–41 and passim.

10. Keeran, *The CP and AWUs*, pp.161–2; Fraser M. Ottanelli, *The Communist Party of the United States from the Depression to World War II* (New Brunswick: Rutgers University Press, 1991), pp.144–6; Edsforth, *Class Conflict*, pp.172, 180; Robert H. Zieger, *The CIO,1935–1955* (Chapel Hill: University of North Carolina Press, 1995), p.53; Fine, *Murphy: New Deal Years*, pp.324, 330; J. Woodford Howard Jr, 'Frank Murphy and the Sit-Down Strikes of 1937', *Labor History* (Spring 1960), 106, 131; *Detroit Free Press*, 8 March 1937.

11. 'Red-Baiting'; *Detroit Times*,18 Jan.1937; *Detroit News*, 11 Jan.1937; Keeran, *The CP and AWUs*, p.161; *Detroit Free Press*, 26 Oct.1958; Richard Gid Powers, *Not Without Honor: The History of American Anticommunism* (New York: Free Press, 1995), p.134; Widick, *Detroit*, p.65; Douglas P. Seaton, *Catholics and Radicals: The Association of Catholic Trade Unionists and the American Labor Movement, from Depression to Cold War* (Lewisburg: Bucknell University Press, 1981), pp.56, 59; David O'Brien, *Public Catholicism* (New York: Macmillan, 1989), p.220; Steve Rosswurm, 'The Catholic Church and the Left-Led Unions: Labor Priests, Labor Schools, and the ACTU', in Rosswurm, (ed.), *The CIO's Left-Led Unions* (New Brunswick: Rutgers University Press, 1992), pp.119–37.

12. *Detroit Free Press*, 20 Aug., 14, 20, 21 Oct.1938; *Detroit News*, 26 Oct.1938; Fine, *Murphy: New Deal Years*, p.484; 'Investigation of Un-American Propaganda Activities in the United States', pp.1–7, typescript of Detroit HUAC Hearing, Oct.1938, in CRC Papers.

13. *Detroit Free Press*, 21, 22, 26 Oct.1938; Howard, 'Murphy and the Sit-Down Strikes', pp.134–5; Frank Donner, *Protectors of Privilege: Red Squads and Police Repression in Urban America* (Berkeley: University of California Press, 1990), pp.56–7.

14. *Detroit Free Press*, 26 Oct.1938; *Detroit News*, 6, 7 Nov.1938; *New York Times*, 5 Nov.1938; J. Woodford Howard, *Mr. Justice Murphy: A Political Biography* (Princeton: Princeton University Press, 1968), pp.166–73; Fine, *Murphy: New Deal Years*, pp.502, 508–15.

15. Jerome M. Britchey to Caroline Parker, 18 Feb.1938, and attached clipping, Vol.2037, 1938, ACLU Records; Fine, *Murphy: New Deal Years*, pp.518–21; Alan Brinkley, *Voices of Protest: Huey Long, Father Coughlin and the Great Depression* (New York: Vintage Books, 1983), pp.266–7; *United Automobile Worker*, 23 June 1937, in 'Red-Baiting'; Keeran, *The CP and AWUs*, p.232; Alan Clive, *State of War: Michigan in World War II* (Ann Arbor: University of Michigan Press, 1979), pp.138–41; *Detroit News*, 3 May 1942; Glen Jeansonne, *Gerald L. K. Smith: Minister of Hate* (New Haven: Yale University Press, 1988), pp.64–71; Widick, *Detroit*, pp.89–90.

16. Edsforth, *Class Conflict*, pp.154–5; Edward Mooney, *Human Relations in Industry – Cooperation Not Conflict* (Washington, DC, 1939), pp.3, 5.

17. 'Red-Baiting'; *Detroit News*, 22 Feb.1939; Keeran, *The CP and AWUs*, pp.199, 205–12; Johnson, *Maurice Sugar*, pp.235–8; *Michigan Catholic*, 3 Aug.1939. See also Nelson Lichtenstein, *The Most Dangerous Man in Detroit: Walter Reuther and the Fate of American Labor* (New York: Basic Books, 1995).

18. 'Report of Civil Rights Federation Activities on Senate Bill 50 (Little Dies Bill), April 24, 1939', in CRC Papers; WHO DEFEATED THE 'LITTLE DIES BILL'? printed leaflet in ibid.; *Detroit News*, 26 April 1939; *Michigan Daily*, 26 April 1939.

19. *Detroit News*, 7, 13 Nov.1939; *Detroit Free Press*, 3, 25 Nov.1939, 29 Feb.1940; 'Red-Baiting'; Keeran, *The CP and AWUs*, p.212; Johnson,

Maurice Sugar, pp.244, 249; 'First Draft of Brief of the Case', pp.1–6, typescript in CRC Papers; Yale Foreman to 'Beatie' (Mrs Robert Kahn), 14 Oct.1940, in ibid.; National Federation for Constitutional Liberties, 'Action Letter', 7 Dec.1940, in ibid.; S. R. Kaye, 'Ann Arbor Hysteria', *The Nation*, 14 Sept.1940, pp.215–16; *New York Times*, 4 July 1940; Maurice Isserman, *Which Side Were You On? The American Communist Party During the Second World War* (Middletown: Wesleyan University Press, 1982), p.70.

20. *Detroit Free Press*, 7 Nov.1939; 'Red-Baiting'; Conot, *American Odyssey*, pp.366–7; typescript carbon headed 'callahan - ...- allan', 10 March [1948], Callahan Act 1947–8 file, CRC Papers; Committee on Free Elections (New York), '1941 Legislative Attacks on Free Elections', mimeograph paper, CRC Papers; Joseph F. Nagel to Owen A. Knox, 8 May 1941, in ibid.; Civil Rights Federation, open letter to legislators, 29 April 1941, in ibid.; *Daily Worker*, 24 June 1940; *Detroit Times*, 15 April 1941; *Detroit News*, 27 May 1941; Mowitz, 'Michigan', p.205; Johnson, *Maurice Sugar*, p.261; Edsforth, *Class Conflict*, p.187; Dunbar, *Michigan*, p.614.Van Wagoner's machine was a personal political apparatus he had built as state highway commissioner: Buffa, *Union Power and Democracy*, p.11.

21. Irving Howe and Lewis Coser, *The American Communist Party* (Boston: Beacon Press, 1957), p.419; Keeran, *The CP and AWUs*, pp.247–9; Edsforth, *Class Conflict*, pp.191, 200–2; Rosswurm, 'The Catholic Church', pp.125–7.

22. George Sirgiovanni, *An Undercurrent of Suspicion: Anti-Communism in America during World War II* (New Brunswick: Transaction Publishers, 1990), pp.47, 48, 56, 73, 78, 90; Brinkley, *Voices of Protest*, p.268; Jeansonne, *Gerald L. K. Smith*, pp.69–80; *Detroit News*, 3 May 1942.

23. *Detroit Free Press*, 14 Oct.1938; *Detroit News*, 3 Nov.1941; *St. Louis Post-Dispatch*, 22 March 1942; Keeran, *The CP and AWUs*, p.232; Johnson, *Maurice Sugar*, pp.274–76; Conot, *American Odyssey*, pp.376–86.

24. Carl O. Smith and Stephen B. Sarasohn, 'Hate Propaganda in Detroit', *Public Opinion Quarterly*, 10 (Spring 1946), 24–52; Conot, *American Odyssey*, pp.376–86, 392–4; Edward C. Banfield, *Big City Politics* (New York: Random House, 1965), pp.51–2; Thomas J. Sugrue, 'Crabgrass Roots Politics: Race, Rights and the Reaction against Liberalism in the Urban North, 1940–1964', *Journal of American History*, 82 (Sept.1995), pp.568–70; Martin Halpern, *UAW Politics in the Cold War Era* (Albany: State University of New York Press, 1988), pp.42–3; Steve Fraser, *Labor Will Rule: Sidney Hillman and the Rise of American Labor* (New York, 1991), p. 570.

5   The Republican Offensive, 1945–1950

1. Alan Harper, *The Politics of Loyalty: The White House and the Communist Issue, 1946–1952* (Westport, Conn.: Greenwood, 1969); Earl Latham, *The Communist Controversy in Washington* (New York: Atheneum, 1969); Robert Griffith, *The Politics of Fear: Joseph R. McCarthy and the Senate*, 2nd edn (Amherst: University of Massachusetts Press, 1987); M. J. Heale, *American Anticommunism: Combating the Enemy Within, 1830–1970* (Baltimore: Johns Hopkins University Press, 1990), esp. ch.8.
2. Roger Keeran, *The Communist Party and the Auto Workers' Unions* (New York: International Publishers, 1980), pp.259–60; Irving Howe and Lewis Coser, *The American Communist Party* (Boston: Beacon Press, 1957), p.424; AYD, *Dust Off Your Dreams; The Story of the American Youth for Democracy* (New York, 1945), p.15; Louis E. Burnham, ... *Smash the Chains* (New York, 1946); AYD, *The Case of the Missing Helicopter, or Youth Wants That Postwar World* (New York, 1946); *Daily Worker*, 3, 28 April 1946.
3. Douglas P. Seaton, *Catholics and Radicals: The Association of Catholic Trade Unionists and the American Labor Movement, from Depression to Cold War* (Lewisburg: Bucknell University Press, 1981), p.203; Thomas Doherty to Joseph S. Lime, 9 April 1946, in ACTU 1942–49 file, Association of Catholic Trade Unionists (ACTU) Papers, Walter Reuther Library, Detroit.
4. Keeran, *The CP and the AWUs*, p.258; *Detroit News*, 19, 20, 29, 31 Oct., 4 Nov.1946.
5. Stephen B. and Vera Sarasohn, *Political Party Patterns in Michigan* (Detroit: Wayne State University Press, 1957), pp.47–8, 53–4; Martin Halpern, *UAW Politics in the Cold War Era* (Albany: State University of New York Press, 1988), p.136; *Detroit News*, 3 Nov.1946; *Michigan Manual, 1947*, pp.275, 555, 557, 651; Frank McNaughton, *Mennen Williams of Michigan: Fighter for Progress* (New York: Oceana Publications, 1960), p.93; Dudley W. Buffa, *Union Power and American Democracy: The UAW and the Democratic Party, 1935–72* (Ann Arbor: University of Michigan Press, 1984), p.11.
6. Harold Mulbar to Floyd Hamacher, 25 Nov.1946, in Communist file, Kim Sigler Papers, State Archives, Lansing; *Detroit News*, 2, 5, 6 Feb.1947; Robert K. Carr, *The House Committee on Un-American Activities, 1945–1950* (Ithaca: Cornell University Press, 1952), p.33; Buffa, *Union Power and Democracy*, p.12; Halpern, *UAW Politics*, pp.112–35.
7. *Detroit News*, 5, 6, 7, 8, 15, 16 Feb.1947; *Labor Action*, 3 March 1947; Foss Baker to Kim Sigler, 8 Feb.1947, Communist file, Sigler Papers; Donald S. Leonard to Kim Sigler, 24 Feb.1947, Communism-General file, in ibid.
8. Civil Rights Congress Open Letter to Gov. Sigler, 22 Feb.1947, Civil Rights Congress (CRC) Papers, Walter Reuther Library; Carl Winter, *19 Questions and Answers About Communist Party Suppressed by the* Detroit

322 Notes and References (pp. 110–14)

News (Detroit, 1947), pp.203; Walter Goodman, *The Committee: The Extraordinary Career of the House Committee on Un-American Activities* (New York: Farrar, Straus and Giroux, 1968), pp.160, 196; Carr, *House Committee on Un-American Activities*, pp.50–1, 327; Richard Gid Powers, *Secrecy and Power: The Life of J. Edgar Hoover* (New York: Free Press, 1987), p.286; *Detroit Times*, 21 Feb.1947; *Detroit News*, 2, 15, 28, 30 March, 2, 3 April 1947; *Detroit Free Press*, 29 March, 4, 5 April 1947; James Truett Selcraig, *The Red Scare in the Midwest, 1945–1955: A State and Local Study* (Ann Arbor: UMI Research Press, 1982), p.5.

9. Halpern, *UAW Politics*, pp.143–4; Keeran, *The CP and the AWUs*, p.265; *Detroit Free Press*, 30, 31 March 1947; *Detroit News*, 29 March, 30 Oct. 1947.

10. *Mich. Sen. J.,1947*, pp.182, 208, 212; *Detroit News*, 11, 12, 20 March, 1, 2 April 1947; *Detroit Free Press*, 21 March, 5, 9 April 1947; *Detroit Collegian* (Wayne University), 3 April 1947; Frank Donner, *Protectors of Privilege: Red Squads and Police Repression in Urban America* (Berkeley: University of California Press, 1990), p.56.

11. *Detroit Free Press*, 5, 9, 16 April, 28 May 1947; Carr, *House Committee on Un-American Activities*, p.351; 'Summary of Current Attacks on Academic Freedom in Michigan', typescript, n.d., in State Committee for Academic Freedom-1947 file, CRC Papers; Selcraig, *Red Scare in Midwest*, p.6; Ellen W. Schrecker, *No Ivory Tower: McCarthyism and the Universities* (New York: Oxford University Press, 1986), pp.85–7.

12. 'The Economic Club of Detroit announces National Affairs Section Group Discussion Meeting Thursday Noon, April 17, 1947...', printed leaflet, CRC Papers; *Detroit News*, 15 March, 4 Sept., 1, 5, 10 Oct.1947; *Mich. House J., 1947*, pp.414, 1726–7, 1964; *Mich. Sen. J., 1947*, pp.735, 958, 1247–8, 1432, 1582; *Mich. Public Acts 1947*, No.270, pp.418–19; Detroit Council To Combat Subversion Activities, *'What To Do'* (Detroit, 1947), p.1, in Sigler Papers; Attorney General Eugene F. Black, Press Statement, 30 Sept.1947, Box 559, Folder 32, ACLU Records, Seeley G. Mudd Library, Princeton University; Committee to Repeal the Callahan Act [CRCA], *REPEAL THE CALLAHAN ACT* (Detroit 1947), and CRCA, *BACK IN THE EARLY DAYS* (Detroit 1947) in CRC Papers.

13. *Detroit News*, 2, 3 April, 16 July, 5 Oct.1947; *Detroit Free Press*, 27, 28 May, 5 Sept.1947; 'Resolutions of Midwest Republican State Chairman's Association', 10 May 1947, Communistic Activities file, Sigler Papers; Governor's Legal Advisor to George A. Dondero, 8 April 1947, Communist file, Sigler Papers; Dondero to Sigler, 24 July 1947, Conference file, Sigler Papers; Jack B. Tenney to Sigler, 29 Jan.1948, Sigler to Tenney, 16 Feb.1948, Sigler to Thomas E. Bienz, 27 Aug.1948, Sigler to Bienz, 18 Oct.1948, Wilmer C. Carter to Sigler, 28April 1948, James F. Magdanz to Carter, 5 May 1948, all in Communism, 1948 file, Sigler Papers.

14. *Detroit News*, 7 March–4 April 1948; James Sweinhart, *Communist Front Exposed!* (Detroit, 1948); Sigler to W.S. Gilmore, 11 March 1948, Sigler to Sweinhart, 17 Feb.1948, Sweinhart to Sigler, 19 Aug.1948, in Communism 1948 file, Sigler Papers; *Detroit News*, 7, 11, 12, 15 March, 1 April 1948.

15. *Detroit News*, 8, 11 March, 1948; see, e.g. Mrs John C. Henderson to Sigler, 10 March 1948, and other letters in Communism 1948 file, Sigler Papers.

16. Typescript carbon headed 'callahan -...-allan', 10 March [1948], in 96-16 Callahan Act, 1947–8 file, CRC Papers; *Detroit News*, 11, 12 March, 7 April 1948; CRC of Michigan, Press Statement, 28 April 1948, in Walter Reuther 1948 file, CRC Papers; *Open Forum*, 15 May 1948; *Detroit Times*, 2 May 1948; *Detroit Free Press*, 13 Aug.1948.

17. Victor G. Reuther, *The Brothers Reuther and the Story of the UAW* (Boston: Houghton Mifflin, 1976), pp.270–81; *Detroit News*, 22, 23 April 1948; CRC Press Statement, 28 April 1948.

18. Michael Paul Rogin, *Ronald Reagan, the Movie and Other Episodes in Political Demonology* (Berkeley: University of California, 1987), p.69.

19. *Mich. House J.,1948*, pp.68, 69, 147–8; *Detroit News*, 7, 16 April 1948; Selcraig, *Red Scare in Midwest*, p.7; *Mich. Sen. J.,1948*, pp.133, 409.

20. *Mich. House J.,1948*, p.225; *Detroit News*, 15, 23, 24 April, 21 Dec.1948; *Detroit Free Press*, 10 March, 15 April 1948, 12, 13, 14 Jan.1949; Detroit Chapter, National Lawyers Guild, *State of Michigan: In the Senate of the State of Michigan, In the Matter of James Zarichny* ... (Detroit, 1948), pp.1-2, 13; *Mich. Sen. J., 1948*, pp.208–11, 302–16, 332–66; Robert J. Mowitz, 'Michigan: State and Local Attacks on Subversion', in Walter Gellhorn (ed.), *The States and Subversion* (Ithaca: Cornell University Press, 1952), p.194n.; *Detroit Times*, 21 Dec.1948.

21. *Muskegan Chronicle*, 6 Nov.1948; *Detroit Free Press*, 13, 23, 29 31 Oct.1948; Williams's campaign speeches in 1948: Democratic Party/Campaign files, G. Mennen Williams Papers, Michigan Historical Collections, University of Michigan; Buffa, *Union Power and Democracy*, pp.12–15; Frank McNaughton, *Mennen Williams of Michigan* (New York: Oceana Publications, 1960), pp.95, 118, 125–6; Sarasohn, *Political Party Patterns*, pp.53–7.

22. Michigan Committee to Defend the Bill of Rights, circular, 29 Oct.1948, Callahan Act 1947 file, CRC Papers; *Detroit Times*,13, 24, 27 Aug.1948; *Mich. Manual,1949*, p.306.

23. Glen Jeansonne, *Gerald L.K. Smith: Minister of Hate* (New Haven: Yale University Press, 1988), p.98; unsigned letter to Father Flanagan, 10 Sept.1948, and W.J. Flanagan, 'LABOR MASS DETROIT SERMON', ACTU: 1942–9 file, and Karl Hubble to 'Dear Father', 12 March 1950, circular, ACTU-1950 file, ACTU Papers. ACTU activities became more narrowly focused on an unrelenting anticommunism after 1945: Steve Rosswurm, 'The Catholic Church and the Left-Led Unions: Labor Priests, Labor Schools, and the ACTU', in Rosswurm (ed.), *The CIO's Left-Led Unions* (New Brunswick: Rutgers University Press, 1992), pp.128–30.

24. *Detroit Free Press*, 21, 23 Oct.1948, 14 April, 2 July 1949; McNaughton, *Mennen Williams*, p.151; Harry S. Toy to Basil L. Walters, 17 Feb.1949, Box 571, Folder 10, ACLU Records; *Detroit Times*, 1, 21 Dec.1948.

25. *Detroit Free Press*, 4, 6, 7, 12 July 1949; Eugene Van Antwerp to Harry S. Toy, 6 July 1949, Van Antwerp to Mennen Williams, 12 July 1949, Williams to Van Antwerp, 20 July 1949, Communism file, Mayors Papers 1949, Detroit Archives.

26. Adelaide G. Geist to Williams, 21 July 1949, Communism file 1949, Williams Papers; Jack Gore to Mayor Van Antwerp, 2 Aug.1949, Communism file, Mayors Papers 1949; Michigan Federation of Teachers, 'A Statement on Proposed Loyalty Commission for City of Detroit Employees', 6 Sept.1949, mimeograph in ibid.; Michigan Committee to Defend the Bill of Rights to Fellow Citizen, 30 Aug.1949, in ibid.; 'By Councilman Smith: An Ordinance to establish a Loyalty Investigating Committee ...', 18 Oct.1949, in Loyalty Investigating Committee file, Mayors Paper 1949; Selcraig, *Red Scare in Midwest*, pp.53, 55; *Detroit News*, 11 Sept.1949; *Detroit Free Press*, 11 March 1950; Buffa, *Union Power and Democracy*, p.138; Thomas J. Sugrue, 'Crabgrass Roots Politics: Race, Rights, and the Reaction against Liberalism in the Urban North, 1940–1964', *Journal of American History*, 82 (Sept.1995), 570–1; Robert Conot, *American Odyssey* (New York: William Morrow, 1976), pp.403–5. The six city councilmen seeking re-election in the 1949 municipal elections were also successful: Mowitz, 'Michigan', p.222.

27. *Michigan Legionnaire* (Jan.1949), p.5, (April 1949), p.1, (July 1949), pp.16, 20, (April 1950), p.1, (May 1950), p.1; programme attached to John Denman to Gov. Williams, 31 March 1950, and Denman to Williams, 17 April 1950, Communism 1950 file, Williams Papers; *Detroit Free Press*, 17, 18, 20, 22, 23 April 1950; *Detroit News*, 24 April 1950; *Mich. Sen. J.*, *1950*, pp.166, 280.

28. On the impulse to restore the initiative to management, see Howell J. Harris, *The Right to Manage: Industrial Relations Policies of American Business in the 1940s* (Madison: University of Wisconsin Press, 1982).

29. Ronald Edsforth, *Class Conflict and Cultural Consensus: The Making of a Mass Consumer Society in Flint, Michigan* (New Brunswick: Rutgers University Press, 1987), pp.191 (citing Serrin), 208–9, 214; Robert H. Zieger, *American Workers, American Unions, 1920–1985* (Baltimore: Johns Hopkins University Press, 1986), p.138.

6   The Triumph of Liberalism? 1950–1954

1. *Detroit Free Press*, 22 April 1950; Communism files (1949) in G. Mennen Williams Papers, Michigan Historical Collections, University of Michigan, and in Kim Sigler Papers, State Archives, Lansing; Frank McNaughton, *Mennen Williams of Michigan* (New York: Oceana Publications, 1960), pp.149, 161–2, 171–2.

2. William W. Keller, *The Liberals and J. Edgar Hoover: Rise and Fall of a Domestic Intelligence State* (Princeton: Princeton University Press, 1989), pp.33, 49. On liberal anticommunism see also Mary Sperling McAuliffe, *Crisis on the Left: Cold War Politics and American Liberals* (Amherst: University of Massachusetts Press, 1978).

3. Legal Advisor to Mr & Mrs Michael J. Cooper, 17 Aug.1950, Communist file 1950, Colin L. Smith to Williams, 25 July 1950, Special Session 3-15-50 file, Williams to Smith, 29 July 1950, ibid., Williams to Leonard, 3 Aug.1950, Police, State, Donald S. Leonard, Commissioner file, 1950, Williams Papers; *Detroit Free Press*, 1 Aug.1950; James Basil Jacobs, 'The Conduct of Local Political Intelligence' (Ph.D diss., Princeton University, 1977), pp.128, 135–7.

4. Colin L. Smith to Williams, 8 Aug.1950, Special Session 3-15-50 file, Williams Papers; Williams to Jefferson Hoxie, 16 Aug.1950, in ibid.; *Mich. Sen. J., 1950*, pp.386–9, 396–8; *Detroit Free Press*, 11, 17, 18, 19 Aug.1950.

5. *Detroit Free Press*, 25, 30, 31 Aug., 1 Sept., 5 Oct.1950; E. Blythe Stason to Williams, 26 Aug.1950, Special Session 3-15-50 file, Talbot Smith et al to Williams, 11 Aug.1950, Special Session Re Subversion file, Williams Papers; Williams to the Senate, 29 Aug.1950, *Mich. Sen. J., Extra Sess. 1950*, p. 402; *Mich. Public Acts,1950*, p.123.

6. *Detroit Free Press*, 12 Aug.1950; James T. Selcraig, *The Red Scare in Midwest* (Ann Arbor: UMI Press, 1982), p.11.

7. *Detroit Free Press*, 10, 16, 26, 27 July, 5, 12, 26 Aug., 26 Sept., 3, 12, 30 Oct., 3 Nov.1950.

8. *Detroit News*, 18, 20 July, 20 Nov.1950; *Detroit Free Press*, 19, 20, 26, 27 July 1950; Edward Lukasik to Mayor Cobo, 3 Aug.1950 – and see B.W. Cooke to Cobo, 21 July 1950, Norman H. Hill to Victor Riesel, 1 Aug.1950, Communist Literature file, Mayors Papers [hereafter MP]1954, Detroit Archives; George F. Boos, Commissioner, to Cobo, 24 May 1950, and Berenice Summer et al. to Cobo, July 1950, in ibid. On Cobo's anti-liberal strategy see Thomas J. Sugrue, 'Crabgrass Roots Politics: Race, Rights, and the Reaction against Liberalism in the Urban North, 1940–1964', *Journal of American History*, 82 (Sept.1995), 571–2.

9. *Detroit Free Press*, 22 Sept., 7, 17 Nov.1950, 21 March 1951; *Detroit Times*, 17 Nov.1950; 'Analysis of Proceedings before the Loyalty Commission Re: Thomas J. Coleman', Loyalty Committee file, MP 1951; Cobo to Norm Hill, 23 Oct.1950, Loyalty Investigating Com. file, MP 1950; John G. Dunn to Loyalty Investigating Committee, 14 Nov.1950, Loyalty Committee file, MP 1953; Jacobs, 'The Conduct of Political Intelligence', pp.126–7.

10. McNaughton, *Mennen Williams*, pp.114-15; Dudley W. Buffa, *Union Power and American Democracy: The UAW and the Democratic Party, 1935-72* (Ann Arbor: University of Michigan Press, 1984), pp.31–3.

11. *Detroit Free Press*, 24, 25 Sept., 6, 11, 17, 25, 27, 31 Oct., 1, 3, 5 Nov.1950; *Detroit News*, 21, 27, 31 Oct.; McNaughton, *Mennen Williams*, p.128.

12. *Detroit Free Press*, 27 Oct., 3, 5 Nov.1950; *Detroit News*, 27, 31 Oct.1950; McNaughton, *Mennen Williams*, p.128; unsigned to Father Flanagan, 10 Sept.1948, ACTU: 1942–9 file, ACTU Papers, Walter Reuther Library, Detroit.

13. *Detroit Free Press*, 11, 12, 13, 14, 16, 19, 27, 30, 31 Oct.1950; *Detroit News*, 19, 20 21, 27, 31 Oct.1950; McNaughton, *Mennen Williams*, pp.114–15.

14. McNaughton, *Mennen Williams*, p.132; *Detroit News*, 20 Nov.1950; *Mich. Manual, 1951–52*, pp.249–51, 513.

15. *Detroit News*, 4, 5 Feb., 28 Sept.1951; *Mich. Sen. J., 1951*, pp.632, 815, 981, 1433, 1646; *Mich. House J. 1951*, pp.679, 996, 1151–2, 1424; Legal Advisor to Mr & Mrs M. Love, 7 June 1951, Walter M. Nelson to Williams, 19 May 1951, and other corr., Legis. Regular Session 1/51 file, Williams Papers; Arthur McPhaul to Williams, 17 May 1951, Hittle Bill-1951 file, and Ernest Goodman to Mr. Segadelli, 28 May 1951, Loyalty 195–3 file, Civil Rights Congress (CRC) Papers, Walter Reuther Library, Detroit; *Detroit Times*, 21 June 1951.

16. *Detroit Free Press*, 13 Jan., 18 Feb., 1–3 March 1952; *Detroit News*, 13 Jan., 11, 26, 28 Feb.1952; *Detroit Times*, 26 Feb., 13 March 1952; B. J. Widick, *Detroit: City of Race and Class Violence* (Chicago: Quadrangle Books, 1972), p.130.

17. E.H.Soderberg to ACLU, 10 April 1952, Box 1040, Folder 8, ACLU Records, Seeley G. Mudd Library, Princeton University; *Detroit Free Press*, 2–6, 17, 18, 24, 29 March, 5 April 1952; *Detroit Times*, 4, 12 March 1952; *Detroit News*, 13 March 1952; Widick, *Detroit* , 132–3; Lorraine F. Meisner, 'An Open Letter To All Students and Faculty', n.d., Academic Freedom – Wayne, U. of M. 1952 file, CRC Papers.

18. *Detroit Free Press*, 3, 4, 17 March 1952; *Detroit News*, 3 March 1952; CRC, Press Release, 19 Dec.1952, Defence 1952 file, CRC Papers; Legal Advisor to Mrs Raine Stepke, 5 March 1952, Communism file, 1952, Williams Papers.

19. CRC, Press Release, 19 Dec.1952; *Detroit Free Press*, 26, 27 March, 10, 17, 22 April, 9 May 1952; *Detroit News*, 1, 2 April 1952; Donald S. Leonard to Frank J. Millard, 25 March 1952, Communism: General Correspondence file, Donald S. Leonard Papers, Michigan Historical Collections, University of Michigan.

20. *Detroit Free Press*, 17, 18, 26 March, 10, 21 April 1952; *Detroit News*, 6 June 1952.

21. *Detroit Free Press*, 1, Feb., 26, 29 March, 4 April 1952; *Mich. Sen. J., 1952*, pp.58, 264, 871, 941, 966, 1507; *Mich. House J., 1952*, pp.10–11, 244, 263, 1274–5; *Detroit News*, 2 April 1952; CRC of Michigan, 'Call To a Lansing Lobby, Tuesday March 24', Truck Act 1952–3 file, CRC Papers; William Albertson, *The Trucks Act* (New York, 1952), p.3; Widick, *Detroit*, p.135; Jeannette Carroll to Gov. Williams, 9 April 1952, Legis. Regular Session 1952 file, Williams Papers. E.H. Soderberg, a Stockbridge minister, complained of the inactivity of the ACLU in Michigan, where the CP-led CRC was often more conspicuous in defending civil liberties: Soderberg to ACLU, 10 April 1952.

22. *Detroit Free Press*, 18 April 1952; *Detroit Times*, 23 April 1952; Albertson, *Trucks Act*, pp.12–13; *Detroit News*, 5 June 1952, 3 May 1954.

23. *Mich. Sen. J., 1952*, pp. 552, 985–6, 1109, 1412; *Detroit News*, 2, 18, 22 April 1952; *Detroit Times*, 5, 6, 12 March 1952; University of Michigan

News Service, Press Release, 23 April 1953, Academic Freedom–Wayne, U of M. 1952 file, CRC Papers; *Michigan Daily*, 1, 22 April 1952.

24. *Detroit News*, 16 April, 2, 11–20 May 1952; *Detroit Free Press*, 20 March, 22 April 1952.

25. *Detroit News*, 12 Oct.1952.

26. *Detroit Times*, 30 Oct., 4 Nov.1952; *Detroit Free Press*, 29, 30 Oct., 2, 4 Nov.1952; *Detroit News*, 22, 23 Oct.1952.

27. *Detroit Times*, 4 Nov.1952; *Detroit Free Press*, 30 Oct., 4 Nov.1952; 'Excerpts from Address by Governor G. Mennen Williams, Knights of Columbus, Pontiac, Michigan, October 11, 1952', Communism file 1952, Williams Papers.

28. McNaughton, *Mennen Williams*, pp.132–3; *Mich. Manual, 1953–54*, pp.215–17.

29. *Detroit Free Press*, 30 Dec.1952; *Detroit Times*, 12 Jan.1953, 6 Feb., 14, 25 April, 1953; *Mich. House J., 1953*, pp.36–7, 800, 837; *Mich. Sen. J., 1953*, pp.739–42, 791; *Mich. Public Acts, 1953*, pp.32–4.

30. Albertson, *Trucks Act*, pp.17–20; Citizens' Committee Against the Trucks Law, *Michigan's Trucks Law: A Totalitarian Measure Violating the Principles of American Freedom* [Detroit, 1953]; *Detroit Free Press*, 2 Feb., 21 Oct.1953; *Detroit News*, 24 March, 2 May 1953, 3 May 1954; Rev. I. Paul Taylor to Dear Friend, 15 Oct.1953, Trucks Act 1952–3 file, CRC Papers; ECLC, *Rights*, July 1956, p.11; Selcraig, *Red Scare in Midwest*, p.14.

31. Ibid., pp.72–3, 126–7; *Detroit Free Press*, 31 Dec.1952, 30 April, 1953; *Detroit News*, 19 Jan.1953, 27 Jan.1954; *Detroit Times*, 12 Jan., 6 Feb.1953; Fact Sheet on Smith Act [1953], and 'Latest Facts on the Appeal to the Supreme Court Against Michigan Smith Act Convictions', March 1956, Nat Ganly Papers, Reuther Library; Ellen W. Schrecker, *No Ivory Tower: McCarthyism and the Universities* (New York: Oxford University Press, 1986), p.221.

32. Frank Donner, *Protectors of Privilege: Red Squads and Police Repression in Urban America* (Berkeley: University of California Press, 1990), pp.58–9; *Detroit News* clipping, 19 March 1953 and attached note dated 24 March 1953, Communist file, Mayors Papers [MP] 1953; Clifford W. Wickman to Clifford Prevost, 12 Jan.1953, Loyalty Committee file, MP 1953; R. Hall to Mayor Cobo, 14 Sept.1954 and Charles Kelly to Cobo, 8 Sept.1954, Police-Subversive-Square D Strikes file, MP 1954; D.E. Moore to George Schudlich, 3 Feb.1953, Loyalty Committee file, MP 1953; *Detroit Times*, 12 Jan.1953, 6 Feb.1953; Selcraig, *Red Scare in Midwest*, p.58; *Detroit News*, 2 May 1952, 25 March 1953, 14 Jan., 9 April 1954; *Detroit Free Press*, 18 April 1953; Loren B. Miller to Mayor and Common Council, 4 Nov.1955, Loyalty Committee file, MP 1955; Clifford W. Wickman, Re: Freedom Agenda of Detroit, 1 March 1955 and Clifford Prevost to Cobo, 7 March 1956, Police Dept.-Subversives file, MP 1955; LIC, 'Annual Report' 13 Dec.1956, Loyalty Committee file, MP 1956; Jacobs, 'Conduct of Political Intelligence', pp.126, 135.

33. Schrecker, *No Ivory Tower*, pp.3, 181–2, 219–33; Lionel S. Lewis, *Cold War on Campus: A Study of the Politics of Organizational Control* (New Brunswick: Transaction Books, 1988), pp.153–7, 172–5, 183–7.

34. Marguerite Gahagan to Dear Friend, 6 Jan.1953, ACTU-1953 file, ACTU Papers; G. Mennen Williams to Thaddeus Machrowicz, 29 June 1953, Communism file, 1953, Williams to John Santieu, 7 April 1953, in ibid., Benjamin C. Stanczyk to Williams, 23 June 1953, Williams to Stanczyk, 29 June 1953, Communism, Gen. Subjects file 1952, Williams Papers; *Mich. House J., 1953*, pp.275, 1686, 1690, 1873; *Mich. House J., 1954*, pp.16, 225, 446, 562, 1588; *Mich. Sen. J., 1954*, pp.692, 1311, 1425; *Mich. Public Acts 1954*, pp.13–14, 69–70.
35. McNaughton, *Mennen Williams*, pp.149, 241–2; Williams to Senate, 30 March 1956, *Mich. Sen. J., 1956*, p.986.
36. *Detroit Free Press*, 1, 2, 4 Nov.1954; see also *Detroit News*, 27 Oct.–3 Nov. 1954

III   Red Scare Politics in Massachusetts

1. Daniel Bell (ed.), *The New American Right* (New York: Criterion, 1955).
2. James Reichley, *States in Crisis: Politics in Ten American States, 1950–1962* (Chapel Hill: University of North Carolina Press, 1963), p.142; Murray B. Levin with George Blackwood, *The Compleat Politician: Political Strategy in Massachusetts* (Indianapolis: Bobbs-Merrill, 1962), pp.17, 28–9; Austin Ranney, 'Parties in State Politics', ch.3 in Herbert Jacob and Kenneth N. Vines (eds), *Politics in the American States: A Comparative Analysis* (Boston: Little, Brown, 1965), pp.61–99; Harmon Ziegler, 'Interest Groups in the States', ch.4 in ibid., esp. p.124. Edgar Litt identifies four political cultures in Massachusetts: the patricians (the old Yankee elite), the yeomen (small-town and rural conservative Yankees), the workers (urban, populist Catholics), and the managers (professionals, intellectuals, suburban): Litt, *The Political Cultures of Massachusetts* (Cambridge: MIT Press, 1965), ch.1.
3. Reichley, *States in Crisis*, p.146; Duane Lockard, *New England State Politics* (Chicago: Henry Regnery, 1959), pp.119–20, 127, 134–5, 141–5, 163–5; Ira Sharkansky, *Regionalism in American Politics* (Indianapolis: Bobbs-Merrill, 1970), p.168; Levin, *Compleat Politician*, pp.22, 52–3.

7   The Contours of Red Scare Politics, 1935–1945

1. John Higham, *Strangers in the Land: American Nativism, 1860–1925* (New York: Atheneum, 1963), pp.240–1; Robert K. Murray, *Red Scare: A Study in National Hysteria, 1919–1920* (Minneapolis: University of Minnesota Press, 1955), pp.134, 159–60, 213; *Tercentenary Edition of the*

General Laws of the Commonwealth of Massachusetts (Boston, 1932), p.3107; Louis Joughin and Edmund M. Morgan, *The Legacy of Sacco & Vanzetti* (Princeton: Princeton University Press, 1978), pp.148, 297.

2. Gerald H. Gamm, *The Making of New Deal Democrats: Voting Behavior and Realignment in Boston, 1920–1940* (Chicago: University of Chicago Press, 1989), p.107.

3. Levin, *Compleat Politician*, p.19; Reichley, *States in Crisis*, p.146; Oscar Handlin, *The Uprooted* (New York: Grosset and Dunlap, 1951), p.217; Sidney E. Ahlstrom, *A Religious History of the American People* (New Haven: Yale University Press, 1972), p.1003; Richard Gid Powers, *Not Without Honor: The History of American Anticommunism* (New York: Free Press, 1995), pp.51–2; Marc Karson, 'Catholic Anti-Socialism', ch.5 in John H. M. Laslett and Seymour Martin Lipset (eds), *Failure of a Dream? Essays in the History of American Socialism* (Garden City: Anchor Press/Doubleday), p.166; James M. O'Toole, *Militant and Triumphant: William Henry O'Connell and the Catholic Church in Boston, 1859–1944* (Notre Dame: University of Notre Dame Press, 1992); Thomas H. O'Connor, *The Boston Irish: A Political History* (Boston: Northeastern University Press, 1995), pp.196–8; Donald F. Crosby, 'Boston's Catholics and the Spanish Civil War, 1936-1939', *New England Quarterly*, 44 (March 1971), 82–100; Francis J. Lally to Richard Cardinal Cushing, 1 Dec.1959, Box 9, Francis J. Lally Papers, Archives of the Archdiocese of Boston; David O'Brien, *Public Catholicism* (New York: Macmillan, 1989), p.220. O'Connor, in *The Boston Irish*, argues that the early painful encounter with an exceptionally Yankee city made the Boston Irish different from the Irish in other American cities, intensifying their religious fidelity and ethnic identity. For a major study of Americanism in another New England Catholic community, Woonsocket, see Gary Gerstle, *Working-Class Americanism: The Politics of Labor in a Textile City, 1914–1960* (Cambridge: Cambridge University Press, 1989).

4. O'Connor, *Boston Irish*, p.198; James M. O'Toole, 'Prelates and Politicos: Catholics and Politics in Massachusetts, 1900–1970', in Robert E. Sullivan and James M. O'Toole (eds), *Catholic Boston: Studies in Religion and Community, 1870–1970* (Boston: Roman Catholic Archbishop of Boston, 1985), pp.15–65.

5. W. A. Swanberg, *Citizen Hearst* (London: Longmans, 1961), p.469; William Pencak, *For God and Country: The American Legion, 1919–1941* (Boston: Northeastern University Press, 1989), p.268.

6. American Legion, Department of Massachusetts, *Annual Proceedings, 1935, Seventeenth Annual Convention*, pp.85–6; *Boston Herald*, 7 April, 25, 27 June 1935; *The Pilot*, 12 Jan., 16 Feb., 9 March, 2 Nov.1935; Massachusetts Society for Freedom in Teaching (MSFT), *How Your Legislators Voted on the Teachers' Oath Law, 1935–1936* (Boston, n.d.), pp.3–5, pamphlet in Civil Liberties Union of Massachusetts [hereafter CLUM] Papers, Massachusetts Historical Society, Boston; David K. Niles to Roger Baldwin, 19 Feb.1935, Vol.841, 1935, ACLU Records, Seeley G. Mudd Library, Princeton University; ACLU, *How Goes The*

Bill of Rights? (New York, 1936), pp.6, 16; S. E. Morison, *Three Oathless Centuries* (Boston, 1936), p.10; Daniel L. Marsh, *Scarlet and White Achievements: Being the Record of the Year 1934–35 at Boston University* (Boston, 1935), pp.17–20; James B. Conant, *My Several Lives: Memoirs of a Social Inventor* (New York: Harper & Row, 1970), p.450; *Boston Globe*, 31 March 1936.

7. American Legion, MA, *Annual Proceedings, 1935*, pp.85–6; Marsh, *Scarlet and White Achievements*, pp.19–20; *Boston Herald*, 7 April 1935; Mrs Francis E. Slattery, Chairman, League of Catholic Women, to Members, 13 Nov.1935, and Lucile A. Harrington to Members of Board of Trustees [1935], Box 2, League of Catholic Women Papers, Archives of the Archdiocese of Boston; *The Pilot*, 4 Jan.1936.

8. *Documents Printed by Order of the Senate of the Commonwealth of Massachusetts during the Session of the General Court 1935* [hereafter *Mass. Legis. Docs*], Senate No. 527, pp.2–4; MSFT, *How Your Legislators Voted*, pp.7–8.There were modest Republican majorities in both houses at this time.

9. *Boston Herald*, 27 June, 1, 2, 7, 8, 12 Dec.1935; *Boston Globe*, 12 Jan.1936; Conant, *My Several Lives*, p.452.

10. Morison, *Three Oathless Centuries*, pp.3, 9; *Boston Globe*, 13, 15 Jan., 6, 11 March, 13 May 1936; MSFT, *Fascism Is Here!* (Boston, 1936), pp.3–6, 8, and League of Women Voters of Massachusetts (LWVM), 'Some Further Observation on the Teachers' Oath Law', Aug.1936, p.1, in LWVM Papers, Schlesinger Library, Cambridge.

11. Rosalind Greene to Mrs Richard H. Field, 6 March 1936, LWVM Papers; CLUM, *Civil Liberties Bulletin*, Nov.1936, p.2; MLWV, 'Further Observations...', p.1; 'Fr Corrigan, S.J., Defends Oath Law', undated news clipping in Newspaper Clippings 1936 file, CLUM Papers; *Boston Globe*, 6, 25 March, 7 April 1936. Some Harvard alumni had been critical of Frankfurter's New Deal activities: Conant, *My Several Lives*, pp.448–9.

12. *Boston Globe*, 7, 8 April 1936, 19, 26 March, 1, 2 April 1937; CLUM, *Civil Liberties Bulletin*, Nov.1936, p.2; Levin, *Compleat Politician*, p.43; LWVM, 'Legislative Newsletter', 9 Feb.1937, p.2 and 21 March 1938, p.5; ACLU, *Let Freedom Ring!* (June 1937), p.2; ACLU, *Local Civil Liberties Committees: Reports 1937–1938* (New York, 1938), p.12; CLUM, *Civil Liberties Bulletin*, April–May 1939, p.11; Charles F. Hurley, *Addresses and Messages to the General Court of ... Massachusetts* (1938), p.47. A repeal attempt in 1939 narrowly failed in the lower house by 105 to 102 votes; the party patterns survived, with 67 Democrats for the oath and 15 against, and 38 Republicans for and 87 against; Rep. Thomas F. Coyne attacked repeal supporters as 'a collection of pinks, reds, crackpot professors and communists': *Boston Herald*, 17 Feb.1939.

13. J. David Valaik, 'American Catholics and the Second Spanish Republic, 1911 [sic]–1936', *Church and State*, 10 (1968), 13–28; Gamm, *Making of New Deal Democrats*, p.155; CLUM, *Civil Liberties Bulletin*, Nov.1936, p.1; Civil Liberties Committee of Massachusetts, *Censorship in Boston*

(May 1938), p.6; CLUM, *Civil Liberties Bulletin*, July 1938, p.1. The influence of the Catholic church was often espied behind the bans on Loyalist and CP meetings: Leo H. Lehmann, 'The Catholic Church in Politics', *New Republic*, 16 Nov.1938, p.34.

14. *Boston Globe*, 12, 19 April 1938; Hurley, *Addresses and Messages to the General Court...* (1938), pp.47, 352, 356, 357; 'Excerpt from speech reported in Boston Globe, April 4, 1938 by Governor Hurley at Communion Breakfast of New York police force Holy Name Society, before 6000 members ...', attached to Phil Frankfeld to Dear Friend, 16 Sept.1938, CLUM Papers.

15. Phil Frankfeld to Dear Friend, 16 Sept.1938, CLUM Papers; *Boston Globe*, 22 April 1938; *Boston American*, 26 April 1938.

16. *The Pilot*, 27 Aug.1938; Thomas H. O'Connor, *South Boston: My Home Town* (Boston: Quinlan Press, 1988), p.189; O'Connor, *Boston Irish*, pp.203–4; John Henry Cutler, *Cardinal Cushing of Boston* (New York: Hawthorn Books, 1970), p.114; Alan Brinkley, *Voices of Protest: Huey Long, Father Coughlin, and the Great Depression* (New York: Knopf, 1982), pp.206, 266–7; Gamm, *Making of New Deal Democrats*, p.154; G. W. Kunze to Dear Sir, 2 Feb.1938, CLUM Papers; Robert Morss Lovett, 'Witch-Hunting in Massachusetts', *New Republic*, 1 Dec.1937, p.97.

17. Lovett, 'Witch-Hunting', p.96; ACLU, *Let Freedom Ring!* p.56; *Mass.Acts and Resolves, 1937*, ch.32, p.629.

18. Citizens Union of Massachusetts, *Voters Guide* (1938), p.4, in CLUM Papers; Joan Hopkinson to Howard Y. Williams, 26 Oct.1938, Kirtley Mather Papers in CLUM Papers; *Boston Globe*, 26 March 1937, 12 April 1938; CLUM Executive Cmte, Minutes, 1930–7, 21 June 1937, CLUM Papers; CLUM, *Civil Liberties Bulletin*, Jan.1938, p.4; Lovett, 'Witch-Hunting', pp.96–7; Orville S. Poland to Roger Baldwin, 25 June 1937, Vol.1045, 1937, ACLU Records; 'Report of the Special Commission to Investigate the Activities ... of Communistic, Fascist, Nazi and Other Subversive Organizations, ... under Chapter 32, Resolves of 1937', 27 May 1938, *Mass. Legis. Docs., House, 1938*, No.2100, pp.9–10; LWVM, 'Legislative News Letter', 18 July 1938, p.5.

19. 'Report of the Special Commission', pp.56, 318, 441–3, 448, 460; *Boston Traveler*, 10 June 1938; Lovett, 'Witch-Hunting', pp.96–7; *New Republic*, 28 June 1938; David Englund, 'Fascism in Massachusetts: State Commission Stages a Red Hunt', *Zion's Herald*, 24 Nov.1937, p.1416; 'Report of the Special Commission', pp.320, 325; William H. Cobb, 'The State Legislature and the "Reds": ... 1935–1937', *Arkansas Historical Review*, 45 (Spring 1986), pp.3–18; Gamm, *Making of New Deal Democrats*, p.172.

20. CLUM, *Civil Liberties Bulletin*, July 1938, p.5; Citizens Union of Mass., *Voters Guide*, p.4; Lovett, 'Witch-Hunting', p.97; 'Report of the Special Commission', pp.578–9, 595, 598; Joan Hopkinson to Roger Baldwin, 13 June 1938, Vol.2036, 1938, ACLU Records. Philip Bowker was later to experience a similar conversion to Holmes: ch.8.

21. *New Republic*, 22 June 1938; S. Ralph Harlow to Florence Luscomb, 19 Feb.1955, Luscomb Papers, Schlesinger Library; *Boston Sunday Post*, 26

June 1938; *Boston Traveler,* 10 June 1938; *Civil Liberties Bulletin,* April–May 1939, pp.5, 11, 12; CLUM, Minutes, 1 June 1938, and Otis Hood and Phil Frankfeld to Dear Friend, 3 June 1938, CLUM Papers; Joan Hopkinson to Howard Y. Williams, 26 Oct.1938, Mather Papers; Civil Liberties Committee of Mass., *To Members and Friends...,* 18 March 1939, pp.1–2; *Mass. Acts and Resolves 1939.*

22. CLUM, *Civil Liberties Bulletin,* Nov.1938, p.5; 'Report of the Special Commission', pp.356, 435; *Civil Liberties Bulletin,* July 1938, p.1 and April–May 1939, pp.4–5, 7; *Boston Globe,* 7 Feb.1939; *Boston Transcript,* 9 Feb.1939; *Christian Science Monitor,* 9 Feb.1939; CLUM Executive Cmte, Minutes, 1939, 9 Feb.1939, CLUM Papers. See ch.1 for the Rapp–Coudert probe.

23. *Daily Worker,* 14 Sept.1940; 'Attacks On The Communist Party', Vol.2203, 1940, ACLU Records.

24. Cutler, *Cushing,* pp.114–16; Wallace Stegner to Teresa S. Fitzpatrick, undated copy attached to Teresa S. Fitzpatrick to Rev. J. J. Wright, 9 Aug.1944, John Joseph Wright Papers, Archives of the Archdiocese of Boston.

25. Cutler, *Cushing,* pp.97, 99; Joseph Dever, *Cushing of Boston: A Candid Portrait* (Boston: Bruce Humphries, 1965), pp.135–6, 156; *The Pilot,* 19 Oct.1946, 12 Dec.1947; Paul Blanshard, *American Freedom and Catholic Power* (Boston: Beacon Press, 1949), partly published in *The Nation,* ending 4 June 1948; Levin, *Compleat Politician,* p.33.

26. Ronald P. Formisano, *Boston Against Busing: Race, Class, and Ethnicity in the 1960s and 1970s* (Chapel Hill: University of North Carolina Press, 1991), uses the term 'reactionary populism' to characterize Boston's later anti-busing movement, which shared some features with popular anticommunism.

8   The Populist Assault, 1945–1952

1. For a historiographical discussion, see the new introduction in Robert Griffith, *The Politics of Fear : Joseph R. McCarthy and the Senate* (2nd edn, Amherst: University of Massachusetts Press, 1987). On the parochial orientation of the lower house, see Edgar Litt, *The Political Cultures of Massachusetts* (Cambridge: MIT Press, 1965), p.205, and on the populistic character of neighbourhood politics see Thomas H. O'Connor, *The Boston Irish: A Political History* (Boston: Northeastern University Press, 1995), pp.189, 202–4, 215, 234–7.

2. *The Pilot,* 19 Oct.1946, 11 Jan., 15 Feb., 1 March, 16 May, 20 June 1947; Joseph Dever, *Cushing of Boston: A Candid Portrait* (Boston: Bruce Humphries, 1965), p.137; *Mass. House J., 1947,* pp.653, 769, 1728; Woonsocket (RI) *Call,* 7 April 1947; *Dorchester Record,* 10 April 1947; *Berkshire Eagle,* 23 April 1947; *Boston Globe,* 9, 22 April 1947; CLUM, 'Seven Bills That Endanger Your Civil Liberties', leaflet, Jan.1948, pp.2–7; 'Report of Executive Secretary, Mary Elizabeth Sanger', 1 May

1947, in Kirtley Mather Papers in CLUM Papers, Massachusetts Historical Society; League of Women Voters of Massachusetts (LWVM), 'Legislative Report for 1947', 22 Aug.1947, in LWVM Papers, Schlesinger Library, Cambridge; *Mass. House J., 1948*, pp.2–10, 52–5, 60, 61, 145, 151; American Jewish Congress, Boston, 'STATEMENT ON H-220 (BARNES BILL)', and CLUM Chairman [Kirtley Mather] to Dear Friend, undated, CLUM Papers.

3. *Boston Daily Record*, 22 Jan.1948; *Boston Globe*, 9 Feb.1948; *Boston American*, 10 Feb.1948; *Boston Herald*, 10, 27 Feb., 3 March 1948; Mrs Kenneth B. Murdoch to Gordon D. Boynton, 8 March 1948, CLUM Papers; *Mass. House J., 1948*, pp.590–2. There were 144 Republicans and 96 Democrats in the house (Levin, *Compleat Politician*, p.50). Two of the bill's sponsors, John F. Collins and Gabriel F. Piemonte, were to emerge as leading politicos: Thomas H. O'Connor, *South Boston: My Home Town* (Boston: Quinlan Press, 1988), p.204 and Levin, *Compleat Politician*, pp.85–6. Several Protestant ministers and a rabbi made clear their opposition to it: 'Statement of Ministers on House Bill 1597', undated, CLUM Papers, and *Boston Herald*, 10 Feb.1948

4. *Who Was Who in America with World Notables*, V, 1969–1973, p.37; Alfred S. Schenkman to Mrs Kenneth B. Murdoch, 4 March 1948, CLUM Papers; *Boston Herald*, 3, 27 Feb., 4 March 1948; *Springfield Union*, 28 Feb.1948; *Boston Globe*, 4 March 1948; *Boston Post*, 3, 10 Feb.1948.

5. *Boston Post*, 10 Feb.1948; *Boston Herald*, 3, 10, 27 Feb., 4 March 1948; *Boston Traveler*, 9 Feb.1948; *Christian Science Monitor*, 9 Feb.1948; Julia Pridden Whitmore to CLUM, 14 Feb.1948, CLUM Papers; *Boston Globe*, 10 Feb., 4 March 1948; James B. Conant, *Laws vs. Communists in Schools and Colleges: Statement of President James Bryant Conant of Harvard University before a Committee of the Massachusetts Legislature, Feb. 9, 1948* (New York: ACLU, 1949), p.5; CLUM, *Civil Liberties Newsletter*, 29 March 1948; *Mass. Acts and Resolves, 1948*, ch.160, p.107.

6. *Boston Herald*, 22 Jan., 10 Feb.1948; *Boston Post*, 22 Jan.1948; *Boston American*, 21 Jan.1948; *Christian Science Monitor*, 21 Jan.1948; *Boston Daily Record*, 22 Jan.1948; *Kill the Barnes Bill*, leaflet in Box 424, Folder 20, ACLU Records, Seeley G. Mudd Library, Princeton University; Statement by Mrs Sheila W. Findly, 21 Jan.1948, CLUM Papers; Mrs Kenneth B. Murdoch to Boynton, 8 March 1948, to Shattuck, 8 March 1948, and to Vaughan, 9 March 1948, CLUM Papers.

7. *Baltimore Sun*, 28 Oct.1948; Samuel Lubell, 'Who *Really* Elected Truman', *Saturday Evening Post*, 22 Jan.1949; Levin, *Compleat Politician*, pp.50–1.

8. *Boston Herald*, 22 Dec.1948, 27 March 1949; *Christian Science Monitor*, 4 March 1949.

9. *Boston Herald*, 22 Dec.1948; *Christian Science Monitor*, 4 March 1949; *Mass. House J., 1949*, pp.101, 188, 1040, 1549–50; American Legion, Department of Masachusetts, *Annual Proceedings ... 1949* (Boston 1951), p.53; VFW, *Annual Proceedings, 1949* (1950), p.66; *Mass. Acts and Resolves, 1949*, ch.263, p.185.

10. *Boston Herald*, 22 Dec.1948, 7 April 1949; *Mass. House J., 1949*, pp.99, 101, 188, 192, 194; LWVM, 'Structure and Administration of

Government – State Legislation for 1949', 11 Feb.1949, LWVM Papers; *Boston Traveler*, 28 March, 6, 13 April 1949; *Christian Science Monitor*, 28 March 1949; *Harvard Crimson*, 26 May 1949; CLUM, 'Legislative Bulletin on Civil Liberties Bills', 12 May 1949, CLUM Papers; Elizabeth B. Roitman to Herbert M. Levy, 23 May 1949, Box 1033, Folder 3, ACLU Records; *Mass. House J., 1949*, pp.101, 1069.

11. *Boston Globe*, 1, 13 July 1949; *Mass. Sen. J., 1949*, pp.1269–70; CLUM, 'Civil Liberties Newsletter', Dec.1949, p.1; *Mass. Acts and Resolves, 1949*, ch.619, p.540.

12. 'Freedom at Harvard: An Exchange of Letters by Frank B. Ober of Baltimore, President Conant, and Grenville Clark, Fellow of Harvard College', *Harvard Alumnae Bulletin*, 25 June 1949, pp.730–5; *Boston Traveler*, 4 Oct.1949; James B. Conant, *My Several Lives: Memoirs of a Social Inventor* (New York: Harper & Row, 1970), pp.454–9; Sigmund Diamond, *Compromised Campus: The Collaboration of Universities with the Intelligence Community, 1945–1955* (New York: Oxford University Press, 1992), pp.116–21.

13. CLUM, 'Report of Planning Conferences on DEFENDING OUR FREEDOM called by the Civil Liberties Union of Massachusetts', CLUM Papers; CLUM, 'Civil Liberties Newsletter', Dec.1949, p.2.

14. Walter Goodman, *The Committee: The Extraordinary Career of the House Committee on Un-American Activities* (New York: Farrar, Straus, Giroux, 1969), p.315; J. R. Killian, Jr, to MIT Alumnae, 27 Sept.1951, Mather Papers.

15. *Mass. House J., 1950*, pp.53, 64, 1704; CLUM Exec. Sec. to Friend of Academic Freedom, 30 Jan.1950, CLUM Papers; CLUM, *Civil Liberties Newsletter: Annual Report, 1950*; *Boston Herald*, 27 Jan.1950.

16. Cornelius Dalton in *Boston Traveler*, 23 March 1951; W. E. Mullins in *Boston Herald*, 2 April 1951, 7 Jan. 1954; *Mass. House J., 1950*, pp.1849–51, 1933; Commonwealth of Massachusetts, *Report of the Committee to Curb Communism, March 30, 1951* (Boston, 1951), pp.8, 9; John L. Carter to Friend of Civil Liberties, 7 Nov.1950, CLUM Papers; *Fitchburg Sentinel*, 14 Dec.1950. The party identities of one voter on each side could not be ascertained.

17. 'Minutes of the meeting of representative organizations, religious groups, and denominations, held on Thursday, October 19, 1950', CLUM Papers; *Boston Traveler*, 23 Nov.1950, 20 March 1951; ACLU, 'Petitioners for the Repeal of the Donlan Order', CLUM Papers; *Boston Post*, 29 Nov.1950; *Boston Globe*, 1 March 1951; Mrs Vincent L. Greene to Dear Madam, 2 Jan.1951, Box 2, League of Catholic Women Papers, Archives of the Archdiocese of Boston; *Boston Sunday Advertiser*, 4 Nov.1951.

18. Thomas H. O'Connor, *The Boston Irish: A Political History* (Boston: Northeastern University Press, 1995), pp.295–6; Paul A. Dever, *Addresses and Messages to the General Court ...* (1952), p.592. See also Litt, *Political Cultures of Massachusetts*, pp.16–25, 51–5, on the tendency for 'managerial' types to overshadow urban workers in the Democratic party in the postwar decades.

19. *Mass. House J., 1951*, pp.56, 64; Kenneth B. Murdoch to W. K. Jordan, 26 March 1951, CLUM Papers; 'Anti-Communism and Civil Rights', *Boston City Reporter*, May 1951, p.1; *Report of the Committee*, pp. 22, 28 and ibid.

20. *Boston Traveler*, 30 March, 2 April 1951; *Boston Herald*, 2 April 1951; *Report of the Committee*, pp.77–80, 84–5.

21. *Boston Traveler*, 23 March, 17 April 1951; *Report of the Committee*, pp.58–71.

22. *Boston Post*, 18, 25 April 1951; *Christian Science Monitor*, 17 April 1951; *Boston Globe*, 25 April 1951; *Boston Herald*, 25, 26 April 1951; Luther Knight Macnair to Members of the General Court, 29 March 1951, Box 1038, Folder 9, ACLU Records; *Mass. House J., 1951*, p.56; *Boston Traveler*, 9 June 1951.

23. *Mass. Sen. J., 1951*, p.1234–5, 1286, 1702, 1822–5; *Boston Herald*, 3 July 1951; *Boston Traveler*, 13 July 1951; *Mass. House J., 1951*, pp.2005, 2266–8, 2451–4; LWVM, *Bulletin*, 29 (Nov.1951), 2; *Boston Globe*, 23 Nov.1951; *Harvard Crimson*, Academic Freedom Survey, 17 June 1952.

24. *Mass. House J., 1951*, p.2096; *Mass. Sen. J., 1951*, p.1823; 'New Anti-Communist Law', *New Republic*, 125 (17 Dec.1951), p.7; *Mass. Acts and Resolves, 1951*, ch.805, pp.821–4.

25. Emergency Civil Liberties Committee, *A Plot Against the Commonwealth of Massachusetts*, (n.p., 1951?), pp.1–2, 6–7; *Boston Traveler*, 12 Sept.1951; 'Red Hunt in Boston', *New Republic*, 125 (24 Dec.1951), 6–7. Struik had also caused offence by his attitude towards the Korean War: Cedric Belfrage, *The American Inquisition, 1945–1960* (Indianapolis: Bobbs Merrill, 1973), p.190n.

26. *Boston Post*, 28 Nov.1951; *Boston Traveler*, 23 Nov.1951; Paul A. Dever, *Addresses and Messages to the General Court* ... (1952), pp.477–9; *Boston Globe*, 23 Nov.1951.

27. *Mass. House J., 1952*, pp.55, 146, 725, 1919; *Mass. House J. Extra Session,1952*, pp.19, 47, 54; Luther Knight Macnair, 'Annual Report' [May, 1952], CLUM Papers; LWVM, 'State Legislative Program 1952', LWVM Papers; *Boston Sunday Herald*, 20 Jan., 5 Oct.1952; VFW of Mass., *Annual Proceedings, 1952* ..., p.28; Cutler, *Cushing*, p.106; *Boston Post*, 27, 30 Sept., 3, 16 Oct.1952; *Boston Globe*, 4 Oct.1952.

28. Herter speeches in Political Parties 1952 file (quotation in 'Speech material'), Christian Herter Papers, Houghton Library, Harvard University; *Worcester Gazette*, 26 Dec.1952; *Worcester Telegram*, 5 Oct.1952; *Christian Science Monitor*, 28 Oct.1952; *Jewish Times*, 30 Oct.1952; *Boston Traveler*, 30 Dec.1952; *Boston Post*, 27 Oct.1952; *The Catholic Mirror* (Springfield, n.d.) in Herter Papers; *Cambridge Chronicle*, 23 Oct.1952; *Mass. House J., 1954*, p.6.

29. *Boston Herald*, 30 Sept.1952.

9   Red Scare and Resolution, 1953–1962

1. *Counterattack*, 16 Jan.1953; Ellen W. Schrecker, *No Ivory Tower: McCarthyism & the Universities* (New York: Oxford University Press, 1986), p.180; *Mass. House J., 1953*, p.348; *Boston Traveler*, 27 Jan.1953.

2. *Boston Globe*, 26 Feb., 27 March 1953; Schrecker, *No Ivory Tower*, pp.194, 200; *Christian Science Monitor*, 14 April 1953; *Boston Sunday Herald*, 19 April 1953; *Boston Traveler*, 22 Dec.1953; David Caute, *The Great Fear: The Anti-Communist Purge Under Truman and Eisenhower* (New York: Simon and Schuster, 1978), pp.410–13; John Henry Cutler, *Cardinal Cushing of Boston* (New York: Hawthorn Books, 1970), p.100.

3. *Mass. House J., 1953*, pp.66, 73, 412, 628; League of Women Voters of Massachusetts [LWVM], 'Proposed Legislative Program, 1953', 21 Jan.1953, LWVM Papers, Schlesinger Library, Cambridge; *Boston Herald*, 17 April, 12 June 1953; Julius Meltzer to Christian A. Herter, 10 June 1953, CLUM Papers, Massachusetts Historical Society; *Boston Globe*, 24 June 1953; *Mass. Sen. J., 1953*, pp.1027–9, 1220–1, 1344; *Boston Evening Globe*, 30 Nov.1953; *Boston Traveler*, 22 June 1953; undated paper in 1953–4 Ad Hoc Watch Dog Committee file, CLUM Papers.

4. Shrecker, *No Ivory Tower*, p.203; Edgar Litt, *The Political Cultures of Massachusetts* (Cambridge: MIT Press, 1965), p.68; Donald Crosby, *God, Church, and Flag: Senator Joseph R. McCarthy and the Catholic Church* (Chapel Hill: University of North Carolina Press, 1978), pp.112–13; *The Pilot*, 27 March 1954; 'Partial Report of the Special Commission Established To Make An Investigation and Study of Communism and Subversive Activities ... in the Commonwealth', 30 March 1954, *Mass. House Docs., 1954*, No.2645.

5. Thomas H. O'Connor, *South Boston: My Home Town* (Boston: Quinlan Press, 1988), p.203; *Boston Globe*, 4 Nov.1955.

6. *Christian Science Monitor*, 12 Nov.1953; *Boston Globe*, 24, 30 Nov.1953; *Boston Herald*, 22 Nov., 7, 9, 10 Dec.1953; Thomas C. Reeves, *The Life and Times of Joe McCarthy* (Melbourne, FL: Krieger, 1982), p.525; David M. Oshinsky, *Senator Joseph McCarthy and the American Labor Movement* (Columbia: University of Missouri Press, 1976), pp.172–3; *Boston Traveler*, 1 Dec.1953; Steve Rosswurm, 'The Catholic Church and the Left-Led Unions', in Rosswurm (ed.), *The CIO's Left-Led Unions* (New Brunswick: Rutgers University Press, 1992), pp.133–4.

7. Joe Hill, 'Anti-Red or Anti-Union? That Boston Labor Probe', *The Nation*, 180 (8 Jan.1955), 32–3; Liberal Citizens of Massachusetts, *Massachusetts Commission on Communism, Subversive Activities and Related Matters* (Waltham, 1955), p.4; Caute, *The Great Fear*, pp.378–9. This sort of collusion was not unusual among redbaiting bodies; HUAC had already shown how UE might be harassed and IUE aided when it had subpoenaed a Lynn UE leader two days before an NLRB election in 1951: Ronald L. Filippelli and Mark D. McColloch, *Cold War in the Working Class: The Rise and Decline of the United Electrical Workers* (Albany:

State University of New York Press, 1995), p.150. On employer–HUAC collusion see also Ellen W. Schrecker, 'McCarthyism and the Labor Movement', in Rosswurm (ed.), *The CIO's Left-Led Unions*, pp.143–4.

8. *Boston Herald*, 15 Dec.1953, 15 Jan.1954; *Boston Evening Globe*, 20 Jan.1954; *Boston Traveler* 25 Jan.1954; *Salem Express*, 6 June 1954; *Boston Post*, 30 Jan.1954; *Boston Globe*, 29 Jan.1954; Liberal Citizens of Mass., *Mass. Commission*; American Legion, Department of Massachusetts, *Annual Proceedings, 1954*, p.164.

9. Christian A. Herter, *Addresses and Messages to the General Court, ...* (Boston, 1956), p.142; *Boston Herald*, 7 Jan., 21 Feb.1954; *New York Times*, 9 Jan.1954; Heseltine to Herter, 8 Jan.1954, Herter Papers, Houghton Library, Harvard University; *Mass. House J., 1954*, pp.667–8, 833; *Christian Science Monitor*, 19 May 1954.

10. *Boston Evening Globe*, 20 Jan.1954; *Boston Herald*, 13 Jan., 2, 25 Feb., 19 March 1954; *Boston Traveler*, 6, 25 Jan., 19 March 1954; *Boston Globe*, 3 April 1954; Litt, *Political Cultures of Massachusetts*, pp.157–8; Hill, 'Anti-Red or Anti-Union?' pp.32–3; Liberal Citizens of Mass., *Mass. Commission*, p.4; Walter A. O'Brien, Jr., to Dear Friend, 4 Nov.1955, Florence Luscomb Papers, Schlesinger Library, Radcliffe College, Cambridge.

11. 'Partial Report of the Special Commission on Communism ...', 18 May 1954, *Mass. Legis. Docs., House, 1954*, No. 2910, p.11; *Christian Science Monitor*, 25 May 1954; 'Fourth Interim Report of the Special Commission on Communism ...', *Mass. Legis. Docs., House, 1955*, No. 3080, pp.7, 8, 87–8, 92, 110, 357; Caute, *The Great Fear*, p.357; Hill, 'Anti-Red or Anti-Union?' p.33.

12. 'Fifth Interim Report of the Special Commission on Communism ...', 10 Nov.1955, *Mass. Legis. Docs., House, 1956*, No. 450, p.216 and passim.

13. *Mass. House J., 1954*, pp.56, 57, 61, 64, 66, 67, 69, 198, 570, 581, 624, 641–2, 1556, 1706, 1725, 1869–70, 2006, 2024–5; CLUM, 'Legislative Bulletin, 1954', 13 April 1954, CLUM Papers; *Boston Herald*, 4, 10 Feb.1954; 'Partial Report', pp.7, 12, 14, 15–19; *Mass. Acts and Resolves, 1954*, ch.92, p.791, ch.454, p.379, ch.584, pp.513–14, ch.650, p.663, ch.654, p.673; 'Annual Report of the Commissioner of Public Safety for the Year Ending June 30, 1956', typescript carbon in Massachusetts State Library, Boston.

14. Crosby, *God, Church, and Flag*, p.194; American Legion, Dept. of Mass., *Annual Proceedings, Thirty-Sixth Annual Convention, 1954*, p.164;VFW, *Annual Proceedings, 1954*, p.13; *Boston Globe*, 21 Oct., 14 Nov.1954; Archbishop Cushing to Very Rev. Francis J. Lally, 9 March 1955, and Lally to Cushing, 14 March 1955, Box 9, Francis J. Lally Papers, Archives of the Archdiocese of Boston; *Mass. House J., 1955*, pp.56, 64–8, 70, 73; CLUM, 'Legislative Bulletin', Feb.1955, CLUM Papers. In Boston by the 1950s traditional Irish ward politics were tending to be displaced by a city-wide managerial style concentrated in the mayor's office, creating resentments in the neighbourhoods: Thomas H. O'Connor, *The Boston Story: A Political History* (Boston: Northeastern University Press, 1995), pp.233–9.

15. *Boston Traveler*, 22 March 1954; *Boston Herald*, 25 May 1954; Gerald Horne, *Communist Front? The Civil Rights Congress, 1944–1956* (Cranbury: Fairleigh Dickinson University Press, 1988), pp.250, 264; *Boston Globe*, 19, 20, 29 Oct.1954; Caute, *The Great Fear*, p.74; 'Legislative Meeting – January 11, 1955', typescript in LWVM Papers.

16. *Congress Shall Make No Law* [Cambridge, 1955], pamphlet in Luscomb Papers; Thelma Dale to Luscomb, 14 Jan.1955, Frank Collier to Luscomb, 14 Jan.1955, Luscomb Papers; Mary Rackliffe, 'Statement to the Massachusetts Commission Investigating Communism', 3 March 1955, CLUM Papers; 'Statement of Laura M. O'Brien Before the Mass. Commission to Investigate Communism and Subversive Activities', 3 March 1955, 'Statement of Walter A. O'Brien, Jr. before Special Commission ...', 3 March 1955, Luscomb Papers.

17. 'Preliminary Report of the Special Commission Established to Study and Investigate Communism ...', 11 April 1955, *Mass. Legis. Docs., Sen., 1955*, No.685, pp.3–11; Florence H. Luscomb, 'Blacklisting the Constitution', leaflet, Luscomb Papers; 'Interim Report of the Special Commission on Communism ...', June 1955, *Mass. Legis. Docs., Sen.,1955*, No.760; Liberal Citizens of Mass., *Mass. Commission*, p.6. One amendment to the Commission's terms, put by Joseph D. Ward (Fitchburg, D), required it to name not only suspected CP members but anyone whom it believed to be 'in any respect a subversive or security risk by reason of disloyalty'. The house first rejected this, but when Ward secured a roll call dutifully passed it by 144 votes to 69. Some 97 Democrats voted in favour, 6 against; Republicans were 46 for and 63 against (one legislator's politics could not be identified); the senate killed the measure: *Mass. House J., 1954*, pp.1808–10, 1873.

18. 'Interim Report', June 1955, pp.84–175; *Boston Evening Globe*, 9 June 1955; *Boston Traveler*, 9 June 1955; 'Web of Circumstances', p.5; 'Not With a Sword', *The Nation*, 181 (30 July 1955), p.86; ACLU, *Thirty-Sixth Annual Report* (New York 1956), p.33; Florence H. Luscomb, press release, 14 June 1955, Luscomb Papers.

19. Florence Luscomb to Dear Friend of Civil Liberties, July 1955, Luscomb Papers; Luscomb, 'Blacklisting'; Liberal Citizens of Mass., *Mass. Commission*, pp.1, 6, 8; *Mass. Reports, Vol.334*, pp. 468–76; Florence Luscomb to Dear Friend, 3 July 1957, and replies, Luscomb Papers. See ch.3 on the *Nelson* decision.

20. Walter A. O'Brien Jr to Dear Friend, 4 Nov.1955, Luscomb Papers; *Boston Globe*, 2 Nov.1955; Thomas H. O'Connor, *Bibles, Brahmins and Bosses: A Short History of Boston* (Boston: Boston Public Library, 2nd edn, 1984), pp.160–5; O'Connor, *South Boston*, pp.203–4.

21. 'Eighth Interim Report of the Commission ...', *Mass. Legis. Docs., House, 1956*, No.3023, pp.9–31, 47; 'Ninth Interim Report of the Commission ...', 21 Jan.1957, *Mass. Legis. Docs., House, 1957*, No.2828, pp.18–19; Cedric Belfrage, *The American Inquisition, 1945–1960* (Indianapolis: Bobbs Merrill, 1973), pp.190, 249–50; Lionel S. Lewis, *Cold War on the Campus* (New Brunswick: Transaction Books), pp.226–32; 'Eleventh Report of the Special Commission ...', 27 Jan.1958, *Mass. Legis. Docs., House, 1958*, No.2626, p.16 and passim.

22. 'Tenth Report of the Special Commission ...', 1 Feb.1957, *Mass. Legis. Docs., House, 1957*, No.3157, p.7; *Boston Traveler*, 3 Dec.1957.

23. Luscomb to Dear Friend, 3 July 1957 and replies, Luscomb Papers; CLUM, Meeting of Exec. Committee, 3 Feb. 1958, CLUM Papers; *Mass. Acts and Resolves, 1958*, ch.34, pp.11–13; *Mass. Acts and Resolves, 1961*, ch.124, p.48.

24. 'Report of Legislative Committee – 1956', CLUM Papers.

25. *Christian Science Monitor*, 16 Jan.1956, 5 Feb.1957, 3, 12 Feb.1958; 'Report of Legislative Committee – 1956', Massachusetts Baptist Convention, 'Resolution adopted at Pittsfield, Massachusetts, November, 1956', Press Statement, 11 Feb.1958, of Prof. James Luther Adams and 28 others, and Statement of B. Loring Young, 10 Feb.1958, all in CLUM Papers; *Berkshire Eagle*, 16 Jan.1957; *Boston Herald*, 16 Jan.1957; *Boston Globe*, 11 Feb.1958; *North American Transcript*, 5 Feb.1957; *Boston Traveler*, 5 Feb.1957; *Boston Record*, 13 Feb.1958.

26. 'Twenty-First Diocesan Congress of the League of Catholic Women', circular [1957], in Box 2, League of Catholic Women Papers, Archives of the Archdiocese of Boston; *Quincy Ledger*, 14 May 1957; Cushing's Pastoral Letters and Statements and his Sermons and Addresses in Richard J. Cushing Papers, Archives of Archdiocese; James M. O'Toole, 'The Church Takes To The Streets: Public Catholicism in Boston, 1945–1960', pp.23–5, unpublished paper in Archives of Archdiocese; *The Pilot*, 28 Feb., 6 June, 8 , 15 Aug.1959; *Boston Herald*, 7 June 1959; Richard Cardinal Cushing, *Comments on Communism* (Boston: Daughters of St. Paul, n.d.), pp.28–40; Captain Harry W. Curtis to Richard Cardinal Cushing, 14 April 1961, Box 10, Lally Papers; Francis J. Lally to Cushing, 24 Feb.1961, and Cushing to Lally, 27 Feb.1961, Box 10, Lally Papers; Richard Cardinal Cushing, *Questions and Answers on Communism* (Boston: Daughters of St Paul, 1960), p.134.

27. CLUM, *Civil Liberties in the Bay State*, Summer 1960, p.4; Commonwealth of Mass., 'Annual Report of the Commissioner of Public Safety for the Year Ending June 30, 1961', typescript in Massachusetts State Library, pp.95–6; 'Fourteenth Report of the Special Commission ...', May 1961, p.5; *Mass. Acts and Resolves, 1962*, ch.62, p.738.

28. 'Annual Report of the Commissioner of Public Safety for the Year Ending June 30, 1956', pp.84–6, Mass. State Library. Subsequent annual reports cited are also found here.

29. 'Annual Report of the Commissioner ...1958', pp.95–7; HUAC, *Investigation of Communist Activities in the New England Area: ...March 14, 18, 19, 20, and 21, 1958* (Washington, 1958), pp.2081, 2084, 2090, 2111, 2230, 2340; 'Annual Report of the Commissioner ...1962', pp.96–7.

30. 'Annual Report of the Commissioner ...1958', pp.94, 99; 'Annual Report of the Commissioner ...1960', pp.102–4; 'Annual Report of the Commissioner ...1965', pp.93–5.

31. ACLU of Sn. Cal., *Open Forum*, Jan.1961; 'Statement by Samuel Bowles Concerning the Massachusetts Teachers' Loyalty Oath', 10 March

1966, and Corliss Lamont to Nathan M. Pusey, 11 March 1966, Day Letter, National Emergency Civil Liberties Committee Papers, Box 2, Columbia University; *New York Tribune*, 20 March 1966; ACLU, 'Bulletin, #2301', 5 June 1967.

32. Litt, *Political Cultures of Massachusetts*, pp.67–70; Crosby, *God, Church, and Flag*, pp.205, 232; Levin, *The Compleat Politician*, pp.50–1.

33. Ronald P. Formisano, *Boston Against Busing: Race, Class, and Ethnicity in the 1960s and 1970s* (Chapel Hill: University of North Carolina Press, 1991); on the populist instincts of Catholic workers in Massachusetts see also Edgar Litt, *Political Cultures of Massachusetts*, pp.18–19; Diamond, *Compromised Campus*, esp. chs 2 and 5.

34. O'Connor, *Boston Irish*, pp.197, 234–9, 291–4; J. Anthony Lukas, 'All in the Family: The Dilemmas of Busing and the Conflict of Values', pp.242, 248, in Ronald P. Formisano and Constance K. Burns (eds), *Boston, 1700–1980: The Evolution of Urban Politics* (Westport, CT: Greenwood Press, 1984); see also essays by Charles H. Trout, William V. Shannon, Martha W. Weinberg and the Conclusion by Formisano in ibid.; O'Connor, *Bibles, Brahmins and Bosses*, pp.153–72, 216–47; Litt, *Political Cultures of Massachusetts*, pp.39–47, 83–6, 92–6, 210. Litt suggests (p.47) that the gubernatorial election of 1952, when Democrat and Irish American Paul Dever lost to Yankee Republican Christian Herter, might be regarded as 'the real "last hurrah" for the urban industrial centers as the unquestioned molders of the Democratic Party, its programs, and candidates'.

IV   Red Scare Politics in Georgia

1. E.g. see Adam Fairclough, *Race & Democracy: The Civil Rights Struggle in Louisiana, 1915–1972* (Athens: University of Georgia Press, 1995), and Patricia Sullivan, *Days of Hope:Race and Democracy in the New Deal Era* (Chapel Hill: University of North Carolina Press, 1996).

2. Earl Black and Merle Black, *Politics and Society in the South* (Cambridge: Harvard University Press, 1987) ; Dewey W. Grantham, *The Life and Death of the Solid South* (Lexington: University of Kentucky Press, 1988); J. Morgan Kousser, *The Shaping of Southern Politics: Suffrage Restriction and the Establishment of the One-Party South, 1880–1910* (New Haven: Yale University Press, 1974); V. O. Key, Jr, *Southern Politics in State and Nation* (New York: Knopf, 1949); Wilbur J. Cash, *The Mind of the South* (New York: Knopf, 1941); Wilson Record, *Race and Radicalism: The NAACP and the Communist Party in Conflict* (Ithaca: Cornell University Press, 1964), pp.52–68.

3. Black and Black, *Politics and Society*, pp.13, 86–7; Numan V. Bartley, *The Creation of Modern Georgia* (Athens: University of Georgia Press, 1983), p.192.

4. Grantham, *Life and Death*, pp.91–2; William Anderson, *The Wild Man from Sugar Creek: The Political Career of Eugene Talmadge* (Baton Rouge: Louisiana State University Press, 1975), pp.96–7 and passim; Key, *Southern Politics*, pp.107–29.

10   Defending the Old Order, 1935–1948

1. Bartley, *Creation of Modern Georgia* (2nd edn, 1990), pp.197–8.
2. M. J. Heale, *American Anticommunism: Combating the Enemy Within, 1830–1970* (Baltimore : Johns Hopkins University Press, 1990), p.101; Kenneth Coleman (ed.), *A History of Georgia* (Athens: University of Georgia Press, 1977), p.294; John Hammond Moore, 'Communists and Fascists in a Southern City: Atlanta, 1930', *South Atlantic Quarterly*, 67 (1968), 437–54; Patricia Sullivan, *Days of Hope: Race and Democracy in the New Deal* Era (Chapel Hill: University of North Carolina Press, 1996), p.21; *Encyclopedia of the American Left*, p.307; *Atlanta Journal*, 3 March 1949.
3. Arthur M. Schlesinger Jr, *The Politics of Upheaval* (Boston: Houghton Mifflin, 1960), pp.521–2; Coleman (ed.), *History of Georgia*, p.314; *Atlanta Constitution*, 23 March 1935; 'Unofficial Observer', *American Messiahs* (Port Washington: Kennikat Press, reissue 1969), p.175; Grantham, *Life and Death*, p.107; Anderson, *The Wild Man*, pp.110–11, 136–40.
4. Coleman (ed.), *History of Georgia*, p.315; Bartley, *Creation of Modern Georgia* (2nd edn), pp.190–2.
5. *Atlanta Journal*, 5 March 1935; *Macon Telegraph*, 6, 20 March 1935; *Georgia House Journal* [hereafter *Ga. House J.*], *1935*, pp.986, 1670, 2672–73; *Georgia Sen. J.*, *1935*, pp.1607, 1848; *Atlanta Constitution*, 19, 22 March 1935; State of Georgia, *Acts and Resolutions of the General Assembly, 1935* (Atlanta 1935), No.54, pp.1305–6; O. E. Petry to Samuel P. Puner, 12 April 1935, and Roger Baldwin to 'Our Friends in Georgia', 18 April 1935, Vol.836, 1935, ACLU Records, Seeley G. Mudd Library, Princeton University.
6. *Ga. Acts and Resolutions, 1937–1938*, pp.189–90, 1425–6; James C. Cobb, 'Not Gone, But Forgotten: Eugene Talmadge and The 1938 Purge Campaign', *Georgia Historical Quarterly*, 59 (1975), 197–209.
7. *The Statesman* (Hapeville, GA), 22 July 1941, 25 Aug.1942; Hugh Clinton Griffis, 'Ethnic Culture and the Political Thought of Georgia's Political Editors: Tom Watson, Eugene Talmadge, and Roy Harris', (MA diss., Emory University, 1978), p.62; Sue Bailes, 'Eugene Talmadge and the Board of Regents Controversy', *Georgia Historical Quarterly*, 53 (1969), 409–23; Bartley, *Creation of Modern Georgia* (2nd edn), pp.193–4; Coleman (ed.), *History of Georgia*, p.379; Anderson, *The Wild Man*, pp.200–12.

8. Sullivan, *Days of Hope*, pp.156–7, 162; *The Statesman*, 25 Jan., 20 Dec.1945; Bartley, *Creation of Modern Georgia*, pp.185–7; Grantham, *Life and Death*, p.115.
9. Ibid., pp.117, 119; William L. Belvin, Jr, 'The Georgia Gubernatorial Primary of 1946', *Georgia Historical Quarterly*, 50 (1966), 37–53; Steve Fraser, *Labor Will Rule: Sidney Hillman and the Rise of American Labor* (New York, 1991), p.571.
10. Barbara S. Griffith, *The Crisis of American Labor: Operation Dixie and the Defeat of the CIO* (Philadelphia, 1988), pp.24–5, 108; Joseph P. Kamp, *Communist Carpetbaggers in Operation Dixie* (New York, 1946); *The Trumpet* (Columbus, GA), 16 Aug.1946; 'Operation Dixie', *Modern Industry*, 15 Aug.1946, pp.49–64; League of Women Voters of Georgia, *Summary of Legislation Passed By General Assembly of the State of Georgia Regular Session 1947* (Atlanta, June 1947), p.19.
11. *West End Eagle* (Atlanta), 8 April 1949, p.1; Emory Burke, *Chain-Ganged By The Jewish Gestapo* (n.p., 1949), pp.5–10; Lorraine Nelson Spritzer, *The Belle of Ashby Street: Helen Douglas Mankin and Georgia Politics* (Athens: University of Georgia Press, 1982), pp.99, 116–17, 126; Ned to AF, 3 Sept.1946, Columbians file, Ralph McGill Papers, Emory University (and see other documents in this file); see also 'Hate at Cut Rates', in Ralph McGill, *No Place to Hide: The South and Human Rights* (Mercer: Mercer University Press, 1984), I, pp.79–88.
12. State of Georgia vs Knights of the Ku Klux Klan, Hearing June 13, 1947, typescript in Ku Klux Klan file, McGill Papers, pp.12, 20 and passim; 'Operation Dixie', *Mod. Industry*, 15 Aug.1946, p.64; Burke, *Chain-Ganged*, pp.4, 10–23; Columbians file, McGill Papers; Dr Samuel Green to Esteemed Klansman, 23 June 1947, Ku Klux Klan file, McGill Papers; 'Klavern No. 1', 19 May 1947, typed report in ibid.; Anderson, *The Wild Man*, pp.224–5. See also Edward C. Banfield, *Big City Politics* (New York: Random House, 1965), pp.19, 32.
13. Bartley, *Creation of Modern Georgia* (2nd edn), pp.198–201; Spritzer, *Belle of Ashby Street*, pp.69–73; *Atlanta Constitution*, 8 Feb.1946.
14. Sullivan, *Days of Hope*, p.211; Spritzer, *Belle of Ashby Street*, pp.82–5, 100–6; Anderson, *The Wild Man*, pp.210–12, 225; Albert B. Saye, *A Constitutional History of Georgia, 1732–1968* (Athens: University of Georgia Press, rev. edn, 1970), p.415; Belvin, 'Georgia Gubernatorial Primary', pp.50–1. Fraud, violence and intimidation also augmented the Talmadge vote: Sullivan, *Days of Hope*, pp.213–14.
15. Spritzer, *Belle of Ashby Street*, pp.109, 116–17, 129–30; Burke, *Chain-Ganged*, pp.6, 10; *Atlanta Constitution*, 11 Oct.1946; Judge Davis Speech #3, 15 Oct.1946, p.3 and Judge Davis Speech #4, 22 Oct.1946, p.1, typescripts in Davis Papers, Emory University, Atlanta; 'For Once And All, Get The TRUTH About the Race For Congress In the 5th Georgia District', leaflet, Helen Douglas Mankin file, McGill Papers.
16. Coleman (ed.), *History of Georgia*, pp.391–2; Herman E. Talmadge, *Talmadge: A Politician's Legacy, A Politician's Life* (Atlanta: Peachtree Publishers, 1987), pp.81–96; *The Statesman*, 25 April 1946, 13 March, 30 Oct., 13 Nov.1947.

17. *The Statesman*, 1 April 1948; Communist Party of Georgia to Dear Friend, 1 Jan.1948, Georgia Communist Party file, McGill Papers; Karl M. Schmidt, *Henry A. Wallace: Quixotic Crusade, 1948* (Syracuse: Syracuse University Press, 1960), p.219.

18. Bartley, *Creation of Modern Georgia* (2nd edn), p.211; *Atlanta Journal*, 2, 13 May 1948, 3 March, 26 May 1949; undated typescript signed by C.H. Gillman and Charles L. Mathias, Georgia Communist Party file, McGill Papers; Ralph McGill to James C. Davis, telegram, 11 June 1948, and Davis to McGill, in ibid.; Robert Carmichael to McGill, 18 June 1948, and John E. Jones to McGill, 28 June 1948, in ibid.; McGill to Henriette S. Bradley, 27 July 1948 in Don West file, McGill Papers; *Atlanta Constitution*, 18 June 1948, 9 Dec.1953. On West's background see John M. Glen, *Highlander* (Lexington, 1988), pp.16–17, 26, Harvey Klehr, John Earl Haynes, & Fridrikh Igorevich Firsov, *The Secret World of American Communism* (New Haven: Yale University Press, 1995), p.287, and Douglas Flamming, 'Christian Radicalism, McCarthyism, and the Dilemma of Organized Labor in Dixie', ch.12 in Gary M. Fink and Merl E. Reed (eds), *Race, Class, and Community in Southern Labor History* (Tuscaloosa: University of Alabama Press, 1994). McGill had also attacked the SCHW as a 'communist infiltrated group' and had thought it was inciting violence in bringing Henry Wallace to Atlanta in 1947: Sullivan, *Days of Hope*, p.246.

19. 'Annual Report of the Atlanta Chapter of the American Civil Liberties Union' [1948], Box 424, Folder 10, and William V. George to Herbert M. Levy, 14 May 1949, Box 1032, Folder 16, ACLU Records.

20. *The Statesman*, 1 April, 15 July, 26 Aug.1948; Coleman (ed.), *History of Georgia*, p.392; Talmadge, *Talmadge*, pp.97, 99; *The Upson County News* in *The Statesman*, 26 Aug.1948; Key, *Southern Politics*, p.127; Spritzer, *Belle of Ashby Street*, pp.136–42.

21. Key, *Southern Politics*, pp.127–8n.; Schmidt, *Henry A. Wallace*, p.332; California Un-American Activities Committee, *Fifth Report, 1949*, p.601; State of Illinois, *Report of the Seditious Activities Investigation Commission* (1949), p.106. Alabama sent one delegate to the Los Angeles conference, which is discussed in ch.1.

11 Controlling Communist Subversion, 1948–1956

1. Morris B. Abram to George E. Rundquist, 11 Feb.1953, Box 1043, Folder 10, ACLU Records, Seeley G. Mudd Library, Princeton University.

2. Dewey W. Grantham, *The Life and Death of the Solid South* (Lexington: University of Kentucky Press, 1988), p.129; *Atlanta Constitution*, 8, 20 Feb.1949; *Ga. House J., 1949*, pp.518, 631; Herman E. Talmadge, *Talmadge: A Politician's Legacy, A Politician's Life* (Atlanta: Peachtree Publishers, 1987), pp.105–6.

3. *The Statesman*, 3 Feb., 10 March 1949; *Atlanta Journal*, 8 Feb., 14 April, 6 May 1949, 12 Jan.1953; *Atlanta Constitution*, 20 Feb.1949; *Ga. House J., 1949*, pp.596–608, 905–6; *Ga. Sen. J., 1949*, pp.259, 300, 372, 692, 727–8; *Ga. Laws, 1949*, pp.960–2; Herbert Levy to William V. George, 3 May 1949, and George to Levy, 14 May 1949, Box 1032, Folder 16, ACLU Records; Paul E. Pfuetze to Patrick Murphy Malin, 3 Feb.1954, Box 882, Folder 2, ACLU Records.The loyalty oath law was formally corrected 1950: *Ga. Laws, 1950*, pp.282–3.

4. *Atlanta Constitution*, 20 Feb.1949; *Georgia Democrat* (Valdosta), 11 Jan., 1 Feb., 1 March 1949; *St Louis Post-Dispatch*, 1 May 1949; *Atlanta Journal*, 18 Aug.1949; *The Statesman*, 5 Jan.1950. The ACLU committee meeting which considered its stand on the loyalty oath also had before it a case involving seven blacks flogged by sheriff's deputies, which it urgently needed funds to pursue: George to Levy, 14 May 1949.

5. *Macon Telegraph*, 8 Feb.1950.

6. *Atlanta Journal*, 11 July, 18, 21, 22, 23 Aug.1950; Robert J. Goldstein, *Political Repression in Modern America: From 1870 to the Present* (Boston: G.K. Hall, 1978), p.358.

7. H.H. Gibson to James C. Davis, 8 Aug.1950 (and similar letters), Walter O. Brooks to Davis, 18 Dec.1950, Communism file, James C. Davis Papers, Emory University, Atlanta; *Atlanta Journal*, 2 Aug., 25 Sept.1951.

8. Talmadge address, 9 Jan.1951, in *Ga. Sen. J., 1951*, pp.14–28; *Ga. Laws, 1951*, pp.224–41; *Atlanta Journal*, 25 Sept.1950, 20 Jan., 12 Sept.1951; *Atlanta Constitution*, 9 Dec.1953.

9. *Atlanta Journal*, 1, 2, 10, 27 March, 31 May, 30 Oct.1951, 15 Jan., 9 Feb.1952; *Ga. Laws, 1951*, pp.6–7.

10. *The Statesman*, 6 March 1952; *Ga. Sen. J., 1951–1952*, p.1338; *Ga. House J., 1951–1952*, pp.1773, 1813; *Ga. Laws, 1952*, p.619; Kenneth Coleman (ed.), *A History of Georgia* (Athens: University of Georgia Press, 1977), p.377; Talmadge, *Talmadge*, pp.134–6.

11. *Atlanta Journal*, 26 Jan., 1, 3, 6 Feb.1953; *Ga. House J., 1953*, pp.606, 613, 892–3, 911.

12. *The Statesman*, 29 Jan.1953; *Atlanta Journal*, 24, 25 Feb., 2 March 1953; Abram to Rundquist, 11 Feb.1953; *The Georgia Journal* (Macon), 28 Feb.1953; *Macon Telegraph*, 24 Feb.1953; *Atlanta Constitution*, 24 Feb.1953.

13. Abram to Rundquist, 11 Feb.1953; *Atlanta Journal*, 1, 12, 24, 25 Feb.1953; *Atlanta Constitution*, 20, 24 Feb.1953; *Macon Telegraph*, 24 Feb.1953.

14. *Atlanta Constitution*, 24 Feb.1953; *The Statesman*, 26 Feb.1953; *Macon Telegraph*, 24 Feb.1953; *Atlanta Journal*, 24 Feb.1953.

15. Charles F. Wittenstein to Alan Reitman, 20 March 1953, Box 1043, Folder 10, ACLU Records; *Atlanta Constitution*, 18, 23, 25, 26 Feb.1953; *Atlanta Journal*, 19, 24, 25 Feb.1953; *Ga. House J., 1953*, pp.225, 657, 661; *Ga. Sen. J., 1953*, pp.493, 541, 602; *Macon News* in *The Georgia Journal*, 21 Feb.1953.

16. *Atlanta Journal*, 25 March, 9 Sept., 26 Oct., 14 Nov.1953, 11 Aug.1965; *The Statesman*, 26 Feb.1953; *Macon Telegraph*, 20 Nov., 1 Dec.1953.

17. *Ga. House J., 1953*, p.952.
18. *Atlanta Constitution*, 20, 24 Nov., 1 Dec.1953; *Atlanta Journal*, 19, 27 Nov.1953; *The Georgia Journal* (Macon), 18 Dec.1953; ACLU, *Report for 1953–54*, p.44; *Ga. House J., 1953*, pp.1021, 1239, 1526, 1603; *Ga. Sen. J., 1953*, pp.493, 545, 602, 720, 744–5, 816; *Ga. Laws, 1953*, p.216; Paul E. Pfuetze to Patrick Murphy Malin, 3 Feb.1954, Box 882, Folder 2, ACLU Records.
19. *Atlanta Journal*, 2 Feb., 4 March, 17 April 1954, 22–4 Aug.1965; *Christian Century*, 71 (14 April 1954), pp.453–4; *Georgia Education Journal*, 47 (May 1954), p.32; State Security Questionnaires, Georgia Education Commission Papers, Georgia Department of Archives, Atlanta.
20. Numan V. Bartley, *The Rise of Massive Resistance* (Baton Rouge: Louisiana State University Press, 1969), p.53; *Atlanta Journal*, 19 Nov.1953; *Atlanta Constitution*, 2 Dec.1953; *Macon Telegraph*, 20 Nov.1953; *Ga. House J., 1953*, pp.935, 1000, 1163–6; *Ga. Sen. J., 1953*, p.982; *Ga. Laws, 1953*, pp.64–7, 241; *The Statesman*, 17 Dec.1953; *Ga. Laws, 1953, Nov.–Dec. sess.*, p.461.
21. *Chattanooga Times*, 8 Feb.1954; *The Statesman*, 25 March 1954; Hollinger F. Barnard (ed.), *Outside the Magic Circle: The Autobiography of Virginia Durr* (University: University of Alabama Press, 1985), ch.18; John A. Salmond, ' "The Great Southern Commie Hunt": Aubrey Williams, the Southern Conference Education Fund, and the Internal Security Subcommittee', *South Atlantic Quarterly*, 77 (Autumn 1978), 433–52; *Atlanta Constitution*, 22 March 1954; *Georgia Journal* (Macon), 26 March 1954.
22. *Morgan County News* in *Georgia Journal*, 29 May 1954, which prints a variety of politician and newspaper reactions to the Brown decision; *Augusta Courier*, 28 June 1954 (see also issues for 2, 9, 30 Aug.1954); *The Statesman*, 1 July 1954; George S. Mitchell to Editor, *Atlanta Constitution*, 6 July 1954, in Southern Regional Council Papers, Atlanta University; Mrs A. N. Horton to Georgia Commission on Education, 25 June 1954 Mrs Della Edwards to GCE, 30 June 1954, Grady Fowler, Chairman, Citizens Crusade, to Durwood T. Pye, 2 July 1954, GCE Papers.
23. Durwood T. Pye to Harold Bradley, 19 July 1954, and see also Pye to Mrs H. M. Kandel, 2 Aug.1954, GCE Papers; GCE, *Report to the Members of the General Assembly by the Georgia Commission on Education, December 1954* (Atlanta, 1954), p.3; Bartley, *Massive Resistance*, pp.54–5.
24. Ibid., pp.68–9, 71; Earl Black, *Southern Governors and Civil Rights* (Cambridge: Harvard University Press, 1976), pp.66–8.
25. *Ga. House J., 1955*, pp.39, 42, 43, 80–1, 741, 879; *Atlanta Journal*, 12 Jan.1953; GCE, *Report, 1954*, p.6; *Ga. Sen. J., 1955*, pp.223, 469.
26. Neil R. McMillen, *The Citizens' Council: Organized Resistance to the Second Reconstruction, 1954–64* (Urbana: University of Illinois Press, 1971), p.82.
27. *Augusta Courier*, 28 June, 2, 9, 30 Aug.1954; Talmadge, *Talmadge*, p.155; Bartley, *Massive Resistance*, pp.186, 377. Copies of the 1955

Talmadge book disappeared from the Georgia public libraries when a reconstructed Talmadge was running for re-election to the US Senate in 1980.

28. Dr J. W. Holley to Eugene Cook, 27 Aug.1955, GCE Papers; *New York Times*, 16 Aug.1955; *Atlanta Constitution*, 3 May 1956; Talmadge, *Talmadge*, pp.62, 157, 200. In 1928 Comintern had defined southern blacks as an oppressed group entitled to their own separate nation, a position published in the US in 1929.

29. Eugene Cook, 'The Ugly Truth About The NAACP', 15 Oct.1955, typescript in SRC Papers; Eugene Cook, *The Ugly Truth About The NAACP* (n.p., n.d.), pp.1, 2, 10; *The Statesman*, 1 Dec.1955.

30. Eugene Cook to James C. Davis, 17 Jan.1956, Davis Papers; Frances E. Walter to George S. Mitchell, 30 Aug.1956, SRC Papers; *Congressional Record: Proceedings and Debates of the 84th Congress, Second Session* (Washington, reprint 1956), pp.1, 4; on Grant, see McMillen, *The Citizens' Council*, pp.81, 83.

31. *Congressman James C. Davis Speaks To The States' Rights Council* (Atlanta: GCE, 1956), pp.3, 8, 10, 21; Eugene Cook to T. V. Williams Jr, 3 Dec.1956, GCE Papers.

32. Coleman (ed.), *History of Georgia*, p.366; Bartley, *Massive Resistance*, pp.69, 71; Talmadge, *Talmadge*, p.340; *Georgia Journal* (Macon), 29 June 1955. McCarthyism also played a major role in destroying the union movement in Dalton, one of its strongholds in the state, in a process driven by local business and press interests and abetted by Governor Griffin in 1955: Douglas Flamming, 'Christian Radicalism, McCarthyism, and the Dilemma of Organized Labor in Dixie', Gary M. Fink and Merl E. Reed, (eds), *Race, Class, and Community in Southern History* (Tuscaloosa: University of Alabama Press, 1994), pp.190–211.

12   The Red Scare as Last Hurrah, 1956–1966

1. Numan V. Bartley, *The Creation of Modern Georgia* (Athens: University of Georgia Press, 1983), pp.192–3, 200–2; Earl Black and Merle Black, *Politics and Society in the South* (Cambridge: Harvard University Press, 1987), pp.13, 30; William Anderson, *The Wild Man fron Sugar Creek: The Political Career of Eugene Talmadge* (Baton Rouge: Louisiana State University Press, 1975), pp.228–9.

2. *Ga. House J., 1957*, pp.27, 28, 99–101, 138–40, 404; *Atlanta Constitution*, 23, 24 Jan.1957; *Ga. Laws, 1957*, pp.56–8. The four opponents of the proposal to strengthen the GCE were from DeKalb and Fulton Counties.

3. Minutes of the GCE Meeting, 3 Jan.1958, GCE Papers, Georgia Archives; Neil R. McMillen, *The Citizens' Council: Organized Resistance to the Second Reconstruction, 1954–64* (Urbana: University of Illinois Press, 1971), p.88.

4. GCE, *Ten Directors of the NAACP* (n.p., 1957); State of Louisiana, Joint Legislative Committee, *Subversion in Racial Unrest* (Baton Rouge, 1957); W. M. Rainach to T. V. Williams Jr, 16 March 1957, Louisiana file, GCE Papers.

5. *The Carnavall Reporter* (Duvall, WA), 12 Sept.1957; T. V. Williams Jr to F. W. Clark, 25 June 1957, Washington file, GCE Papers; Will Beck to T.V. Williams Jr, 6 June 1957; Williams to Beck, 2 July 1957, Georgia file, GCE Papers; T.V. Williams Jr, to Robert L. Storey, 21 Oct.1957, Alabama file, GCE Papers (see also files for other states); *Atlanta Journal and Constitution*, 25 Dec.1957. GCE minutes refer to a more modest mailing list of 30000: Minutes, 3 Jan.1958, GCE Papers.

6. John M. Glen, *Highlander: No Ordinary School, 1932–1962* (Lexington, 1988), pp.181–3; GCE, *Highlander Folk School* (1957), pp.1–4.

7. Ibid., p.4; Glen, *Highlander*, p.183; *Augusta Courier*, 8 July 1963; *Birmingham News*, 6 Oct.1957.

8. T. V. Williams Jr to Tommy Tibbs, 25 Nov.1957, Georgia file, GCE Papers; *Maryville-Alcoa Daily Times*, 16 Dec.1957; Marvin Griffin to Courtney C. Pace, 25 Nov.1957, T.V. Williams Jr to J. G. Sourwine, 21 Oct.1957, Gale Arbuckle Higgean to Williams, 25 Nov.1957, E. J. Roese to GCE, 29 Oct.1957, Joseph A. Malone to T.V. Williams Jr, 15 Oct.1957, E. D. Stoetzel to GCE, 13 March 1958, Ira H. Latimer to T.V. Williams Jr, 8 Jan.1958, H.U. Warner to Marvin Griffin, 5 Dec.1957, Bella V. Dodd to GCE, 4 Nov.1957, Alfred Kohlberg to GCE, 31 Oct.1957, T. V. Williams Jr to William R. John, undated, John to Williams, 29 Nov.1957, Williams to John, 3 Dec.1957, all in GCE Papers.

9. *The Atlanta Journal and Constitution*, 15 Dec.1957; *Atlanta Constitution*, 16, 17, 19, 20, 21 Dec.1957; Minutes of GCE Meeting, 3 Jan.1958, GCE Papers; John Constable to Harold Fleming, undated memorandum, GCE Papers.

10. Herman E. Talmadge to Richard Arens, 3 July 1957, Washington DC (Senators and James C. Davis) file, GCE Papers [all files in this note in GCE Papers unless otherwise stated]; T. V. Williams Jr to S. G. Sourwine, 21 Oct.1957, and Sourwine to Williams, 15 Oct.1957, Washington DC file; *Atlanta Journal*, 29 Oct.1957, 28 Jan.1958; T. V. Williams Jr to Hugh M. Burns, 25 Sept.1957, California file; W. M. Rainach to Williams, 19 Oct.1957, Correspondence A–M 1957 file; R. J. Strickland to Harvey Chandler, 28 May 1958, Florida Legislative Investigation Committee file; Chandler to Strickland, 23 June 1958, Florida file; Billy James Hargis to James C. Davis, 23 May 1958, Communism–General 1958–9 file, James C. Davis Papers, Emory University, Atlanta; Lester L. Buttram to Harvey H. Chandler, 5 Aug.1958, Arkansas file; William A. Lufburrow to T. V. Williams Jr, 26 June 1958, and see also George D. Stewart to Williams, 31 Jan.1958, GCE Papers. In November 1957 the States Rights Council made a loan of $2000 to T. V. Williams Jr, allegedly in connection with the investigation of NAACP activity in Florida: *Atlanta Constitution*, 24 June 1958.

11. Harold C. Fleming to Arnold Foster, 14 March 1957, SRC Papers, Atlanta University; SRC press release, 8 July 1957, 'An Analysis of the Attack on SRC in The Firing Line of May 15, 1957', Hate Groups file, Ralph McGill Papers, Emory University; *Atlanta Journal and Constitution*, 25 Dec.1957; Methodist Secretaries Annual Conference file, GCE Papers; T. V. Williams Jr to E. J. Hammond, 20 Nov.1957, T. V. Williams Jr to Douglas Carlisle, 3 Dec.1957, Georgia file, GCE Papers; C. C. Perkins to T. V. Williams Jr, 24 Feb.1958, C. C. Perkins typewritten affadavit, 4 April 1958, GCE Papers; John Constable to Harold Fleming, undated memorandum, SRC Papers.

12. McMillen, *Citizens' Council*, pp.272–3; Marvin Griffin's Speech, 2 Oct.1957, Correspondence A–M 1957 file, GCE Papers; *Atlanta Constitution*, 31 Oct, 1, 2, 5, 6 Nov.1957; Minutes of GCE Meeting, 3 Jan.1958, GCE Papers; John Constable to Harold Fleming, undated memorandum, SRC Papers; *Augusta Courier*, 24 March 1958; *New York Herald Tribune*, 17 Feb.1958; T. V. Williams Jr to James C. Davis, 17 Jan.1958, GCE Papers.

13. Harvey Chandler to Dr Granville F. Knight, 4 June 1958, GCE Papers; Glen, *Highlander*, p.183; GCE, *Communism and the NAACP* (2 vols, Atlanta, n.d.); Bartley, *Massive Resistance*, p.223; *Atlanta Constitution*, 24 June 1958, 3 June 1959; Roy Longbottom to GCE, 16 July 1958, R. A. Francis to GCE, 8 Aug.1958, Mrs Baldwin Bridges to GCE, 12 June 1958, Wilder G. Little to GCE, 4 June 1958, E. L. Perry to GCE, 10 March 1958, L. Frederick Meyer to GCE, 18 May 1958, W. Thomas Morgan to GCE, 28 Aug.1958, all in GCE Papers; *Macon News*, 2 June 1958; Walter F. Murphy, 'The South Counterattacks: The Anti-NAACP Laws', *Western Political Quarterly*, 12 (June 1959), 378. Curiously, *Communism and the NAACP* conceded that the NAACP was 'not a Communist front': I, p.40, cited in Murphy, 'The South Counterattacks', p.388n. Segregationist leaders in Louisiana also significantly weakened the NAACP through a similar campaign of harassment: Adam Fairclough, *Race & Democracy: The Civil Rights Struggle in Louisiana, 1915–1972* (Athens: University of Georgia Press, 1995), pp.187, 193–7, 205, 208–11.

14. Eugene Cook to Marvin Griffin, 10 Oct.1957, GCE Papers; Address of Louis C. Wyman, Attorney General of New Hampshire to the General Assembly of Georgia ... February 18, 1958, typescript copy, GCE Papers; *Ga. Sen. J., 1958*, pp.221–31; *Atlanta Constitution*, 22 May 1958; *Southern American* (Columbus), June 1958.

15. *Atlanta Journal*, 11, 27–31 July, 4 Dec.1958, 23 Jan.1959; *Washington Post and Times Herald*, 13 July 1958.

16. *Atlanta Constitution*, 1, 2 Nov.1957, 25 June, 7, 14, 22–6, 29 July, 5, 6 Aug.1958, 17 Jan.1959; *Atlanta Journal-Constitution*, 6 July 1958; *Macon Telegraph*, 8, 13 July 1958; *Atlanta Journal*, 28, 30 July 1958; Bartley, *Massive Resistance*, p.183; Numan V. Bartley, *From Thurmond to Wallace: Political Tendencies in Georgia, 1948–1968* (Baltimore: Johns Hopkins University Press, 1970), p.32; McMillen, *Citizens' Council*, pp.85–7.

17. Vandiver address, 15 Jan.1959, *Ga. Sen. J.*, *1959*, p.43; *Ga. Sen. J.*, *1959*, pp.17, 22, 23, 34, 44, 72, 93, 405; *Ga. House J.*, *1959*, pp.83, 121–2, 136, 162, 204–5; *Ga. Laws, 1959*, pp.5-6, 21; *Atlanta Constitution*, 23, 24 July 1958, 21, 28 Jan.1959; *Atlanta Journal*, 28 Jan.1959; Bartley, *Massive Resistance*, pp.183, 334–5.

18. Bartley, *Massive Resistance*, p.334; Kenneth Coleman (ed.), *A History of Georgia* (Athens: University of Georgia Press, 1977), pp.368–70; on Vandiver, see his address, 18 Jan.1961, *Ga. Sen. J.*, *1961*, pp.83–90.

19. Bartley, *From Thurmond to Wallace*, p.52; Coleman (ed.), *History of Georgia*, pp.395–400; *Atlanta Journal*, 11 Aug.1965; Albert B. Saye, *A Constitutional History of Georgia, 1732–1968* (Athens: University of Georgia Press, rev. edn, 1970), pp.421–6.

20. *Ga. House J.*, *1962*, pp.292, 316, 726, 983, 1220–1, 2071; *Ga. Sen. J.*, *1962*, p.54; *Atlanta Constitution*, 18 Jan.1962; *Atlanta Journal*, 9 Dec.1962.

21. *Atlanta Journal*, 1 May, 9 Dec.1962, 18 Nov.1963; West Georgia College, *Studies in the Social Sciences* (Carrollton, Ga), vol. 1, no. 1 (May 1962), pp.1–2; 'Conflicting Ideologies', *Georgia Education Journal* [hereafter *Ga. Educ. J.*], 56 (Sept.1962), 38; Lutian R. Wootton, 'Conflicting Ideologies Taught in Georgia Schools', *Ga. Educ.J.*, 57 (Feb.1964), 12.

22. *Atlanta Journal*, 9 Dec.1962, 18 Nov.1963; *State Journal*, 10 March 1963; *Ga. Educ.J.*, 56 (Sept.1962), 38; 'Georgia Teachers Begin Fighting Cold War', *Ga. Educ.J.*, 57 (Sept.1963), 20–1; Wootton, 'Conflicting Ideologies', pp.12–13; *State Journal and Constitution*, 27 Oct.1963; Claude Purcell and James S. Peters, *Time for a New Break-Through in Education in Georgia* (Atlanta, 1963), p.19. Educators elsewhere too were striving to introduce professional standards into teaching on communism in the early 1960s: Rodger Swearingen, 'Teaching About Communism in the American Schools', *Social Education*, 28 (Feb.1964), 68–70.

23. Earl Black, *Southern Governors and Civil Rights* (Cambridge: Harvard University Press, 1976), pp.177–81; Bartley, *Thurmond to Wallace*, pp.67–78; Bartley, *Creation of Modern Georgia*, 2nd edn, pp.229–31; Coleman (ed.), *History of Georgia*, pp.398–402; Ralph Cregar to Paul, n.d., appended to typescript headed 'maddox', Administrative Records, SRC Papers.

24. *Ga. House J.*, *1963*, pp.385, 1078–80, 1153–54, 1249–53; *Atlanta Constitution*, 14 Feb.1963; *Augusta Courier*, 8 July, 5, 12 Aug.1963.

25. Robert Weisbrot, *Freedom Bound: A History of America's Civil Rights Movement* (New York: W. W. Norton, 1990), pp.191–2; James F. Cook, *Carl Sanders: Spokesman of the New South* (Macon: Mercer University Press, 1993), p.260; *Atlanta Constitution*, 11, 20, 22, 25, 26, 28, 31 Jan., 1, 11 Feb.1966; *Atlanta Journal*, 17, 18, 21, 22, 24, 25 Jan., 1, 2 Feb.1966; *Ga. House J.*, *1966*, pp.318, 352. Bond was eventually seated by court order.

26. Florence B. Robin to Alan Reitman, 23 Aug.1965, and American Civil Liberties of Georgia, 'Civil Liberties', Sept.1965, Box 182, Folder 8,

ACLU Records, Seeley G. Mudd Library, Princeton University; *Atlanta Journal*, 11, 12, 15, 17 Aug.1965.

27. Robin to Reitman, 23 Aug.1965; *Atlanta Journal*, 22–4, 29 Aug., 7, 28 Sept., 1, 2 Oct., 2 Dec.1965, 6 Feb.1968, 13 April 1969, 26 Sept., 12 Oct.1972; *Ga. House J., 1966*, pp.307, 311, 1367; *Ga. Sen. J., 1966*, pp.12, 89, 90, 119; *Atlanta Constitution*, 11, 21 Jan., 18 April 1966.

28. Karl M. Schmidt, *Henry A. Wallace: Quixotic Crusader 1948* (Syracuse: Syracuse University Press, 1960), p.219; Patricia Sullivan, *Days of Hope:Race and Democracy in the New Deal Era* (Chapel Hill: University of North Carolina Press, 1996), p.257; Coleman (ed.), *History of Georgia*, p.366.

29. Georgia appears to have been unusual for the *extent* to which red scare tactics were deployed, but several southern states were using them to protect segregation and the old political order. For Louisiana, another state in which anticommunism was used with some effect, see Fairclough, *Race & Democracy*, esp. chs 6–8.

V   Conclusion

1. This summary of the anticommunist tradition largely follows M. J. Heale, *American Anticommunism: Combating the Enemy Within, 1830–1970* (Baltimore: Johns Hopkins University Press, 1990). For a provocative interpretation which relates the counter-subversive impulse in American political culture to the historic repression of Native Americans and African Americans – symbols of disorder which had to be controlled by state violence – see Michael Paul Rogin, 'Political Repression in the United States', ch.2 in Rogin, *Ronald Reagan, the Movie and Other Episodes in Political Demonology* (Berkeley: University of California Press, 1987), pp.44–80.

2. Daniel Bell (ed.), *The New American Right* (New York: Criterion, 1955); Richard Hofstadter, *The Paranoid Style in American Politics* (New York: Knopf, 1964); Michael Rogin, *The Intellectuals and McCarthy: The Radical Specter* (Cambridge: MIT Press, 1967); Robert Griffith, *The Politics of Fear: Joseph R. McCarthy and the Senate* (1970; 2nd edn, Amherst: University of Massachusetts Press, 1987). Studies emphasizing the responsibility of the Truman administration include Athan Theoharis, *Seeds of Repression: Harry S. Truman and the Origin of McCarthyism* (New York: Times Books, 1971) and Richard Freeland, *The Truman Doctrine and the Origins of McCarthyism* (New York: Knopf, 1972), while the essays in Robert Griffith and Allan Theoharis (eds), *The Specter: Original Essays on the Cold War and the Origins of McCarthyism* (New York: Watts, 1974) lay responsibility on various elites; the Republicans are implicated in Earl Latham, *The Communist Controversy in Washington: From the New Deal to McCarthy* (Cambridge: Harvard

University Press, 1966) and Michael Miles, *The Odyssey of the American Right* (New York: Oxford University Press, 1980). On the FBI, see, for example, Athan Theoharis and John Stuart Cox, *The Boss: J. Edgar Hoover and the Great American Inquisition* (Philadelphia: Temple University Press, 1988); federal government responsibility is crisply delineated in Ellen Schrecker, *The Age of McCarthyism* (Boston: Bedford Books, 1994). The view that much of anticommunism was a reasonable response to a real threat is presented most boldly in the writings of John Earl Haynes, e.g. 'The New History of the Communist Party in State Politics: The Implications for Mainstream Political History', *Labor History*, 27 (Fall 1986), 549–63, and *Red Scare or Red Menace? American Communism and Anticommunism in the Cold War Era* (Chicago: Ivan R. Dee, 1996), though for more complex and qualified analyses issuing from a similar standpoint, see e.g. Guenter Lewy, *The Cause That Failed: Communism in American Political Life* (New York: Oxford University Press, 1990), Harvey Klehr and John Earl Haynes, *The American Communist Movement: Storming Heaven Itself* (New York: Twayne Publishers, 1992), and particularly Richard Gid Powers, *Not Without Honor: The History of American Anticommunism* (New York: Free Press, 1995). A recent study from a leftist perspective is Joel Kovel, *Red Hunting in the Promised Land: Anticommunism and the Making of America* (New York: Basic Books, 1994), which equates American anticommunism with a 'black hole', a mindless abyss in which reasoned discussion is impossible, though this metaphor may confuse as much as it illuminates. For fuller discussions, see the bibliographical essays in Griffith (2nd edn) and Schrecker cited above, and Heale, *American Anticommunism*.

13   McCarthysim in State and Nation

1. Except where otherwise indicated, the data in this chapter are drawn from earlier chapters. The Arizona lower house also briefly sported a little HUAC, but it seems to have done little.
2. Austin Ranney, 'Parties in State Politics', in Herbert Jacob and Kenneth N. Vines (eds), *Politics in the American States: A Comparative Analysis* (Boston: Little, Brown, 1965), p.65.
3. David Caute, *The Great Fear: The Anti-Communist Purge Under Truman and Eisenhower* (New York: Simon and Schuster, 1978), pp.216–23, 431–45; Herman Kogan, 'The Sucker State Sees Red', *The New Republic*, 11 April 1949, pp.18–19; James O'Gara, 'What Price Anti-Sedition?' *The Commonweal*, 50 (8 July 1949), 312–15; Karl M. Schmidt, *Henry A. Wallace: Quixotic Crusade, 1948* (Binghamton: Syracuse University Press, 1960), p.79; Don E. Carleton, *Red Scare! Right-wing Hysteria, Fifties Fanaticism, and Their Legacy in Texas* (Austin: Texas

Monthly Press, 1985); James A. Maxwell, 'Cincinnati's Phantom Reds', *The Reporter*, 3 (26 Sept.1950), 28–30.

4. Walter Gellhorn, 'A General View', in Gellhorn (ed.), *The States and Subversion* (Ithaca: Cornell University Press, 1952), p.376; E. Edmund Reutter, Jr, *The School Administrator and Subversive Activities* (New York: Teachers College, Columbia University, 1951), p.23; Frederick K. Beutel to Alan Reitman, 25 Oct.1961, Box 900, Folder 14, ACLU Records, Seeley G. Mudd Library, Princeton University; William B. Prendergast, 'Maryland: The Ober Anti-Communist Law', in Gellhorn (ed.), *The States and Subversion*, p.161; M. J. Heale, 'Red Scare Politics: California's Campaign Against Un-American Activities, 1940–1970', *Journal of American Studies*, 20 (April 1986), 16.

5. Powers, *Not Without Honor*, esp. ch.3; contributions of Hirsch, Sugrue and Gary Gerstle to the 'Round Table', *Journal of American History*, 82 (Sept.1995), 522–86. Also suggestive on the grievances of white ethnics are Thomas H. O'Connor, *The Boston Irish: A Political History* (Boston: Northeastern University Press, 1995), pp.233–41, Ronald P. Formisano, *Boston Against Busing: Race, Class, and Ethnicity in the 1960s and 1970s* (Chapel Hill: University of North Carolina Press, 1991), and Michael Kazin, *The Populist Persuasion* (New York: Basic Books,1995), pp.192–3, 225–42.

6. See Jon C. Teaford, *Cities of the Heartland: The Rise and Fall of the Industrial Midwest* (Bloomington: Indiana University Press, 1993), pp.193–6, on the impact of southern whites on Midwestern cities.

7. 'Round Table', *Journal of American History*, 82 (Sept.1995), 522–86; Thomas J. Sugrue, 'Reassessing the History of Cold War America', *Prospects*, 20 (1995), 493–509; Kazin, *The Populist Persuasion*, pp.193, 226–7; Dan T. Carter, *The Politics of Rage: George Wallace, the Origins of the New Conservatism, and the Transformation of American Politics* (New York: Simon & Schuster, 1995), p.306. See also Leonard J. Moore, 'Good Old-Fashioned New Social History and the Twentieth-Century American Right', *Reviews in American History*, 24 (Dec.1996), 555–73 on the persistence of 'populist' conservatism from the 1920s onwards.

8. Heale, 'Red Scare Politics', pp.9–13.

9. George Sirgiovanni, *An Undercurrent of Suspicion: Anti-Communism in America during World War II* (New Brunswick: Transaction Publishers, 1990).

10. John Earl Haynes, *Dubious Alliance: The Making of Minnesota's DFL Party* (Minneapolis: University of Minnesota Press, 1984); Alonzo L. Hamby, *Beyond the New Deal: Harry S. Truman and American Liberalism* (New York: Columbia University Press, 1973), pp.16, 135–6, 218–19, 269; Powers, *Not Without Honor*, p.188; Haynes, *Red Scare or Red Menace?* p.127. See also Patricia Sullivan, *Days of Hope: Race and Democracy in the New Deal Era* (Chapel Hill: University of North Carolina Press, 1996), pp.8–9, 241–73, on progressive politics and anticommunist reactions in Georgia and the South generally.

11. *The Firing Line*, 1 Sept.1953; R. Will Burnett and Henrietta DeBoes, 'Resistance in Illinois: Is the Tide Turning?' *The Nation*, 177 (8

Aug.1953), 112–13; *Report of the Un-American Activities Commission, State of Ohio, 1951–52*, pp.11–13; Heale, 'Red Scare Politics', pp.26–7.

12. Ellen W. Schrecker, *No Ivory Tower: McCarthyism and the Universities* (New York: Oxford University Press, 1986); Sigmund Diamond, *Compromised Campus: The Collaboration of Universities with the Intelligence Community, 1945–1955* (New York: Oxford University Press, 1992). The accommodation of universities did not mean that intellectuals more generally put their talents at the disposal of the national security state; see, e.g. Hugh Wilford, *The New York Intellectuals: From Vanguard to Institution* (Manchester: Manchester University Press, 1995).

13. Frank Donner, *Protectors of Privilege: Red Squads and Police Repression in Urban America* (Berkeley: University of California Press, 1990), p.296n and passim.

14. State of Louisiana Joint Legislative Committee, *Subversion in Racial Unrest: An Outline of a Strategic Weapon to Destroy the Governments of Louisiana and the United States* (1957), pp.1–3, 17–135, and see also Louisiana Joint Legislative Committee on Un-American Activities, *Report No.1* (8 May 1961) and *Report No.2* (24 April 1962); George B. Weaver, 'Liberation – Red Bait for Negroes', *American Mercury*, 87 (Nov.1958), 37; Numan V. Bartley, *The Rise of Massive Resistance* (Baton Rouge: Louisiana State University Press, 1969), pp.180–3, 188. Matthews testified before committees in Florida, Mississippi and Arkansas.

15. Arnold Forster and Benjamin R. Epstein, *Danger on the Right* (New York: Random House,1964), ch.4 and pp.87–8; Powers, *Not Without Honor*, p.278; Betty E. Chmaj, 'Paranoid Patriotism: The Radical Right and the South', *Atlantic*, 210 (Nov.1962), pp.91–7; State of South Carolina, *Report of the Committee To Investigate Communist Activities in South Carolina, March 26, 1963* (n.p.), pp.1–2.

16. Lawrence Lowther and Floyd Rodine, 'History Teaching in the High School', *Pacific Northwest Quarterly*, (July 1968), 147–52; Chmaj, 'Paranoid Patriotism', p.94; Florida State Department of Education, *A Resource Unit: Americanism vs Communism* (Tallahassee, 1962), pp.68–9; State of South Carolina, *Report of the Committee ...March 26, 1963*, p.2 and *Report of the Committee ...South Carolina, April 8, 1964* (n.p.), passim; Arkansas State Department of Education, *Strengthening America: A Resource Booklet for Teaching the American Way of Life* (Little Rock, 1963) pp.57, 64; Roland F. Gray, 'Teaching About Communism: A Survey of Objectives', *Social Education*, 28 (Feb.1964), 71–2, 80; Jack Nelson and Gene Roberts, Jr, *The Censors and the Schools* (Boston: Little, Brown, 1963), pp.75, 89–96, 159–61. Louisiana required universities to teach a course on 'Americanism vs Communism', although Louisiana State University substituted a course on US history, 'the greatest success story the world has ever known': Adam Fairclough, *Race & Democracy: The Civil Rights Struggle in Louisiana, 1915–1972* (Athens: Georgia University Press, 1995), p.324. The involvement of the military in anticommunist politics became a national issue in 1961–62, when Senator J. William Fulbright in particular drew attention to it and the

Kennedy administration sought to put an end to it; see Powers, *Not Without Honor*, pp.297–303. Southern state authorities seem to have been unusually receptive to courses on the evils of communism, but such units also appeared in other parts of the Union; in Canada, on the other hand, the provincial authorities did not prescribe such teaching: Gray, 'Teaching About Communism'.

17. Heale, 'Red Scare Politics', pp.7–8, 31–2; Don Edward Carleton, 'A Crisis of Rapid Change: The Red Scare in Houston, 1945–1955' (Ph.D diss., University of Houston, 1978), p.25.
18. On the role of the South, see e.g. Margaret Weir, Ann Shola Orloff and Theda Skocpol (eds), *The Politics of Social Policy in the United States* (Princeton: Princeton University Press, 1988).
19. Carter, *Politics of Rage,* esp. chs 10 and 11; Kazin, *The Populist Persuasion,* esp. chs 7, 9, 10.

INDEX